On the Origin of Objects

On the Origin of Objects

Brian Cantwell Smith

A Bradford Book

The MIT Press
Cambridge, Massachusetts
London, England

First MIT Press paperback edition, 1998

Copyright © 1996 Brian Cantwell Smith

Library of Congress Cataloging-in-Publication Data

Smith, Brian Cantwell.
    On the origin of objects / Brian Cantwell Smith.
    p.   cm.
    Includes bibliographical references.
    ISBN 0-262-19363-9 (HB), 0-262-69209-0 (PB)
    1. Metaphysics.   2. Object (Philosophy).   I. Title.
BD111.S573   1996
111—dc20   95-37637
                                         CIP

Contents

Preface

A few years ago, at a workshop on the perception of objects, I raised a question about one of the philosophers' ontological assumptions, which seemed to me altogether too neat. I was concerned about basic issues of object identity—about what makes a newspaper into a single entity as opposed to a large number of separate pieces of paper, what distinguishes the headache that I had this morning from the one I had last night, what it is for Microsoft Word on PCs to be "the same program" as Microsoft Word on the Macintosh. I was particularly troubled by how ready most of the other workshop participants were to base their perceptual theories on the presumption that such ontological questions had clear, determinate answers.

Over lunch, several people pushed the worry aside, as if it were a matter of internal theoretical hygiene. "Don't worry," someone assured me; "most philosophers would insist on precise individuation criteria." Sure enough, most do—I knew that. My question was *why*—whether such presumptions were warranted. And I had a special reason for asking. Having spent more than twenty-five years working in the trenches of practicing computer science, in a long-term effort to develop an empirically re-

It is difficult to find in life any event which so effectually condenses intense nervous sensation into the shortest possible space of time as does the work of shooting or running an immense rapid. There is no toil, no heart breaking labour about it, but as much coolness, dexterity, and skill as [a person] can throw into the work of hand, eye, and head; knowledge of when to strike and how to do it; knowledge of water and rock, and of the one hundred combinations which rock and water can assume—for these two things, rock and water, taken in the abstract, fail as completely to convey any idea of their fierce embracings in the throes of a rapid as the fire burning quietly in a drawing-room fireplace fails to convey the idea of a house wrapped and sheeted in flames.

—Sir William Francis Butler (1982)

sponsible theory of computation, I had never met such a logically pure entity, never met such a lapidary individual thing. And computation, alleged to be one of science's most dazzling achievements, is presumably as promising a site as any for ontological clarity and distinctness. Moreover, those few objects that are possessed of anything like crystalline ontological coherence, such as numbers, and perhaps the underlying bits and bytes, are manifest exceptions, no matter how highly prized. By and large, or so at least my experience suggests, the world is an unruly place—much messier than reigning ontological and scientific myths would lead one to suspect.

The workshop where this all took place was held at King's College, Cambridge, in 250-year-old hand-cut stone buildings, surrounded by immaculate English gardens. The setting was ironically apposite. Looking out the window, I felt like an eighteenth-century explorer, newly returned from the New World, faced with the task of explaining, over tea and crumpets, the stark and searing beauty of the arctic, with its thousands of miles of desolate rock and wild rivers, unchecked ranges of lapped, craggy mountains, vast outcroppings of exfoliating granite, and millions upon millions of acres of profusely variegated and often impenetrable lichen, brambles, and muskeg. It is hard to imagine a more vivid contrast. And for better or worse—but mostly, I believe, for worse—the conception of "object" that has been enshrined in present-day science and analytic philosophy, with its presumptive underlying precision and clarity, is more reminiscent of fastidiously cropped hedge rows, carefully weeded rose gardens, and individually labeled decorative trees, than it is of the endless and rough arctic plain, or of a million-ton iceberg midwifed with a deafening crack and splintering spray from a grimy 10,000-year-old ice flow.

It is not wildness, per se, that differentiates the cases. No one travels the arctic without tools and equipment, endless preparation, and companions—or escapes an enmeshing web of social and political influences. But even the artifacts, on an expedition, are to a degree unstable, contingent, in flux. It is not just the dirt and grease ground into endlessly mended paddles—paddles grasped and worked by salty hands of people with sunburnt skin and densely matted hair. Think also of late-night conversations around the campfire, about possible routes and upcoming dangers (are we following "the same route" as Sir John Franklin?), about how to make one's way across fifty-seven miles of partially frozen swamp. Landscapes, plans, even material ordnance, are fecund masses of jumbled identity.

A far cry from a meticulous bed of yellow jonquils. Or so at least I thought. But then, while I watched, the Cambridge garden began to yield up its secrets, and the world fell back into its usual restless semblance of place. It was obvious, first, that the perfection with which I felt so at odds was in large part an idealization, if not illusory—that crumbly earth and erupting masses of new shoots are as essential to the life of a garden as cut stems or kempt grounds. Moreover, as I was mulling on the role of tamed wildness in English horticulture, a gardener came into view, and patiently bent down to work. Of course! That is what is profound about gardens: *they have to be maintained*. It takes continuous, sometimes violent, and often grueling, work, work that is in general nowhere near as neat as its intended result, to maintain gardens as the kind of thing that they are. Neither discovered, nor in any simple sense merely constructed, gardens, in order to be gardens, must be cared for, tended—even loved. What more could one ask for, by way of ontological moral?

This is a book about metaphysics—one that attempts to do justice to the tundra, to gardening, to politics, to rock. As indicated, my path into these subjects has come through computer science, but that is mostly by the way. Although some technical material is reviewed in chapter 1, computational considerations are largely set aside, in order to tell a tale about the territory into which that long exploration has led. The result is something of a metaphysical romp—occasionally riding rough-shod over turf already well explored (and well tilled) by generations of writers: from philosophy, feminism, theology, science studies, physics, poetry. Notwithstanding the germ of truth in the remark that "progress is made by stepping on the toes of giants," links with these literatures need to, and at some later point will, be forged. Nevertheless, my aim for the present text is simple: by presenting the story stripped of its computational heritage, to open up a conversation about perspectives, requirements, insights, and struggles—a conversation with others who have been led, via different routes, to this same metaphysical terrain.

To those inspired to take the trip—whether from explicit professional wrestling with such issues, or as the result of late-night reservations about how to participate authentically in academic life—I hope to say two things. First: *yes*, it is possible to base uncompromising theoretical inquiry on alternative foundations: messier foundations, contested foundations, foundations that run closer to the wry and weathered texture of ordinary life. No one, least of all God, has decreed that intellectual rigor must (or even can) be founded on a pristine foundational atomism. Second, though, I also want to make evident just how much such a transformation costs. Politics, creativity, ambiguity, irreverence—none of these can be grafted, at a later stage, onto a silent steel core, or even poured, like life-giving water, over inherently desiccated foundations. The whole story has to be turned upside down.

As is inevitable for a project under way for decades, I owe more debts to more people than possibly can, or should, be said here. I trust they know who they are, and why.

With respect to this particular manuscript, the initial suggestion to write it, and much subsequent encouragement, came from long-time friend and colleague Kathleen Akins, who organized a conference in Vancouver in January 1992 on "The Perception of Objects," as part of the Simon Fraser University Cognitive Science Series, where the material was first presented. Since then I have benefited greatly from the workshop participants at King's, as well as from audiences at the University of Illinois, Indiana University, Stanford University, and the Xerox Palo Alto Research Center. All these groups, it must be said, were subjected to pell-mell presentations of a view that cannot, it seems, be conveyed in an hour. I hope this book goes some way towards explaining what happened.

I am also extremely grateful to Adrian Cussins, and to the singular group of fellow travelers he assembled—Adam Lowe, Bruno Latour, and Charis Cussins—each of whom in his or her own way is telling a similar story, though Adam tends to do so in acrylic and epoxy. The first full draft of the manuscript was prepared for a meeting of this small group at ChatelPerron, an eleventh-century castle south of Paris—an idyllic setting for naturalized theology.

Closer to home, I have worked for many years in collaboration with colleagues at the Xerox Palo Alto Research Center: Mike Dixon, Gregor Kiczales, John Lamping, Jim des Rivières, and other members (past and present) of the Embedded Computation Area—and many other members of the wider PARC community, for whom this in part was written: Annette Adler, Bob Anderson, Bob Bauer, Danny Bobrow, Austin Henderson, Dan Huttenlocher, Gitte Jordan, Geoff Nunberg, Estee Solomon-Gray, Lucy Suchman, and Mark Weiser, to name just a few.

Special thanks also to: John Haugeland, co-presenter at the Vancouver conference and long-time metaphysical companion, and Adrian Cussins, again, for trenchant, detailed reviews of an earlier draft, without which the present version would be far more obscure; Teri Mendelsohn and Betty and Harry Bradford Stanton of the MIT Press, for faith in the project and stewardship of the manuscript; Shelley Evenson and John Rheinfrank, for layout, typography, and the world of design, as well as for their help in designing this manuscript; Helga Wild, for all the artwork; and Sharon Olson, for editing. And to John Batali, Niklas Damiris, Güven Güzeldere, Stefan Heck, Mimi Ito, Natalie Jeremijenko, Joanna Rączaszek, Arnold Smith, Kären Weickert, and (again) Helga Wild, fellow travelers, sustaining friends, and stalwart coconspirators. Also to Charles Smith, for early faith; Barbara Grosz, for the original CSLI; Susan Newman, for help with the social; Walter Fontana, for chemistry and biology; Meg Graham, for reliance; Jon Barwise, for surety; Peter Finkelstein, for balance; Tytti Solantaus, for identity; Leigh Star, for bravery; Stefano Franchi, for play; and Jim Mahoney, who understands improvisation.

I also want to give this to David Levy, Marcia Lind, Mitch Marcus, Susan Stucky, and Henry and Catharine Thompson, separately and together, because of what it is. It is for my parents, too, Wilfred and Muriel Smith (to whom I have added little)— and above all, again, for Susan. Finally, a very warm thank you to John Seely Brown, for fifteen years of sustaining friendship— to say nothing of running the best place in the world to do research on the edge.

On the Origin of Objects

Introduction

This book introduces a new metaphysics—a philosophy of presence—that aims to steer a path between the Scylla of naive realism and the Charybdis of pure constructivism. The goal is to develop an integral account that retains the essential humility underlying each tradition: a form of epistemic deference to the world that underlies realism, and a respect for the constitutive human involvement in the world that underwrites constructivism.[1] The proposal is also intended to be neutral with respect to (a late twentieth-century update of) C P Snow's famous two cultures—serving equally as a foundation for the academic, intellectual, and technological, on the one hand, and for the curious, the moral, the erotic, the political, the artistic, and the sheerly obstreperous, on the other.

Fundamental to the view is a claim that objects, properties, practice, and politics—indeed everything ontological—live in what is called the "middle distance": an intermediate realm between a proximal though ultimately ineffable *connection*, reminiscent of the familiar physical bumping and shoving of the world, and a more remote *disconnection*, a form of unbridgeable separation that lies at the root of abstraction and of the partial (and painful) subject-object divide. No sense attends to the idea of complete connection or complete disconnection; limit idealizations are outmoded. Yet an essential interplay of patterns of partial connection and partial disconnection—restless figures

The footnotes in this book, positioned here in the bottom left corner of the page, are intended to be contrapuntal to the main body of the text. As well as supplying the usual references and other supporting material, they are used to fill in certain details, particularly philosophical details, that only some readers will view as essential to the argument.

[1] "Constructivism" is intended to signify not only what is known as *social constructionism*, but a more widespread constructive metaphysical stance especially prevalent in artificial intelligence and cognitive science.

of separation and engagement—is shown to underlie a single notion taken to unify representation and ontology: that of a subject's *registration* of the world.

The notion of metaphysics is itself overhauled in the process. For the project requires finding something whose existence (even possibility) is not obvious in advance: a way to feed our undiminished yearning for foundations and grounding, while at the same time avoiding the reductionism and ideological fundamentalism that have so bedeviled prior foundationalist approaches. Doing so (this is the same fact) answers the fundamental open challenge to pluralism, by making it evident how an integral metaphysical reality can simultaneously underwrite our unutterable differences and uniqueness, and at the same time sustain basic notions of worth and value, standards and significance, truth and even beauty. Thus the proposal shows what any successful metaphysics must show: how an irrevocable commitment to pluralism is compatible with the recognition that not all stories are equally good.[2]

Perhaps surprisingly, the end result is a picture of rather stark simplicity. Simplicity, though, is more a retrospective than a prospective quality—and anyway it is not a picture of a simple world, but a simple picture of a world of surpassing richness.

1 The foundations of computation

It may help, first, to explain how a computer scientist has come to tell such a bluntly metaphysical tale.

The interest in metaphysics and ontology has grown rather

---

[2]Thus Haraway: "So I think my problem and 'our' problem is how to have *simultaneously* an account of radical historical contingency for all knowledge claims and knowing subjects, a critical practice for recognizing our own 'semiotic technologies' for making meanings, *and* a no-nonsense commitment to faithful accounts of a 'real' world, one that can be partially shared and friendly to earth-wide projects of finite freedom, adequate material abundance, modest meaning in suffering, and limited happiness." Haraway (1991), p. 187, italics in the original.

straightforwardly out of a long-term (and ongoing) concern with the foundations of computer science and artificial intelligence. For more than twenty-five years I have been striving to develop an adequate and comprehensive theory of computation, one able to meet two essential criteria:

1. **Empirical:** It must do justice to computational practice (e.g., be capable of explaining Microsoft Word—including, for reasons that will emerge, the program itself, its construction, maintenance, and use);[3] and

2. **Conceptual:** It must provide a tenable foundation for the computational theory of mind—the thesis, sometimes known as "cognitivism,"[4] that underlies artificial intelligence and cognitive science.

The first, empirical, requirement, of doing justice to practice, helps to keep the analysis grounded in real-world examples, as a guard against excessive abstraction. It is humbling, too, since if anything is reliable about the computer revolution, it is its unerring ability to adapt, expand, dodge expectations, and generally outstrip our theoretical grasp. The criterion's primary advantage, however, is to provide a vantage point from which to question the legitimacy of all theoretical perspectives. For I take it as a tenet that what Silicon Valley *treats* as computational, in practice, *is* computational, in fact; to deny that would be considered sufficient grounds for rejection. But no such a priori com-

---

[3] To require that an account of computation *do justice* to a program's design, use, construction, repair, etc., is not to insist that a theory of computation *be* a theory of use (design, repair, etc.). For any technology or tool or equipment, there is almost certainly no limit to, and therefore no theory of, the uses to which it can be put. The idea, rather, is to make it a criterion on a successful theory of a technology that it explain or make intelligible how it is that the technology can subserve or play the roles that it does, while recognizing that they will be essentially open-ended. Thus if the materiality of computation is essential to a non-trivial fraction of the roles to which it is put, then an adequate theory, by these lights, will have to treat of its materiality.

[4] Cf. for example Haugeland (1978).

mitment is given to any story about computation, including the widely held Turing-theoretic conception of computability that currently goes by the name "the theory of computation." By the same token, I reject all proposals that assume that computation can be defined. By my lights, an adequate theory must make a substantive empirical claim about what I call *computation in the wild*:[5] that eruptive body of practices, techniques, networks, machines, and behavior that has so palpably revolutionized late-twentieth-century life.

The second condition, that an adequate theory of computation provide a tenable foundation for a theory of mind, is of a rather different character. Here labeled *conceptual*, it is more a metatheoretic requirement on the form or status of the theory than a constraint on its substantive content. In committing myself to honor the criterion, in particular, I make no advance commitment to cognitivism's being true (or false); I just want to know what it says.

That is not to say that the content of cognitivism is left open. Cognitivism's fundamental thesis—that the mind is computational—is given substance by the first, empirical criterion. The point is only that cognitivism, as I read it, is not a theory-laden claim, in the sense of framing specific hypotheses about what computers are. Rather, it has a more of an ostensive character: that people (i.e., us) are computers in whatever way that computers (i.e., those things over there) are computers, or at least in whatever way some of those things are computers.[6] In my view,

---

[5] With a nod to Hutchins' *Cognition in the Wild* (1995).

[6] To say that people, or minds, or intelligence, are computational is an asymmetrical claim: it is not, conversely, to say that to be computational is to be a person, or mind, or intelligent. Patently, some computers are impersonal, non-mental, and stupid. That raises a question about the status of the identifying characteristic of the subset. The strongest version of the computational claim, to which I believe most artificial intelligence advocates would subscribe, should be reconstructed along something like the following lines: (i) that people, minds, etc., are a subclass of the set of computers—implying that the property of being a computer is necessarily ex-

that is, cognitivism holds that people manifest, or exemplify, or are, or can be explained by, or can be illuminatingly understood in terms of, *whatever properties it is that characterize some identifiable species of the genus exemplified by computation-in-the-wild.* It would not be very interesting, or at least I would not consider it very interesting, for someone to argue that people are (or are not) "computers" according to a notion of computation that does not apply to present-day practice—does not apply to Unix, say, or to the PowerPC, or to the embedded controllers in a computerized lathe. Such a claim would be uninteresting because the hunch that has motivated artificial intelligence and propelled computational psychology into the mainstream of intellectual life—the hunch that has excited several generations of graduate students—is ultimately grounded in practice. Two weeks in any artificial intelligence laboratory is enough to demonstrate this. The cognitive revolution is fueled, both directly and indirectly, by an embodied and enthusiastically endorsed, but as-yet largely tacit, intuition based on many years of practical computational experience.

It follows that any theoretical formulation of cognitivism is doubly contingent. Thus consider Newell and Simon's popular "physical symbol system hypothesis," or Fodor's claim that thinking consists of formal symbol manipulation, or Dreyfus' assertion that cognitivism (as opposed to connectionism) re-

---

hibited by every mind; and (ii) that the property that distinguishes that subset—i.e., its characteristic function—is itself also a computational property (i.e., is computationally defined, occurs as part of a theory of computation, involves a computational regularity, whatever). Clearly, other variants are possible, such as that being a mind involves being computational *plus something else*, where that "something else" is noncomputational: having transducers of a certain form (on the assumption that 'transducer' is not a computational property), being conscious, or whatever. However this goes, a more finely textured characterization is needed than is captured for example in Searle's binary distinction between "strong" vs. "weak" AI (Searle 1980, 1984). See also Jackendoff (1987).

quires the explicit manipulation of explicit symbols.[7] Not only do these writers make a hypothetical statement about *people*, that they are physical, formal, or explicit symbol manipulators, respectively; they do so by making a hypothetical statement about *computers*, that they are in some essential or illuminating way characterizable in the same way. Because I take the latter claim to be as subservient to empirical adequacy as the former, there are two ways in which these writers could be wrong. In claiming that people are formal symbol manipulators, for example, Fodor would naturally be wrong if computers were formal symbol manipulators and people were not. But he would also be wrong, even though cognitivism itself might still be true, if computers were not formal symbol manipulators, either.

That, then, constitutes what I will call the *computational project*: to formulate a true and satisfying theory of computation that honors these two criteria. Needless to say, neither criterion is easy to meet. Elsewhere, I report on a study of half a dozen reigning construals of computation, with reference to both criteria—formal symbol manipulation, automata theory, information processing, digital state machines, recursion theory, Turing machines, the theory of effective computability, complexity theory, the assumptions underlying programming language semantics, and the like—and argue, in brief, that *each fails*, on *both counts*.[8] These are non-standard conclusions, and I do not press the present reader even to suspend reasonable disbelief, let alone to accept them. To understand the present book, however, and especially to understand why I use the examples that I do, it helps to know that they are, in fact, conclusions that I hold. To begin with, that is, I believe that each of the enumer-

[7]Newell & Simon (1976), Newell (1980), Fodor (1975, 1980), Dreyfus & Dreyfus (1988), and "Introduction to the MIT Press Edition" in Dreyfus (1992).

[8] *The Middle Distance* (forthcoming); henceforth TMD. The present volume can be seen as a travel brochure for a new land to which that study takes a full-fledged trip.

ated construals is inadequate to explain practice, being incapable of making sense of current systems, much less of unleashing a new generation. As a result, each fails the empirical criterion. For various theoretical reasons, moreover, even if they were empirically adequate, no one of them alone, nor any group in combination, would provide a tenable foundation for a theory of mind. So none of them meets the conceptual criterion, either.

What is the problem? Why do these theories all fail?

The most celebrated difficulties have to do with semantics. It is widely recognized that computation is in one way or another a symbolic or representational or information-based or semantical—i.e., as philosophers would say, an *intentional*—phenomenon.[9] Somehow or other, though in ways we do not yet understand, the states of a computer can model or simulate or represent or stand for or carry information about or signify other states in the world (or at least can be taken by people to do so—see the sidebar on original vs. derivative semantics, page 10). This semantical or intentional character of computation is betrayed by such phrases as *symbol* manipulation, *information* processing, programming *languages*, *knowledge representation*, *data* bases, etc. Furthermore, it is the intentionality of the computational that motivates the cognitivist thesis. The only compelling reason to suppose that we (or minds or intelligence)

---

[9]Although the term 'intentional' is philosophical, there are many philosophers, to say nothing of some computer and cognitive scientists, who would deny that computation is an intentional phenomenon. Reasons vary, but the most common go something like this: (i) that computation is both *syntactic* and *formal*, where 'formal' means "independent of semantics"; and (ii) that intentionality has fundamentally to do with semantics; and therefore (iii) that computation is thereby not intentional. I believe this is wrong, both empirically (that computation is purely syntactic) and conceptually (that being syntactic is a way of not being intentional); I also disagree that being intentional has *only* to do with semantics, which the denial requires. See the "Independent of semantics" sidebar on page 15, as well as TMD·II.

Original vs. derivative semantics

Many people have argued that the semantics of computational systems is intrinsically *derivative* or *attributed*—i.e., of the sort that books and signs have, in the sense of being ascribed by outside observers or users—as opposed to that of human thought and language, which in contrast is assumed to be *original* or *authentic*.* I am dubious about the ultimate utility (and sharpness) of this distinction, and also about its applicability to computers—for a cluster of reasons, having to do partly with the fact that computers are increasingly being embedded in real systems, and can thus directly sense and affect what their symbols denote, and partly with arguments about the division of linguistic labor, or the division of labor more generally, arguments implying that some of our referential capacities are inherited from the communities of which we are a part.

Even if the distinction were useful, however, and even if the claim based on it were true—even if computational intentionality were in point of fact derivative—that would take nothing away from the point made in the text, that a theory of computation needs a theory of intentionality. First, it would be absurd to take derivativeness to be a *defining* characteristic of computation; if, in fact, derivativeness is a property of computers, that fact ought to be demonstrable—derivable from an account of what computers are like, to say nothing of an account of what originality and derivativeness are like. Such an argument would require a prior theory of intentionality. Second, derivative semantics is still real semantics—and of a quite complex kind. *Derivative*, after all, does not mean *fake* or *unreal*.

*Searle and Haugeland are the primary proponents of this distinction; see Searle (1980, 1982, 1984) and Haugeland (1981 p. 32–33; and 1985 p. 25–28, 87, & 119–123). For another very clear application to computers see Dretske (1985). An opposing (nondifferentiated) view is argued by Dennett; e.g., in chapter 8 of (1987).

might be computers stems from the fact that we, too, deal with representations, symbols, meaning, information, and the like.

For someone with cognitivist leanings, therefore—as opposed, say, to an eliminative materialist,[10] or to some types of connectionist—it is natural to expect that a comprehensive theory of computation will have to focus on its semantical aspects. This raises problems enough. Consider just the issue of representation. In order to meet the first criterion, of empirical adequacy, a successful candidate will have to make sense of the myriad kinds of representation that saturate practical systems—from bit maps and images to knowledge representations and data bases; from caches to backup tapes; from low-level finite-element models used in simulation to high-level analytic descriptions supporting reasoning and inference; from text to graphics to audio to video to virtual reality. As well as being vast in scope, it will also have to combine decisive theoretical bite with exquisite resolution, in order to distinguish models from implementations, analyses from simulations, and virtual machines at one level of abstraction from virtual machines at another level of abstraction in terms of which the former may be implemented.

---

[10] Strictly speaking, an eliminative materialist—or rather, in the vocabulary of chapter 5, an eliminative physicalist—would be someone who thinks that in due course (e.g., in millennial science) all non-physical levels of explanation, presumably including intentional, computational, and psychological varieties, will be "eliminated" in favor of physicalist or materialist alternatives. This strong form of eliminativism is further from common sense than reductionism: whereas the reductionist expects (or at least allows) higher-level notions, such as belief and truth, to survive but to be reducible to lower-level material accounts, the eliminativist in contrast expects the higher-level account to be replaced or discarded.

Not all self-proclaimed eliminativists are this thorough-going, though. It all depends on what is in line for elimination. Thus the Churchlands, well-known defenders of an eliminativist position, are more committed to the elimination of propositional attitude psychology than they are to the elimination of all intentional (semantic) vocabulary and/or ontology. See, e.g., Patricia Churchland (1986, 1992) and Paul Churchland (1989).

In order to meet the second, conceptual, criterion, moreover, any account of this profusion of representational practice must be grounded on, or at least defined in terms of, a theory of semantics or content. This is necessary in part in order that the concomitant psychological theory avoid vacuity or circularity, and in part in order that the main theory meet a minimal kind of naturalistic criterion: that we understand how computation is part of the natural world.[11] This is made all the more difficult by the fact that the word 'semantics' is used in an incredible variety of different senses across the range of the intentional sciences. Indeed, in my experience it is virtually impossible from any one location within that range to understand the full significance of the term, so disparate is that practice in toto.[12]

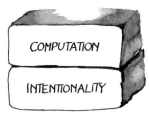

FIGURE 0·1 FIRST CUT

Genuine theories of content, moreover—of what it is that makes a given symbol or structure or patch of the world be *about*

---

[11] My use of 'naturalism' is non-standard: although it is a (metatheoretic) criterion I embrace, I do not thereby mean to lend support to physicalist explanation, or indeed to give any special status to what are known as the natural sciences. As explained in §1.a of chapter 3, all I am really committed to is that the account show how computation is not, as it were, *supernatural*: mysterious, spooky, or otherwise intellectually disreputable.

[12] In computer science, to take just one salient example, the term "the semantics of α," where α is an expression or construct in a programming language, means approximately the following: the topological (not geometrical) temporal profile of the behavior to which execution of this program fragment gives rise. By "topological" I mean that the overall temporal order of events is typically dictated, but that their absolute time-structure (e.g., exactly how fast the program runs) is not. As a result, a program can typically be sped up, either by adjusting the code, or by running it on a faster processor, without, as it is said, "changing the semantics." This reading is discussed further in chapter 1, §2. For an historical analysis of how the word 'semantics' has come to be used for such an effective kind of phenomenon—something that, at least to a traditional logician, sounds more like proof theory than model theory—see TMD·III.

or *oriented towards* some other entity or structure or patch—are notoriously hard to come by.[13] What is needed, to put a Husserlian spin on it, is an account of why, when we look out the window, we see a tree—i.e., have a (potentially) conscious experience of or about a tree, not of a two-dimensional leafy and barked surface, let alone of a pattern of incident electromagnetic radiation, or even have no experience at all, but instead just participate in an electromagnetically-mediated causal loop. Some putatively foundational construals of computation are implicitly defined in terms of just such a background theory of semantics, but do not explain what semantics is, and thus fail the second conceptual criterion. This group includes the "formal symbol manipulation" construal so favored in the cognitive sciences, in spite of its superficial formulation as being "independent of semantics" (see the sidebar on page 15). Other construals, such as those that view computation as the behavior of discrete automata—and also, I would argue, even if this is not immediately evident, the recursion-theoretic one that describes such behavior as the calculation of effective functions—fail to deal with computation's semantical aspect at all, in spite of sometimes using semantical vocabulary, and so fail the first empirical criterion. In the end, I find myself driven to the conclusion represented in figure 0·1, which for discussion I will call a "first cut" on the computational project: that, in spite of the advance press, especially from cognitivist quarters, computer science, far from supplying answers to the fundamental intentional mysteries, must, like cognitive science, await the development of a satisfying theory of intentionality.[14]

[13] Best known are Dretske's semantic theory of information (1981), which has more generally given rise to what is known as "indicator semantics," Fodor's "asymmetrical-dependence" theory (1987), and Millikan's "teleo-semantics" or "biosemantics" (1984, 1989). For comparison among these alternatives see, e.g., Fodor (1984) and Millikan (1990).

[14] As suggested in footnote 9 (p. 9) and in the "Independent of semantics" sidebar on page 15, philosophers are less likely than computer scientists to expect a theory of computation to be, or to supply, a theory of

2 The ontological wall

This, then, was my position for almost twenty years: (i) I was in awe of the depth, texture, scope, pluck, and impact of practice; (ii) I was critical of the inadequate state of current theory; and (iii) I was sure in my belief that what was needed, above all else, was a (situated, embodied, embedded, indexical, critical, reflexive, and all sorts of other things) theory of representation and semantics. In line with this metatheoretic attitude, I kept semantical and representational issues in primary theoretical focus.[15] Since, as already indicated, what currently goes by the name "the theory of computation"—essentially a derivative of recursion and complexity theory—pays very little attention to such intentional problems, to strike even this much of a semantical stance was to part company with the center of gravity of the received theoretical tradition.

And yet, in spite of the importance and magnitude of these intentional difficulties, I have gradually come to believe something even more sobering: that the most serious problems standing in the way of developing an adequate theory of computation are as much *ontological* as they are semantical. It is not that the semantic problems go away; they remain as challenging as ever. It is just that they are joined—on center stage, as it were—by even more demanding problems of ontology.

Except that to say "joined" is misleading, as if it were a matter of simple addition—i.e., as if now there were two problems on

···

intentionality. Thus they would not expect the metatheoretic structure to be as expected by most computer scientists and artificial intelligence researchers—namely, as indicated in the diagram to the right, with a theory of intentionality resting on a theory of computation. But that does not mean they would necessarily agree with figure 0·1. As discussed in TMD·II, many philosophers seem to think that a theory of computation can be *independent* of a theory of intentionality. Clearly, I do not believe this is correct.

[15] As is typical of those who work in artificial intelligence, I also paid more attention to representation than to algorithms.

Independent of semantics

Because formal symbol manipulation is usually defined as "manipulation of symbols independent of their interpretation," some people believe that the formal symbol manipulation construal of computation does not rest on a theory of semantics. But that is simply an elementary, though apparently very common, conceptual mistake.

The "independence of semantics" postulated as essential to the formal symbol construal is independence at the level of the phenomenon; it is a claim about how symbol manipulation *works*. Or so at least I have come to believe, based on more than twenty years of investigating what version of formality practitioners are actually committed to. (Whether the condition holds of computation-in-the-wild is a separate issue.) The intuition is simple enough: that semantic properties, such as referring to the Sphinx, or being true, are not of the right sort to do effective work. So it cannot be by exemplifying them that computers run. At issue in the present discussion, in contrast, is independence *at the level of the theory*—or, perhaps, to put it less epistemically and more ontologically, independence at the level of the *types*. And here the formal symbol manipulation construal is as dependent on semantics as it is possible to be: *it is defined in terms of it*. And defining yourself in terms of something is not a very good way to be independent of it, as the parent of any teenager knows.

Symbols must have a semantics—i.e., have an actual interpretation, be interpretable, whatever—in order for there to be something substantive for their formal manipulation to proceed independently of. Without a semantic character to be kept crucially in the wings, the formal symbol manipulation construal would collapse in vacuity. It would degenerate into something like "the manipulation of structure," or, as I put it in TMD·II, *stuff manipulation*—i.e., materialism.

the table, where before there had been just one. No such luck. The two issues are inextricably entangled—a fact of obstinate theoretical and metatheoretical consequence. This book can be viewed as an attempt to follow out, as simply but as rigorously as possible, the consequences of this entanglement.

A methodological consequence will illustrate the problem. Within the analytic tradition (by which I mean to include not just analytic philosophy, e.g. of language and mind, but most of modern science as well, complete with its formal/mathematical methods), it is traditional to analyze semantical or intentional systems, such as computers or people, under the following presupposition: (i) that one can parse or register the relevant theoretical situation in advance into a set of objects, properties, types, relations, equivalence classes, and the like (e.g., into people, heads, sentences, real-world referents, etc.), as if this were theoretically innocuous; and then (ii), with that ontological parse in hand, go on to proclaim this or that or the other thing as an empirically justified result. Thus for example one might describe a mail-delivering robot by first describing an environment of offices, hallways, people, staircases, litter, and the like, through which it is supposed to navigate; and then, taking this characterization of its context as given, ask how or whether the creature represents routes, say, or offices, or the location of mail delivery stations.

If one adopts a reflexively critical point of view, however, as I will try to do in chapter 1, one is inexorably led to the following conclusion: that, in that allegedly innocent pretheoretical "set-up" stage, one is liable, even if unwittingly, to project so many presuppositions, biases, blindnesses, and advance clues about the "answer," and in general to so thoroughly prefigure the target situation, without either apparent or genuine justification, that one cannot, or at least should not, take any of the subsequent "analysis" seriously. And that is problematic, in turn, not just because it rejects standard analyses, but because it seems to shut all inquiry down. What else can one do, after all? How can one not parse the situation in advance (since it will hardly do to merely whistle and walk away)? And if, undaunted, one were to go ahead and parse it anyway, what kind of story could possibly serve as a justification? It seems that any conceivable form of defense would devolve into another instance of the same problem.

In sum, the experience is less one of facing an ontological challenge than of running up against an ontological wall. Perhaps not quite of slamming into it, at least in my own case, since recognition dawned slowly. But neither is the encounter exactly gentle. It is difficult to exaggerate the sense of frustration that can come, once the conceptual fog begins to clear, from seeing one's theoretical progress blocked by what seems to be an insurmountable metaphysical obstacle.

Like the prior claim that all extant theories of computation are inadequate to reconstruct practice, this last claim, that theoretical progress is stymied for lack of an adequate theory of ontology, is a strong statement, in need of correspondingly strong defense. Again, this book does not present rigorous arguments for it, though I hope chapter 1 goes some way towards suggesting why it is true. I mention it only in order to motivate the present project. In my judgment, that is, despite the progress that has been made so far, we are not going to get to the heart of computation, representation, cognition, information, semantics, or intentionality, until the ontological wall is scaled, penetrated, dismantled, or in some other way defused.

3 A convergence of fields

One reaction to the wall might be depression. Fortunately, the prospects are not so bleak. For starters, there is some solace in company. It is perfectly evident, once one raises one's head from the specifically computational situation and looks around, that computer scientists, cognitive scientists, and artificial intelligence researchers are not the only ones running up against the demands of ontology. Similar conclusions are being reported from many other quarters. The words are different, and the perspectives complementary, but the underlying phenomena are the same.

The concerns are perhaps most pressing for literary critics, anthropologists, and other social theorists, vexed by what analytic categories to use in understanding people or cultures that, by the theorists' own admission, comprehend and constitute the world using concepts alien to the theorists' own. What makes the problem particularly obvious, in these cases, is the potential for *conceptual clash* between theorist's and subject's worldview[16]—a clash that can easily seem paralyzing. One's own categories are hard to justify, and reek of imperialism; it is at best presumptuous, and at worst impossible, to try to adopt the categories of one's subjects; and it is manifestly impossible to work with no concepts at all. So it is unclear how, or even whether, to proceed.

But conceptual clash, at least outright conceptual clash, is

---

[16]It is hardly surprising that among the first writers to recognize the potential of undischarged bias in their theoretical equipment were those, including many comparative humanists, social scientists, theologians, etc., whose task it was to characterize other people or cultures that lived by different conceptual schemes. But the fact that ontological problems are obvious in such cases does not mean that such difficulties are unique to them. For example, it is traditional within the humanities to suppose that univocal, objectivist, monist, or "scientific" approaches are fine for rocks, but inapplicable in human affairs. It is true, of course, that rocks' lack of a conceptual system obviates the possibility of conceptual clash—and rocks will not complain, either, being mute. It would take a lot more work than this, however, to show that methodological monism can do a rock justice.

Computers are not cultures, at least not yet, but neither are they rocks. As chapter 1 tries to demonstrate, problems analogous to conceptual clash arise for any intentional subject matter, no matter how modest.

not the only form in which the ontological problem presents. Consider the burgeoning interest in "complex systems" coalescing in a somewhat renegade subdiscipline at the intersection of dynamics, theoretical biology, and artificial life. This community debates the "emergence of organization," the units that selection operates on, the structure of self-organizing systems, the smoothness or roughness of what are called "fitness landscapes," and the like.[17] In spite of being virtually constitutive of the discipline, these discussions are conducted in the absence of adequate theories of what organization comes to, of what a "unit" consists in, of how "entities" arise (as opposed to how they survive), of how it is determined what predicates should figure in characterizing a fitness landscape as rough or smooth, etc. The ontological lack is to some extent recognized in increasingly vocal calls for "theories of organization" (a theory of organization is nothing but a metaphysics with a business plan). But the calls have not yet been answered.[18]

Ontological problems have also plagued physics for years, at least since foundational issues of interpretation were thrown into relief by the developments of relativity and quantum me-

---

[17] See for example Kaufmann (1993), Gell-Mann (1994), and Gleick (1984).

[18] A dramatic historical example involves the development of graphics displays. It is relatively easy to program cellular automata with various kinds of rule, and to see—palpably, in front of one's own eyes—little "organisms" and other organized or patterned entities emerge—dynamically, like worms or clusters or hives of activity. But when one "sees" such a creature emerge, one is relying on one's perceptual apparatus. No one yet has a theory that, given a field of cellular activity, can reliably identify such "objects" or "emergent entities." And *identification* is not really the problem, anyway. If the underlying theory—of selection, say, or organization, or behavioral emergence, or evolution—is to be worth its salt, it should be defined in terms of a theory of such things. (It has even been speculated that the entire field of non-linear dynamics, popularly called "chaos theory," could not have happened without the development of such displays. No one would have "seen" the patterns in textual lists of numbers.)

chanics (including the perplexing wave-particle duality, and the distinction between "classical" and "quantum" world views[19]). They face connectionist psychologists, who, proud of having developed architectures that do not rely on the manipulation of formal symbol structures encoding high-level concepts, and thus of having thereby rejected propositional content, are nevertheless at a loss as to say what their architectures *do* represent.[20] And then there are communities that tackle ontological questions directly—not just philosophy, but poetry and art, where attempts to get in or around or under objects and ontology have been pursued for centuries.

So there are fellow travelers (perhaps even fellow readers). In this book, however, at least for one more chapter, I will remain focused on the case with which I started: computation in the wild. For the plan for the book is to respond to the encounter with the ontological wall by developing an actual, concrete, metaphysical proposal—not simply to press for properties or features that an adequate metaphysics must have. Unlike at least some arguments for realism or irrealism, and also unlike some treatises pro or con this or that philosophy of science, the present project is not intended to be *meta*-metaphysical. But answering the concrete demand requires detailed, representative examples—examples, as one says, that "go the distance." And for this purpose the computational realm has unparalleled advantage. Midway between matter and mind, computation stands in excellent stead as a supply of concrete cases of middling complexity—what in computer science is called a "validation suite"—against which to test specific metaphysical hypotheses. "Middling" in the sense of being neither so simple as to invite caricature, nor so complex as to defy comprehension. Crucially, too, they are cases with which we are as much practically as theoreti-

---

[19] See the sidebar on page 146.
[20] See e.g. Smolensky (1988) and Cussins (1990). Though not, strictly speaking, a connectionist, Brooks' (1991) proposal to set aside representation entirely can be viewed as an extreme version of this view.

cally familiar (we build systems better than we understand them[21]).

The end result is intended to be general, however—i.e., to cope as well with other fields' ontological problems as with computation's—so I have tried to present the examples in chapter 1 in a straightforward enough way that readers from other disciplines can understand what is going on. As far as possible, technical details have been restricted to a series of sidebars. As a result, the text should be accessible to anyone even moderately familiar with conceptual issues in computation, artificial intelligence, or cognitive science. Still, in places chapter 1 is rough going. If computers are not your cup of tea, do not fret the details. Better to identify situations in your own experience that exhibit analogous (or disanalogous) structure than to try to figure these out, which will anyway not work if they are not "in the bones" familiar. Computation is *an* example, throughout; it is never *the* example.

At the beginning of chapter 2, with motivation and examples in place, I set aside any further consideration of computational issues per se, and for the remainder of the book go straight for the metaphysical jugular. The project from that point forward remains as described at the outset: to develop a new metaphysical/ontological account—an account adequate, at a minimum, though that will turn out to be much less of a minimum than anyone would have had any right to expect, to the computational task.

4 Rhetoric

One final comment, on writing. It turns out that the normative demands on writing in computer science and philosophy are

---

[21] In the spirit of Vico's "verum et factum convertuntur" (1744/1984), Dretske (1994) argues that to understand a mechanism is to know how to build one. I am sympathetic to a necessity reading of the claim, expressed for example in Dretske's title: "If You Can't Make One, You Don't Know How It Works." But present computational practice, in my view, defies a sufficiency reading.

rather different. In computer science, a text is treated as something like a map or travel guide: it gives you a route to the author's real contribution, but once that contribution is reached (understood, implemented), the text has served its purpose, and might as well be thrown away. It is assumed that the destination can be evaluated on autonomous criteria—of elegance, utility, practicality, etc. (how fast it runs, how easy it is to use, how many people will buy it). Part of what it is to be a professional computer scientist is to know how to perform this kind of on-location property assessment. It would seem as bizarre for serious normative criteria to be applied to the guiding text as for the capabilities of a sports car to be confused with the merits of its owner's manual, or the value of a buried treasure to be confused with the merits of the path through the jungle one was forced to take to reach it.

The situation in philosophy is a little different. Here the text, or perhaps the argument that the text expresses, is subject to more serious normative evaluation. At its worst, this can sometimes make it seem as if conclusions are held to no higher (e.g., ethical) standard than the quality of the technical arguments that have been offered in their favor. But even at its best there remains a substantial difference between the two fields—a difference reflected in the fact that texts, at least arguably, are the primary product in philosophy, but of secondary importance in computer science.

This book may look like philosophy, but do not be fooled. Although in many ways it takes the form of an argument, if you scratch its surface it will betray its computational roots. It is only as much of an argument as I thought was necessary in order to show the reader the direction I was headed. I was less interested, this time around, in developing watertight arguments than in introducing a new territory—a territory that I believe is worth exploring on its own merits.[22] The particular path I follow is by no means the only one to that territory; nor do I have any reason to suppose that it is necessarily the best. It is one of the routes I have traveled, however; I hope it is one that others find worthwhile as well.

[22] The TMD series presents a more rigorous and detailed argument.

Part I · Analysis

1 · Computation

Turn, then, to computation, and to the sorts of ontological problem that arise. As this chapter will show, they infect the subject at every level. I start (in §1 and §2) by addressing some evident ontological issues in the realm of computation itself, and go on (in §3) to claim that, first appearances notwithstanding, the discussion must be broadened to include general issues in ontology as a whole, because of computation's representational character. The ante is upped (in §4) in an argument that these two issues interact—that what we theorists take our systems to *represent* depends on how we take our systems to *be*—leading to the conclusion (in §5 and §6) that developing an adequate theory of computation requires developing a full theory of ontology.

Throughout, the aim is not only to show that a theory of computation requires a theory of ontology, but to develop some sense of what such a theory of ontology will have to be like.

1   The ontology of computation

The first set of ontological problems that a theorist of computation encounters has to do with the nature of computation itself—with the kind and character of the workaday entities of professional computational practice. What are *programs*, for example, really; and how do they differ from *data structures*? What is an *implementation level*? What is an *abstraction boundary*? What is the relation between *hardware* and *software* (the mind/body problem for machines)? In what ways are *interpreters*, *compilers*, and *emulators* alike, and in what ways different? Are *virtual machines* physical or abstract? What exactly is *state*? What are the identity conditions on *functions*, *algorithms*, *programs*, and *implementations*? What is the difference between an *effect* and a *side-effect*? How do *computer*, *computation*, and *comput-ability* relate?

Every one of these questions is one about which working pro-grammers have deep-seated intuitions. Nor, except in tricky sit-uations, is there much disagreement; the field is characterized by a remarkably robust, though rough and tacit, working con-sensus. Thus it is rare for someone to complain, outright, that something advertised as a compiler is really an emulator or an algorithm, even if no one can say exactly what a compiler, emu-lator, or algorithm is. This confluence of practical opinion is important—though it is also important that it not be misun-derstood. It consists less of a prior agreement on everything, in principle, so much as an ability, in specific cases, to negotiate or work through to consensus. Thus, to take a current example, debates rage about how (and even whether) scripting languages do or should differ from programming languages. Over time, though, these debates often converge. What we have been un-able to do, at least so far, is to give adequate voice to the intu-itions on which such agreements are based—i.e., to develop an appropriately fine-grained articulated account of computation that does them all justice.

To say this is not intended to be critical or discouraging; it is simply a recognition that computer science is still in its infancy. Nevertheless, to see just how inchoate our present understand-ing is, one only needs to see what happens when one tries to "lift" this tacit understanding outside its natural context—and redeploy it somewhere as nearby as in the debate about the com-putational theory of mind.

Thus consider Searle's characterization of cognitivism as the idea "that the mind is to the brain as software is to hardware."[1] Based on this analogy, Searle goes on to claim that cognitivism must consequently be false, because programs, being syntactic entities, are abstract, and hence lack the requisite causal powers

---

[1] Searle (1980, 1984).

to be a mind.[2] Is this a sound argument? Recall what was said in the introduction, about how such claims can fail in two different ways. Quite apart from the merits of the main premise (that the relation of mind to brain is that of software to hardware), the truth of the conclusion depends on the additional claim that being a program is an abstract property. But is this true?

It is not clear. Imagine two programmers—I will call them McMath and McPhysics—who disagree. McPhysics argues against Searle, denying that programs are abstract. Instead, they[3] claim, to be a program is to be a physical object, or at least to be as physical as any arrangement of physical things counts as physical. In order to be a program, that is, something must be able to be used as a causally efficacious ingredient with which to engender behavior by a concrete machine. Au fond, programs have to work. So even if a purely abstract structure, such as one made up in the universe of pure set theory, might be a (set-theoretic)

[2]Or, more sophisticatedly, that *as syntactic entities* they are abstract—i.e., that the theory of them *as* syntactic is not a theory that can explain their causal powers. See Searle (1992).

[3]Throughout, I will use 'they' and 'them' as syntactically plural but semantically singular third-person personal pronouns of unmarked sex. It seems the best alternative. 'He/she' and 'his or her' are irretrievably awkward, and it seems unlikely that any entirely new or invented word will ever be satisfactory. And there is precedent. In the second person case, we are entirely accustomed to using the syntactically plural 'you' to convey semantically singular as well as semantically plural meanings. In formal writing, the syntactically plural 'we' is even sometimes used as a stylized and somewhat detached form of singular first-person reference (though in this book I will use the grammatically singular 'I'). So using 'they' fits into a general pattern of employing the plural form when pointed, individual reference is not justified. It appears moreover that exactly this pattern is naturally evolving in informal speech.

None of this is to deny that 'the painter picked up their brush' sounds awkward and informal—to say nothing of 'the barber shaved themself.' The awkwardness may pass, however, and anyway informality is better than artifice.

model of a program, it could no more *be* a program than a mathematical model of a rainstorm could itself be a storm, could itself cause things to get wet.[4]

McMath, however, takes the opposite view, claiming that programs are as abstract as any of the sets and numbers and other first-order structures we studied in graduate school. Sure enough, McMath agrees, no program that is not physically instantiated (modeled?) can be useful, in the sense of doing material work. And yes, it might be that no one would (literally) pay for it unless it could be so realized. But that is a practical consideration, they go on, having nothing to with the abstract theory of programs itself. In fact theoretical computer science, on McMath's view, is very close to, and might even be profitably merged with, intuitionistic logic and constructive mathematics.[5]

It is hard to predict how real-world programmers would vote if presented with this question directly—especially in the absence of any surrounding discussion. A majority might initially agree with McMath, in no small measure because the reigning "theory of computation" treats computation (or at least computability) as a purely abstract mathematical subject matter. But suppose one were to press on this intuition, by elaborating Searle's claim that on such a view the wall of his office could, without contradiction, be interpreted as a running implementation of WordPerfect, by employing sufficiently outlandish "physical" properties in support of the instantiation relation (such as by defining P to be "is 8 feet tall until 9:23:07 A.M. on July 23, 1995, but 9 feet tall thereafter"—so that the wall would change state, from being-in-state-P to not-being-in-state-P, at

---

[4] The rainstorm example is also from Searle (1980), p. 423.
[5] The convergence of these two fields, noted informally by Dana Scott and others in the 1970s, is reflected for example by the use of Martin-Löf's intuitionistic type-theories by Constable and others. See, e.g., Constable et al. (1986).

the appropriate moment without any expenditure of energy whatsoever).[6]

All programmers, in my experience, balk at this suggestion, rejecting the use of such physically meaningless predicates. Under pressure, that is—though, notably, without supporting theory—just about all working computationalists will not only admit but insist that there must be causal constraints underwriting the notion of what counts as computationally legitimate. Admittedly, it is not clear at what level these constraints should be stated. They will have to be at least somewhat abstract, in the face of what are called "multiple realizability" arguments: that there is nothing special about any particular implementing medium—nothing unique about silicon, or vacuum tubes, or gallium arsenide. But neither can they be so abstract as to let Searle's perverse wall predicate through. Even if we do not quite know how to formulate them, these views support McPhysics' contention that to be a program intrinsically involves at least some kind of physical or causal property.[7]

Programs are not the only kind of computational entity for which fundamental ontological problems remain unanswered. In a similar vein, the connections remain to be clarified about the relation between these computational categories and semantics, such as about what happens to the ineliminably semantical aspect of information—the fact that information is information *about* something—in popular reductions of information to an almost physical notion of complexity, such as Kolmogorov complexity.[8] We do not even yet have a good understanding

[6] Searle (1992). See Goodman (1983), pp. 74–81, for a discussion of predicates of this odd sort—his examples are 'grue' and 'bleen,' for "green if examined before time T, else blue," and vice versa—and Fodor (1987), p. 33, for a comment on their irrelevance in causal explanation.

[7] As much as anything is intrinsic to anything else; see e.g. §4 of chapter 8, chapter 9, and chapter 11.

[8] For various attempts to deal with the semantic nature of information, see Dretske (1981), Barwise & Perry (1983), Rosenschein (1985), and Halpern (1987).

The seriousness of programs

Asking the sorts of questions posed in the text, especially of working programmers, reveals a normative dimension to the topic not usually accounted for in theoretical accounts. Physicality seems not to be the only thing that is violated in Searle's suggestion; so is seriousness. If we are genuinely to do justice to computational practice—and that remains the primary methodological mandate—we must also recognize that a decision to register or take something as this or that kind of machine, this or that kind of program, is not merely a theoretical exercise, but a matter of commitment, complete with associated benefits and trade-offs. What programmers find most disturbing about Searle's thought experiment, in other words, is not simply the conclusion in itself that an ordinary wall could literally implement a word processor, but the idea that one could reach a conclusion about what program something was running with so little apparent personal or professional cost. The problem is not so much that the proposal treats computation as abstract, to put it another way; it is that the question itself is so abstract. It has something of a Teflon feel to it: abstruse and disconnected from anything real. Programs in the wild, in contrast, are more consequential than this, more entrenched and connected into the fabric of surrounding events.

of *process*, arguably the most potent notion in all of computer science.

2 The use of metaphorical terms

Rather than merely recite more examples, it will help to get at a pattern that underlies this general inarticulateness. As so often happens, especially when a field is young, computer science employs terms and concepts borrowed from another place and time, using them initially in an essentially metaphorical way, but so as gradually to stretch their meaning, until, as the community develops a surer sense of the layout and geography of the new terrain, they come to have literal, but computationally specific, meanings.[9] Given the intellectual origins of computer science, it is no surprise that much of our present-day computational vocabulary was lifted from the study of logic, mathematics, and formal languages. And the objects that occupied the foreground in those traditions were, among other things, by and large either (i) *linguistic* or *grammatical*—written formulae or sentences, with a grammar and constituent structure, such as are familiar from the ordinary quantificational calculi—or (ii) *abstract*, such as the numbers and sets and functions that they have usually been taken to denote. Moreover, the virtually universal and by-now mythologized semantical model, which I will call the "binary model of semantics," involved mapping elements of the first onto elements of the second.[10]

Unfortunately, in my opinion, the uncritical attempt to fit computation into this typology has obscured, rather than illuminated, the true nature of the computational situation. The fundamental problem stems from the fact that the paradigmatic computational situation involves at least three types of entity, not just two. The situation is caricatured in figure 1·1, which discriminates among: (i) a *program*, of the sort that might be edited with a text editor; (ii) the *process* or *computation* to which that program gives rise, upon being executed; and (iii) some (often external) *domain* or *subject matter* that the computation is about. Three objects naturally give rise to three binary relations, of which I will take two to be of primary importance: the

---

[9] See Boyd (1979). To the extent that the later metaphysical story involves us in considerations of reference, this kind of wholesale adoption and revision of a set of technical terminology is something that must be accounted for.

[10] For the moment I am ignoring the way in which intensional contexts are dealt with, which almost always involves positing an intermediate realm— of senses, intensions, propositions, "meanings," or whatever—between the realm of grammatical items and the realm of their denotations. The kind of triple model discussed in the text involves a deeper and more primary division into three.

program-process relation, labeled 'α' in the diagram; and the *process-subject matter* relation, labeled 'β'.

If you adopt the simple binary model, you are forced either to ignore or to elide one of these distinctions, and (usually) thereby to conflate two of the three fundamental types of entity. In cognitive science and the philosophy of mind—and more generally, I think, in disciplines surrounding computer science—it is the distinction between program and process that is elided. This leads people to adopt two very familiar views: (i) that computation is fundamentally syntactic (the manipulation of structures that are in some essential sense like written tokens); and that it can therefore be adequately characterized using concepts that were developed for written languages, such as a simple type/token distinction, a notion of (lexical) constituent, etc.; and (ii) that 'semantics' refers to the relation β between "computation" (the conflation of program and process) and the world in which that computation is embedded. Theoretical computer science, however, takes the opposite tack: it focuses on the program-process relation α, not so much eliding as setting aside the process-subject matter relation. As a result, computer scientists view programs, not processes, as syntactic, but treat computation itself abstractly; and, more seriously, take the word 'semantics' to refer to the program-process relation (α), not to that between process and subject matter (β).

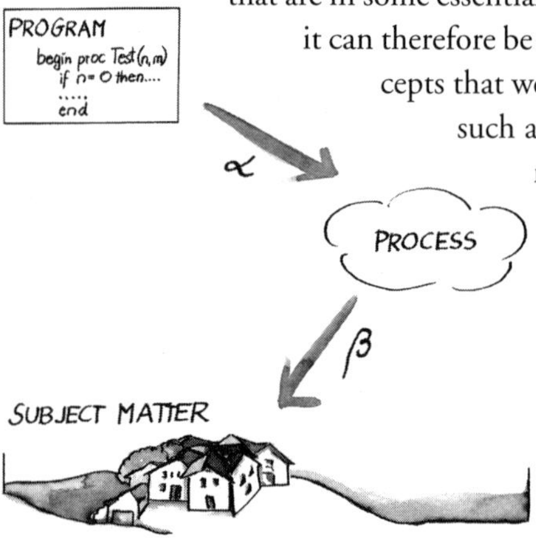

FIGURE 1·1 PROCESS VS. PROGRAM SEMANTICS

Naturally, this characterization is far too simple; it ignores numerous crucial subtleties.[11] Still, it is enough to explain a raft

---

[11] Primary among these is the fact that programs, in some cases, can be understood in terms of the resulting processes' semantic domain—i.e., as if α and β could be *composed*. See for example Smith (1987), TMD·IV, and

of rampant theoretical confusions. The fact that cognitive science treats computations not just as concrete but as syntactic has misled a generation of philosophers into thinking that all standard architectures—von Neumann machines, Lisp, just about everything except connectionist networks—involve the explicit manipulation of formal symbols. This I believe is simply false.[12] It has also led them to presume that such predicates as "concatenation" and "constituent" are appropriate for describing the relationships among a computational process's causal or effective ingredients. In point of fact, however, it is impossible to say what "contains" what is inside a computer—e.g., inside what is called the Lisp "heap," essentially a large directed and potentially cyclic pointer graph. Nor, again contrary to many current discussions in the philosophy of mind, is there any clear sense to be made of the notion of a data structure's being "tokened." But entire debates—such as that between connectionists and so-called "classicists" (defenders of a Language of Thought)—have been conducted as if this grammatical intellectual heritage from formal logic could unproblematically be carried over.[13]

Perhaps the most unfortunate consequence of the adoption of the traditional binary semantic model, however, has been in outsiders' tendency to elide *program* and *process,* and thereby to miss an extraordinarily important ontological shift in focus at

...———————————————

Dixon (1991). Nevertheless, I maintain that the characterization in the text exemplifies what ought to be an important predicate in the philosophy of science: of being truer than anything else this short.

[12] By analogy, it would patently be a mistake to conclude, from the fact that a blueprint for a gasoline engine was covered with words ('injector,' 'driveshaft,' etc.), that the specified engine was an internal symbol combustion machine. Although I believe that computational processes *are* intentional—even representational, on a sufficiently wide reading of 'representation'—to conclude that they are representational from the fact that *programs* are manifestly syntactic is (to at least a first order of approximation) an equivalent use/mention mistake.

[13] Fodor and Pylyshyn (1988), Smolensky (1991), Fodor and McLaughlin (1990), Aydede (1993).

the heart of computer science. This is a very deeply entrenched change away from treating the world in terms of static entities instantiating properties and standing in relation, and towards a view that is much more intrinsically dynamic and active. Later on, for example, I will argue that we should not think about what it is to *be an object*, but should instead focus on what it is to *behave or act or participate or be treated as an object* (this without abandoning appropriate notions of objectivity and realism). By the same token, intentionality will be reconstructed not so much in terms of a static notion of meaning or significance, but instead in active terms of *being meaningful* or *being significant*.[14] Activities and/or processes will be intentional "first," as it were, with more static states and objects deriving their intentionality from them. It is important to realize that this adjustment in focus will seem natural—indeed, almost boring—to practicing computer scientists.

By the same token, the theoretical point of view in computer science has led to equally curious views, including for example the idea that all semantic relations must be effective, since programs would not be of much use unless they could be used to engender (not just to describe) computations. Programs, that is, are treated as much as *prescriptions* as *descriptions*. And of course it is natural to restrict your attention to effective relations, if you restrict your focus in this way to the program-process relation α. This explains the increasing intimacy, noticed above, between theoretical computer science and intuitionistic mathematics. But there is of course no requirement that the process-world relation β be effective (unless one is *metaphysically* intuitionistic). It is hard to understand how one could refer to something outside one's light cone, for example, or even how the notion of a light cone could ever have been made coherent, if *all* semantical relations had to be effective.[15]

---

[14] See e.g. Wenger (forthcoming).
[15] The notion of a light cone of an object **x**, at a position in space-time, is from relativity theory, referring to that part of the space-time universe with

Clearing up these confusions would seem to be a minimal first step towards a better understanding of computational ontology. But even that is not so easy. In 1981, as something of a design exercise, I developed a programming language called 2-Lisp, with the explicit aim of exhibiting within the context of a programming language a degree of semantical clarity about these very semantical issues.[16] More particularly, I identified two different semantical relationships: one, approximately α in the diagram, between external expressions and internal computational structures that I called *impressions* (i.e., using the word 'impression' to designate *process* ingredients); and another, approximately β, between those impressions and such external, Platonic entities as sets, numbers, and functions.

Some 2-Lisp details are presented in the sidebar (page 39), but it is the morals of that experiment that are important here. First, in part because I myself came from an artificial intelligence and cognitive science background, like many others in the philosophy of mind I was too ready to use grammatical concepts to

...

which x could potentially interact in the future, or could potentially have interacted in the past, without violating the prohibition against signals traveling at greater than the speed of light. Light cones are challenging to causal theorists, or at least should be challenging, because it is hard to understand what causal chain could ever have led back to a dubbing of a light cone *as* a light cone—or equivalently, how light cones, as figures, could ever have been causally distinguished from their backgrounds.

[16] Smith (1984). 2-Lisp was a stepping-stone en route to 3-Lisp, a so-called "reflective" programming language, which was partially constituted with respect to an effective internal model of its own structure, operations, and behavior. The thesis embodied in 3-Lisp was that reflection, a much more substantial form of self-reference than the mere referential cyclicity of such antinomies as "I am lying," more like what philosophy would call self-knowledge than self-reference, was relatively simple if based on a semantically rationalized base. 2-Lisp was offered as that semantically cleaned-up predecessor. I still believe that 2-Lisp is closer to being "right," semantically, than any other dialect of Lisp, before or since. But it was nevertheless a failure, for reasons adumbrated in the text.

characterize the innards of a computational process. To consider just a small example, I used the term 'numeral' for those inner "impressions" that canonically designated numbers, rather than for the "expressions" that notated them. This turned out to be ill-advised. At the time the choice had seemed reasonable, because these process-internal structures possessed what I took to be the most important characteristic of numerals: namely, of being canonical witnesses to, and standing in a one-to-one correspondence with, and being effectively usable in engendering calculations about, but nonetheless of not actually being, numbers. On the other hand they did *not* have another property widely taken to be characteristic of numerals: namely, that of having a base (being roman, arabic, binary, whatever), or of being visible marks in a consensually shared medium of expression. Whatever its merits, this choice of terminology sowed a certain amount of confusion. It was especially confusing to theoretical computer scientists—because of their tendency, alluded to above, to conflate the ingredient elements of a computation with the corresponding elements of their subject matter (this is especially common when the two are approximately isomorphic, as they often are in cases like this, when the process is defined over a purely mathematical subject matter). It is not unusual for computer scientists, that is, to think of these canonical internal witnesses as actual numbers. To me, that seemed to require a much more solipsist or idealist metaphysics than anything I was willing to credit—indeed, an at least residual realism was something I was fighting for in designing 2-Lisp in the first place.

What morals should be drawn from this experience? I believe there are two. First, all three domains relevant to a computation—program, process, and semantic domain (task domain, domain of interpretation)—must be recognized by an adequate theory of computation as first-class realms in their own right. Moreover, they should also be classified with properties they ac-

In logic, we are taught to be strict about the familiar distinction between numerals and numbers. Numerals, on the standard story, are canonical designators of numbers, though they come in various varieties: arabic, roman, binary, etc. (there is no such thing, on at least a standard reading, as a binary *number*; numbers are numbers, without a "base," but they can be *represented* in any number of bases). Although informal discussion is often sloppy, maintaining a clear distinction between the two is considered an elementary case of semantical hygiene. Computation, for example, is on such a view crucially numeral-crunching, not number-crunching.

Given this general mandate, and the three-way distinction depicted in figure 1·1 (on page 34), the design of 2-Lisp made, and forced its users to make and forever maintain, a strict distinction among at least the following types of object:

1. *Numbers* and *sequences*, abstract entities outside the machine;
2. Canonical impressions, called *numerals* and *rails*, that *designated* those numbers and sequences, respectively;
3. *Notations*, such as the three-character string '475', or the eight-character string '[2 7 13]', that (as I put it at the time) *notated* these impressions; and
4. *Handles*, another kind of internal structure or impression, notated with a single leading quotation mark, that (at a meta-level) in turn canonically designated the internal structures described in (2), or the notations described in (3).

This typology was recursive, enabling one to say such baroquely complicated things as the following: that the four-character string "'345" was a *notation* that *expressed* the internal *handle* that *designated* the canonical internal *impression* that in turn *designated* the *number 345*. Or, in turn: that the six-character string "''345'" was a *notation* that *expressed* the internal *impression* that *designated* the previously described four-character string. And so on and so forth. Note, too, that this entire matrix of distinctions is cross-cut by yet a fifth: that between types and their instances (thus "'345'" and "'345'" are two instances of the same string type)—leading to the untenable complexity described in the text.

tually exhibit, rather than classified metaphorically, with properties lifted from a merely analogous domain.

The second moral is much more serious. In practice, 2-Lisp's semantical strictness was unbearable. When it mattered, it was very convenient to have a rigorous way to distinguish among number, numeral, impression, string, type, token, character, etc. And it did sometimes matter. It mattered to the routines (what computer scientists would call coercion routines) that translated or moved around among these various kinds. It also mattered when the one-to-one correspondence broke down. From a practical point of view, however—which is to say, for virtually all purposes—it was almost essential to elide many of these distinctions (although which distinctions to elide, at any given point, depended on the specifics of the case). And yet, at the very same time, there sometimes arose other types of situations—such as during garbage collection, or when handling side-effects—when even more distinctions were required than 2-Lisp made, such as between different copies of the internal impressions.

It was soon clear that what was wanted, even if I did not at the time know how to provide it, was a way of allowing distinctions to be made on the fly, as appropriate to the circumstances, in something of a type-coercive style—and also, tellingly, in a manner reminiscent of Heideggerian breakdown. Representational objects needed to become visible only when the use of them ceased to be transparent. Reason, moreover, argued against the conceit of ever being able to make *all* necessary distinctions in advance—i.e., against the presumption that the original designer could foresee the finest-grain distinction anyone would ever need, and thus supply the rest through a series of partitions or equivalence classes. Rather, what was required was a sense of identity that would support dynamic, on-the-fly problem-specific or task-specific differentiation—including differentiation according to distinctions that had not even been imagined at a prior, safe, detached, "design" time.

It was sobering, moreover, to encounter this moral (which many social theorists would argue for in much more complex settings) even in such simple arithmetic cases as essential arithmetic calculation— *allegedly the paradigmatic case of formal symbol manipulation construal of computation.* If even arithmetic generates this much complexity, that lends strong support to the idea that in more general situations it will be even more inadequate to treat objects as having stable purpose-independent identities, without regard to the functions or regularities in which they participate.

Any programmer could go on and on supplying such examples. One more is presented in the "Crossing the implicit–explicit boundary" sidebar on page 43. And the lessons in other realms are similar. One can easily construct cases in which a structure that is side-effect-free, from one perspective, crucially

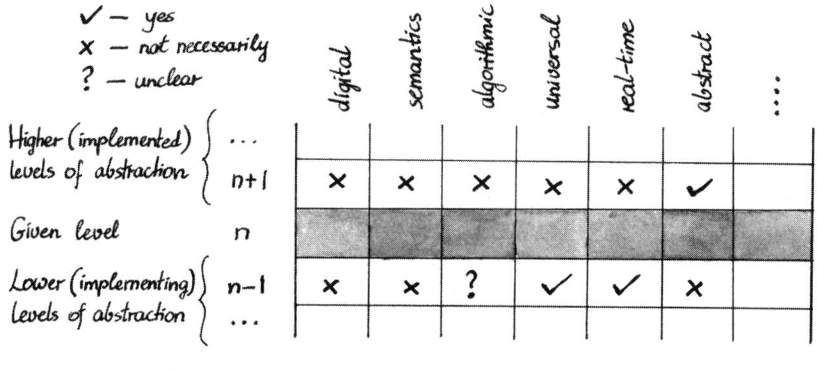

		digital	semantics	algorithmic	universal	real-time	abstract	…
Higher (implemented) levels of abstraction {	…							
	n+1	✗	✗	✗	✗	✗	✓	
Given level	n							
Lower (implementing) levels of abstraction {	n−1	✗	✗	?	✓	✓	✗	
	…							

Legend:
✓ — yes
✗ — not necessarily
? — unclear

FIGURE 1·2 IMPLEMENTATION BOUNDARIES

involves a side-effect, from another (such as setting up a circular data structure)—a situation that leads one to wonder what it is to say that state is a perspectival property.[17] Other examples

[17] See chapter 6 of Bawden (1993) for a radically non-traditional theory of state, including an analysis of how state appears to different observers, especially observers embedded within the system itself.

demonstrate the complication involved in the notion of implementation. As suggested in figure 1·2, for example, there are some properties, such as being Turing-complete, that cross implementation boundaries "downwards," but not "upwards": if language l_1 is implemented in language l_2, l_1's being Turing-complete implies that l_2 is Turing-complete, but not the other way around. Other properties, such as being discrete and thereby proscribing chaotic turbulence, go upwards but not downwards. Still others, such as using heuristics or supporting recursion—and perhaps also semantics—need not cross in either direction. Where is the account of implementation boundaries that will make sense of all this?

3 Computational ontology

Challenging as it may be, this first set of ontological issues, about the nature of computation itself, pales in importance in the face of a second one. Computer scientists wrestle not just with notions of computation itself, but with deeper questions of how to understand the ontology of the worlds in which their systems are embedded. This is so not just for the elementary (if significant) reason that anyone building a functioning system must understand the context in which it will be deployed, but for the additional one that computational systems in general, being intentional, will *represent* at least some aspects of those contexts. The representational nature of computation implies something very strong: that *it is not just the ontology of computation that is at stake; it is the nature of ontology itself.*

Since this is far from an obvious conclusion,[18] it is worth unpacking a bit. The way that task domain ontology enters the

---

[18] In philosophy, it is traditional to view representation as independent of ontology. The examples in this section can be taken as intuitive evidence against this conclusion; and the rest of the book as a proposal for the consequences of its being false. A substantive argument to this effect—i.e., against the independence of representation and ontology (and thus for their interdependence)—is given in TMD·IV. See also Cussins (forthcoming).

Crossing the implicit–explicit boundary

One more quick example may strengthen the moral that one cannot, in designing computational structures, presume to think in advance of everything that will ever be important or needed. Suppose you were to develop a record system for all graduate students in your university. For each student you assign a record that includes name, social security number, year, and department. At first everything works swimmingly well. Your program becomes famous—so much so that all the other schools in your neighborhood decide to use it. So far there is no problem. But now suppose a motion is introduced to allow students to cross-register among schools, requiring all the various copies of the program to be able to communicate. It is clear that to support this expanded use, another entry will be needed in the data base—a new field, per student-class-registration, to identify the school at which they are registered.

This example illustrates a situation that is tremendously widespread in real-world practice: of needing to *add a field* (slot, variable, whatever) to a representational data structure so as to make explicit something that was previously implicit, so as in turn to allow the record or system to be used in settings in which a property that was originally and tacitly assumed to be fixed, can now be changed to one in which it is explicitly recognized to be variable. And one can *never* know all the slots one might need in advance.

computational arena has to do with the *sense*, the *mode of presentation*, or what Searle calls the "aspectual shape" of representation: the fact the you represent the relevant part of the world *as being a certain way*.[19] How this goes will depend on your ontological commitments. In one situation you may represent it as consisting of objects, properties, and relations; in another, as a superposition of waves; in a third, as a two-dimensional matrix of light intensities. I am not here concerned with the case-specific details, which will always depend on facts about the sub-

---

[19] Frege (1892/1993), p. 24; Searle (1992), p. 155.

ject matter at hand—bank balances, say, voter registration records, or flight schedules. Rather, I am concerned with the more general ontological assumptions that control the categories in terms of which these details are formulated (categories like *object*, *property*, *relation*, and *wave*); and higher-order properties of those properties, having for example to do with issues of *negation*, *parameterization*, *instantiation*, etc.

To make this concrete, consider the exploding interest, both theoretical and practical, in the development of object-oriented languages. Even if not advertised as such, this turn of events has led computer science squarely into the business of doing research in ontology. This is an unavoidable conclusion of taking a serious look at practice.

As with any strong conclusion, this is a claim that invites detraction. In an attempt to counter it, for example, someone might argue that this computational practice is just an effort to represent the ontology of specific subject domains: bank accounts, say, or airplane flights, or window systems. But that is wrong; coding up the details of task-specific domains is the job of *users* of object-oriented languages, not of their designers. Someone else might claim that these computational designers are just concerned with providing effective supporting structures (control strategies, efficient access algorithms, strategies for defining problems in ontological terms, etc.), but that the real ontological issues (what objects are, for example, and how they relate to types, concepts, and abstraction; whether there are negative facts and propositions, or only denials of positive ones; and so on) would all be inherited, like semantics, from an appropriate philosophical backdrop. But that, too, I believe, is false. Computers are used in real, non-mythologized domains—a fact that puts extraordinary pressure on their ontological sophistication. An appropriately flexible philosophical backdrop simply does not exist.

As a result, computer scientists have ended up having to face all sorts of unabashedly metaphysical questions: about the nature of mereology (part/whole relations); about whether or not object identity within a system crosses different levels of abstraction or implementation, relevant to questions of theoretic reduction; about the nature of type/token distinctions; about individuation criteria, including the establishing of identity, for example in self-organizing systems; about the nature of parameterization; about the similarities and differences among sets, classes, and types; and so on and so forth. Nor are object-oriented system designers the only people involved in these issues; currently they are just the most visible. The same questions have been under investigation for decades by developers of knowledge representation schemes, data base designers, people worrying about strongly typed languages, and the rest. More recently they have been taken up anew by network designers wrestling with the relations among identifiers, names, references, locations, handles, etc., on the World Wide Web. Moreover, this ontological emphasis meshes in complex ways with computation's intentional character, for example in attempts to sort out the relation between higher-order vs. meta-level predicates or concepts—i.e., between $P(R)$ and $P('R')$, a distinction that seems clear enough in lexical representational vehicles, but whose clarity erodes when dealing with internal arrangements.[20]

Perhaps the most interesting thing about this ontological effort, moreover, has been the ways in which it has failed. The problem is that, upon encounter with real-world problems, it is hard for practitioners to avoid realizing that such traditional ontological categories as discrete countable objects, clear and precise categories, and other products of received ontological myth, are both too brittle and too restrictive.

The traditional categories are too detailed, for one thing: programmers are frustrated at having to decide whether men and

---

[20] Necessity and possibility are sometimes analyzed as syntactic operators, but more often as semantic modalities; for a discussion of the differences see e.g. Quine (1953), Montague (1963), and Kripke (1976).

women are different types, or a single type marked by a distinguishing feature (technically, do you create two classes, MAN and WOMAN, or a single class PERSON with a slot for gender?). They are also too narrow: as I will argue below, connectionists and others interested in "sub-symbolic" representation despair of being able to characterize the content of their networks in anything like familiar "object + property" fashion—and, lacking a richer ontological repertoire, are reduced to thinking that the networks must not be interpretable at all.[21] The traditional categories are also too committing: trying to say whether frogs track flies or only track black spots can be a scholastic exercise, an overinterpretation of the situation in terms of our own conceptual scheme, and yet we lack the resources to know how to characterize the situation differently, in sufficiently neutral terms.

By the same token, as suggested earlier, programmers have to deal with representations as varied as those that occur on architectural blueprints—mixes of images, icons, sketches, labels, brands, diagrams, figures, annotations, texts, etc. They need intellectual tools with which to characterize their content or representational import (how does one describe the content of the vague and tentative sketches that are so crucial in early stages of architectural design, for example? and how do they relate to the later-stage fully worked-out CAD structures?).[22] Designers of machine perception systems similarly want notions of objects that are fluid, dynamic, negotiated, ambiguous, and context-dependent (in part in order to represent fluid, dynamic, negotiated, ambiguous, and context-dependent objects!), rather than the black-and-white models inherited from logic and model-theory. So do engineers dealing with software re-use, user-friendliness, and portability—to say nothing of intellectual-

[21] Smolensky (1988), Cussins (1990), Kirsh (1991), p. 26. For a positive alternative, in which networks *are* interpreted or assigned semantics, but not in "object + property" form, see e.g. Churchland (1995), pp. 21–53, and Haugeland (1991).

[22] Goel (1995).

property-rights lawyers. To decide whether a given system is or is not an implementation of a standard program (Unix, say), or whether or not one company's chip violates a competitor's copyright (as for example whether AMD violated Intel's copyright on the i486), requires more sophisticated individuation criteria, and more subtle understandings of issues of reduction and supervenience (e.g., do identity conditions cross implementation or abstraction boundaries?) than are supplied by any known ontological theory.[23] Indeed, trying to force fit the political structure of a live and dynamic organization into a predefined set of discrete objects and categories is about as alluring as proposing that the US Army Corps of Engineers level the surface of North America into equal-area discrete strata with elevations that are exact multiples of 1000 feet.

Even what the issues are is only beginning to be appreciated. In part, it is increasingly recognized not only that the represented categories have context-dependent meanings, but that the question of what the categories are can only be answered dynamically, within the settings in which the computational systems are deployed. This presses for a kind of representational flexibility that current object-oriented systems lack. Indeed, as suggested in the "Objects in knowledge representation" sidebar (page 48), the challenges that this observation raises cut very deep, and even call into question some of the most basic assumptions on which this practice is based.

Even in situations where it would seem as if the techniques would apply, however, many current systems are not only remarkably inflexible, but tend to hang on to ontological commitments more than is necessary. Thus consider the sequence of drawings shown in figure 1.3 (page 49). Suppose that the figure shown in step 2 was created—in MacDraw, for example—by

---

[23] In fact the Intel-AMD suit depends on what the word 'microcode' denotes: whether, as Intel argues, it refers only to the "operating code" used in a *micro*processor or *micro*computer, or whether, as AMD contends, it includes the lower-level floating-point firmware.

Objects in knowledge representation

As much as twenty years ago, members of the knowledge representation community in artificial intelligence, and also a number of researchers working on data bases, began to wrestle with many of the same problems as now face object-oriented system designers. In part as a reaction to the insuperable difficulties they encountered, many people in the knowledge representation community abandoned the idea that a system's ontological categories (those in terms of which it deals with its primary subject matter) should be explicitly represented at all. Instead, they viewed them as emerging in constant and dynamic renegotiation with the environments in which these systems play or are deployed. It is interesting to speculate on how the mainstream programming community will rise to this challenge of developing external, social, and negotiated categories.

first drawing a square, then duplicating it, as suggested in step 1, and then placing the second square so as to superimpose its left edge on the right edge of the first one. If you or I were to draw this, we could then coherently say: now let us take out the middle vertical line, and leave a rectangle with a 2:1 aspect ratio, as suggested in step 3. But only recently have we begun to know how to build systems that support these kinds of multiple perspective on a single situation (even multiple perspectives of much the same kind, let alone perspectives in different, or even incommensurable, conceptual schemes).[24]

It should not be inferred from any of these comments that

---

[24]The MacDraw example is from Levy et al. (1988). Note that EMACS, a popular text and programming editor, derives much of its power from supporting multiple simultaneous "takes" on the string of characters in its buffer, in just the way suggested in the text. One command can view the buffer as a Lisp program definition; another, as a linear sequence of characters; another, as bracketed or parenthesized region. In order to support these multiple simultaneous views, EMACS in effect "lets go" of its parse of the buffer after every single keystroke, and re-parses all over again the next time a key is struck—possibly with respect to a wholly different grammar.

these theoretical inadequacies have stood in the way of progress. Computer science does what it always does in the face of such difficulties: it makes up the answers as it goes along—inventive, specific, and pragmatic, even if not necessarily well explicated. But that leads in turn to the third broad class of ontological problem—a problem with a methodological as well as a substantive dimension.

4 Inscription errors

So far I have discussed two problems: specific issues in the ontology of computation, in §1 and §2, and general issues in ontology as a whole, in §3, the latter relevant to a computer scientist because of computation's inherently representational character. It turns out that these two issues interact.

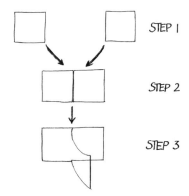

FIGURE 1·3 COMPUTER-DRAWN FIGURE

Although the details can get tricky, it is not hard to see some evidence of this interaction. As I will show in a moment, though it is hardly surprising, the choices one makes about the *content* of the various pieces of a representational system—how the representation represents its subject matter as being—are often affected by how one describes the computational structures themselves, the structures that have or carry that content. Thus we will see an example with the following structure: if we describe a system in one way, there is a very natural tendency to suppose that it represents an object; however, if we describe the very same system in another way, equally plausible, then this leads more naturally to the idea that what is being represented is not the object itself, but rather something more fine-grained, such as episodes in that object's life, or even discrete time-slices.

This is problematic because of the danger that one will unwittingly impose unjustified ontological categories onto the computational device, and as a result misclassify its semantic content. This leads, I believe, to one of the most important stumbling blocks that stand in the way of our ability to understand the true nature of computation (and, by implication, other intentional systems). It is a phenomenon that I will in general call an *inscription error*:[25] a tendency for a theorist or observer, first, to write or project or impose or inscribe a set of ontological assumptions onto a computational system (onto the system itself, onto the task domain, onto the relation between the two, and so forth), and then, second, to read those assumptions or their consequences back off the system, *as if that constituted an independent empirical discovery or theoretical result.*[26]

I will consider a number of examples, more or less briefly, to show how this works. Suppose, first, as depicted in figure 1·4, that, in a manner reminiscent of Brooks,[27] one were to build a

[25] Using a term I introduce in chapter 6, Cussins (forthcoming) calls this form of theoretical presumptuousness "pre-emptive registration."

[26] Inscription per se is not an error. In any situation, more or less "writing on the world" is invariably necessary—as much will be a mainstay of the metaphysical account to be proposed. What constitutes what I am calling an inscription *error*, in a particular case, is a failure to recognize a particularly blatant dependence of a claim or result on the original inscription, especially when that inscription is not appropriately warranted—e.g., in a case of chauvinism, projection, or naiveté. The notion is not intended to be black and white, though the cases I will explicitly cite throughout the book are pretty egregious.

'Inscription' connotes writing. Although, as just indicated, I am using the term to imply writing onto the world, not merely onto a representation, there is good reason to believe that the particular ontological frameworks most commonly adopted in current (especially formal) theoretical analysis, involving a strict distinction among objects, properties, and relations, and strict separation between entities of each type, is at least in part a product of writing, and even more specifically of printing. By the end of the book, moreover, I want to undermine the strict distinction between representation and ontology, thereby giving inscription a more general sense.

[27] Brooks (1986).

robot to pick up stray Coke cans. Whenever the robot first sees a can **x** feet in front of it and **y** to the right, it writes the pair <**x**, **y**> into an internal memory register. Then, as it approaches the can, it decrements the two parts of this pair appropriately, until it reaches <0, 0>. At that point it reaches down, picks up the can, tosses it into its hopper, and sets off in search of another one.

The question is what one wants to say about the representational content of this memory register. Here are some alternatives:

1. It egocentrically represents *a particular place*: that stable point on the floor **x** feet in front and **y** feet to the right of the robot's current position.

2. It egocentrically represents *the Coke can* lying at that position. The memory register is only used when there is a Coke can there, after all, and it is Coke cans, not positions, towards which the overall behavior of the system is directed.

FIGURE 1·4 COKE-CAN
COLLECTING ROBOT

3. Rather than egocentrically representing the position of either a place or a can, it *allocentrically* represents the position of *the robot itself*, with reference to the position of the Coke can (in much the way that, upon encountering a familiar landmark, one often represents one's own position with respect to it: "I see; I am still a quarter of a mile from the edge of the lake").

4. Rather than having any particular content, in terms of specific individuals or places, it instead represents the generic property of *being* **x** *feet in front and* **y** *to the right*.

5. It is not a representation at all, and so has *no* content. Rather, it is a simple control state in a digital servo mechanism.

Without more information, it is impossible to say which of these alternatives is right, although first-class metaphysical issues of reidentifiability, objectivity, and the like (all subjects to be addressed in later chapters) would have to be addressed in any serious analysis. Here I only want to make two points. The first one is relatively straightforward. If, in analyzing or describing such a system, one were simply to adopt one alternative or other, without clear justification, then any ensuing putative "facts" about the ontological and semantic character of the system would run the risk of being derailed by arbitrary choices imposed from the outside.[28]

The second point is more substantial. Even if one recognizes that the choice among these alternatives is problematic, and therefore engages in the sort of analysis suggested above, e.g., of reidentifiability, objectivity, etc., *one does not thereby escape the possibility of committing inscription errors.* Since the reason for this is very important, I want to step through the argument relatively carefully. The crucial thing, at any given point, is to pay attention to how one individuates the data structure about which the question of representational content is being asked. In the previous paragraph I took that question to be about a memory register—or rather, about a pair $<x, y>$ written into that register. Suppose, based on this description, one were to argue that this register represented the generic property of being x *feet in front* and y *to the right* of the robot. The problem is that this conclusion is liable to depend on the assumption that the memory register was a single individual, and *that* choice was in turn neither clarified nor justified.

More specifically: if one takes the overarching semantical question to be a question about the representational content of

---

[28] Arbitrary choice need not be problematic. In "arithmetized" physics, for example, we arbitrarily pick an origin and a set of units, without "derailing analysis." But such cases are special, and deserve special attention. In physics, the arbitrariness of a reference frame is well understood (and explicitly taught), and effort is expended to ensure that theoretical results do not depend "in bad ways" on such choices (involving what is known as renormalization). Risk was run; what makes the case special is that an acceptable outcome was nevertheless ensured.

a single enduring entity, one that lasts over time, through encounters with multiple different Coke cans, then one is much more likely, on analysis, to select the generic-content alternative (#4) from among the representational candidates listed above. But there are other possibilities. Suppose, for example, that one were instead to take a more punctuated approach to the robot's mental life, and were to take the subject matter of the question about content not to be the memory register as a whole, but different episodes in its life—episodes lasting from an initial sighting of the can until the point at which the can is picked up. On this second alternative, that is, each new episode is to be viewed as a new and different data structure. Given *this* approach, one would have more warrant for choosing one of the more particular interpretations of representational content (#1, #2, or #3). The justification for assigning different kinds of content to a system, that is, is vulnerable to the ways in which we (perhaps unwittingly) individuate the system itself. Even though one may *think* one is doing justice to the question about the proper ascription of content, by engaging in sophisticated arguments about reidentification and the like, that alone does not suffice to guarantee that inscription errors will not be made, unless one does the same for the internal arrangements of the system. And, to belabor the obvious, it is not clear in this internal case what justifies making one individuating choice over another—i.e., between a single data structure, and a temporal sequence of different ones.

A similar example is provided by analyses of conditions under which a system is able to reidentify a given object as being the same as one it saw before, rather than being a new one of the same type—e.g., the sort of argument that would be used to support the conclusion that the system is capable of particular, not just generic, reference. Again, this is worth going through slowly, because the moral only emerges from the details. Thus suppose someone were to claim that a system **r** was able to reidentify, at time t_2, an object **y** that it had previously encountered at time t_1. And suppose, further, that this claim were supported by an observation that, at time t_2, the system tied its perception of **y** to *the very same mental data structure* **x** that it had established on first encounter with **y**, at time t_1. For example, suppose one were to argue that a cat recognized its owner as a single and stable enduring individual, by showing that the same cells were activated upon each encounter with that person, and not with anyone else.

This form of argument proves nothing. *All it does is to piggyback the alleged identity of the content off the presumed identity of the representation.* The problem is that nothing has been provided to justify the claim that the manifestation of **x** at t_1 (e.g., the activity in the specific cells) and the manifestation of **x** at t_2 are in fact the same mental data structure (are one and the same set of cells)! Along the lines indicated above, one might instead have parsed the system differently, taking **x**-at-t_1 and **x**-at-t_2 to be different entities in the system's mental life, of a more dynamic or episodic nature, and taking the relation between them to be one of instantiating a common type ("being of type **x**"). This would lead more naturally to a generic, non-reidentification reading—e.g., that the cat's cells activate upon encounter with an instance of a particular-person-type—thereby defeating the proposed argument in support of reidentification.

It may help, in order to be clear, to treat two possible counter-intuitions, neither of which in fact succeeds in getting around the problem. Those of an engineering bent, first, might try to argue that this is a non-issue. Sure enough, they might agree, we observers rely on potentially ad hoc inscriptions in building systems and getting them to work. But who cares? The systems get the job done—do what they do, picking up Coke cans or whatever—independent of how we individuate them. This may be partially true, but it misses the point. I will give substantial credit to such constructive attitudes in a moment, but their contribution is subtle; they are not a wholesale way to duck theoretical problems. The primary question, after all, was how to understand the systems we build, not simply how to get them to behave.

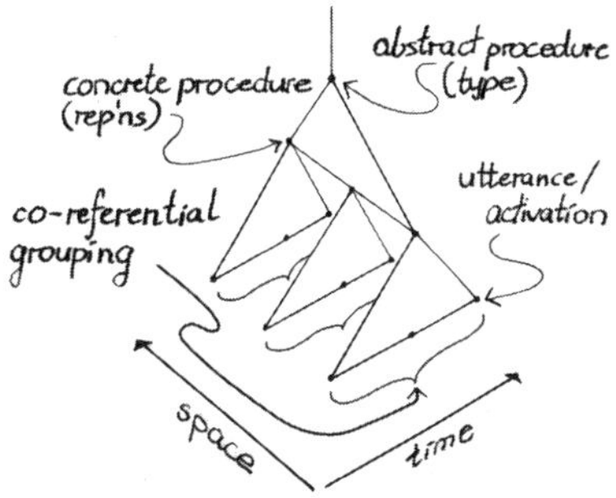

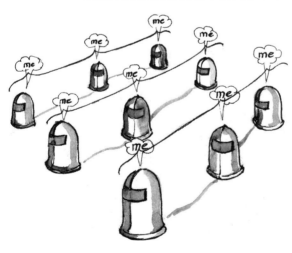

FIGURE 1·6   THE LOGIC OF "ME"

Second, others might be prepared to admit that *our* inscriptions are necessarily ad hoc, and hence should be inadmissible in a proper theoretical account, but might point instead to the creatures themselves, as if they could provide a defensible way to ground the individuation. The content of a critter's representation should not depend on how *we* individuate structural patterns in its brain, they might claim; the question is what these patterns are like *for the critter itself*. But this goes from bad to worse. For if the warrant for individuation criteria on mental episodes is unclear for observers, it is even less clear — in fact there may not be any compelling reason to believe there is even a metaphysical fact of the matter—for the system in question, e.g. for the cat. As intentional creatures, in representing the world we commit ourselves to taking

FIGURE 1·5   "ME": TIME-SPANNING REFERENCE

55

the *world* to be a certain way, but we do not thereby commit ourselves to any specific ontological parse of our own representational capacities. So there is no ready way to look to the system
itself for aid. Moreover, which makes a difficult problem even
more serious, someone might reasonably propose that the depen-
dency should go exactly the opposite way: that the warrant for
calling **x**-at-t_1 and **x**-at-t_2 different manifestations of one mental
representation, rather than different representations instantiating a common type, should depend on the fact that they are used,
by the system in question, to represent one reidentifiable entity in
the world. If such a suggestion were right, it would show the piggyback argument to be vacuous and backwards at the same time.

A different kind of example will substantiate this claim that
choices about system individuation can affect semantical analysis. Suppose one were to design a class of computers that have an
internal way of referring to themselves—say, by calling some
specially named procedure ME. And suppose one were to ask
whether this form of self-reference is indexical, in the familiar
"token-reflexive" way: that is, whether different instances of a
common type refer to different entities, in a way that is a systematic function of the instantiation context.[29]

Given this distinction, consider two ways of typing the situation:

1. Take the relevant type to be the general procedure type
   shared by all machines in the class, and the relevant instances
   to be the machine-specific copies of that procedure.

---

[29]The English pronoun 'I' is considered to be indexical on this metric,
since different utterances of it refer to different speakers in a systematic way
that depends on the context of use. In particular, on at least the simple-
minded theory, in each context a use of 'I' refers to whomever is speaking.
So the *meaning*—the aspect that is assumed to be the same in all these different cases, and what is described in the dictionary—is the general fact:
that the referent of 'I' is a function of its context of utterance, that function
that maps an utterance context onto the person who is speaking in it. In a
particular situation, the referent or *interpretation* will be different—sometimes me, sometimes you.

2. Take each machine-specific procedure to be the relevant type, and each occasion on which that procedure is executed to be the relevant instances.

On the first alternative, the self-reference *does* count as indexical, since different instances (copies) of a single type would systematically be used to name different objects (machines) in a way that depends systematically on the context of use. On the second alternative, however, the scheme is *not* indexical: each execution of a given procedure-copy results in the machine's referring to itself as the same extended temporal unity. Each specific call, across the life of a given machine, refers to the same thing as every other call during that same lifetime.

The "real" structure of the situation, in other words, is as depicted in figures 1·5 and 1·6 (p. 55). There is a two-stage fan-out, first from abstract procedure to copy, then from copy to use. What is to be semantically evaluated are the uses, at the bottom of the second fan-out. In the case of self-reference, the semantic value is (by assumption) shared by all uses of a given copy, but different from one copy to another—implying that the first fan-out is indexical, the second, not. If we replace "me" with "now," however, as in figures 1·7 and 1·8 (p. 60), the situation is transformed into an approximate dual: the semantic value will in general not be shared by different uses of a given copy, but may be shared from one copy to another (in particular, if two or more robots utter the word 'now' at the same time). Theoretically, it is clear that no binary "type-instance" distinction is sufficient to analyze these cases; at least a three-stage categorization is required. Moreover, as indicated in the "Cross-cutting fan-out" sidebar (p. 59), this is just the tip of the iceberg; real-world programs require even more complex analyses to deal with cross-cutting fan-outs, so that entities that look more abstract than others from one point of view (i.e., make fewer distinctions), look less abstract from another (make more distinctions).[30]

[30] Someone might recommend what seems an obvious solution: to define types for each of these species (the type *abstract variable*, the type *lexical oc-*

Two final examples will drive the point home. During the early 1980s I spent some time trying to work out a theory of representation,[31] somewhat Peircian in flavor, in terms of which to make the following sorts of intuitive claim: that the ordinary syntax of first-order logic *objectifies* properties and relations, because it represents them with objects. Thus I noted that the formula 'R(A,B)' itself consisted of three objects, 'R', 'A', and 'B', held together by a three-place grammatical construction, ' __ (__ , __)', but that it *represented* a two-place relation (call it **r**) between only two objects, the first, **a**, represented by 'A', the second, **b**, represented by 'B'. Since **a** and **b** were themselves objects, and were represented by objects ('A' and 'B'), I said they were represented *directly*. Since **r**, however, was not an object but a relation, but was represented by an object ('R'), I said that **r** was *objectified*.[32]

Sensible as this project might sound, or even if it sounds nonsensible, it was at any rate doomed. It was doomed for exactly the reason now under consideration. The problem was that the

· · ·

currence, the type *activation instance*, etc.), and then simply to axiomatize the various relations among them. This is unsatisfying because of the background suggestion that a theory of computation might be relevant to a theory of intentionality. The forms of instantiation to be found in the subject matter are supposed to illuminate how we understand types and their instances. To follow the given suggestion, therefore, would be to use, as part of one's theoretic machinery, what one might think of as a *red* type-instance relation, between these various objects and the suggested theoretic types, but then to color as *green* the relations among them. Sure enough, if red and green are kept wholly separate, confusion would not reign. But neither would understanding. At least within the context of cognitivism, the whole point of studying these systems is to understand *how red and green relate*. It would be bizarre to suppose that the instantiation structure of computer systems was entirely orthogonal to the instantiation structure of theoretical analysis.

[31] Smith (1987), TMD·IV.

[32] In this text I of course am referring to **r** as if it were an object; if possible, that fact should not be allowed to obscure the main point.

Cross-cutting fan-out

Consider the following definition of factorial, containing 3 lexical occurrences of the variable **n**:

```
define factorial (n)::-
    if n = 1
    then 1
    else n * factorial (n − 1)
```

Imagine calling it with an argument of 5. On each call (each activation frame) there is one value for **n**, so that *temporally* the variable has a fan-out of 5. *Spatially*, however, the fan-out is 3. The total number of variable-lookups is the product, 15.

For some purposes (e.g., program editing), the spatial fan-out is salient; for other purposes (e.g., debugging) the temporal fan-out is more important. Or to put it more ontologically, there is/are:

1. Something of which there is 1;
2. Something of which there are 3;
3. Something of which there are 5; and
4. Something of which there are 15.

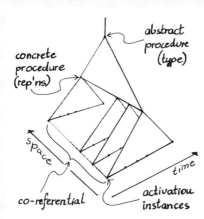

With respect to indexical reference, the factorial situation is thus the dual of figure 1.5's self-referential robot. Whereas the robot example illustrated temporal but not spatial co-reference, in the case of factorial the situation is opposite: the coreference is spatial but not temporal— and is thus more like the use of 'now' illustrated in figures 1.7 and 1.8.

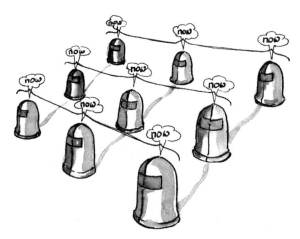

FIGURE 1·7   "NOW": SPACE-SPANNING REFERENCE

way the theory classified a semantic mapping was vulnerable to how the theorist classified the representational structures that were so mapped. And in many cases there was no way to decide. Thus consider ordinary road maps. If you take streets in the world to be objects, and lines in the map to be objects, then the representation is direct. But you can also take points on the map to be objects, and lines to be relations between them; in that case the classification of the map's semantics is different. It was not so much that there was no way to classify the representation (thus the example was different from that facing connectionists); it was just that there was no way to justify taking it one way over another.[33]

Informally, when I have made these claims of ambiguity, I am sometimes asked which way of registering the situation is *right*, or am asked—what amounts to the same thing, but is

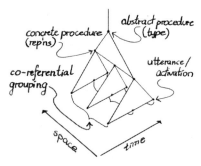

FIGURE 1·8   THE LOGIC OF "NOW"

[33]That is not to say that this problem would always defeat practice. In a given situation, a "user" might, tacitly or even with good explicit reason, make one choice over another. That would change the question only slightly: to inquire about how such choices can legitimately be made.

more cleverly packaged—to demonstrate a situation in which registering the situation incorrectly has led a theorist to make a false claim. *But of course I have no way of knowing!* That is the whole point. Nevertheless, it may help to conclude with a real-world example. In the late 1970s, Mitch Marcus, in developing a computational system for parsing natural language, defended the following strong claim: that human languages could be parsed by parsers that never "backed up"—i.e., that never rescinded any decisions they had made. This stood in stark contrast to standard practice at the time, in which parsers usually

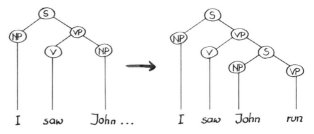

FIGURE 1·9 DETERMINISTIC PARSING

explored hundreds of alternative parses in the course of analyzing a single sentence, eventually throwing most of them away. In later work, Marcus devised a follow-on parser that sometimes was in fact forced to insert a node into the middle of a graph where one had not been before—e.g., to undergo a state change of the sort depicted in figure 1·9. The question was whether this new system violated the original mandate. Does moving from left to right in the figure constitute the system's "changing its mind"?[34]

Initially, it seemed that the answer had to be *yes*, since the tree, after all, which was taken to represent the grammatical structure of the incoming sentence, undeniably suffered a side effect. It was soon realized, however, that there was a different way of interpreting the graph. According to the initial and seem-

[34]The original parser is described in Marcus (1980); for the later work, see Marcus et al. (1983) and Marcus & Hindle (1990).

ingly most natural interpretation, for a node **b** to be the daughter of a node **a** (in the graph) meant that the grammatical
fragment represented by **b** must be an immediate constituent of
the grammatical fragment represented by **a**. On this interpretation, the parser had indeed "changed its mind." Suppose, however, one were to adjust the semantical interpretation function,
so that a node **b**'s being a daughter of a node **a** in a graph was instead taken to mean that the grammatical fragment represented
by **b** was "dominated" by the grammatical fragment represented
by **a**—where to be dominated meant that it was either an immediate constituent, or a constituent of a constituent, etc. *Voilà!*
Now the "information," as it is convenient to call it, represented
by the changed graph is compatible with the information represented by the graph on the left. So the parser has not changed its
mind after all! It has just learned some more precise facts.[35]

For parsers this adjustment in theoretic glasses may be fine; I
am in no way criticizing Marcus' work. But it does leave one
wondering how one is supposed to know which of the two interpretations, if either, is right. And although the example is particular, the issue is very general. If we are going to take cognitivism
seriously—i.e., the claim that computational mechanisms can
underwrite or exhibit intentional capacities—then something
must settle the matter as to the nature of such intentional contents. Being able to have content, after all, is what it is to be an
intentional capacity. So it is not an issue that can be left to arbitrary choice. *We* may not know what it is, but that does not
mean God leaves the content indeterminate.

5 Theorist's vs. subject's perspective

I have now argued: (i) that the ontological status of computation
itself is somewhat in disarray, at least as regards our ability to ar-
ticulate what is in the blood and bones of a working program-

---

[35] The following proviso needs to be added: that, at the end, the interpretation is the simplest possible one consistent with the conveyed information,
along appropriately defined lines.

mer; (ii) that the ontological status of the representational content that we ascribe to computation is also problematic; and (iii) that the two interact—our choices for the latter being troublingly affected by our choices for the former. So far, however, I have written as if this instability about the content of a representational system were simply an issue of our choosing among alternatives, each conceptually clear enough on its own. But as many readers will have realized, the problem is more difficult than that. Something more troubling, but also more interesting, is at stake.

This is easiest to see in the case of autonomous computational agents (the development of which is a substantial goal, but still more modest than that of full artificial intelligence). The issue is not how the world seems to us, but *how it is for the constructed agent*. And there is no a priori reason to suppose that *any* of the choices that the theorist is likely to entertain, or is even capable of entertaining, will be the right one. There is no reason to suppose that it will share our conceptual scheme—no reason to suppose that there need be any way to resolve a potential conflict between two ontological perspectives on the world: what the world is like for us, as users or designers, and what it is like for the systems we thereby use or design.

Some people may feel that we *must* share a world-view with computers, in part because they are our own creations, and in part because it might seem as if there would otherwise be no way to understand them. But that is a mistake. Logically, first, nothing prevents us from constructing machines, and even understanding those machines, at a level of analysis that is "lower"— i.e., closer to their physical constitution—than that at which they are representational (especially that at which they have representational content). The most dramatic example is the familiar science-fiction image of someone's constructing a brain, or something with a brain, and then being surprised, displaced, or otherwise overpowered by the behavior of the resulting monster.

The logical requirements of this possibility are very weak; not only does it not depend on a reductionist theory of representation or content; it does not even depend on physicalism. Just as an employee of the Philadelphia Mint can make real money without in the least understanding the overall social structures, including issues of authority, democracy, perceived value, and the like, that cause it to *be* money; and just as someone can put a stop sign up by painting the word 'STOP' onto a red octagonal sign and posting it at the street corner, without understanding anything about language, semantics, commands, or traffic tickets; so too someone in a computer science or artificial intelligence laboratory could in principle build a genuinely intentional robot without understanding why, or in virtue of what, it *was* intentional.[36]

From the fact that we can build something that is ϕ, that is, it does not follow that we understand what it is to be ϕ. Recent work on connectionist systems, furthermore, suggests that with respect to the property of having representational content this possibility may not be all that remote. As mentioned above, devices have already been built with inner states (primarily patterns of activation values of hidden units) to which their designers despair of assigning content.[37] Some have concluded that therefore these systems do not *have* any content, but no very convincing reason has been proffered as to why that should be so, and indeed it seems hard to imagine that there *could* be such an argument until we have an acceptable theory as to what it is

[36] How likely is this in practice—that someone build a system without understanding why it is intentional? That is hard to say. It might seem more likely to happen in molecular genetics than in artificial intelligence. I am not sure, however—especially because there is every reason to believe that semantic content, and perhaps even semantic prowess, may arise relationally; and engineering practice typically takes place in settings in which the requisite relational structures are already tacitly in place. This is why the highway worker can put up a stop sign without understanding legal authority.

[37] For discussion see Smolensky (1988) and Bechtel & Abrahamsen (1991).

for a state to carry content. Furthermore, if Kirsh is right to characterize the research strategy of modern interactionist roboticists (such as Brooks) with the slogan "Today the earwig, tomorrow man,"[38] then we had better assume that it is possible to build systems the contents of whose representational states we do not understand. For just about everyone, researcher or philosopher, would agree that there is some critter in the presumed continuum between earwigs and man (i) that has genuinely representational or at least proto-representational states, and (ii) that does not share with us our highly-articulated and conceptualized representational schemes.

Some writers have taken this possibility of non-conceptual (or "sub-symbolic") content to be one of connectionism's most attractive features—and have even argued, somewhat in the spirit of Evans and Cussins, that much of our *own* representational content is similarly non-conceptual (though just how much such human non-conceptual content should be expected to overlap with the content of the representational states of a creature that was incapable of conceptual representation is not, as far as I know, a question that has been much addressed).[39] I am sympathetic to the claim that the content of many human intentional experiences, even including conscious experiences (such as memories of the smell of nutmeg, knowledge of the direction in which one has suddenly heard a door open, and musings about the sting of wind-driven salt spray), are not "conceptual," in the sense of being combinatorially constructed out of anything remotely like the meanings of words. My present aim, however, is not so much to take a stand on how the human case goes. Rather, I want to draw three conclusions that will matter to the later metaphysical story.

First, I simply want to acknowledge and record the possibility—in fact the likelihood, I believe—of there being a gulf be-

---

[38] Kirsh (1991).
[39] Cussins (1990), Smolensky (1988), Evans (1982), Strawson (1959).

tween the representational content of creatures we build and any content that we ourselves can entertain.

Second, hand in hand with this observation, I want to emphasize, especially for readers outside the field, that computer science and artificial intelligence are, by their own admission, largely *engineering* disciplines. The relationship that professional practitioners bear to the systems that constitute their subject matter is not an entirely descriptive, theoretical, or indeed intentional one at all. The seemingly mundane fact that we design, build, use, test, repair, modify, dismantle, and update those systems is extremely important, methodologically.

The juxtaposition of these two facts leads to an important point that Cussins has made: that the way to understand the intentional capacity of creatures with which one does not share a conceptual scheme may involve understanding how to construct them, understanding how they behave, their routines, and the like. But I want to assert something stronger: that it is intellectually essential not just that we *understand* how to build them, but that we *actually* build and modify and use them—because of the fact that, in so building and modifying and using, we become enmeshed with them in a participatory fashion, in a way that both transcends and also grounds the representational attitudes we bear towards them. It is this, I believe, though of course it is not usually formulated in this way, that underlies the common wisdom in computer science that anyone who has not written a substantial amount of code, no matter how otherwise brilliant and educated, lacks something essential to the understanding of computers. One reason this is true we have already seen: the modest state of extant theory. But there is reason to believe that in substance and reach it goes considerably beyond this.

Third, no one would argue that all devices that computationalists make are equally impressive. Indeed it is at least arguable that some extremely simple ones, like automatic light switches, may not have any representational content at all. Another important consequence of computer science's methodological stance is that we have, or at least potentially have, experience with an entire range of mechanical creatures, spanning the gamut from those that warrant a "merely physical" analysis, up through and including those that are in some sense genuinely intentional.

The most important conclusion, however, has to do with the relation between: (i) that participatory stance that we, as designers, bear to our machines; and (ii) the conceptual point made in the last section, about how our ascription of representational content is vulnerable to how we register or individuate the representing structure. I opened this section with the question of how the world may seem *for the machines themselves*, not for us. I cannot answer this question.[40] But surely it is possible to put this constraint on it: that except in rarefied cases of introspection and reflection, the machines do not register or individuate their own representational mechanisms. As a result, their conception of the world cannot be relativized to any way in which their representing mechanisms are registered or individuated, for the simple reason that, except in those rarefied introspective cases, they need not represent their internal workings at all (even if, as some have suggested, they do need to represent themselves in other ways). The point is easier to see in our own case. How *we* take the world to be—to consist of objects, properties, and relations, or of other things, or whatever—cannot depend on how we take our *minds or brains* to be, since most of us do not take our minds or brains to be any way at all.[41]

However the question is to be answered about what the world

---

[40] Nagel (1974).

[41] The beauty of indirectly classifying people's mental or psychological states in terms of *content*—that she believed that ϕ, for some ϕ—is that it sidesteps the issue of how the representational states that carry that content are structured or individuated.

is like for our machines, therefore, and even whether we answer that question or not, it will not be able to be anything at all like what was imagined in §4, above. While it was right to be stopped short by the recognition that the ascription of content depended on the way in which the machine was registered, it was a mistake to assume that the way to repair that situation was to choose the correct way to register the machine. Somehow or other—and this I take to be the most important and difficult task facing the cognitive sciences—*it must be possible to have determinate representational content, i.e., for there to be a fact of the matter as to how the world is represented*, without that analysis depending on *any* way of taking the internal structures in the mind that does the analysis. That is not to say that it will not depend on those struc-

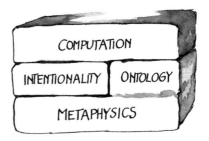

FIGURE 1·10   SECOND CUT

tures, or on how they work; this is absolutely not a recommendation for a return to behaviorism. I am in no way denying that internal mechanisms are useful, or central, or essential. All I am claiming, though it is enough to claim, is that it will have to be an answer that does not depend on how anyone registers or individuates those mechanisms—again, for the simple reason that it happens in people, for example, without anyone doing that. Naturally, understanding those mechanisms may be extraordinarily important—again, may even be essential—in order for us even to *begin* to get a sense of what the world must be like, for them.[42] But the fact remains that the answer, whatever it is, and whether or not it is conceptually accessible to us, must not depend on how it is that we do that individuation.

---

[42] Akins (1993).

6 Participation

Where does that leave things? It leads to a single inescapable conclusion:

There is no way to proceed on the overall project, of developing a comprehensive theory of computation that meets both the empirical and conceptual criteria, except by taking on metaphysics and ontology directly.[43]

Moreover, this conclusion has to be integrated into the earlier result, described in the introduction as a "first cut" on the overall project, that an adequate theory of computation will have to rest on a theory of semantics and intentionality. The present conclusion leads to what I will call a "second cut," depicted in figure 1·10. If there is ever going to be a satisfying theory of computation, it will have to rest on theories of both intentionality and ontology — or else (I will be recommending this alternative) a single integrated theory that covers both subject matters. Either way, there is no way to sidestep the metaphysical challenge.

Even this, however, is not the last word on the layout of the intellectual terrain. To see why, it helps to go back to the beginning. I said at the outset that my interest in metaphysics had arisen out of an analysis of computation.[44] In the intervening

---

[43] Or "metaphysics, including ontology," if you view ontology as a species of metaphysics.

[44] This is not quite right. In fact the opposite is closer to the truth. Ever since the fall of 1967, when I first took up this project, and learned how to program, my primary interest in computation has been in the potential window it might (may) give us on a new way of understanding — one with all the rigor and power and penetration of the natural sciences, but one that at the same time could do justice to the richness and complexity and sheer vivacity of human life. That, moreover, or at least so it has always seemed to me, is the only really interesting promise behind the cognitivist thesis. I still believe it; what has changed, if anything, is a recognition that, in order to do these things, the "new way of understanding" will have to reach all the way down (i.e., will require, or be, a complete metaphysical overhaul), rather than being a new form of empirical account on top of a traditional (or modernist) metaphysical base.

Cross-cutting boundaries

Consider two "boundaries" or divides that figure in the characterization of a computer as a symbol manipulating system:

1. A *physical* boundary—roughly, the divide between "inside" and "outside," between what is part of the system and what is part of its environment, necessary in order to warrant the label 'system'; and
2. A *semantic* boundary, between the realm of the symbols and the realm of the referents, necessary in order to warrant the identifying phrase "symbol manipulating."

The plausibility of the "theorem prover plus transducer" model of computation depends on a rarely articulated assumption: that these two boundaries align, with the symbols inside the head or machine, and the referents outside, in the environment. *But this alleged alignment does not occur.* In real-world systems the boundaries *cross-cut* in myriad complex ways. For starters, all four possibilities exist: internal symbols and internal referents (introspection); external symbols and external referents (encyclopedias); external symbols and internal referents (psychotherapy); as well as the presumptive base case, internal symbols and external referents (thoughts about dinner). Mechanisms that cross the physical boundary, moreover, from outside to in and inside to out, differ from mechanisms that cross the semantic boundary, from referents to symbols and symbols to referents (note that transducers are traditionally thought to do *both*). I even believe that the four categories are occupied *essentially*, in the sense that the warrant for calling computers intentional at all depends on the two boundaries cross-cutting.*

All sorts of entailments flow from this cross-cutting of boundaries, a characteristic I take to be essential to participatory systems in general. A specifically ontological one is this: computational types—i.e., the categories in terms of which the ingredients of a computational process are identified—are, as it is said, functionally defined, in terms of their role and behavior in the overall range of settings in which the system is deployed (or is imagined to be deployed, or is designed for, or whatever). If it were true (i) that the two boundaries were aligned, and (ii) that the constitutive types were internally definable, then there would be a chance of the constitutive types being, as again it is often said, "formally" definable, definable independent of interpretation. But since both assumptions are false, it follows that the functional constitution of a computational type can make essential reference to its semantical significance. This is not uniquely characteristic of highly-evolved or complex cases, such as the category of person. Think of a simple counter: a module that, given a series of inputs, yields as output a *numeral* (not number!) that denotes the *number* (not numeral!) of elements in the input. Counters are devices that *mediate a semantic boundary* (though they are not traditionally viewed as transducers): they go from an exemplified property ("threeness," say, if given '**<a b c>**' as input) to a canonical representation of that exemplified property (the numeral '3'). If a counter is *defined* to be a device with this property of crossing the referent-symbol divide, then it is *semantically* individuated.

Not only does the way in which we assign semantics to computational states depend on how we individuate them, in other words, as argued in §4, but individuation is a *hybrid process*, making essential reference to both sides of the presumed symbol-reference divide. It is not even clear, when one does individuate or type a system, that any special role is played by that divide—or even, which is even more metaphysically challenging, whether that distinction is clear. In a sense this was one of the lessons of 2-Lisp: not only do semantical and ontological distinctions need to be made on-the-fly, in situation- and perspective-relative fashion, but the very distinction between what is symbol, what is referent, ultimately comes to seem far more a subsequent and contingent matter of degree than a prior and necessary matter of black-and-white.

*If they were aligned, then what one might think of as the terrible worry of the formalist—that there is no way to connect the inner realm of symbols (or thoughts) with the outer realm of things (or substances)—would be legitimate: sure enough, there wouldn't be any way to get the two together. Fortunately, the worry is based on a false presumption.

pages I have identified both semantical and ontological concerns that have arisen as part of that study. But these meta-theoretic morals are not the only ones to have emerged from that work. Three more will affect the stance towards ontological and metaphysical questions I adopt in the coming chapters.

First, it turns out that issues of physical embodiment are essential. McPhysics was right: there *are* physical constraints on what it is to be a program. Indeed, the remark made at the outset about recursion theory and the theory of effective computability's not being able to account for computation's semantical aspect is in part compensated for by a recognition that this theory—of "effective computability," as it is said—is, and ought to be understood as, a non-semantical *theory of the effective*: a theory of whether one can transform one physical (i.e., causally efficacious) configuration of the world into another, and if so, at what physical cost. It is a theory of the *flow of effect*, in other words—and as such, even though it is not so advertised, is probably the best candidate yet for a scientific theory of causality.[45]

Second, fitting in with this essential materiality and locatedness is perhaps the most ramifying consequence of investigating computation in the wild: the recognition that computers are

---

[45] There is a terrific irony here. The formal symbol manipulation construal of computation claims to be a theory of computation "independent of semantics," but fails; it is constitutively defined in terms of semantics, contrary to its by-line. The recursion-theoretic construal makes no such claim, but in so (not) doing, perversely meets the criterion (i.e., of not having to do with semantics). But before according recursion theory victory, note that fate is ultimately balanced: what the recursion-theoretic tradition does claim to be independent of are the *details of physical realization*—but there, in its own way, it fails. The fact that non-linear dynamics and quantum theory both require computation theory to be revised is only the beginning of the evidence that, on the contrary, recursion theory is almost directly about physical effect. Moreover, if anything can lay legitimate claim to non-physicality, because of its ancestral reliance on mathematical logic, it is the formal symbol manipulation construal! See TMD·1.

inextricably involved in their subject matters. It is not just that they do not merely reason about those subject matters, in other words, in the way suggested by the formal symbol manipulation hypothesis (and all other positions that view computation as a form of logic). Neither is it possible, for reasons explained in the sidebar on "cross-cutting boundaries" on page 70, to understand them by amplifying an inner realm of reasoning with boundaries mediated by sensors and effectors—i.e., by expanding the domain of their operations to satisfy the equation "computation = perception + reasoning + action" (or as Dennett has put it, that computers are theorem provers wrapped in transducer overcoats[46]).[47] Nor, even more seriously, is it enough to enlarge the scope of the discussion from reason and perception and action to a more general notion of *experience.* Experience, in any intuitively recognizable form, is too passive or receptive a category to do justice to the sorts of activity that computers engender. Injecting dioxin into a patient, like cutting down a tree, is a full-blooded intentional action, and thus will require analysis; it would be odd to call it an *experience,* at least for us (even if it is an experience for the patient, or the tree). In the end one can only conclude that any semantical theory adequate to practice will have to be a full-blooded theory of *participatory engagement,* not just of reasoning or representation, or even of perception, action, and experience.

For present purposes, however, both these results pale in importance compared with a third and final lesson:

Computation is not a subject matter.

In spite of everything I have said about a "theory of computation," in other words, and in spite of everything I myself

---

[46]Dennett (1987), pp. 149–50 and 160.

[47]For starters, it is often impossible to decide which of the three categories (perception, reasoning, action) to assign a given computational operation to, such as instantiating an X window system object type, or shifting from compiled to interpreted code, or doing what is known as a "level-shift" in a reflective architecture such as 3-Lisp. There is no evidence that the tripar-

thought for almost twenty years, I no longer believe that there is a distinct ontological category of computation, one that will be the subject matter of a deep and explanatory and intellectually satisfying theory. Close and sustained analysis suggests that the things that Silicon Valley calls computers do not form an intellectually delimited class. Computers turn out in the end to be rather like cars: objects of inestimable social and political and economic and personal importance, but not the focus of enduring scientific or intellectual inquiry.

This is yet another extremely strong claim. If I am right, it implies that there will never be a satisfying and intellectually productive "theory of computation" of the sort I initially set out to find. It is not just that a theory of computation will not *supply* a theory of semantics, in other words, as Newell has suggested; nor that it will not *replace* a theory of semantics, nor will it *depend or rest on* a theory of semantics, as intimated in figure 0·1, in the introduction, or even here in figure 1·10. It will do none of these things because *there will be no theory of computation at all.*

Especially given the weight that has been placed on the notion of computation by the cognitive sciences, this might seem like a negative conclusion. Indeed, you might conclude that I have spent these twenty-five years in vain. But in fact I firmly believe the opposite: that this superficially negative conclusion makes the late-twentieth-century arrival of computation onto the intellectual scene a much more interesting phenomenon than it would otherwise have been. In retrospect, in fact, it is far and away the most exciting conclusion of all.

For I am not saying that the phenomena of computation in

...

tite division would facilitate analysis of real systems, if it were used (which it is not), and good reason to believe that it would impede it, supporting a sense that the categorization does not get at any fundamental empirical regularity. And finally, there is a whole class of operations, such as timekeeping (as performed by clocks), that does not seem to naturally fit into any one of the three categories, suggesting that they are also too narrow. See Smith (1988).

the wild are intrinsically atheoretical—and thus that there will be no theory, altogether. Rather, the claim is that such theory as there is, and there is surely good chance of that, as much as in any domain of human activity, will not be a theory of *computation*. It will not be a theory of computation because *computers per se*—computers qua computers—do not constitute a subject matter. Rather, what computers are, I now believe, and what the considerable and impressive body of practice associated with them amounts to, is neither more nor less than the full-fledged social construction and development of intentional artifacts.[48] That means that the range of experience and skills that have been developed within computer science—remarkably complex and far-reaching, if still inadequately articulated—is best understood as practical, synthetic, raw material for no less than full theories of semantics and ontology.

Where does that leave things? Substantively, it leads to the third and final cut on the intellectual project, depicted in figure 1·11: that metaphysics, ontology, and intentionality are the only integral intellectual subject matters in the vicinity. This book can be understood as an attempt to undertake the project conceived in this third and final way. Methodologically, it means that our experience with constructing computational (i.e., intentional) systems may open a window onto something to which we would not otherwise have any access: the chance to witness, with our own eyes, how intentional capacities can arise in a "merely" physical mechanism. It is sobering, in retrospect, to realize that the fact that computers are computational has placed a major theoretical block in the way of our understanding how important they are. They are computational, of course; that much is tautological. But only when we let

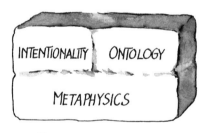

FIGURE 1·11 THIRD CUT

---

[48] By 'social construction,' here, I refer not to a metaphysical philosophy, but to a public enterprise.

go of the conceit that that fact is theoretically important will we finally be able to see, *without distraction*—and thereby, perhaps, at least partially to understand—how a structured lump of clay can sit up and think.

2 · Irreduction

Time and again, over a period of almost twenty years, my efforts at computational theorizing were defeated by ontological problems of the sort raised in the last chapter. In one case I was focusing on reflection, introspection, and computational self-reference, in an attempt to build systems that would benefit from substantial forms of self-knowledge. A second project centered on the design of "semantically rationalized" programming languages (including 2-Lisp, described in the last chapter). A third started out in knowledge representation, but quickly devolved into an attempt to formulate a general theory of representation and correspondence.[1] In each case, attempts at coherent analysis soon mired in apparently irresolvable issues of ontology (this is what I meant by running into the ontological wall). It soon became evident, too, that the fundamental problems were not so much with the ontological structures of the systems under investigation, though those were difficult enough, as with the ontological *assumptions* that I often pre-emptively imposed or inscribed on the problem domain.

Finally, in an attempt to face the problem straight on, I embraced a methodological criterion that, following Latour, I call a *principle of irreduction*.[2] Essentially a standard of metatheoretic accountability, it mandates that no theoretical assumption—empirical premise, ontological framework, analytic device, investigative equipment, laboratory tool, mathematical technique, or other methodological paraphernalia—be given a priori pride of place. Every piece of metatheoretic apparatus

---

[1] For introspection, etc., see Smith (1984 & 1986); for semantically rationalized languages, Smith (1984) and Dixon (1991); for a theory of representation, Smith (1987) and TMD·IV. Very little of the total work was published, though, for the reasons identified here.

[2] The term 'irreduction' is from Latour (1988); its commercial characterization, from personal conversation with Latour in the spring of 1992.

should be "left open" in order to be subjected to critical assessment, raised up for skeptical analysis, and potentially revamped or set aside. Unless one is willing to adopt this strict a standard of suspicion, ontological biases and unwarranted metaphysical assumptions will slip through and derail subsequent analysis.

1 Commercial metaphor

The irreduction mandate is something I will embrace. What it comes to in detail will emerge over the course of the book. To keep it vivid, it helps to summarize it as a simple commercial slogan: that for each theoretical assumption (premise, framework, etc.), one be prepared to say:

1. Where one bought it;
2. How much one paid; and
3. How one got it from there to here.

"Where one bought it" simply means that one understand the situation and setting in which the device or distinction arose. Thus it is easy to imagine analyses that rest on a distinction between natives and immigrants, that accept the "mutually assured destruction" premises of nuclear deterrence, that assume that nightmares about nuclear war are pathological, or that accept the formal conception of 'game' underlying so much artificial intelligence, economic modeling, and structuralism. In each case, irreduction first requires that, before one accept such a premise, one understand the political context, intellectual agendas, metaphysical presuppositions, and other contextual factors that gave rise to the premise or distinction in the first place. Irreduction is not a stance against making or using distinctions—merely an injunction to acknowledge that one is doing so.

By "how much one paid," analogously, the idea is to admit, and perhaps even to compensate for, the consequences of adopting this piece of theoretical ordnance—for example by taking responsibility for those aspects or features of the subject matter that the technique ignores or idealizes away from, or by re-pairing or at least adjusting for any violence it does to the under-lying subject matter. Thus consider how the binary categories *male* and *female* idealize away from (and thus "disappear") the almost 4 percent of the population who in one way or another are physiologically hermaphroditic.[3] Any theoretical construct defined in terms of this binarism, in fact any theoretical con-struct at all, will pay a certain cost associated with this failure to get the world exactly right. Irreduction's second requirement is that one own up to that price.

Finally, by "how one got it from there to here" the aim is to recognize the potential distortion that comes from using tech-niques in situations different from those in which they were originally developed—i.e., from "translating"[4] them away from their original context. The use of formal methods in computer science, for example, derives in part from the fact that Turing was a mathematician, and that the development of the so-called theory of computation took place primarily in the mathematical part of the academy. In retrospect, it seems as if a wider semiotic tradition, perhaps in the spirit of Pierce, Dewey, and Mead, might have done more justice to the complexities of present-day practice. But the route from those alternative forebears is not as well traveled as that from the ancestors of modern logic and the foundations of mathematics. Unless one recognizes the his-torical contingency of this development, one is liable, perhaps without realizing it, to give undue weight to the ontological per-spectives of the formal, logical, set-theoretic tradition (e.g., to accept the mistaken idea, in my view, that computation is ab-stract).

2 Ideology and reduction

In part, owning up to irreduction's three requirements is a mat-ter of intellectual honesty. In such cases the mandate can be

---

[3] Fausto-Sterling (1993).
[4] Latour (1987), pp. 108 ff.

viewed as simply a reminder to be modest and fair. But the criterion has special bite when applied to premises and presuppositions taken to be methodologically primitive. For if there is any aspect of one's analytic stance about which these questions cannot be answered—i.e., if there is some assumption whose price one is not prepared to pay—then that is suggestive of a lurking inscription error.

The connection is not a logical one; reductionism and inscription errors are not the same thing. But suppose an account unquestioningly relies on some category α—by blindly imposing it, deferring to it, reducing other phenomena to it, or in any other way using it without explanation. It is not too much of a stretch to realize that the ontology of the target subject matter is liable as a result to be biased in α's favor. Moreover, this is likely to be true *independent of α's category or type*.[5] Thus if one is committed to the use of mathematical or statistical methods, chances are that one will find the phenomena in one's area of inquiry to be of the sort to which mathematical methods apply. If one is pretheoretically committed to formal methods, certain kinds of ambiguity are less likely to be accorded theoretical centrality. If one starts out making a sharp distinction between people and computers, one is almost sure to misconstrue median cases of only emergently intelligent capacities. More graphically: if one views the distinction between having a child and making something with one's hands—i.e., between kid and artifact—to be prior, sacred, and immune from intellectual scrutiny, then one should expect to be broadsided on the fateful day when artificial intelligence succeeds in its titular quest.

The point of these examples is to show that ideology and reductionism, in their reliance on protected, unexplained categories, are ultimately more similar than they are different (modulo the argument given in the sidebar on page 82). For it does not much matter what *kind* of category α is, in terms of

---

[5] Maslow was right: if your only tool is a hammer, the world is liable to look like a nail.

which a phenomenon is explained, if that category is committed to in advance, and thereafter held immune from doubt, scrutiny, and question. All sorts of categories have historically played such a role. For some, it has been electrons or brains; for others, logic and set theory; for others, political power and male indoctrination. Still others have relied on the materiality of our bodies, on the waves and particles of quantum physics, on the products of our labor, on the human condition in toto, or on some absolute form of spirit or religious belief. The problem is not with any of these categories, per se. What is at issue, especially when the ontological status of the subject matter is fragile, is any a priori or advance commitment to such categories. However we label the alternatives—political correctness or ideological zealotry, scientific rigor or desiccating reductionism, or even just methodological purity—to give prior allegiance to any such categories or techniques is, strictly speaking, prejudice, in the etymologically literal sense of being "pre-judged." The irreduction criterion, therefore, which could as well be called an anti-ideology mandate (and perhaps, though more contentiously, a brief against methodology[6]), is simply a useful formulation of a commitment to stand on constant guard against any such simplifying seduction.

Although the irreductionist mandate affects everyone, it is especially stringent for a foundationalist. So stringent as to be impossible to meet, some would say. For how can one possibly provide foundations if one does not have an advance sense of

---

[6]Methodology is widely considered to be a good thing, so it is important to be clear on what is being said. I have no complaint about commitment to rigorous *methods*; my concern has to do with the locus of primary theoretical allegiance. What an irreductionist approach would recommend is that one's commitment be to a subject matter or phenomenon, and that one use whatever methods do that subject matter justice—as opposed to what one might call a methodological allegiance, which would put a particular method or technique in the driving seat, and then search for a phenomenon to which that technique is applicable. Among other problems, I claim, the latter is far more likely than the former to lead to inscription errors.

A priori and *a posteriori* reduction

Strictly speaking, especially at this pretheoretic (methodological) point in the argument, valid complaints cannot be raised against reductive explanation per se, but only against a *doctrine* of reductionism—i.e., against an advance or pre-theoretic commitment to the idea that proper scientific explanation will or must take reductive form. At least logically, it would seem possible that some category or type of phenomenon β might turn out, empirically, to depend wholly on, and thus to be theoretically reducible to, some other category or type α. Independent of theoretic bias, that is—or so at least someone might argue—reductive explanation, at least some reductive explanation, might turn out to be *true*. And that might seem to argue against the validity of the irreduction mandate. Surely an advance commitment against the possibility of reductive explanation is as ideological (and hence as methodologically suspect) as an advance commitment for it.

Logically, there is much that is right in this argument. No doubt many anti-reductionist positions are as ideological—and hence, by my lights, as guilty of prejudice—as any of their pro-reductionist counterparts, and thus stand in equal violation of the spirit motivating the irreductionist mandate. In practice, however, two considerations weaken the force of this distinction between what might be called *a priori reductionism* (bad) and *a posteriori reduction* (presumptively okay). First, at least in my own experience, few advocates of reductive positions derive their allegiance to those positions from the world independent of prior methodological commitment. Non-ideological, a posteriori reduction may be logically possible, that is, but my guess is that it is empirically rare. Second, and this gives credence to the first claim, it is a consequence of the metaphysical view to be advanced in this book that reductive explanations are, in point of fact, false. Although they are not logically precluded, they are metaphysically precluded—or so at least I will claim. If that is so, then it (ironically) becomes an almost logical claim, rather than an empirical one, that reductive allegiance must stem from methodological bias. Together, at any rate, these two considerations support the assumption made in the text: that, at least in practice, only deleterious forms of explanation will be blocked by commitment to the irreductionist mandate. Hence its name.

what foundations are made of? But to conclude that foundationalism implies either reductionism or ideology would be a terrible mistake. Just as Sir Francis Drake, in heavy fog, is rumored to have sailed right on past the entrance of San Francisco Bay, to accept that conclusion would be to miss the one navigable route through these tortuous straits into satisfying metaphysical waters. Yes, we need something that will satisfy our yearning for foundations. And *no, it must not be grounded in* α, *for any* α. But there is another possibility. Why can we not just be grounded, *simpliciter?*[7]

---

[7] Some readers will assume (some historical traditions have assumed) that the word 'grounded' *means* grounded in some primitive category α. Clearly, I do not believe that; or at least I am using the term in a broader sense. But for those who take 'grounded' to mean "grounded in α," the book should instead be understood as a search for a non-grounded foundational metaphysics. And for those who insist that "foundations," too, require grounding in some privileged category α, then they and I should have a drink. (See the discussion of *immanent induction* on page 373.)

3 · Realism

What, then, of a non-question-begging nature, can be said about the notion of an object? Can an object be an object on its own? Or, in order to *be* an object, must it be taken *as* an object by a subject? If a subject views an object as an object in this way, what relation binds them? And what about these subjects, anyway—are they objects too?

The strategy is to move in on the answers, by triangulation. This chapter starts at the top, identifying a set of requirements to which any successful metaphysical candidate must be held accountable. Of special importance is the development of a workable characterization of something I will call *symmetrical realism*—a construal of (non-naive) realism that not only establishes some of the background assumptions or metaphysical preconditions on the existence of objects, but places equally strong preconditions on the existence and nature of subjects, including on their epistemic achievements, with particular reference to the recalcitrant notion of objectivity.

To stay too long at this level would be to engage in meta-metaphysics, however. So chapters 4 and 5 are something of a bridge. In chapter 4, the discussion is narrowed down to focus in on two ideas—*particularity* and *individuality*—ideas which, though still of an overarching metaphysical character, are best understood as (rather abstract) features of objects themselves. Both, I argue, can be seen to underwrite our ordinary understanding of simple concrete objects—especially material things such as tables and chairs, plants and trees, and people, and perhaps even less clearly concrete things, such as musings and nations.

Chapter 5 mines the current status of physics, to see what insights can be extracted from this most prestigious of sciences—partly in general, but also with special reference to these two criterial notions. Then, in Part II, I begin working much more bottom-up, by setting out to assemble a first cut at a new metaphysical story, pretty much from scratch. By the time we reach chapters 11 and 12, the incremental process of metaphysical construction will have reached far enough up that, with one final stretch, it will make contact with the present chapter's requirements, reaching down from the top. Only in those final chapters will an "answer" be arrived at, and the rhetorical circle closed.

Three things about this chapter's top-down approach. First, although I claim it is grounded in common sense, the stance I embrace is not going to be traditionally scientific or formalist or modern. My intent is to retain what is most important about a realist orientation, though it will be a version of realism most familiar to those acquainted with science studies, feminist critiques of science, Putnam's internal realism, debates about social constructionism, and the like.[1] Second, nothing I say here will be very precise. Especially at the beginning, exactness should be no one's goal; all I want are initial spurs to thought, to get the project going.[2] Third, and most important, the properties to be

[1] For discussions of the metaphysical and epistemological implications of science studies see e.g. Bloor (1976/1991), Latour and Woolgar (1979), Knorr-Cetina (1981), Shapin and Schaffer (1985), Rudwick (1985), Callon (1986), and Latour (1987 & 1988); for feminist critiques of science see Harding (1986 & 1991), Longino (1990), Keller (1985), Haraway (1991); for Putnam on internal realism see Putnam (1981, 1987, & 1990); for social constructionism more generally see e.g. Berger & Luckmann (1966/1980), Kuhn (1962/1970).

[2] This lack of precision is already evident. I opened the chapter by asking about the *notion* of an object, for example, rather than about objects per se. Given an alleged interest in ontology, rather than in psychology or epistemics, would it not have been better to ask about objects themselves—or at least, more abstractly, about the *type 'object'*? Perhaps. And what do I mean by introducing individuality as an *idea*, and then by sentence's end claiming that it is a *property*? Nothing much. In part, this equivocation merely reflects the point made in the text: that since any initial framework will soon have to be overhauled, there is little to be gained, and much to be lost,

laid out in this chapter are to be viewed as *requirements* on a successful metaphysics. Not only are they not themselves metaphysics, as has already been indicated, but neither do I take them as starting points or premises. I will endorse a highly local and constantly renegotiated form of pluralism, for example, and will agree that an ineliminable sense of "other" is implicated in taking something to be an object. By the same token, some sympathy will be shown for the partial transcendence yet inexorable immanence of the world, for the inherently participatory, embodied, located nature of a responsible subject, and for a feisty, contested notion of objectivity. All these features are to be taken as goals or desiderata, as properties that an adequate metaphysics should manifest. Simply to assert them as conditions in advance, or to take them as premises, would somewhat ironically be (ideologically) reductionist. And to argue that they must be true, but then simply to leave it at that, would be too expensive.

Perhaps the best approach is to view advocates of such high-level metaphysical conditions (e.g., those who ask how science would be conducted, and what content it would have, if it were founded on alternative metaphysical foundations) as potential customers for the present account. The aim of the book is to paint a picture of the world that entails that all these things are true—a picture in which all these various post- or non-modernist[3] metatheoretic properties, as it were, "fall out."

1 Successor metaphysics

Two sensibilities, then, drive the metaphysical story to be told. First, although the aim is to steer a 'strait and narrow' path between realism and constructionism,[4] it is not to aim for an aver-

...

by pressing for accuracy early on. But it also represents something more serious: a sharp distinction between concepts and types will not be a feature of the final story, so why pretend that it is a feature here?

[3] See Latour (1993).

[4] Not, as some people think, '*straight* and narrow' (see Matthew 7:14). It is a conceit to imagine that the way to make safe passage through these tortured metaphysical waters is to put on blinders and sail stubbornly in some

age of the two, or to suggest that the result need in any other way be a compromise. On the contrary, the goal is to show two things: (i) that the classical positions do not conflict, *au fond*, but instead can be reconstructed under a single more powerful conception; and (ii) that the best of each is a form of deference or located responsibility, an epistemic deference to the transcendence of the world underlying realism, and a similar "fessing up" to the importance of human involvement in the world that underwrites social construc-

One notices, if one will trust one's eyes, the shadow cast by language upon truth."
—Auden, "Kairos & Logos"

tionism—a recognition that our practices, our words, our histories, and our cultures not only affect, but partially constitute, the ways we take the world to be, even the way the world is. "We are here," says the constructionist. "We are not the only things here," says the realist. No serious metaphysical proposal, especially this late in the century, can afford to ignore either insight.

The second goal is more social or political: to show that doing metaphysics is not only intellectually and politically viable, but intellectually and politically urgent as well—and quite concrete. It has become fashionable to be "antifoundationalist"—in part because all prior attempts at foundations have in one or another way failed. I have already said that I want to rescue foundationalism, at least foundationalism of a very special irreductionist sort ("grounded, but not grounded in α, for any α"). But current metaphysical suspicion is more than a mistrust of particular proposals, or even of particular kinds of proposal. It has grown into a mistrust of the enterprise itself, because of a very general and by now deep-seated belief that no single story—no master narrative—can ever be strong or universal enough to do

· · · ————————————————————

unswerving direction. Rather, it is a job for a good river pilot, someone with the skill to steer and twist and turn appropriately, so as to avoid foundering on contradictions and conundrums, getting caught in vicious circularities, or otherwise being seduced by reductionism, ideology, and other high-priced sirens of the deep.

the whole metaphysical job. First, it is thought, no story could ever be sufficiently universal in *content*: broad and rich and flexible and deep enough to get at, or even to sustain, everything that matters. Second, no story could ever be sufficiently universal in *perspective*: free of influences and interests and assumptions and biases of the particular cultural or disciplinary or personal perspective from which it was told. And if all these things are true, it is assumed, metaphysics must be impossible.[5]

I believe both claims—about the inherent limits of all stories, and about their ineliminably perspectival or situated nature. Both claims will be retained in, and will be consequences of, the metaphysical picture to be painted here. In fact I will argue something stronger: that all stories, simply in virtue of being stories, are not only inherently partial and intrinsically perspectival, but in addition must do a certain amount of violence to their subject matters. The mistake, however, is to assume or to allow oneself to be convinced that any of these facts undermines the legitimacy of telling metaphysical tales. In fact the point can be put even more strongly:

The idea that metaphysics must be univocal, perspective-independent, from-nowhere, value-free, and the like, is itself a relic of the old (predecessor) metaphysics; it is not an inherent truth.[6]

[5]Moreover, and more radically, it is also argued there would be no great point in having such an account, even if it were possible to obtain one, because of the fact that there is no way such a thing could ever mesh with practical action. On this view metaphysics is useless, as well as being impossible.

[6]Some readers may assume that metaphysics *must* be objective, non-perspectival, value-free, and the like—i.e., will assume that the word 'metaphysics' means, or can only be used to refer to, a "from nowhere" enterprise, or an irreducibly rational account, or something of that ilk. If I were to agree with such a view, then I too would rail against its viability and vitality. My brief in this book, however, is to argue an alternative conclusion. For the sake of the reading, however, those who make such an assumption should simply assume that I am using the term 'metaphysics' to

To see how this could be so, it helps to appreciate something that underlies the current antifoundationalist/antimetaphysical mood. In this era of modern science—independent of whether one views science as in ascendancy, zenith, or decline—the very idea of foundations, and of metaphysics more generally, tends to connote *scientific* foundations: quantum mechanics, relativity, set theory, mathematics, and logic. For lack of alternatives this narrow scientific focus has for a long time seemed inevitable, but at the same time disturbing. No matter how otherwise modern, and no matter how strong their apparent physicalist or materialist commitments, most people retain a residual and ineliminable intuition that these sorts of technical foundation will never be able to support or sustain or give rise to everything of significance. Especially as regards the ability to sustain moral and political and spiritual values, scientific and mathematical foundations have at best seemed impotent, at worse nihilist. Many of us, perhaps even most of us, long for validation of the *non-scientific*—the historical and artistic and ethical and political, the texture and spirit and puckish humor of the human condition.

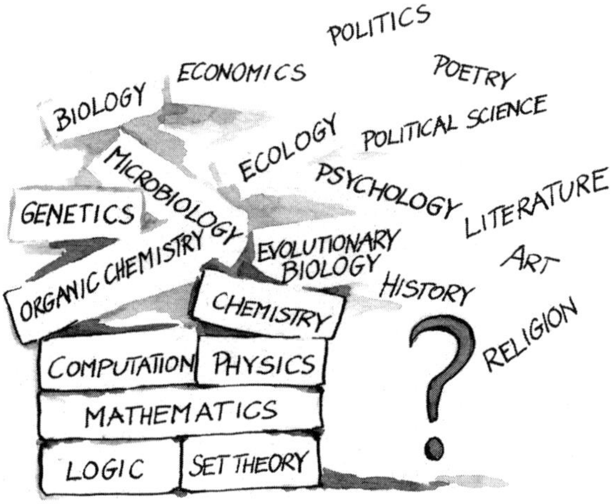

FIGURE 3·1   MODERN METAPHYSICS

In our current modernist imaginations, in other words, the terms 'foundation' and 'metaphysics' suggest a situation rather like that depicted in figure 3·1. The problem, indicated by the

...

mean something different from what they would normally take it to signify. It should be evident by the end of the book what it is that I take the word 'metaphysics' to signify, which is anyway non-standard.

question mark, is that nothing holds up the right hand side, the realm of the humane or the spiritual. This is what leaves us with an intense unsatisfied hunger. And if it is presumed that foundations must exhibit this bimodal character, it would be natural, and perhaps even correct, to be suspicious of any proposal that fits into such an overall framework. I agree; I am also left unsatisfied by this picture. And I do not believe I am alone. As numerous commentators have noted, this sense of deprivation, this longing for ethical grounding or aesthetic and political vision, is extraordinarily widespread.[7]

Antifoundationalism, post-modernism, and other more general antimetaphysical stances, are represented in figure 3·2. Sure enough, these approaches remove one of the difficulties of the classical picture, and restore symmetry to the situation. They are more integrated, in other words, and perhaps more well-rounded. But they do so not by putting foundations under the right, but by removing foundations from the left. Their argument is probably correct: that science, too, in its own way, is as much a product of social institutions and political power as literature or art, and cannot be understood in a "purely objectivist" manner. Furthermore, their result has the virtue of suggesting that art and politics and literature are no more metaphysically adrift than science and technology—and can thus, at least potentially, be restored to a position of equal importance and power. But this kind of unifi-

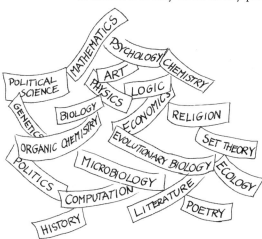

FIGURE 3·2 POST-MODERN METAPHYSICS

[7] See for example Bellah (1985 & 1991).

cation, this tearing down of the intellectual equivalent of the Berlin Wall, is achieved at unimaginable cost. It is exactly backwards: it aims to achieve parity by casting *everything* adrift, rather than by anchoring the right-hand side.[8]

How does the present project fit into this debate? Clearly, I admit to doing metaphysics. Does that make the project foundationalist, and therefore suspect, and therefore bad? It depends on what is being asked—on what language is being spoken. If by "foundations" one (prejudicially) means a rationally articulable, fully conceptualized, completely objective,[9] "scientific" basis, out of which all else is a rational or logical or physical or mathematical construction, then *no*, the project is certainly not that. I agree with those who deny there ever will, can, or should be such a thing. As much is implied by the "grounded but not grounded in α, for any α" interpretation of irreduction. Yet in a deeper sense, both in feel and in fact, the investigation remains indelibly foundational. Perhaps the best way to characterize it is as the positive version of what the universal longing for foundations turns into, according to the new story to be told.

This is not what metaphysics was constrained to be, in the old metaphysics; this is what metaphysics is allowed to be, in the new.[10]

"Successor metaphysics," one might call it, or "metaphysics for the 21st century"—although to say such things is mostly to incur a debt: to explain, before the story is done, what such a phrase

---

[8] No wonder the religious right are on the rise. It can sometimes seem as if they, alone, recognize the power and depth of the unsatisfied longing. Appalling as their answers may seem, at least to some of us, no one can deny, or at least no serious person should deny, that they respond to a genuine human—and, presumably, intellectual—need. We critics should do as well.

[9] In terms of a distinction to be made in a moment, this should read 'Objective,' not 'objective.'

[10] By "old" I really mean modern, and by "modern" I probably mean 20th century. The story being told here is more like 17th-, 18th-, and 19th-century metaphysics than it is like set theory or quantum mechanics.

might mean.[11] The irreduction mandate banishes so many familiar variations that it seems as if nothing may be left. Thus the assumption is dismissed that foundations need to deal with the vanishingly *small*, for example, in the sense of coming up with the world's fundamental physical constituents (so no version of quantum mechanics is even a candidate[12]). Similarly excluded is the presupposition that foundations must be *rational*, in the sense of coming up with the basic logical constituents of reason. Logic, truth, and mathematics will not even be available en route; they are prizes to be won from the contest, not stage props or road equipment brought along for the journey—not illicit steroids taken on the sly, to give unfair advantage. But if these traditional foundational characteristics are all rejected, then it is incumbent to explain what coherent sense of "being a foundation" is intended. It is not enough to provide irreductionist foundations, in other words; it is also necessary, because it is so far from being clear in advance, to explain what irreductionist foundations are.

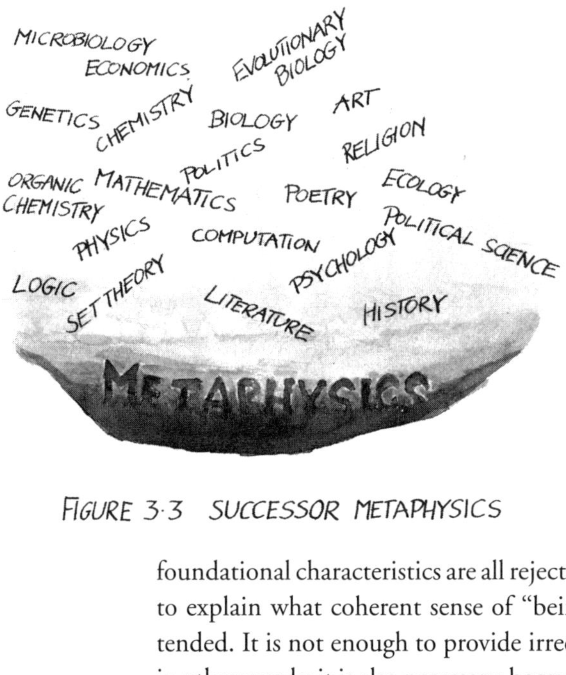

FIGURE 3·3   SUCCESSOR METAPHYSICS

In the main the answer will emerge slowly, as appropriate vocabularies and intuitions are developed. But one thing can be

---

[11] Cf. the discussion of "successor science" in Harding (1986), p. 142.

[12] Why anyone should think physics *is* a candidate is the interesting issue. Physical laws do not apply to physical laws, to take just one obvious example, and so if physical laws are real *in any sense at all* then that would seem to entail that physics cannot be a theory of everything.

said here. To the extent that the project is foundationalist or has foundationalist leanings on anyone's conception, it is intended to be a common foundation for everything, not just, nor even preferentially, for the technical or scientific or "objective." Thus the aim of the project is as pictured in figure 3.3. Hence the reference to C P Snow in the opening paragraph:[13] the story is intended to be neutral with respect to—and thereby, perhaps, to help heal—the schism between the sciences and the humanities. But as the century draws to a close that is no longer the right way to put it, since the word 'humanities' has come to signify a largely academic and highly intellectualized activity, not so distinguishable from science. Better to say that the story to be told represents an attempt to unify, and therefore with luck to help heal, the schism between the academic-cum-intellectual-cum-technological, on the one hand, and the curious, the erotic, the spiritual, the playful, the humane, the moral, the artistic, the political, and the sheerly obstreperous, on the other. That is the divide that tears us apart; not the walls between this and that academic department.

So here is the situation. Nothing has yet been said about how it might be possible to accomplish this task of providing a grounded, successor metaphysics. But it is important to be clear on which gauntlet is being taken up. With respect to naive realism and social constructionism, I accept neither, and want instead to steer a tenable course between the two. With respect to the intellectual and the obstreperous, I embrace both, and aim for a common foundation.

2 Realism

To raise the level of discourse to the metatheoretic level, in the way that is being done in this chapter, and thus to talk about realism, objectivity, truth, and the like (instead of reidentification and indexical fan-out), is to enter the well-traveled and several-thousand-year-old terrain of philosophical metaphysics. To a

[13] Snow (1964).

working scientist, it is a little like lifting the man-hole cover over one's head and finding oneself in front of Grand Central Station. The territory is if anything over-developed. This makes it difficult for anyone to speak without, by sentence's end, being classified as adhering to this or that doctrine, believing this or that creed, belonging to this or that school. This may already have happened, in virtue of my using 'realism' and 'objectivity,' for example—or perhaps in virtue of *not* using 'social' or 'material.' All these terms carry a considerable weight of connotation, only part of which any sane person would want to shoulder.

I say this in order to distinguish two tasks, only one of which this chapter will address. The one I will not take up here is to locate the story within the landscape of intellectual history. There are many reasons why that would (and will) be an important thing to do, but it is also necessary to understand that any attempt to do so might be *wrong*.[14] It might be wrong because the content of the account does not derive from such classification. One of the whole points of resuscitating foundationalism is to show that an account need not "hang from above" in this way, but can be grounded in its own terms. Better to tell the story first, in other words, and analyze it later.

---

[14] For example, it is natural to ask whether the account argued in this book is idealist, since I claim that the ontological warrant for an object's being an object depends in part on a subject's taking it to be so. But all sorts of questions would need to be answered first, before one could tell. The warrant I embrace, for starters, is no *more* the subject's than the object's; it is claimed to be collaborative between the two. And so whether my account is idealist, or has idealist overtones, depends on whether the idealist's grounding of objectivity in a subject's intuition is symmetrical or asymmetrical (to say nothing of whether the *distinction* between subject and object is presumed in idealism, counter to the irreductionist mandate, or is wrested from the metaphysical account itself, as I will argue that it must be). There is also a question as to what *kinds* of subject activity or capacity are ontologically implicated: mental capacities, as intuition is most often construed, or, as I will claim here, life practices, including the collective practices of the embedding historical community.

The task I will take up is more modest: of motivating some driving intuitions. Following Putnam, therefore,[15] I will use capitalized versions of various familiar meta-metaphysical terms—Realism, Pragmatism, Idealism, Objectivity, etc.—to denote familiar philosophical positions, and lower-case versions to get at the meanings I want to lean on, which arise out of much more rudimentary and commonplace sets of intuitions. As Putnam remarks, it is especially important to do this with the term 'Realism,' because of the gap that has opened up, in this century, between that philosophical doctrine and anything recognizable to common sense. Thus Realism-with-a-capital-'R' has come to be closely associated with the natural sciences, meaning something very much like what I associated with modern foundationalism: that everything that exists or is metaphysically legitimate either rests on, or is built up out of, or can ultimately be explained in terms of, or is a (perhaps epiphenomenal) consequence of, the world as described in the natural sciences, especially including, or perhaps *only* including, physics (plus mathematics, perhaps, though people differ as to whether this mathematics is an enthusiastically embraced or reluctantly admitted bride). Given the sheer oddness of modern physics, however—including not only the original quantum mechanics and relativity, but more modern developments, such as ten- or eleven-dimensional string-theory and quantum chromodynamics—this puts common sense into something of a conundrum. What is *Real* has become at the very least challenging to, and at worst outright incompatible with, what is *real*.[16]

By realism, on the other hand—the version with the lower-

---

[15] See for example chapter 1 (the title essay) of Putnam's *Realism with a Human Face* (1990).

[16] This is tricky ground. In point of fact Realism is more closely associated with a *mythology* of science—i.e., with Science—than it is with what actually happens in lived laboratories. As a result, the alleged standards of value-free "objectivity" and the like, embraced by Realists, are much more stringent than anything actually true of quantum mechanics "in the wild."

case 'r', and the version to which I want to hold the story accountable—I simply want to get at the familiar and virtually unshakable commonsense intuition that, as it is said, there is "a world out there," a world beyond our fingertips and imaginations, a world at once utterly familiar, totally enveloping, and unfailingly surprising—a world of breakfast and skateboards, scandals and melancholy, DNA and falling interest rates. There is *more* to the world than us, in other words; more than our imaginations, more than our experience, more than our thoughts and dreams. And that "more" matters. It matters pragmatically, it matters aesthetically, it matters epistemically. If we should ever make the mistake of thinking that we are the whole story, moreover—that we "have it down," that we are in control—then the world has a fortunate habit of tripping us up, of reminding us that our perspective is both flawed and partial, that ours is not the only game in town.

This familiar sense of "moreness"—a kind of simple transcendence of the world—is something any metaphysical account must retain. On the other hand I want to resist two common ways in which realism (or Realism) is often described: (i) a formulation that takes it to be a claim that the world exists *independent* of the experiencing subject, and (ii) a formulation that takes it to be a claim about the existence of an *external* world.

Start with the claim that the world exists independent of the experiencing subject. This is immediately untenable for irreductionist reasons: the distinction between world and subject (whether that distinction is assumed to be logical, metaphysical, or epistemic) needs to be paid for; it cannot be assumed. Worse, it is also too strong, because of the nonsensical quandary into which it places subjects. It is an elementary observation, after all, though still a consequential fact (indeed, partially constitutive of constructionism), that intentional subjects, including us, are full-blooded, embodied, effective *participants* in the world.[17] We are made of the stuff of, and inhabit, and seriously mess with, the very world that the doctrine of realism is intended to establish. *And wholes are not independent of their parts.* Think of how odd it would be to think or pretend that your body was independent of your arm.[18] A subject cannot have a perspective on an object, or pick it up, or make it out of clay, or be wrong about it, if the two do not share a common ground. And they cannot share a common ground unless they are part of the same world. But if that is true—that they are part of the same world—that is enough to invalidate the "independence" construal of realism. The world they are part of, the world to which realism is committed, must be an encompassing whole. On pain of conceptual confusion, it cannot be construed as independent of what it comprises.

Some readers may object. In response to this last claim, that subject and object are part of the *same* world, they may argue that there is no "same world"—that worlds are inherently many. But that is not my present concern. Pluralism, which I will consider in a moment, is crucial, but it is irrelevant to the present point, in part because we are talking about a single instance of a person's (subject's) taking the world to be a certain way—e.g., a single person's perceiving or thinking about a single object. There are not enough actors on stage for pluralism to get into the picture.

More relevant is the following complaint: that the independence claim was intended to be more focused. It was never

---

[17] This is an "elementary observation" only for realists, of course. But they are my present target. I am claiming that the independence formulation is too strong to adequately represent the intuition or commitment of realists; it is a separate, and subsequent, question whether, once that intuition is properly expressed, it then carries any weight with, say, skeptics or idealists.

[18] And how gruesome. In trying to make sense of a claim that **a** is independent of **b**, one automatically imagines a situation in which **b** is *separated* from **a**—even if **b** is normally a *part* of **a**.

claimed, such an objector will insist, that the world as a whole be independent of the subject; rather, the requisite intuition is only that there exist pieces of the world, distinct from the experiencing subject, that enjoy an independent existence—pieces such as the tree outside the window, or the table in the room across the hall, pieces such as the referent or object of the person's intentional state. The "independence" construal of realism, the critic might suggest, should be read as a condition that holds between two parts of the world—subject and object—not as a condition between one part of the world, subject, and the encompassing world as a whole.

But the "piecemeal" suggestion fails, for a spate of important reasons. First, it is absolutely not innocent to change the topic in this way. The intuitive notion of realism, of the small-'r' variety, really is a single thesis about the world in general—a thesis about the world as an entirety. There is no reason to suppose, and good reason not to suppose, that it is a schema for an indefinite number of specific claims about the world's multiplicitous ingredients. For one thing, the resulting set of piecemeal independence claims is too wimpy to be the basis of a comprehensive metaphysics. Realism was supposed to be a strong enough doctrine to serve as a backdrop against which to develop an understanding of individual objects; if one needs to have the objects (i.e., the pieces) separated out in order to state it, the proposal collapses in circularity (to say nothing of massively violating the irreduction mandate). Moreover, to turn to an epistemic consideration, a subject can legitimately be said to have an objective conception of an existing object *just in case they recognize, understand, or take it to be part of that unifying entirety.* That is what it is to be "real": to be part of the encompassing whole, to take a place alongside, and thus potentially to interact with, everything else that there is—including, not least, with the subject. And a metaphysical position on realism should at a minimum be strong enough to support its counterpart epistemic position on objectivity. If objectivity is going to make reference to a unifying entirety, a proper analysis of realism should embrace that entirety explicitly.

A piecemeal independence schema, to put the same point more ontologically, would be unable to explain how it is that everything stands in an infinite number of relations with everything else—including, crucially, how it is that objects resist or fight back against subjects, a kind of spat or contention necessary for an object to be real, as well as for a subject to be right or wrong. Nor is it possible to avoid this last conclusion—that everything potentially interacts with everything else—by invoking the potential incommensurability of conceptual schemes or world views. Once again, pluralism is not an answer here. Just because you and I use alien concepts to understand the world does not mean that my car bomb won't rain on your parade.

Finally, it is not clear that the piecemeal interpretation of (the independence formulation of) realism is even true. Social constructionists will not think it is true, of course, arguing that how the world is, as well as how we take it to be, is partially determined by our collective social or historical or cultural practices. But it is unclear that realists should accept it, either. Consider tables. The problem is not just that tables are almost certainly individuated functionally, where we as subjects figure in the establishment of the social practices in terms of which they are functionally individuated. A defender of (again, the independence formulation of) realism might accept that, but try to duck such epistemic or classificatory involvement by saying that "that which we take to be a table" exists independently of our so taking it, even if our taking it *as* a table depends in part on us (because of those constitutive social practices that are implicated in its function). But that does not work, either. "That which we take to be a table" does not exist independent of us for the almost pedantically simple fact that *tables are things that we build.*

The problem is that artifacts, to broaden the case a bit, are by definition products of human labor; there is no way to claim that they exist independently of us. And artifacts, qua objects, are not exactly outré. On the contrary, they are among the most paradigmatic objects of all—at worst taking second place to such high-level biological entities as people and animals. Remove the animals, artifacts, and perhaps the trees, and just try to individuate what remains: infinitely variegated but not very cleanly divided rock outcroppings, muskeg, bramble patches, cloud formations, lichen, and the rest.[19] Nor does it help the cause, when the issue of artifacts is raised, to retreat to putatively more "natural" objects, such as the polar ice cap, or the atomic structure of gold, which at least arguably have some sort of existence independent of our so taking them. Even if one could defend an independence construal of realism on these or other similar examples (by ignoring global warming, in the case of the ice cap), to do so would weaken the claim beyond recognition. A metaphysical doctrine that did not apply to pen and paper would not be worth the writing down.

In sum, independence of subject and world is somewhere between incoherent and too strong.[20] Similar considerations militate against the other most familiar characterization of realism: the idea that there is a world "out there"—i.e., that realism is a claim about the existence of an *external world*, and thus that a subject's developing an objective commitment to realism has to do with their building up a conception of, or otherwise being engaged with, the existence of a world taken as external. This fails because of the ultimate incoherence of the idea that the world as a whole—and again it is the world as a whole we are talking about—is external to anything. Or else, to put the same

[19] One way to understand this book is as the metaphysics of a northerner— and as such much more aimed at rock than at rocks.

[20] The view I will eventually develop will mandate *partial* independence of subject and object (not partial independence of subject and world; that I will still hold as incoherent).

101

point a different way, it fails because of the existential difficulties
it imposes on whatever it is that the world is thought to be external *to*. Not only is the "internal" world of a subject as real as anything else, but developing anything that could justifiably be
called an objective conception of it—in introspection or reflection, for example—is as much an achievement as developing a

View	Characterization	Relation to subject	Form of separation
1	World independent of the experiencing subject	Independent	Logical
2	External world	External	Physical

FIGURE 3·4   UNTENABLE READINGS OF "REALISM"

conception of an external reality. Possibly more so, in fact, since
subject and object, being identical, inevitably end up tripping
over each other.[21] So the internal world should neither be for-
gotten about nor abandoned. Even if *access* to one's self is in
some sense privileged, because of the causal proximity of reflective mind and reflected-upon mind, that does not mean that developing a perspective on yourself, or seeing yourself as part of
the world, is anything like automatic (if it were, psychiatrists
would be redundant).

There is an important parallel between these last two charac-
terizations—first, of a world independent of the subject, and
second, of a world external to the subject—that shows why both
fail. As indicated in figure 3·4, the problem is that both char-
acterizations take subject and world to be *two*—logically
separated, according to the "independent of the subject" formulation; physically separated, according to the claim about an
"external world." But both dualities are false. There is nothing

[21] This fact, evident from psychoanalysis, is also a prime architectural concern in reflective computer systems. See Smith (1984).

for the world to be separate from, logically, physically, meta-physically, or in any other way. And there is no way for us sub-jects to be separate from it either. That is what it is to be the world. The conclusion is actually very simple: the world, our world, is *one*.

And this oneness goes deep. Thus the world is not "one" in any ordinary sense of that word. It is not one, for example, in a sense in which it could have been two, or indeed in a sense in which *counting* makes any sense at all. Nor is it one in the way in which a single object can be singled out and called one, in dis-tinction from a background; thus in the next chapter I will deny that the world is an *individual*. Nor is it one in the sense of being unified or homogenous: the world's local unutterable variety will play a significant role in the upcoming metaphysical pro-posal. What is meant, rather, is: (i) that the world is nowhere clo-ven wholly in two, neither between subject and object, nor between concrete and abstract, nor between empirical and logi-cal, nor between any two other kinds of things; and (ii) that there is nothing other than it. Maybe this is a technical enough meaning that I should capitalize it: and say that the world is One. On the other hand, if it turns out to be true that every word, in order to be meaningful, must carve out or identify a "figure" to be drawn into the foreground, and thereby distin-guished from a necessary backdrop or background or horizon, then it may follow that *no* word, capitalized or not, can denote or even convey the encompassing totality to which the realist is committed. We can still point at it indirectly, for example by saying that the world is *complete*. Or if 'complete' connotes too much of a sense of closedness or finality, in the sense of being finished off or shut down or exhausted, then perhaps 'entire.' Or we could abandon common terms, or even abandon the idea that it can be referred to at all, even with the term 'world,' and therefore avoid naming it. Or we could call it *God*, or *Ayn Sof*—

or more whimsically, just *The*.[22] No matter; vocabulary is not
what matters. For one thing (this will surface later), the idea of
this totality is in fact easier to grasp, internally and bodily, than
to express in consensual language. For now I will leave it at this:
that there is nothing in fact, or in logical possibility, or in metaphysical possibility, or accessible to the imagination, or in any
other form, for the world to be dependent on, independent of,
separated from, or external to. The world has no "other."

3 Application to subjects and objects

Given this overarching view of a single and entire encompassing
reality, what can be said, more specifically, about the subjects
and objects that inhabit it?

   In a sense, the rest of the book is an attempt to answer that
question. Here I will simply identify seven constraints that this
construal of realism places on subjects and objects—constraints, as mentioned at the beginning of the chapter, to which
the subsequent metaphysics will be held accountable.

3a Symmetric Realism

The most important fact about this conception of realism is its
inherent symmetry. As an overarching condition, that is, it is
uniformly applicable to the full intentional situation, including
subject, object, and whatever relation binds them (including the
full historical embedding context). Hence the phrase *symmetrical realism*. Of particular importance is the fact that it is not especially oriented towards or relevant to the *object* side of this
most famous of divides. Realism is no more a precondition on

---

[22] 'The' for three reasons: (i) because the reference is determinate, no matter
how otherwise ineffable, because of its inexorable immanence; (ii) because
what is referred to is referable-to in virtue of one's situation or context—
being in and of it—so that it is appropriate to signal the indexicality of the
determinate reference; and (iii) because the world cannot be 'the ϕ,' for any
ϕ, since ϕs in such constructions invariably filter or place restrictions, and
the whole point is to get at the world unfiltered and unrestricted. (Cf. the
commitment to not be grounded in α, for any α.)

objectivity than a precondition on subjectivity; no more a condition on the realm of reference than a condition on the realm of sense or of subject or of sign. To think otherwise is to fail to take responsibility for what I claim to be the constructionists' fundamental insight: that we, too, as subjects, are as much "here" as are the objects of our thoughts.

It is fortunate that it works out in this symmetric way, too, because of what has already been said: that having one's metaphysical doctrine commit in advance to a division of the situation into subjects and objects would cost too much. Where would that distinction have come from? Who would have paid for it?

This is not to say that no subject/object distinction will ever be drawn. It will be, and crucially. Irreduction, as I have already said, is not an injunction to block distinctions; its demand is simply that we own up to drawing them. So we can identify that as the first requirement on a successful metaphysics: it must supply resources with which to draw a distinction between subject and object. On the other hand subject and object will *never* be viewed as independent; the arguments given above continue to hold. Rather, the separation between the two will be inherently partial. It is not just that the *notions* of 'subject' and 'object' will be interdefined, which many would expect. As much could be said about the length and width of a rectangle: a width cannot be a width without a length's being a length; yet length and width remain, famously, independent, in at least some sense. The non-independence of subjects and objects goes deeper. The actual *distinction* between subject and object, as phenomena on the ground—physical distinction, logical distinction, conceptual distinction, whatever sort of distinction it is—will be intrinsically partial. Any successful metaphysics must provide resources for subject and object to be *separated*, in other words; but at the same time must never go so far as to wholly sever them. Like neighboring sand dunes, their being two (as opposed to one, One, or Two!) can never be entirely assured, never be one hundred percent true.

3b A Single Cup

I said above that the notion of world is prior to the subject/object distinction, and that the metaphysics must provide resources for that distinction to be drawn within the world. But of course the subject/object divide is not special in this way; every distinction must be wrested from the same metaphysical flux. We can label this as the second requirement: everything, including physical objects, human societies, truth, beauty, reason, and mathematics—i.e., both might and right—are to be drunk from this one same cup. To assume, just because they are (allegedly) abstract, that any of these latter notions escapes the world's confines, is, curiously enough, to commit oneself to an untenably physical view of the world. It is doubly reductionist: physically reductionist with regards to the world itself, because of an advance prejudice as to what sorts of things the world does (and does not) contain; and ideologically reductionist with respect to the paraphernalia of extra-world notions, such as mathematical entities, types, laws, and the like (including the laws that govern the physical world), to which the metaphysician or ontologist or scientist or God is thought to have free access, on a privileged side channel, immune from theoretical scrutiny.

3c Objectivity

Realism's encompassing wholeness will limit the possible extent of intentional achievement—basically because there is no way to "step outside" reality in order to see it entire. Realism-with-a-small-'r', that is, spells defeat for Objectivity: the mythological idea that there is an attainable or coherent form of knowledge that is independent of any bias, interest, position, perspective, or other fact of subjective particularity. Given that subjects inhabit the world, which I have already said, and is anyway implied by the world's totality, and given also that subjects develop perspectives on things in virtue of "looking out" at those things from a vantage point, which I have not yet said, but will say, and also follows from the fact that they inhabit the world, it will rather directly follow that there is no position from which the whole is visible. It has not yet been argued, in other words, but will be argued, that the totality of the world is by itself enough to imply that there is no such thing as a "from nowhere" perspective or universal viewpoint. Making sense of the fact that the perspectival character of knowledge is never entirely eliminable is realism's third requirement.

3d objectivity

If Objectivity is doomed, which is hardly a surprise, what about objectivity—objectivity with a small-'o'? Does the incoherence of the idea of a view from nowhere, and a concomitant commitment to view knowledge as inexorably situated, located, embodied, perspectival, contested, and so forth—do these things undermine the possibility of any notion of objectivity at all? It is extremely important that the answer to this question is *no*. This can be taken as the fourth requirement. It is essential, that is, that the eventual metaphysical story retain, or perhaps regain, some form of "successor objectivity." For all sorts of reasons, ranging from a desire not to relinquish the English language to predecessor science or metaphysics, to a need to guard against the ravages of a bankrupt, vapid, "anything goes" kind of relativism, to a desire to hold onto what is best about the humility or deference of the empirical method, it is essential to retain an appropriately sensitive but appropriately robust species of objectivity as a lived and livable option.

Lots of challenges will have to be addressed en route to such a notion, including basic issues about the range of its application, including whether, for example, as is often thought, objectivity should be viewed as a (valorous) property of propositional representation in language and thought, or whether it should be extended to cover full-bodied social and historical activity—i.e., ultimately construed as a way of *living right*, rather than merely a way of speaking truthfully. The relation between objectivity and objects will similarly have to be clarified, as well as what it is to have an objective conception of the world.

Perhaps the toughest challenge to a notion of objectivity, however—or perhaps the toughest context in which to develop such a sense—involves the question of pluralism. To put it more specifically, one of the most difficult challenges a metaphysical theory must face is how to do justice to what is right about pluralist intuitions, cultural sensitivity, and infinite variability, on the one hand, while at the same time retaining an appropriately rigorous notion of virtue or standards or worth, on the other. Especially in these late-twentieth-century times, either without the other is by now too easy: univocal or monist truth, on the one hand; or laissez-faire "I'm OK; you're OK" pluralism, on the other. As history has repeatedly shown, both one-sided variants are politically dangerous as well: univocal truth being a recipe for cultural imperialism and blindness to alternative voices; laissez-faire pluralism, a way of defusing the seriousness of any discourse whatsoever.

The challenge is to combine virtue and pluralism in a single coherent vision. Honoring this duality is what tests the mettle of a theory of the real.

3e Pluralism

By *pluralism*, in the sense that I embrace, I mean something constantly lived and multiply textured: a dynamic, day-by-day, in-the-rough, wrestling and struggling with the *fit* of one's concepts and actions and thoughts into the world surrounding them—fit with the rest of one's beliefs and hopes and desires, fit with the ideas and desires of one's fellows, fit with one's community and history—and by no means least, fit with the subject matters they are about.

Thus the picture I have in mind views pluralism as active, political, violent, and feisty—a kind of negotiated plasticity (but not indeterminacy) of reference that can affect the meaning of words from the beginning to end of a single utterance, and that is not even close to being stable across a whole culture. Perhaps its most enduring quality is of *locality*: justice to the particular, the specific, the located. As such, it differs from another view sometimes associated with the same name—something I will call "pluralism-in-the-large," and might have even called Pluralism, since in some quarters it verges on received mythology. By pluralism-in-the-large, in particular, I refer to a position that admits that, yes, sure enough, the words or concepts of a given people or society are not absolute or God-given, but that nonetheless maintains that they are relatively stable across some identifiable (and expensive) unit of analysis: stable across a populace, say, or across a culture, or across a given historical period.

The major theoretical difference between the two positions (for a political difference see the sidebar on page 112) is that pluralism as I mean it—pluralism-in-the-small—is a phenomenon that must be *dealt with at the center*, whereas pluralism-in-the-large, although it admits pluralism to be *true* at the center, claims that it only needs to be *dealt with at the edges*.[23] And that conclusion I believe is false. On the contrary, that pluralism be dealt with at the center can be identified as our fifth realist requirement.

The following will thus be a consequence of the metaphysical story to be told: not only (i) that all intentional processes—discourse, thinking, computation, conversation, etc.—are located and embodied and perspectival, but also (ii) that their located,

---

[23] Pluralism-in-the-large admits that language, discourse, thoughts, etc., are culturally relative at the center; that comes with the territory. But since it typically assumes (i) that conceptual systems are approximately uniform, across the population under study, and (ii) that one is studying this population *from the inside*, it does not need to do more than admit it. It does not change the *work*, in other words; it just changes one's stance towards it. Whereas what I am arguing for will change the way we do business, materially change the way we theorists conduct our affairs.

embodied, perspectival, pluralist aspect is dynamic and everywhere potentially unstable;[24] and also (iii) that it is in the intrinsic nature of language, thinking, concepts, etc., that they are designed to wrestle with these dynamic and unstable features of intentional life. The sorts of constitutive regularity that, according to the picture I will paint, undergird thought, representation, conversation, and the like, involve essential strategies for adjusting and negotiating and enforcing and ripping apart and otherwise *struggling* with the fit of one's conceptual system to the in-part differently conceptualized, and in-part unconceptualized, world.

The wrestling is not optional, in other words. Nor is it an inevitable but unfortunate complication. Struggling in and around and with and through and underneath concepts is the very essence of intentionality.

3f Directedness

What then of the other half of the critical duality: pluralism's partner, the notion of virtue or worth?

Note, for starters, that I have several times claimed that realism's most important consequence is the deference or respect it engenders in us for the "wider world"—or at least the deference or respect that underlies a living commitment to it. But so far that has just been extra-theoretical motivation for embracing a realist position. Nothing has yet been said about how realism itself, the symmetrical encompassing entirety, causes or constrains or catalyses such deference. It is not enough for a metaphysical account to *be realist*, in other words; it must also *explain realism*, in the sense of showing how, why, and what it is for an

---

[24] It cannot be everywhere unstable all at once, of course—or everything would be chaos. Nothing in what I am saying denies that a great deal of what we do and talk about and collaborate on is relatively stable most of the time. I would only deny: (i) that any of it need ever be *perfectly* stable; (ii) that all of it ever be even roughly stable; and (iii) that any of it be immune from variation or risk. This makes clear what should anyway be evident: that this dynamic conception of pluralism is closely related to irreduction.

intentional agent to have a world-directed commitment. This is the sixth requirement.

World-directedness takes many forms. The version we are most theoretically familiar with is semantic directedness—the fact, famous since Brentano,[25] that subjects (their experiences, representations, documents, intentions, thoughts, etc.) point or are directed towards the transcendent-but-immanent world that surrounds them. A symmetrically realist account per se supplies two of the requisite ingredients in this pointing: (i) the fact that subjects are *in* an enveloping world, which gives them a place to point *from*; and (ii) the fact that they are *made of* that same enveloping world, which gives them the wherewithal to point *with*. What a theory of intentionality needs to add is the far-from-obvious third ingredient: (iii) a way for subjects to orient *towards* that enveloping world, the world of which they are constituted and in which they live.

Many familiar milestones demarcate this road. The metaphysics will have to show that there is *more* to what is pointed at than the subject grasps, for example, in at least two senses: more to the world, in toto, than the particular fragment towards which the subject is directed (precursor of the notion of *part*); and more to that fragment—more qualities it manifests, for example—than experience relates (precursor of the notion of *aspect*). It will involve explaining what it is to point to fictional entities, and to entities that do not yet exist. It will need as well to recognize that the subject, that which points, and the object, that which is pointed at, can and often do part company. Beliefs are not always right; intended actions do not always succeed; perception is not always veridical. This potential for "coming apart" is very basic, underwriting not only the possibility for error, but the very possibility of entertaining a hypothetical. And it is not a painless separation, a casual no-fault divorce. When

---

[25] Or at least since Chisholm's misinterpretation of Brentano; see Chisholm (1957), pp. 168 ff., Franchi (forthcoming·a), McAlister (1974), and Dupuy (1994), p. 105.

Politics of pluralism-in-the-large

My ultimate disagreement with the large-scale reading of pluralism stems, naturally enough, from my belief that it is false. The metaphysical system developed in this book implies that it is false. Specifically, the view I argue for contradicts its major tenet: that it is harmless to view conceptual schemes as constant across even small groups. At the same time, however, it is hard to ignore the fact that pluralism-in-the-large is politically distressing.

To see why, note first that pluralism-in-the-large lets theoreticians off lightly, by allowing them to pledge allegiance to a degree of cultural sensitivity, but at the same time to view that sensitivity, as it were, as extra-theoretical—i.e., as if cultural or situational dependence were an independent parameter, to be set once for a given language or people or period of history, but then thereafter ignored. Furthermore, although one is supposed to *imagine* this parameter being set, no one can say anything more specific than that, such as what it would be set *to*, because the requisite thing to say is required, by the view's own commitments, to be metaphysically ineffable. If your culture is different from mine, I can say that we are incommensurable, but I can say nothing more, nor can I learn anything from you, nor can I interpret my scheme for you, or anything else. In spite of its protestations, pluralism-in-the-large does not require a theoretical commitment to make diversity a central metaphysical focus.

But the real problem is not with its theoretical consequences; it is in the image of what it would be to live by such an account. Nor is it clear that Putnam's internal realism escapes this danger: his picture of truth subject and object part company, *the object wins*. This merciless insight is what underlies the empirical method.

All these things will need to be explored. What is important here is to recognize that the fundamentally asymmetrical and potentially separated world-directedness is much deeper than just semantic. Subject really is *less*; world, *more*—as much in terms of potency and worth as in terms of content or substance.

relative to, and therefore only assayable from within, a governing language community, seems to exhibit this unsettling, black-and-white character. It is too easy to imagine its being interpreted by a privileged "conceptual" elite (i.e., the members of whatever governing social unit is in power, presumed to share a conceptual or at least linguistic scheme) as implying that they can assess the truth of an internally articulated proposition *simpliciter*, without challenge to their own conceptual schemes, while simultaneously banishing those who are not within their group—the culturally disadvantaged, as it were—to the other side of an metaphysically unbridgeable gulf of incomprehension.* Outsiders will intrinsically be unable to understand what is being said by people on the inside; and since no one on the inside will ever be able to understand the outsiders, they therefore need not even try.

It is dangerous to build into one's metaphysics such an unassailable strategy for being able to ignore external criticism and cultural diversity—especially since, as mentioned above, how it is to live by a claim will figure in the ultimate story to be told about "virtue" and objectivity. At least Realism and Objectivity had the merit of requiring that culturally diverse voices be taken somewhat seriously, in the sense that the doctrine at least accorded them comprehensibility, even if its adherents (mistakenly) argued that most or all alien views were false. Pluralism-in-the-large does not even extend to outsiders the respect of allowing them to be wrong.

*It is a little unclear how one would know this; no clear test is provided for telling whether or not someone shares one's conceptual system.

This indelible asymmetry, this risk of losing, this higher significance of the world, far transcends the merely semantic. Subjects, intentions, and the like are *normatively* subservient to that towards which they are directed. It will even turn out—in "the primordial case," as it were—that the normative aspect of directedness, which I earlier called deference and respect, and the semantic directedness, normally thought of in terms of reference or 'aboutness,' are not originally different.

This unification should come as no surprise. If for no other reason than irreduction, there had better be no distinction between the natural and the normative in the metaphysician's analogue of the physicists' first 10^{-23} seconds. Who knows? Perhaps the explanation of world-directedness, and the story of how it has come to manifest in semantic, normative, and other varieties, can take a lead from the way in which one unified physical force bifurcated into strong, weak, electromagnetic, etc., at the beginning of time.

3g Objects

Seventh, and finally, a metaphysical account must do justice to the widespread recognition that part of what it is for an object to be an object—part of what it is for an object to be real, part of what it is for a subject to have an objective conception of an object—is for the object to *resist* us: to fight, to be scrappy, to refuse to be wholly controlled. Except with this caveat: that the talk of resistance applies in general to everything in the world; it is not the unique province of objects. It is only in virtue of difference or separation or otherness, after all, that we tear apart properties or qualities: "mom" from woman in general, mass from weight, ethics from self-righteousness. It is a very general fact that only in virtue of difference and separation do we recognize the world as world.

The particular emphasis on objects, therefore—including their mention in the book's title—is in part a concession to the centrality they are accorded in the traditional (predecessor) metaphysical picture: the familiar picture of discrete objects and properties and relations, tied together with set-theoretic glue. I use the term 'object' reluctantly, because it figures so prominently in this classical story, the very story to which I am dedicated to constructing an alternative. On the other hand, this reluctance is perhaps temporary; there is no more reason to relinquish the term 'object' to predecessor philosophy than there is to relinquish 'objectivity.' So I will henceforth use 'Object' for the set-theoretic consort of Properties and Relations, and continue to give objects prominent billing—in part because they are common, in part because we are thick with intuitions about them, and in part because it will be possible, using them, to get at much more general characteristics of how we take the world to be.[26] They also have the advantage of being, by and large, small, local, and urgent. There is a pragmatic immediacy to objects, not theirs alone, that would be lost by unrealistically raising the topic to that of the structure of the world as a whole.

[26] Pace typography, this book should have been called "On the origin of objects."

115

4 · Particularity

There is a sense in which everything so far has been preparatory. The introduction presented the project; chapter 1 described the computational background and supplied some examples; chapter 2 endorsed an overall methodological stance; and chapter 3 laid down a set of operative metatheoretic and metaphysical requirements. We have done a lot of work, but we have not yet begun to build. Nor are we quite ready to do so. We still need to see how these requirements can all be met.

1 Particularity and individuality

In this chapter I turn to *particularity* and *individuality*—two overarching metaphysical characteristics mentioned at the beginning of chapter 3 that are essential to our everyday conception of at least ordinary material objects. Both ideas, I will argue, come together when we conceive of a stable and enduring thing, such as a table, an old notebook, or a favorite bristlecone pine. Both are involved, too, in the useful motto that an object is *something on which one can have a perspective.* It is helpful to separate them, however, not only because they have different conceptual structures, but also because, as I will argue, they stem from different sources.

1a Particularity

By *particularity*, first, I mean simply that our everyday notion of an object—the base case, on which any more abstract versions rest—is of a located patch of metaphysical flux. By 'particular,' that is, I mean something like 'occurrent': something that is located or that happens, something that is embodied, something for which there is a Steinian "there there." The intent is to capture a root (and rooted) sense of inexorable specificity, as when we talk about a *particular person* or *particular reason* or *particular insight*, or refer to the *particular circumstances* surrounding an accident, say, or a decision. This is also the sense we get at when we say "in particular," as for example in "Let's not worry about our general hiring policy; let's talk about Isaac's situation in particular." Throughout, the emphasis is on the located, the specific, the singular—as opposed to (sometimes even in defiance of) the generic or universal.

Just what particularity comes to depends on how one understands the rest of the metaphysical picture. If one is a physicalist, which most people are at least in part, particularity will at a minimum hold of anything that occupies or has any claim on space-time. If one is a physicalist, that is, a possible alternative for 'particular' might be 'concrete.' Certainly the implication goes one way: physicalist and non-physicalist alike can agree that everything that is concrete is particular. But since, as already indicated, I do not want to give the physical inappropriate pride of place,[1] I do not want to assert the opposite—at least not in advance, and also not later on. So I will use the term 'particular' in a broad sense, to include phenomena whose concreteness rational people might reasonably doubt: events, such as the start of the Olympics or the knock at the door, and processes, such as Joanna's writing or Isaac's tenure fight, as well as such arguably ephemeral phenomena as Leigh's curiosity last night, the collapse of Cold War diplomacy, and the burgeoning interest in the information superhighway. More contentiously, perhaps, but no less importantly, thoughts and ideas will be taken as particular as well: her thoughts about how to build a dock, his ideas about what counts as messy, your dreams about vacation (not her thoughts in the sense that someone else might have those same thoughts, but her instantiated, lived thoughts, those "thinkings" she had on Wednesday afternoon). Indeed, just about the only things that are not particular, and they only arguably, are universals, generics, and (if there are any) pure ab-

---

[1] The physical undeniably deserves appropriate place; less clear is the pride. See §1 of chapter 11, and the sidebar on pp. 320–21.

stractions—the type *canoe*, for example; the number 4; the abstract property of being chartreuse.

In sum, I mean by particularity to get at approximately what philosophers would say distinguishes so-called "bare particulars," or just particulars in general, from such putatively non-particular entities as types or universals. And yet, as I will argue in a moment, there is more to the traditional notion of a (bare) particular than its manifestation of the more abstract character I am calling particularity.

1b Individuality

By *individuality*, on the other hand, I mean whatever it is about an entity that supports the notion of individuation criteria—something that makes 'object' a count noun, something that makes objects discrete. Somehow or other, an individual object is taken to be something of coherent unity, separated out from a background, in the familiar "figure-ground" fashion. Think of reaching into a wet vat and pulling out a handful of clay, watching it break off from the mass of clay that is left behind, and fashioning it into a unitary whole, patting the sides, neatening it up, knocking messy bits off into the vat, and forming a stable *thing*, something that can be put on a table and admired. To take something to be an individual object, or to make something into an individual, or however one likes to put it, is to do something similar. *Individuality is what allows one to say of one object that it is one; or of two, that they are two.* That is not to say that individuals are One, in the sense used in the last chapter. On the contrary, individuals are exactly what do have all of the properties of ordinary "oneness" lacked by the world as a whole.

Etymologically, individual means *indivisible*: not to be divided. That should not be taken as implying that individuals cannot be chopped up at all—as if they were metaphysically pointillist. Rather, it is to imply that, *qua* individuals, they have an overall integrity or unity that is liable to be violated by taking them apart. Because they are discrete, in other words, individuals support a notion of half, as well as of two.[2] Unlike water, if you put individual and individual together, you get two individuals, not just more. By the same token, if you take an individual apart, you get parts or fragments, not just less.

It must be said, however, that the term 'particular' has similar etymological associations, of "particulateness," which I explicitly want to block. Particulateness, that is, is something I am not associating with particularity, but rather with individuality. In fact that is the whole point, really: to separate the sense of the very specific or local or "peculiar," to be associated with particularity, from the quite different sense of being discrete or chopped up into distinct units or wholes, to be associated with individuality. Thus the toys strewn around on the lawn outside, as I write, have both properties: they are *particular individuals*; whereas the water lapping on the rocks far below them remains particular—even exquisitely so—without thereby requiring any such "division" into discrete individual parts.

Whereas the most intuitively accessible individuals are material objects—toys, chairs and tables, people, and the like—I will also countenance abstract objects such as types, properties, and relations as first-class individuals. In doing semantics, for example, we talk about the successor function, the arithmetic relation of divisibility, the move type "pawn-to-king-4." These

[2]Given this, the fact that you can have two lumps of clay, but not (at least not so easily) half a lump of clay, would seem to undermine a lump of clay's grip on individuality. But that is not so clear. Given a particular lump of clay, there is no difficulty in having half of *that* lump. So particular lumps of clay seem to be in good shape, *qua* individuals. The problem is rather at the level of the type: since half of any lump, because of the nature of clay, is itself also a whole lump, it is odd, in the absence of any compelling reason, to call something half a lump. On the other hand it is easy to construct circumstances in which one would naturally do just that—for example, if one were (contextually) working with a specific size of lump. If an assistant has regularly been handing lumps of mortar to a bricklayer, it would make perfect sense for the bricklayer to say, at the end of a row, "I think we can finish this out with just half a lump."

sorts of entity, along with the 1957 T-bird (in the sense of being the most beautiful car Ford ever designed), to say nothing of Frege's "concept horse," are by my lights legitimate individuals. They certainly stake a far higher claim to indivisibility than does anything concrete.

1c Sameness and difference

Individuality rests on background notions of sameness and difference. The structure of this sameness and difference is of the utmost importance. It will be asked to underwrite a calculus—a "story about the one and the many"—that will occupy center stage later on. The point is actually very simple. In order to be distinguished from a background, a given (individual) object must be viewed as different from that background: *qualitative* difference, difference in the sense of being differentiable. In order to be distinguished from other objects of the same type, an individual must similarly be viewed as different from them: *quantitative* difference, difference in the sense of being distinct. Moreover, these two (qualitatively) different senses of difference are undergirded by a more fundamental and unified sense of metaphysical difference overall.[3] Thus a cloud is different from the sky; and the keyboard I am now typing on is different from the monitor, different from the mouse, different from another keyboard, of the same make and model, that sits broken behind me on a shelf. And such difference is not hard to find; it is no metaphysical rarity. Difference is endemic.

By the same token, however, in order for an individual to be

---

[3]The claim that differentiability and distinctness are distinct notions—i.e., that qualitative and quantitative differences are qualitatively different—is what I will call a *post-ontological* claim: something that requires a prior identification of (individual) objects in order to be made out. It is a distinction that can only be made after metaphysics is done; it cannot be used as a basis for the metaphysics itself. I also do not believe that the difference between differentiability and distinctness is all that sharp. What is needed, anyway, is a metaphysically powerful enough notion of difference to use to register the objects in the first place.

taken as a unity, any internal variation in behavior or constitution must be ignored, or at least contained, so that the whole can be treated as one thing—and in that sense the *same*. Thus the keyboard is the same individual object, whether or not the 's' key is held down, whether it is in my lap or resting on the desk, whether or not I spill coffee on it. Difference from *without* is essential to an individual's being an individual; difference *within* at least some difference within, must be ignored, temporarily set aside, viewed as a different "mode of being" for one and the same enduring entity. The internal difference that is caused by my thumb's striking the space bar does not violate the keyboard's logical integrity, its integrity as a spatio-temporally enduring individual.

This sameness across difference—sameness for difference to be difference of—shows that abstraction is intrinsically implicated in the notion of an individual. It will also be required in order to support a notion of reidentifying the same object, at a different place or time.

Note the striking similarity between the structure of sameness and difference at the level of an individual object, and the analogous story of sameness and difference one level higher, having to do with different instances (tokens) of a common type. There is a sameness in common across all different instances of the species *Maine Coon Cat*, for example; that is exactly what it is to say that these animals are all of the same type. On the other hand there is also fundamental difference: your cat and my cat are different cats—different *particular* cats, as we say—even if they are of the same species. So a story about the constitution of individuals should be expected to have something in common with, even if in other ways it is different from, the analogous story about the constitution of types. It was partly in order to demonstrate the similarity of these two structuring devices, and at the same time to question their ultimate adequacy— i.e., to challenge the (formal) neatness of the traditional characterization of Tokens/Instances and Types—that some of the "fan-out" examples in chapter 1 were presented. If difference is metaphysically endemic, then structured sameness, dynamic patterns of fan-out and fan-in, is concomitantly endemic to ontology.

2 Bare particulars

It is non-standard to distinguish particularity and individuality in the way I have just done. In uppercase dress, the two notions are almost always combined in the traditional philosophical notion of what is called a "bare particular" (or even just "particular," on its own). The traditional treatment is pictured in part (a) of figure 4·1: particulars are viewed as a kind of individual, even if they are perhaps a crucial kind, or at least paradigmatic. Nonparticulars, however—generics, for example, and/or abstract entities—are (or at least can be) counted as individuals, but not as particulars, and therefore are within the outer but outside the inner circles. Thus a particularly ornery tiger, the one that snarled at your Land Rover yesterday, would be a

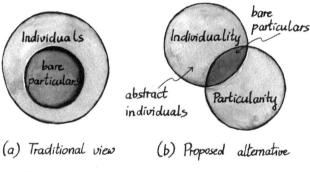

(a) Traditional view   (b) Proposed alternative

FIGURE 4·1 INDIVIDUALITY AND PARTICULARITY

(bare) particular, and thus inside the inner circle. The type tiger, being abstract, would still be an individual, but since it is not a particular, it would be located outside the inner circle, though still inside the outer one. The same would be true of the generic tiger, the tiger that is threatened with extinction.

It is traditional, in other words, to take the word 'individual'

to be essentially synonymous with 'object' or 'entity'—i.e., as denoting the most general class, of which particulars are taken to be an important, or even the paradigmatic, species.

The picture I am arguing for, in contrast, is better diagrammed in part (b) of the figure. The overlapping but symmetrical structure is intended to reflect the fact that particularity and individuality, as I am using the terms, are conceptually orthogonal. This can be seen by observing that they occur differentially, or at least potentially occur differentially.[4]

2a Particularity without individuality

As an example of particularity without individuality, consider Strawson's analysis of the reference or content of what he calls *feature-placing* sentences, such as "it is foggy" or "it is raining."[5] In saying such a thing, Strawson says, we commit ourselves to the existence—"on the ground," as it were, in the world's trenches—of some amount of exemplification of what Strawson calls a *feature*, but without any concomitant commitment to discrete objects. If it rains, and, noticing that fact, you say, "It's raining"—something simpler than, but similar to, a kind of ostensive "Raining! here! now!"—then what you are saying is that the feature of "raining" is being exemplified, around here and about now. You do so, however, without identifying or individuating any *object* or individual of which that feature or quality holds. "*What's* raining?" is not a sensible question to ask. It cannot be answered, indeed it has no answer, because the 'it' in "It's raining" does not refer. In this construction, to say the same thing in a different way, rain is not a property. It is not a property because it is not being predicated of any (individual) object.

To be careful in the saying, I will follow Strawson in using the word 'feature' for the sorts of thing, like rain, that in this way do not require individual objects for their exemplification, and 'property,' in contrast, for the more familiar notion of some-

---

[4] In setting things out this way I take a lead from Strawson (1959)—though he himself does not go this far.

[5] A construct that linguists call the "weather 'it'."

thing that does require an object. Thus if I say that it is raining, I use the word 'raining' to signify a *feature*, a feature that, in making my utterance, I *place* here and now around me (or, perhaps—I do not want to take a stand on this just yet—that is so placed by the weather gods). If, in reply, you say that you will therefore bring your green umbrella, you thereby use the word 'green' and, perhaps, the word 'umbrella,' to signify *properties*, properties that *hold* of the umbrella that you bring along. So the term 'property' is reserved, at least informally, for qualities or ways of being or types that do require objects for their exemplification; the term 'feature,' for things that do not. Features, on this analysis, are thus in some metaphysical sense simpler than properties—and perhaps, though it is less clear on what metric, more basic as well.[6]

It is not features themselves that exhibit particularity without individuality. Rather, what is particular but not individual is the metaphysical patch or disturbance or stuff in the world that warrants the feature placement. Thus suppose that last night you drove for three long hours through the rain. There is no denying that the rain you drove through was concrete (and thus particular). Suppose, however, that, while staring out the windshield, you thought "it's too bad that it is raining"—thereby engaging in an intentional act of feature placing. The feature that you "placed" remains somehow universal or abstract (whatever sort of thing a feature is, and however it is abstract). What is particular-but-not-individual, in the described situation, is *that towards which your feature-placing was directed*. Or so at least we

[6]This characterization implies that objects and properties are in some logical sense interdependent: to be an object is to be something that a property can be predicated of; to be an object (i.e., an individual, in my scheme) is to be something of which a property can be predicated. Ontologically, however, rather than logically, objects and properties are thought to be at least relatively *independent*, in the sense that any property can coherently be predicated of any object—what Evans calls a "generality constraint" (1982, pp. 100–105). See §1 of chapter 9.

theorists or observers would say, although to do so is distracting, in a way, because it is so tempting for us, from our different theoretical position, simply to call that towards which your feature-placing is directed "the rain." But nothing follows from that; all it means, to echo the introduction's discussion about conceptual clash between theorist and subject matter, is that we theorists have individuated the rain, not that you have. Still, one can try to put the same point more indirectly, and simply say this: that utterances of feature-placing sentences share with utterances of predicative sentences the property of being true or false. It is what makes a (particular) act of feature-placing true that is particular but not individual.

Although the feature/property distinction will come up again later, it was introduced here primarily in order to motivate the more important (for present purposes) distinction between particularity and individuality. Before returning to that main topic, however, I should add that it would be a mistake, especially in light of our overall project, to cast the feature-property distinction in stone. It is not just that I do not want to do so at this early stage, because that would be too expensive. The more serious problem is that doing so would only necessitate a troublesome later retreat. The problem is easy enough to see. Everything that was just said about the distinction between features and properties was really a discussion about the distinction between features and *Properties*—i.e., between things that do and do not require (mythologized) Objects for their exemplification, rather than, as I have been putting it, between things that do and do not require *individuals* for their exemplification. The problem is that we are not yet clear enough—and it is also not obvious that it will ever be possible to be clear enough—to make the distinction between features and lowercase properties anything like absolute. Suppose after walking back to your Cairo hotel on an August afternoon you say, "It is hot." By the lights of the foregoing discussion, this counts as feature-placing.

If, after you sit down for tea, the waiter says, "Be careful; the tea-pot is hot!"—that in contrast involves (i.e., is directed towards) the use of a property: the property of being hot, a property that holds of an individual tea-pot. But what if, instead, after pouring the cup of tea, they say, "Be careful; it's hot!" Is this feature-placing or predication? Or is it something halfway in between?

Or suppose, to take another example, that in response to a woman's saying, "It is foggy" (feature-placing), a man agrees by replying, "Yes, I guess the fog has come in." According to the present analysis, the second statement is not a perfect translation of the former. In virtue of saying "the fog," it (or he) commits an additional act of individuation—something like an ontological analogue of semantic ascent. But what is the man referring to, and how does that relate to what the woman said? That is not so clear. One would be hard-pressed to say that the word "fog" is ambiguous, as between denoting a feature and denoting a property. Or suppose, even worse, that he were instead to reply, "Yes, it's the same fog as yesterday." In this case it is hard to say definitely, one way or the other, whether he is referring to anything particular, individual or no, or whether instead he means something like the same *type* of fog—or even, which seems intuitively more plausible, if metaphysically more problematic, whether the difference between the two options (particular and type) is perhaps not so hard-and-fast.

As any number of such examples show, things can (and will, and do) get messy—quite messy, very fast. That in itself is a fact to remember. That the distinction between features and properties and objects is not sharp, on the other hand—that logic is messy, not just finger paints—will not ultimately be a problem, at least not for us. It is more of a problem for Ontology than for ontology, since it is Objects, not objects, that have determinate boundary conditions; Logic, not logic, that requires "clear and distinct" boundaries between Properties and the Individuals they hold of. Just as in the desert a lack of determinate boundaries need not undermine the sand dunes' claim on plurality, so too there is no reason to suppose that a lack of precise boundary, or the existence of an intermediate grey area, need undermine the distinction between particularity and individuality.

2b Individuality without particularity

Feature-placing was introduced to illustrate the possibility or at least coherence of particularity without individuality. What would it be to have the converse: individuality without particularity? Again, the answer depends on the underlying metaphysics. It depends, that is, on whether one takes abstract entities, universals, and the like, to occur.[7] But on at least the familiar stance that separates abstract entities from particulars, this one is easy, and in fact has already been answered. (Lowercase) objects of the sort cited above—the type *anger*, the number 4, the 1957 T-Bird—would count as exactly non-particular individuals.

2c Higher-order individuation

All I have argued, so far, is that it is possible to utter feature-placing sentences without committing any acts of individuation at the "base" or "particular" level (i.e., at what would traditionally be called the "object" level—but of course that is not a phrasing I can use). In order to make such feature-placing claims, however, it appears that we must engage in some form of higher-order individuation *of the features themselves*. Thus in taking it to be foggy, but not raining, we commit ourselves to some kind of distinction—arguably an individual distinction—between the feature fog and the feature rain.

The nature of this distinction, however, is not yet clear. It is not obvious, that is, exactly what kind of "unity and integrity" of the features themselves someone is committed to who utters a feature-placing sentence, or thinks a feature-placing thought. For that matter, it is equally unclear what kind of unity and in-

---

[7] Ultra-intuitionists might be sympathetic to the view that occurrence is a prerequisite to all existence. Perhaps ultra-intuitionism is a claim that *everything* is particular.

tegrity of properties one is committed to in making an ordinary statement predicating a property of an individual. And murkiness threatens. For consider the wide range of intonations in which the sentence "It's raining" can be uttered—from an emphatic assertion about a torrential downpour, to a hesitant comment as a shower shades off to a drizzle. What kind of unity, and what kind of boundaries, inhere in the feature of rain, across these utterances? Is it the same feature, in both cases, more and less strongly exemplified? Or should the situations be analyzed, apparently conversely, as cases of equal-strength exemplification of a varying feature (with the property-level variation signified by the utterance's intonation)? Or is there no variation, in either feature or exemplification; but rather a higher-order strength property, superimposed by the intonation? But if so, then where is the edge of the rain? When does it stop being rain, and start being drizzle?

God only knows. This is not an issue I am yet ready to answer; we lack anything like adequate tools. But neither fact should be allowed to hide the question's centrality. The order of phenomena at the level of properties and types is a recalcitrant but essential topic—one that any eventual metaphysical reconstruction will have to address. It is also, just to give a hint of what is to come, the place where letting go of uppercase assumptions will have the most profound consequences.

3 Individuality and identity

Return, then, to particularity and individuality, the main topic on the table. These two notions will play an important role in the metaphysical reconstruction, starting in the next chapter. In order to see how that goes, it is important to distinguish the second of these, individuality, from the notion of identity. Or rather, to be more accurate, it is important to distinguish 'individuality,' 'identity,' and 'Identity.' There is a three-way thicket to untangle.

Consider Identity, first. It is traditional in philosophy to take Identity to be a property, for any individual, of "being that individual." Formally, one could make this specific by taking Identity to be a family of properties, one per individual in the universe, such that each individual's identity property is just that unique property that holds of it and of no other. It is more convenient, however, to take Identity to be a single binary relation "between one thing," as it were—i.e., that two-place relation that each (particular) individual stands in with, and only with, itself.

From a metaphysical point of view, a number of things are striking about this notion. Foremost is its adherence to a sharp individual/property distinction. As with any property or relation, it makes essential (logical) reference to individuals; without them, it would not get any purchase. In spite of taking individuals to be essential, however, it is not otherwise committed to essentialism. Even on the family of properties proposal, the identity property of an individual would simply be the property of being the individual in question, not the essential property in virtue of which this individual is the individual that it is, even if there were such an essence. Suppose, as some have thought, that it is essential to any given person that they be the child of their actual parents. Even so, Chelsea's identity property would be the property of being Chelsea; it would not involve Bill or Hillary, their modal importance notwithstanding.[8]

Identity is thus thoroughly extensional; it is not traditionally assumed to be a property with much of a Fregean "sense" or other intensional content. It is also a yes/no affair: either the saucepan on the stove is the one they borrowed last week, or it

---

[8]This argument requires that properties be individuated more fine-grainedly than by considerations of what is essential. But that I take it is both intuitive and standard. Or at least it is for necessity. Many people would argue that the property of being the sum of 2 and 2 is different from the property of being the positive square root of 16, even if it is necessary that the two properties hold of one and the same individual.

is not the one they borrowed. But if any features or substantial properties of the saucepan should be relevant to the question—not just relevant to determining whether it is the same saucepan, which is an epistemic issue of identification (not, I would claim, at least not in the first instance, an issue of Identity or individuality), but metaphysically relevant to whether it actually is or is not the same saucepan—then those properties must be something other than the saucepan's Identity property. Identity, to repeat, is simply the property of *being* the individual in question; it is not a feature or property relevant to *whether* it is the individual in question.

Given this picture, the traditional notion of Identity can be glossed as a notion of self-identity—or, as I would rather put it, of *identicality*. Furthermore, as I will argue in a moment, since there is something else that I want to use the term 'identity' for—or rather, since there is more to it than Carrollian wish, something else important that the English word 'identity' *means*—I will from this point forward use 'identicality' to signify the traditional philosophical notion of Identity.[9]

There are two reasons for adjusting (professional) terminology in this way. First, serious questions will need to be asked about what use this "sense-less" notion of identicality will be for a metaphysician with even slight constructionist leanings. For if there is any story to be told about how objects arise—what they are, what constitutes them, how social practices figure in their constitution, etc.—identicality, because of its pure extensionality, is not a notion that will play much of a role. It will not play a role because it is too much after-the-fact; as was said in footnote 3 on page 121, it is "post-ontological." Rather like a report card, identicality reflects the result of the metaphysical process; it can be used to reveal how the individuation process went. Because it presumes the answer, however, it cannot have done any of the work in getting there.

[9] Cf. Frege's distinction between 'identity' and 'sameness' (Frege 1893/1980, pp. 46 and 76).

But that alone is not enough reason to disrupt current usage. The second and more important reason has to do with the fact that hidden underneath the philosophical notion of Identity lies the prior notion of identity in ordinary English—a notion of considerable metaphysical interest, that will be especially useful in the story to be told here. It will be of use, moreover, exactly because of how it differs from identicality (Identity). So what is being proposed is not so much a change in terminology, as a return to natural terminology. It is only in order to rescue an original use from the weight of philosophical jargon that such a change is justifiable. Only by relieving the press of philosophical usage can we give the lay notion a chance to breathe.

What then is the lay conception of identity, the one I will now adopt? It has to do with what makes something be the thing that it is, more than with any claim that the thereby-constituted thing is discrete and unitary.

Thus note, for starters, that this unmarked notion is not necessarily restricted to individuals. Because objects (individuals) play such a central ontological role, not only in current analytic frameworks but also in popular imagination, questions of identity are often assumed, by default, to be questions about the identity *of an individual*. But the fact that we are so quick to make that inference, from identity to individuality, is more an unfortunate artifact of our object-oriented (Object-oriented) ontological attitude, than it is a metaphysical necessity or even recommendation. It may also stem from an overly deferential attitude to writing. In practice, however, it is easy to see that it is not always justified. Diffusions (such as fog), abstractions (such as melancholy), and collectives (such as of people) can have identities without necessarily being individuals, or supporting individuation criteria.

Identity also differs from identicality in having something of a Fregean sense—and also, which is even stronger, an ineliminably intentional-with-a-t (as well as intensional-with-an-s) aspect. The lay notion of identity has intuitively to do with how things are taken or represented, not only with aspects of them. This is why 'identity' is cognate with 'identify.' It is also why identity is so much more metaphysically useful than identicality for someone attempting to do justice to constructivist ontology.

These characteristics can be seen in a wide range of settings. An application to our understanding of ordinary equations is given in the sidebar on page 134. But many of the same issues are evident psychologically. For people, issues of identity have to do with how they take themselves as being; that is why it is natural to speak of a "sense of identity" (and meaningless to talk of a "sense of identicality"). Issues of individuality, in contrast, have to do with autonomy. Thus people in communities or groups can have a very strong sense of identity, even if, or perhaps even especially if, their individuality is weak. From this point of view, in fact, identity, by signifying belonging, and individuality, by signifying separateness, can start to seem in tension—tension that is grist for the metaphysical mill.

4 Terminology

In order to help keep the distinction between particularity and individuality in view, I will use (and have been using) the words 'individual' and 'particular' as adjectives, whenever possible, when issues of individuation or particularity are in focus. It is trickier to do the same with nouns. Individuality is not a problem; whenever possible I say "an individual," rather than "an object," when the individuality of the referent is important, for whatever reason. The problem, however, is that the expression 'a particular,' being not only a singular term, but a singular count noun phrase, is more specific than 'particularity'; it seems to carry an evident commitment to the referent's *also being an individual.* The grammar of English, that is to say, puts pressure on

Identity, identity & individuality in equations

Think about how we read equations, and about the meaning of the '=' sign.* Although most people intuitively understand this sign to signify a relation between two things, it is hard to say exactly what those two things actually are—unless of course equality is interpreted syntactically as a relationship between two *terms*: namely, the relation of designating one and the same individual. When pressed, however, most semantically minded theorists reject the syntactic interpretation, claiming that '=' does not signify a binary relation between *two* things, but instead denotes a binary relation "between one thing," as it were—i.e., the relation, called Identity in the text, that each (particular) individual in the universe stands in with, and only with, itself. In sum, the '=' sign is taken to denote a (referentially transparent) relation of self-identicality.

Analyzing equations with a notion of identity (as well as identicality), however, not only allows one to preserve more of the informal intuition, but results in a more penetrating understanding as well. Assume in particular that equations consist of two terms designating individuals, which is certainly how they are normally understood. Then an equation of the form $\alpha = \beta$ can be interpreted as saying that *the individual identified as α is (numerically) identical to the individual identified as* β, where α and β are in turn interpreted in a way that makes reference to the terms' intensions or sense. Without necessarily taking the things that are identified to be individuals (notice how automatic the tendency is, as soon as the discussion gets technical, to invoke the Ontology of Objects, Properties, and Relations), it is right to say that '=' has to do with identity, and also right to say that identity is in some way aspectual, and in some ways intentional. Analyzing the situation in terms of a notion of identity allows one to preserve information content without having to go syntactic. (It is a confusion to try to read the '=' sign as representing individuality, of course.)

*Throughout this sidebar, the phrase "the meaning of the '=' sign" could be replaced with the word 'equality'—i.e., by claiming, by stipulation, that equality is what '=' means, and then inquiring, more ontologically and less semantically, into the nature of equality. Ultimately, this would be a better way to do things, but trying to disentangle a four-way relation among identity, Identity, individuality, and equality is a heavier load than two paragraphs can bear.

the distinction: the singular term 'a particular' can only be used to refer to something that I would deem as both particular *and* individual. I will therefore continue to use 'particularity,' sans determiner, when no commitment to individuality is warranted or implied.

More generally, I will as far as possible avoid the use of determiners and plurals except when individuality is definitely implicated. Thus in talking about how coherence is sustained, for example, I will talk of the world's *regularity*, rather than of the existence of *regularities*, in order to avoid the presumption that those ways are intrinsically plural or discretely countable. By itself, this seemingly minor linguistic convention can substantially affect the overall picture and connotations of a proposed account.

Yet the correlation between grammar and ontology should not be overinterpreted, even for someone of constructionist, let alone deconstructionist, leanings. An informal use of "this morning's fog" entails no precise individuation criteria; nor does "there are lots of clouds in the sky" commit one to the existence of a metaphysical warrant for discrete cloud countability. Moreover, nothing in what I have said implies that issues of individuality come all or nothing, as in mathematics. As suggested earlier, questions about what "It's hot" describes, and about what 'the rain' refers to in a statement such as "The rain is coming back," make it evident that there is no reason to suppose that individuality, such as of fogs or of colors, as opposed to Individuality, may not itself be a matter of degree.[10]

---

[10] These distinctions and ambiguities and gradualities are cross-cut by the meta-linguistic or meta-conceptual problems that plague any theorist who contends with this issues. When, qua theorist, I say that *rain* is used as a feature in the statement "It's raining," I objectify that feature—i.e., give it, in my metatheoretical discourse, the status of +INDIVIDUAL and –PARTICULAR. This is in contrast to the rain that the utterer of the sentence was drawing attention to; that rain was –INDIVIDUAL and +PARTICULAR.

If these two aspects—particularity and individuality—are essential characteristics of at least ordinary material objects, where do they come from? Are they an intrinsic part of the structure of the world, to which the subject need merely be attuned? Or are they achievements? They might be achievements of the subject, to be explained in terms of representational prowess, linguistic capacity, or social skill. They might be achievements of society as a whole, especially the analytic West. Or perhaps they are achievements of the object—or even of all three in collaboration. What store were they bought at; and how much did they cost?

We need to find out. And there is one store we must look in first: physics—or at least the physical substrate. It is impossible, this late in the century, to ask about the origins of anything without casting a long, hard look at what is often called "the material world." In this chapter, therefore, I will consider this modern mythical clay, out of which so many people think that both subject and object must ultimately be fashioned.

Two problems, right away. First, some readers, especially antifoundationalists, will already have been made uneasy, in virtue of the question's being framed in terms of the word 'physics.' Not to worry. My plan is only to go into this store and look around. I am not now claiming, nor will I claim later, that this one establishment sells all the provisions that a metaphysician needs. Second, to generalize from *physics* to *the material world* is to move from the excessively narrow to the excessively broad. Some notion of physicality underlies just about all modern debates, after all—from quantum mechanics to the materiality of language, from cosmology to embodied cognition, from eco-politics to the abstract notions of space and time in complexity theory. So the first task is to impose some order on this diversity.

137

1 Living in the material world

There are at least four reasons why someone interested in metaphysics and intentionality might turn to the physical or the material as a source of theoretical or ontological grounding.

1a Naturalism

The first reason has to do with *naturalism*—except that to say
that is not to say anything very specific, since the term is used to
cover a multitude of sins. In some quarters, especially in analytic
philosophy, naturalism is interpreted methodologically, as a requirement on theories: that they somehow be tied, by reduction
or supervenience or implementation, to the natural sciences in
general, and especially to physics (or even, unfortunately, to
Physics—see the sidebar on page 139).[1] But a physics-directed
interpretation of naturalism is both historically and intellectually specific, the result of a series of inferential steps.

The most overarching notion, I take it, to back up to the beginning, simply takes 'natural' to mean *of nature*. On this reading naturalism is simply the requirement that an intellectually
satisfying account of whatever (intentionality, culture, death
and taxes, bent spoons) must show how it is that the phenomenon in question is part of reality, belongs to the world. As suggested earlier,[2] this is close to the lay sense of 'natural,' as that to
which *supernatural* things are "super": weird, mysterious, alien,
metaphysically spooky. To be natural, in contrast, is to be okay:
here with us, part of commonsense or consensual reality—
made up of, or at least continuous with, what we know and
trust.

This reading is neither theory-laden nor narrow. But that
does not make it weak. One of the points of the discussion of
realism in chapter 3 was to demonstrate the opposite: that a rigorous commitment to a single encompassing reality places substantial constraints on both subjects and objects, and also on the
form of an intentional theory. This is especially true if the word

---

[1] See for example Quine (1964), Kitcher (1992).
[2] Footnote 11, p. 12.

On physics vs. Physics

In virtue of its almost mythic prominence among the sciences, someone might suggest that the academic discipline that studies quarks and neutrinos should be called Physics, rather than physics. That would be a mistake, however. It would set one up to miss the subject's general interest, to say nothing of misunderstanding important contributions from recent science criticism.

Rather, I will reserve the upper-case 'Physics' for our modernist *myths* about what science is like: i.e., for the supposedly value-free, Objective, True, Rational, dispassionate, empirical inquiry that figures in our naive but collective imaginations. It was 'Physics,' that is, that was vaunted at the end of the last century to be the Queen of the Sciences; that is committed to Realism; that works with Objects, Properties, and Relations; whose confirmation rests purely on predicative accuracy; that employs the Empirical Method. By 'physics,' in contrast—the workaday, lower-case version—I will refer to physics-as-it-actually-practiced, complete with political battles, elaborate and often messy laboratory procedures, complex instruments and documents, power struggles, aesthetic judgments, and other paraphernalia of a socially engrained and highly professionalized discipline.

It is a reductionist myth that Physics can supply the ground or basic elements out of which everything else is constructed. My interest in looking to the physical, however—in order to discover what it can contribute, and what will have to be purchased elsewhere—is an interest in what physics departments have actually seen and understood. We need real, not mythologized, contributions.

'everything' is taken seriously, to include mathematical and logical entities—types, laws, reason, beauty—as well as electrons, thoughts, and those spoons. Abstract entities, too, must not be treated as in any way "supernatural." So the reading has bite.

Moreover, since this is as strong a reading of naturalism as I myself am prepared to endorse, I will use the term with this sense

139

in what follows. From here forward, that is, 'nature' will be taken to be another name for the unnameable world, 'natural' to mean part of this unnameable world, and 'naturalism,' to shift back to its epistemic or metatheoretic sense, to be our mandate, as theorists, to show how everything is part of this world—i.e., to show how the world is One, in chapter 3's sense of being entire or complete. In sum:

Naturalism is realism's methodological correlate.

Note that this construal does not give the physical any logical or metaphysical pride of place. Nor does it imply the existence of, or probability of, or even the commitment to look for, anything that would warrant being called a "unified theory of science." To think that would be to commit an error of scope. Naturalism as I understand it, that is, is not so much a desire for an integrated understanding of nature, as a desire for *an understanding of an integral nature*. To see how the world is One, however that is accomplished.[3]

More specific readings of naturalism differ on how they see this being accomplished—on how they think one demonstrates (reassures oneself, convinces one's peers) that something is, as required, part of the real.

First is something I will call *commonsense naturalism*: the requirement that accounts mesh into our native workaday grasp of (or participation in) the world around us, the world into which we get up each morning, the world of our daily routines.[4] What *that* means depends on what embodied local practice is actually like. On this view, a seventeenth-century Spaniard, in contrast to a modern secularist, might view as "natural" something that was integrated into daily prayers or garden-variety piety. An-

[3] Ultimately, the distinction between an understanding of an integrated nature and an integrated understanding of nature will hinge, at least in part, on a distinction to be drawn between ontological pluralism and metaphysical monism. See §7 of chapter 12.

[4] Kitcher (1992), Cussins (forthcoming), Agre (1996).

cient Greeks would similarly count the actions of the fates as natural; Australian natives, the song-lines that traverse the outback. So in a way the strength of this proposal is also its weakness: it is as varied as human life. And it does nothing to *explain* that life, varied or otherwise. It merely mandates that other things be grounded in it, as convivial cohabitants.[5]

Per se, commonsense naturalism still gives the physical no special status. But many would go further, especially in the secular West, and accord the physical pride of place. In some unique and essential way, such people would argue, the physical world is more real than any other — the one true foundation, the basic stuff out of which everything else is built. On the surface, that sounds reasonable, but what it comes to in detail depends on what 'physical' is taken to mean. To avoid confusion, therefore, I will separate two senses, even if they are joined by areas of grey, using:

1. '*material*' to signify our ordinary commonsense notion of physicality, as for example in the sense in which everyday concrete objects are physical, such as tables and chairs, fields and hospitals — the so-called "furniture of everyday life"; and

2. '*physical*' for "as in physics."

In addition, when necessary, I will use 'physical-in-general' for the union of the two, and 'Physical' for "as in reigning modernist myths about physics." So toasters and hospitals and stop signs and dollar bills are by these lights material; leptons and gravity waves, physical.

The material/physical distinction leads in turn to two species of naturalism. *Material naturalism*, on the one hand, rather than setting up long-distance relations to the remote quanta and differential equations of physicists (for example with bridge laws), requires accounts to be grounded in the material world as it is

---

[5] Commonsense naturalism can in turn be opened out across a continuum: from one end, that grounds explanations in our lay *understanding* of the world, to another that places less emphasis on articulation and understanding, requiring instead a grounding in lay unreflective practice.

right here and now in front of us. As indicated in figure 5·1, material naturalism is a variety of commonsense naturalism; what distinguishes it is its emphasis on the "physical-in-general," as opposed, say, to giving top billing to the political, or religious, or psychological. Material naturalism is thus a doctrine one might point at with the phrase 'lay physicalism.' Contrasting with it is *physical naturalism*, a version that, in a significant and (especially in retrospect) far-from-obvious step, defers commonsense intuitions about the physical world to reigning scientific theories—especially

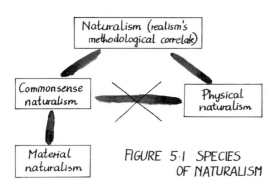

FIGURE 5·1 SPECIES OF NATURALISM

to physics. "In the end all there is is atoms and molecules," perhaps; or "Everything, ultimately, is *made* of atoms and molecules"; or, "All there really *are* are atoms and molecules." The constitutive intuitions come in a myriad flavors, though most of them can be more or less associated with a range of theoretically recognizable metaphysical views: brute or eliminative physicalism; type or token reductionism; or, weakest of the lot, a form of global or holistic physical supervenience.

No one would deny that these two forms of grounding (the material, in everyday experience; the physical, in the rarefied discourse of academic physics departments) have something to do with each other. But it would be bizarre to conflate them, especially for a metaphysician. For the entire present question, of whether the objects of everyday life can be bought at physics' store, hinges on the nature of their relation. And whereas material naturalism is a species of commonsense naturalism, physical naturalism is *not* such a species—or at least not obviously. This was essentially Putnam's point in distinguishing 'Real' from 'real.' And as much will be the brunt of much of this chapter. As we will see, the ontological commitments of physics are nothing like adequate to the task of reconstructing even material ontology, let alone commonsense ontology more generally.

A final comment. In the interests of open-mindedness, I have been vague about just what relation "everything" is thought to bear to what each view, respectively, takes as basic. It is especially important that neither species of naturalism be construed strongly enough to entail eliminativism (even if they are compatible with it). Thus material naturalists need not weigh toasters against détente, with respect to their respective claims on reality or existence, and decide in favor of toasters—or deny that ideas are real, just because they do not weigh anything. Nor do physical naturalists need to champion theoretical reduction, inveigh against psychology or semantics, or hold non-physical categories suspect. Rather, physical naturalism is usually taken to be a claim that the world can be completely characterized at an appropriate level of physical abstraction, usually at a very *low* level, with detailed questions being deferred to professional physicists (hence the reference to atoms and molecules, above; perhaps it would have been better to say fermions and bosons). There is still assumed to be room at "higher levels" for more complex phenomena: psychology, semantics, intentionality, and the like. The point is only that physical naturalism, and perhaps material naturalism as well, spring from a general sense of a "hierarchy of nature"—with physics or the physical at the bottom, and more sophisticated things, like people and traffic laws and economic policy, higher up.

But liberalism at the level of the type is different from liberalism at the level of the instance. It is one thing to define naturalistic categories widely enough to take in a variety of metaphysical views; another to let any given proposal off the metaphysical hook. Thus if someone stakes a claim to a physicalist position, it is incumbent on them to make that claim stick—including, for irreductionist reasons, being able to explain all the paraphernalia and equipment used in defending that view. For that, I take it, is what it is to raise an allegiance to the physical to the status of a metaphysical claim (to say nothing of being the only conceivable justification for writing books with such titles as *Theories of Everything* and *Dreams of a Final Theory*[6]).

1b Ontological hygiene

Return to the original question: of why someone interested in metaphysics or intentionality would turn to the physical. This digression on naturalism makes it clear that we need to split that question into two: of why or whether they would turn to the material world, and why or whether they would turn to the physical world.

One reason for turning to the physical-in-general we have just considered: a pre-theoretic allegiance to some species of naturalism;[7] this falls approximately evenly across the physical/material divide. A second, essentially a matter of ontological hygiene, lies solely on the side of physics. The discourse of modern physics is conducted in terms of an ontology that is by all accounts bizarre—widely alleged to be discordant with that of common sense (though see the "Classical vs. quantum ontology" sidebar on page 146). For metaphysical purposes this discord has a certain appeal: it suggests that it may be possible to use the ontology of physics as a kind of reality check—as a discipline to guard against the unwarranted imposition of individuation conditions onto the metaphysical realm. In sum, checking in with physics from time to time seems like a good way to avoid inscription errors. That is not to deny that physics' ontology is as suspect as any other; nor is it a sneaky way to avoid paying its

---

[6] Barrow (1991) and Weinberg (1993).

[7] It is easier to understand how a commitment to material naturalism could be "pretheoretic" than a commitment to physical naturalism. On the other hand, the idea that physics is in fact (or at least in potential) a theory of everything has turned into something like folk mythology—so calling it pretheoretic may not be far off base, at least for many adherents.

price. Nevertheless, to the extent that the ontology of physics is *different* from the commonsense material one that we might otherwise be likely to impose, taking a preparatory look at the situation in physical terms is a useful way to unseat stubbornly residual ontological presumptions. Two different perspectives is a lot more than one if your goal is to triangulate onto a third and previously unknown spot.

1c Implementation

A third reason to be interested in the physical-in-general is evident in the current explosion of interest in understanding the physiological or, as I will say, the *implementational* basis of intentional or other "subject" capacities—from psychophysics to robotics to neurophilosophy to connectionism. What is in common to these projects is the idea that building a φ (e.g., a mind), or understanding how a φ works, is a good way to understand what it is to be a φ.

Are these implementational projects material or physical? Lord only knows. Some considerations push towards interpreting them physically. Their adherents would undoubtedly identify with overarching physicalist intuitions, especially in the broad "hierarchy of nature" sense. By most accounts their efforts would be counted as attempts to "naturalize" psychology, representation, etc. And whereas implementations are not full-scale theory reductions, they do lend themselves to the idea that the salient regularities in their field will succumb to implementational or causal explanation. Thus some imagine that consciousness, though not itself obviously material, let alone physical, will be explained by adverting to the 40 HZ cycles in the brain that (may) realize it; others, that intentionality will be shown to be a species of causal interaction; still others, that the crucial missing ingredient in current cognitivist approaches to mind is a form of "causal power."[8] Such intuitions are not just "physicalist" in the

---

[8] For discussions of causal powers and physicality of the mind, see Searle (1984 & 1992); for the suggestion of a 40 HZ oscillatory basis for consciousness, Crick & Koch (1992).

Classical vs. quantum ontology

It is famously alleged that the ontology of quantum mechanics is incompatible with common sense or, as it is called, "classical" ontology. The aim of the diagram below is to suggest that the ontology with which quantum mechanics clashes may in fact be Commonsense Ontology, not commonsense ontology—i.e., may have more to do with reigning *myths* about what commonsense ontology is like (the usual capitalized myths about discrete Objects, well-defined Properties, clear and distinct Categories, perfect Boundaries, and the like), rather than having anything to do with

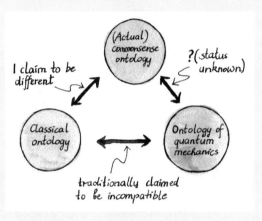

the unreflective person's everyday use of material objects.

The picture of objects, individuals, and so forth presented in this book differs radically from that of Commonsense Ontology, especially with respect to issues of boundary, determinacy of identity, and the like (see for example §s 2 & 3 of chapter 11). Naturally I claim that this alternative account stakes a higher claim on how we think of and treat objects in our daily routines—i.e., that it does a better job of "doing justice" to ordinary material objects. If this is so, then the interesting question, with respect to quantum mechanics and other ontological challenges from the sciences, is to ask how—to what extent, whether, and so forth—the view of objects laid out here (not the traditional myth of Objects) meshes with the findings of quantum mechanics. The differences may not be as great as we have been led to think.

sense of providing physical explanations, but shade into even stronger reductive form, by suggesting that the phenomenon in question actually *is* physical, rather than just having a physical basis.

But there are also reasons to understand implementation as *material*—and therefore, at least on current understanding, as much less methodologically secure.[9] First, implementors are not inevitably driven by an interest in extra-theoretical bridge laws. They are at least as likely to base their accounts in common sense as to hand over responsibility to neighboring academic departments. Second, it is not clear that implementation projects are wholly descriptive: as suggested in chapter 1, they may instead ground out in practices of synthesis and construction. Implementation may be distinguished by the kind, not the content, of its knowledge: knowledge *how*, rather than knowledge *that*. One would expect as much in engineering disciplines (such as artificial intelligence), but the same point has been made in philosophy, e.g., by Dretske, who argues that we will only understand intentionality when we know how to buy the parts in a hardware store—Fry's Electronics, for example—and build it.[10] Third, hardware stores sell *material*, not *physical*, objects. Their wares are functionally individuated, and coherent with respect to use; they are not theoretically individuated, and coherent with respect to physics. Fourth, and finally, as explored in more detail in the sidebar on page 148 ("The limits of material implementation"), even if an implementation project works, it does not follow that to understand the implementation is to understand what has been implemented. This is true for all sorts of reasons. Creating a Frankenstein monster (mentioned in chapter 1) is implementation, where the creator understands things at the wrong level. Having a child is implementation, but is not theoretical at all. Drawing up a blueprint for a hospital, or even

---

[9] Material implementation is given more due in chapter 9, e.g. in §5a.
[10] Dretske, "If You Can't Make One, You Don't Know How It Works" (1994).

The limits of material implementation

Computational experience raises a cautionary flag with respect to too great a materialist enthusiasm about cognition, or intentional phenomena more generally. When listening to reports about the search for the structure of the human genome, for example, or to neurophysiologists' and neurophilosophers' enthusiasm about the prospects of finally understanding the wiring of the human brain, it is hard not to reflect on the following fact: that with respect to computer systems *we already know the answers to all the physiological questions* (we have the source code and wiring diagram), without that necessarily leading to any serious understanding, at the right explanatory level, of "what the program is doing."

That is not to say that physiological analysis (electronic or biological) cannot or will not be part of a full explanation, or may not aid in such an explanation. I would be as loathe as the next person to relinquish my source code listing, when debugging a faulty program. But the gap between code listings and wiring diagrams, on the one hand, and the intentional issues that characterize computation but bedevil analysis, on the other hand, remains extremely impressive. The well-known lack of a full theory of reliability is just one of many issues that stand witness to this gap. So while no one would reasonably doubt that physicalist and/or materialist investigations of the human case should be pursued, we should be cautious about any hope that by understanding the brain we will thereby automatically understand the mind—especially in regard to the sorts of semantic and intentional questions under investigation here.

building one, is implementation, but remains blind to the wealth of surrounding social and political and economic forces that are in part constitutive of what it is to be hospital.

In a way, this is simply to agree with one of social construction's essential insights: that the kinds of thing you buy in a hardware store, to say nothing of what you pay for them with, are sustained and supported by extraordinarily more complex social and political and institutional forces than the naive observer (or customer) might guess. Think about a worker at the Philadelphia Mint, or a civil servant who paints 'STOP' on a red octagon and mounts it on a pole at the end of the street. Yes, there is a sense in which both have performed material jobs—jobs that the rest of us can readily imagine doing. But from the fact that we can make a dollar bill or a stop sign, it in no way follows that we know how either of them works. Extraordinarily complex issues of semantics and authority cry out for analysis, as well as ontological questions about the status of the letters 's', 'T', 'O', and 'P', to say nothing of why drivers stop their cars when they see such displays. As many have reminded us, it is not even clear who pays for *red*.[11]

1d Practice

A fourth reason why a student of intentionality and metaphysics might be interested in the physical-in-general is not at all the implementationalist's idea that intentionality, representation, etc. are themselves physical or material, or that they can be explained (by theorists) in physical or material terms. Rather, it is the claim that a subject's possession of intentional capacities is ultimately grounded in *practice*—in their daily routines of moving around, making breakfast, being hired and fired, talking with people around the coffeepot, and in general pushing on and being pushed back upon by the world. In one form or other this is an extraordinarily widespread intuition. From Heidegger to Vygotsky to Strawson to Dreyfus to post-modern robotics, it is virtually unanimous that a subject's crafts, skills, and everyday routines are essential to its development of a full-blooded intentional capability. And there is no reason to suppose that this conclusion is uniquely human. A similar moral arises from chapter 1's analysis of computation as intrinsically participatory.

The third and fourth intuitions, implementation and practice, differ in an important way (even if they shade into one an-

---

[11] For reasons as diverse as considerations of its being a Lockean secondary property to neurophysiological arguments of the sort advanced by Lettvin et al. (1959).

other). The concern with practice focuses on *part* of what it is to be intentional, but does so at the *same* level of analysis as that at which we think, refer, and wonder. Thus someone in this camp might argue that the ability to intend to withdraw $300 from a bank account depends on being able to participate in, or on having participated in, some form of commercial exchange: earning money and paying it out, being refused something because of inadequate resources, and the like. The implementationalist, in contrast, aims to give an analysis of *all* of what is involved in being intentional—including, that is, an analysis of thinking about and referring to money—but at a *different* level of analysis (presumably a lower one, such as in the example of taking consciousness to occur in virtue of the existence of a 40 HZ wave). As a result, they differ with respect to their degree of implied reduction. The implementor's belief that thinking about money can be explained physically or materially is a more reductionist position than the belief that humans' intentional capacities are grounded in material practice.

In sum, whereas it was unclear whether implementation should be analyzed as material or physical, this fourth intuition is less ambiguous. It clearly rests on a material, rather than physical, notion of routine or practice. "Participating in a commercial exchange" is no predicate of any present or future physics.[12] So whereas the first reason to be interested in the physical-in-gen-

---

[12] To be fair, even within this group there is room for difference. Social theorists, for example, are liable to emphasize the *historicity* and *sociality* of activities and routines—the fact that they arise out of, happen within, and are sustained by, culture and community. Far from taking historicity or sociality to undermine materiality, they would be among the first to argue that every one of these things—even language use—is material, in the sense of crucially depending on the body, its location and history and capacities and context. An artificial intelligence researcher, on the other hand, even if they agreed that historicity and sociality are essential, would want to understand how that historicity and sociality take effective, present form (e.g., through memory, communication, etc.), since the physical substrate is by definition local and ahistorical.

eral (naturalism) comes in both physical and material versions, and the second (ontological hygiene) is unambiguously physical, the third and fourth (implementation and practice) tend to shade away from the physical and towards the material. In ambiguous cases, moreover, as was betrayed as early as chapter 1, my own tendencies lean towards the material: i.e., towards a synthetic or constructive reading of implementation, and towards a social and historical interpretation of practice and routine.

1e Strategy

Where does this leave us? With respect to the present metaphysical project, all materialist ontology must be set aside. This is not to say that all forms of materialism are false. It may well be that our intentional capacities, our ability to represent the world as being a certain way, and the like, are essentially intertwined with our daily routines—habits of cooking breakfast, going shopping, navigating through the world. Ontologically, too, it may be that most material objects are functionally defined in terms of such practices. And such practices may even figure (though not primitively) in an ultimate metaphysical reconstruction. None of this is being denied. What must be set aside, rather, is their *advance characterization as material*—as centered in the body, for example, as routine, as habits. None of these concepts—'body,' 'habit,' 'routine,' etc.—are notions we can afford. We especially cannot afford them in advance, for fear of becoming ideological. In spite of its apparent seduction, a metaphysics of the body is as reductionist as one grounded on the electron.[13]

Ironically, in other words, we have to avoid all stores that traffic in material objects exactly because material objects are the most likely things to be particular and individual. What we are looking for is a store that sells the *notions* of particularity and individuality—or, failing that, a store that sells things from which

---

[13] To thematize the body is just to commit to yet another α—an α, like any other, grounding in which is ideologically reductionist. But see the discussion of immanent induction in chapter 11, which attempts to retain what is right about grounding in bodily practice, without paying its price.

to learn about particularity and individuality. And for these purposes the already-constructed material world is of no help. It is too expensive, for one thing. And it is also too late. Like Athena, it enters our imaginations already formed.

With respect to physicalism-in-general, therefore, implementation and practice must both be deferred. That leaves two other options. The one we considered second is the simplest— the suggestion of using the ontology of physics as a rhetorically instructive contrapuntal ontology. That one is easy to accept. The more difficult issue regards the first one, about naturalism. Material naturalism has already been set aside. But what about physicalist naturalism: the idea that everything, somehow, at least supervenes on the world-according-to-physicists?

It should be clear that physicalism cannot be accepted in advance. That would be ideologically reductionist. Nor, to point forward a bit, will it be accepted later on—though that will have to be argued. Nor, in the interim, will it be seriously entertained. From these three things its fate might seem doomed. But in a way that misses the point. The question on the table is not whether physicalism is right. As I said at the outset, the question is merely one of going into its store and looking around. And that is worth doing. It will pay to look closely at the wares on display: at this most famous of master narratives, this allegedly all-conquering physical level of analysis. The aim is not so much to see whether it is complete, which is doubtful, but rather to see *what contribution it can make towards metaphysical understanding*, especially as regards the two notions in primary focus, of particularity and individuality. Which aspects of the problem of ontology are "provided for" by physics, since physics is presumably *some* part of the story? And which require further work?

This rhetorical strategy is depicted in figure 5.2. Because of the prominence to be given to physical considerations in the next three chapters, it would be easy for a reader to mistakenly think that the view I eventually end up with is in some way, even if only in a relatively weak supervenientist way, physicalist. But that is not so (it is not entirely clear to me whether it is even compatible with supervenience). Furthermore, it should be evident from the rhetorical strategy that I am not committed to a physicalist result. The aim is to lean on physics—or at least on some of its ontological commitments—only in order to make some points in terms of which (in chapter 11) to describe the metaphysical view to which in fact I am ultimately committed. In doing so I will care as much about what physics is not as what it is. And anyway the strategy is temporary. As soon as we step off the with-reference-to-physics boat and back onto solid ground, we will be able to turn around and briefly look back at physics in order to see, from that perspective, how it fits in its appropriate, indeed its natural, place. Or to change the metaphor, physics can be viewed as a ladder—not a ladder to be kicked away, but neither to be confused with the higher ground reached with its aid.

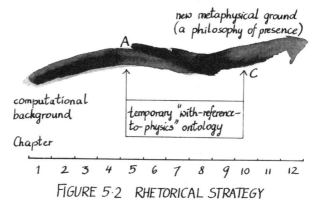

FIGURE 5·2   RHETORICAL STRATEGY

Ironically, moreover, the lessons to be drawn from physics are almost diametrically opposed to what is standard. It is normal to interpret physicalism as the idea that everything, from light bulbs to bus routes to foreign policy, is somehow *based* on the underlying physical substrate, but on top of that to nonetheless believe that these higher-level entities are very different in char-

153

acter from what can be found in a graduate textbook on relativistic quantum mechanics. The traditional position, that is, is one of *metaphysical supervenience without ontological similarity*. My position is almost exactly the opposite: that there *are* things we can learn from the ontology of physics, even rather abstract physics, that are directly relevant to the commonsense ontology of our ordinary lives—and furthermore that this is true quite apart from any reason to believe that our lives supervene on that physical substrate.

Two more quick preparatory comments. First, I am a tourist in the realm of physics; I claim no special expertise, and require none of the reader, beyond that covered in a first-year course in mechanics. No essential reference will be made to either relativity or quantum mechanics. Within the classical realm, moreover, for reasons that will soon be apparent, I will focus primarily on field-theoretic interpretations. Far from undermining the potential significance of the analysis, I believe that the points made here about field-theoretical interpretations should bolster the argument for their general foundational role.

Second, I take it that physical *laws*—whether one views these ontologically, as abstract regularities in the world, or epistemically, as conceptual or theoretic descriptions—have at least four properties. Famously, first, they are universal in content, in the sense of not themselves referring to or containing particulars. They *apply* to particulars, of course, in ways that will need to be explicated, but they are phrased or formulated in terms of abstract types. So whereas they apply to the sun, they do not mention the sun explicitly; whatever is true of the sun is required, by prior if not explicit stipulation, to be captured in properties such that any object possessing those properties would behave in indiscriminable ways. Second, they are intensional-with-an-s, in the sense of getting at properties of the world, not just at objects that possess them, or even at sets of objects. This has to do with their ineliminably modal character, in the sense of applying not just to the world as it happens to be, but of providing a clear indication of what a "physically possible" world could be like. Third, at least in classical physics, the laws are by and large continuous, not involving any discrete edges or sharp discontinuities. This continuity will not matter in any essential sense, but it will be rhetorically helpful in unseating ordinary intuitions about individuality.[14] Fourth, and finally, they are traditionally formulated in terms of differential equations; the laws or regularities have to do not so much with how the world is, at any given point, but with how it changes, given that it is this or that way to start with.

Given those preliminaries, I now want to argue that *physics sustains a basic notion of particularity, but not of individuality*. It is because of this fundamental asymmetry that it was so important to separate these two aspects at the outset.

2 Particularity

What, then, does physics have to say about particularity? A great deal, as it happens. To get at it, we need some conceptual typology.

2a Three realms

Even though the laws of physics are themselves particular-free, the opposite is true of the world they govern or describe.[15] Far from being universal, the physical world itself is a realm of *complete and total particularity*. This may seem tautologous, since the notion of particularity was in part motivated with reference to spatio-temporal occurrence, and space-time is first and foremost a physical (and material) construct. Nevertheless, this pic-

---

[14] This rhetorical reliance on continuity carries dangers; see §3.b, below.

[15] There are as many ways to describe the relation between the laws and the world as there are metaphysical positions. Some will be happiest saying that the laws *hold of* the world; others, that they *describe* it; others, that they *structure* or even *construct* it; others, that they *govern* it. I will set out my own metaphysical views in chapter 11; for now I want to be as inclusive as possible.

ture of encompassing particularity is worth holding clearly in mind: of a very large space or manifold—perhaps infinite, perhaps curved, or whatever—of particular phenomena or fields, ebbing and flowing, perhaps exploding or disintegrating, coalescing into stability or fomenting in chaotic turbulence.

Something else is worth holding in mind. Along with this primary image of world-extensive cosmic particularity, which I will call the *first realm*, there is also a *third realm* (why 'third' in a moment), an allegedly abstract realm containing universal objects: the types, the numbers and sets, and the physical laws themselves, *qua laws*. This situation is depicted in figure 5·3. Moreover, the relation between the third realm, of universals, and the first realm, of cosmic particularity—a relation labeled γ in the diagram, and variously called 'holding' or 'governing' or 'exemplifying' or 'manifesting'—is mediated or negotiated or maintained by the logic of property instantiation, or perhaps by the theoretical apparatus of physics-the-discipline, or perhaps by God. Either way, and this is the important point here, neither the third realm itself, nor the relation it bears to the first realm, is part of the subject matter of physics itself.

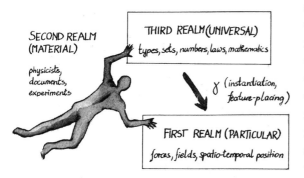

FIGURE 5·3   PHYSICS' THREE REALMS

This is not to claim that a physicist cannot be a realist about laws or numbers or types or property exemplification. Perhaps they too exist, as surely as any proton or table. The point is only that *nothing non-particular is itself governed by physical law*.[16] Physical laws occupy the third realm, but they do not apply to

[16]That is not to deny the possibility of higher-order laws; it is only to say that such laws will not be *physical* laws.

the third realm. They are abstract, but they do not govern the abstract, and therefore they do not govern themselves (and thus are in no sense "token-reflexive," to use Reichenbach's term[17]). This is why the question of the ontological status of laws is a subject of philosophical or metatheoretic debate, not something one expects to find explicated within the substantive part of the discipline itself—i.e., as the subject matter of textbook equations, alongside the laws of motion.

But universal laws and cosmic particularity are not the only things in physics. What about the physicists—the people, their experimental apparatus, their books and papers, their conferences and tenure battles? In the figure, I have labeled the lot of these things a *second realm*, and represented it as spanning between the first and third, since it needs access to both. Physicists must have some kind of physical or effective access to the first realm in order to conduct their experiments, take their measurements, and check their hypotheses. This necessary involvement in the physical situation is what raises such perplexing questions in both relativity theory and quantum mechanics (e.g., about the collapse of the wave function). On the other hand, it is equally necessary for physicists to have at least semantic access to the third realm in order to publish papers discussing or representing or stating those laws. If physicists could not represent or otherwise stand in an intentional relation to the third realm, they could not be *right*; neither would there be any warrant in calling them *physicists*.

Distinguishing the three realms is metaphysically useful because each is populated by different ontological types. Thus: (i) the first realm is *particular* and *physical*; (ii) the second realm is *material*; and (iii) the third realm is *abstract* and *universal*. Moreover, I take it that a metaphysical account of physics, as opposed to a physical account of reality, must account for how the three relate.

With respect to realms number one and two, the physical and

Popper's three worlds

Because of an at least superficial similarity, it is natural to enquire into the relation between the three realms identified in the text and Karl Popper's "Worlds 1, 2, and 3."*

At first blush the two categorizations seem almost orthogonal. Thus my second realm, for example, includes elements of all three of Popper's Worlds:

a. *Physicists*: living organisms, and hence elements of Popper's World 1 of physical objects;

b. *Theories*: elements of Popper's World 2 of "subjective experiences"; and

c. *Artifacts*: products of the human "mind," and hence elements of Popper's World 3.

By the same token, what I take to be paradigmatic inhabitants of my third realm—types, numbers, laws, and other abstract ontological paraphernalia—are not clearly located anywhere in Popper's typology. Issues of particularity (or of type vs. token) are not his primary concern, perhaps not his concern at all.

On further reflection, though, confidence in this orthogonality fades, and deeper similarities surface. Although Popper initially locates artifacts in World 3, in later passages he seems to expand the scope of World 1 to include all physical objects, or perhaps all of physical "object-hood," claiming (e.g., p. 47) that all World 3 objects, qua being part of World 3, are abstract.† While it is surely false, on the face of it, that hammers, say, are abstract (at least if abstract is understood as the opposite of concrete or physical), one can nevertheless discern in his remark an inchoate version of the sort of claim I make later in this book: that, as I will put it, *all* "ob-

the material, some starting positions can be identified. Physical naturalists must believe that the second realm (people, laboratory equipment, etc.) is *part* of the first realm (the domain of physics), since they believe that material phenomena can be reduced to, or at least supervene on, the physical. In contrast, material naturalists must believe approximately the converse: that

jects"—hammers, yes, but trees as well—qua registered objects, involve a degree of abstraction. Whereas Popper's World 2 is a world of subjective experience, I identify the second realm as the realm of the *subject full bore*, again including bodily material and concrete practices, as well as more ephemeral conscious states. Finally, Popper's World 1 and my first realm share the intuitive property of being intended to hold what one might think of as the concrete (particular) physical world, prior, in some vague logical or evolutionary sense, to human intentional practices. That he populates World 1 with objects, whereas I claim that the first realm contains no objects, represents a substantive empirical claim, rather than a difference in conception of realm or world.

To the extent that this diagnosis of common purpose is correct, I then offer my metaphysical picture and analysis of registration (and redistribution of bodies, abstraction, materiality, etc.) as a better way to do justice to Popper's underlying intuition. Yet it should also be said that dividing the world into three realms in this (or any other) way is not, for me, of ultimate interest. Not only does categorization into realms not play any crucial role in my positive picture, but allegiance to any such metaphysical typology runs the danger of violating irreduction.‡ I invoke the three-way distinction here only as a way to explain the structure—and to some extent to reveal the difficulties—of physics as traditionally conceived.

*See for example Popper & Eccles (1977), pp. 16 ff. and 36–50.
†Popper defines World 3 as products of the human *mind*—not, tellingly, as products of *body* or human *activity*, to say nothing of factories.
‡And the Criterion of Ultimate Concreteness; see p. 184.

rather than reducing the second realm to the first, the first should instead be grounded in the second.

As for the third realm, home of mathematics and the universal, the situation is much less clear. In some very lofty sense the most elegant solution would be to treat it in the same way as the first and second. On this view the physicalist should treat the

Inter-realm relations

Suppose what is anyway easy to imagine: that a physical naturalist were to reject the idea of reducing the third realm to the first (i.e., of reducing universals and types and numbers and the like to the realm of physical particulars), and instead: (i) were to commit to the existence of *two* realms: the first realm of physical particulars, and the third realm of mathematical laws and numbers and types; and (ii) were to believe that the second realm, of physicists and papers in *Physical Review Letters* and laboratory notebooks and the like, supervened on the first. In spite of its great familiarity, this stance faces two very serious, perhaps even insurmountable, problems.

It violates what I am calling naturalism, for starters—the mandate to show how the world is One. For what we have is not a picture of a single, integral world. On the contrary, this is a world that is by explicit stipulation *two*. And it is far from clear how the two parts relate. It may be thought that they relate by *logic*: i.e., by something like an instantiation relation, tying first-realm physical particulars to third-realm universal physical types. Perhaps—although to say that is to expand the metaphysical picture to include a third thing, instantiation, along with the two primitive realms (so now it is a world that is *three*). But there is a worse problem: how do the second-realm physicists, when writing their second-realm papers, manage to *represent* the third-realm laws? Representation is as close to a core intentional phenomenon as there is. But representation is not a species of instantiation. There must be *another* relation, of representation, between the first-cum-second realm and the third. Perhaps we

third realm as reducible to or supervenient on the first—i.e., should derive the universal from the particular. The materialist, correspondingly, should treat the third as reducible to or supervenient on the second—i.e., ground the universal in material practice. On the other hand, in neither case is it clear how the argument would go, especially because of the third realm's alleged abstractness. This is a question I will mostly defer, because it behave to make room for a distinct realm of the mental or semantic or intentional. So now we have a world that is *four*.

And that is not the end of the trouble. It was claimed in the text that physical naturalists are committed to the idea that second-realm physicists supervene on first-realm particulars. But if, as suggested earlier, and is surely at least plausible, being able to represent is constitutive of being a physicist, then according to this unfolding story physicists must *not* supervene on first-realm physical particulars, after all—but instead on first-realm particulars plus this new and rather mysterious representational or semantic relation holding between (arrangements, say, of) physical particulars and universal laws. But now things are starting to look bad. Because if representation has to be added on, as a metaphysical extra, to that which supervenes on the physical, then the view's original claim to being *physically naturalistic* starts seriously to erode. Nor are we done. For what about representation relations to particulars—as for example when a physicist writes a paper about a particular experiment? Does this form of representation "escape" the confines of the first realm, like the representation relation to types, and then re-enter it, at the point of reference? Or does the representation of particulars somehow supervene on the physically particular, even if the representation of universals does not? The former option has the merit of consistency, but the demerit of not being physically naturalistic after all; the latter fares better on naturalism, but at the cost of driving a fundamental metaphysical wedge between the representation of particulars and the representation of universals. Hardly a recommendation.

longs not so much to the philosophy of physics as to the philosophy of mathematics. I do want to make clear, though (as explained in more depth in the sidebar on inter-realm relations, above), how much there is for a reductionist program to explain. Moreover the tripartite typology can also help us understand the nature of particularity itself.

2b Particular and universal interpretations

Ontologically, I have suggested that the relation between the universal and particular may be mediated by God or by logic, but is anyway outside the purview of the physical laws themselves. What is more interesting is the way in which the relation between the (third-realm) universal and the (first-realm) particular is mediated in the practice of (second-realm) physicists.

As a simple example, consider the problem set in figure 5·4, of the sort that might be given in a first-year course in mechanics. It will help to step through this analysis slowly, paying special attention to the semantic interpretation of both text and diagram—i.e., to the representational artifacts consisting of a diagram and various simple equations, using **h** for the height of the table, **g** for the acceleration due to gravity, **t** for the time in flight, and **d** for the distance from the end of the table to the point of impact. Suppose, moreover, for the sake of discussion, that this example, or something like it, is being worked out for a real situation—say, in order to make sure that a room under construction is large enough to house some sort of game.

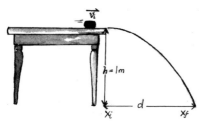

A frictionless puck moving at 3m/sec falls off a table 1m high. Where does it land?

$$y_f = y_i + v_{iy}t + \tfrac{1}{2}a_y t^2 \qquad x_f = x_i + v_{ix}t + \tfrac{1}{2}a_x t^2$$

$$y_f - y_i = h = 1m = \tfrac{1}{2}(9.86)t^2 \qquad x_f - x_i = d = v_{ix}t$$

$$t = \sqrt{\tfrac{2}{9.86}} = 0.45 \, sec \qquad d = 3(0.45) = 1.35m$$

FIGURE 5·4 A SIMPLE MECHANICS PROBLEM

Consider, more specifically, the singular terms **h**, **t**, **d**, $\mathbf{x}_i$, and $\mathbf{x}_f$. It turns out that they are crucially but curiously ambiguous, in a systematic way, as between a universal and a particular reading. Moreover, this ambiguity is an essential feature in allowing the problem to be worked. When we interpret the equations as describing some situation at hand—e.g., as applying to the distance between the table and the wall[18]—we take the terms as having *particular* reference, reference in the first realm. So $\mathbf{x}_i$ and $\mathbf{x}_f$ would be names of particular locations: one at the edge of the table, one at the point on the floor where the puck will land. Similarly, on at least a natural interpretation, $\mathbf{h}$ would also be taken, or at least could be taken, to have particular reference: namely, as referring to *the height of this particular table*, in the sense that that names a different thing from the height of some other table, even if, though perhaps only in this possible world, those two heights are of equal measure.

With respect to the official interpretation of equations, however, the situation immediately changes color. The particular interpretation vanishes, and all terms are instead interpreted as having purely universal interpretation, interpretation in the third realm. They are taken as referring to properties or features—measurable features, admittedly, in the sense of having a given magnitude, but features nonetheless, that could be exemplified by any number of other particular phenomena. Thus $\mathbf{d}$, for example, which works out on the official interpretation to be 1.35 meters, refers to an *amount of distance*, not to the unique particular spatial separation between the edge of the table and the point of impact. Variable $\mathbf{d}$ does not refer to that located separation in the world, in other words; rather, from this point of view it *applies* to that separation in virtue of being a *measure* of that separation, a measure that would be exemplified by any other separation between two particular locations that were also 1.35 meters apart. Similarly, if, on the particular interpretation, $\mathbf{h}$ referred to the height of this table, and $\mathbf{h}'$ to that of another table of the same extent, then on the universal interpretation the equation $\mathbf{h} = \mathbf{h}'$ would not be a claim of the common extent of two particulars, but rather an assertion of identicality between one and the same abstract measure.

[18] Tables and walls are of course material, not physical.

On the mathematization of position

Points or positions, in elementary physics, are traditionally modeled as vectors, which even at an abstract level requires the imposition (inscription) of an *origin*. Vectors can in turn be broken down into axial components, mandating the additional imposition of a reference-frame *orientation* with one axis for each of the underlying number of dimensions. Finally, the measure (length) of a vector, or of its components, requires imposing the third defining characteristic of a reference frame: that of *units* or *scale*. To an extent, these three characteristics—origin, orientation, and scale—are orthogonal. Thus the measure (length) of an arbitrary vector requires the last of the three (scale), but is independent of the first two (origin and orientation).

Given these facts, positional vectors can be added and subtracted arbitrarily. Curiously, however, with respect to dependence on reference frame, the difference between two positions-taken-as-vectors **a** and **b** has a different status from their sum. The sum, first, has the same status as the addends: it is intrinsically origin-relative, requires units for measure or length, and similarly requires frame orientation in order to be broken down into axial components. Although it is also a vector, the difference between **a** and **b** points from **b** to **a**, rather than originating at the origin— and therefore, at the most abstract level, depends on *none* of the three properties of the reference frame (though, again, it will depend on units for measure, and orientation for axial componentry).

In a sense, what is going on here is that **a** − **b** is associated with a *translation* from **a** to **b**, where translations are a different kind of thing from

Even the position terms x_i and x_f receive universal (third-realm) interpretations on the official view: as designating the abstract measure of the distance between the two points in question and some putative "origin." The position terms have to be interpreted in this way, moreover, since subtraction, normally defined over numbers, is understood as extended to arithme-

points or positions (even if they are modeled by the same kind of thing—namely, by vectors). Thus you can add and subtract translations to get more translations, subtract positions to get translations, and add positions to translations to get positions—but at least on this non-origin reading, you cannot add positions, at all.

Alas, the subtleties do not stop there. For note that translations, in the sense just defined, *lose particularity*. Thus, in a vector-space model (and in most more abstract mathematical models as well) the difference between positions-as-vectors **a** and **b** is considered to be identical to the difference between positions-as-vectors **c** and **d**, so long as **d** is the same distance and direction from **c** that **b** is from **a**. The *particular path* from **a** to **b**, however, remains different from that from **c** to **d** (except where **a** *is* **c** and **b** *is* **d**). If I were to walk from **a** to **b**, and you from **d** to **c**, we would not in general pass each other along the way.

What this all shows, I suppose, is that mathematical modeling is more of a gradual than an all-or-nothing affair. Nevertheless, I stand by the statement in the text: that mathematical operations, of which addition and subtraction are simple examples, are still only defined over positions-as-modeled, not over positions-in-and-of-themselves. In order for things to be added or subtracted—in order, that is, for things to be of the right form for the relevant arithmetic operations to be coherently defined—they must be modeled with *non-particular abstractions*, not directly treated as *concrete in-the-world particulars*. That, after all, or so at least it is plausible to argue, is what it *is* to be mathematized.

ticized measures, but is not normally thought of as applying to *locations*. In fact it is meaningless to think that it applies to locations; what sense is there in imagining subtracting the position of the Statue of Liberty, say, from the position of the World Trade Center? One needs origins, orientations, and measures for mathematics to get a grip. The fact that the terms are given in

units betrays this fact of measurement; if they genuinely designated particular locations, units would not be necessary. Units
figure only in the universal interpretation.[19]

Two morals. Some theory—perhaps a theory of intentionality, or a theory of science, or a theory of measurement, but anyway a theory sustained by an adequate metaphysics—is going
to have to deal with the complexity of how we as participant
observers (we must be participants, if we are to build the room)
negotiate so seamlessly and almost unconsciously between universal and particular interpretation. Being able to slide back and
forth in this way, between the particular interpretation, of type
"2nd ⇒ 1st realm," and the universal interpretation, of type
"2nd ⇒ 3rd," is a genuine and hard-won skill—one that must
be learned, one at which some people are better than others, one
that ties into differences between narrative and abstract readings
of word problems.[20] The second moral is to recognize, as well,
that nothing has been said about how we are able to perform this
feat. We know that, as intentional subjects, we *can* interpret
terms as having particular (1st realm) reference. That comes
with, or at least is dependent on, our ability to take the objects
in question (positions, heights, etc.) as particulars. And that aspect of our ability to register the world in terms of concrete objects has been admitted since the outset; indeed, that has been
one of my main claims. But *how* we can do so has not yet been
explained. Nor has it been explained how we can interpret terms
as having universal (3rd realm) reference. Certainly neither ability has yet been illuminated by what we know about the physics
of the situation.

[19]Things are actually trickier than this paragraph suggests; see the sidebar
"On the mathematization of position" on page 164.

It is also interesting to consider whether the units and position of the
origin matter to the "answer." In one sense they clearly do, since "1.35 meters" is couched in terms of them. In another sense they do not—the sense
in which the answer "4.43 feet" is the same as "1.35 meters."

[20]Perhaps if word problems were explained in this way, they would be easier
to learn.

In a moment I will set people aside and turn to the pure physics of the situation—to the table and the puck alone, independent of theorists, equations, or terms. One final comment, though, is worth bringing to the surface. From a semantical point of view, the nature of the "language of physics" differs markedly, depending on whether one considers the universal or the particular interpretation. With respect to the universal interpretation, the one that normally receives official blessing, the language of physics is at least allegedly formal or context-independent (though that can, and of course has been, denied). But the particular interpretation is more interesting. It gives rise to a vaguely "token-reflexive" intuition in the Reichenbachian sense mentioned earlier: that we may be able to refer to these particular positions on the floor because of our *own* particularity. But however the story goes, whether or not it involves indexicality or token-reflexivity, it is at least clear that the particular interpretation is context-dependent. So if being able to read the equations both ways is constitutive to being a physicist, even the language of equations may not be so formal, after all.

2c Deixis

Turn, then, to the world itself, sans theorist or observer, sans written equation or diagram. Set the entire second realm aside. What remains?

Although the laws themselves are wholly abstract, and in and of themselves have no particular purchase, I have already said that the "first-realm" world they apply to is one of pure particularity. Not only that; it is a realm of particularity unfolding in time. And not only does it unfold in time, but how it is at any future moment differs from the way it was at a previous moment in a regular way. As far as physics is considered, in fact, that is the only thing that is regular. That is why physical laws take the form of temporal differential equations. The particular state at any given moment is mapped onto a new particular state, in a way that is governed (dictated, described, etc.) by universal laws. *Particularity breeds particularity.*

Consider the situation from the puck's "point of view." It launches from the table's edge, and heads towards a landing point downwards and in front of it. Which point, exactly? Whatever point is determined to be the point of impact, as dictated by the laws of physics. But the laws are universal; is there any problem with their "specifying" a particular point? None whatsoever. We *say* that the point of impact is determined by the laws of physics; what we *mean* is that it is determined by two things in combination: the laws, which are universal, and the launching point, which is particular.[21] The laws themselves are universal, and they apply universally; but in their application they are functions from particularity to particularity.

All of this is so obvious and familiar that it can seem insignificant, or anyway banal. The way it works is so thoroughly engrained in the metatheoretic apparatus in terms of which we formulate the laws (differential equations, the calculus, etc.) that the underlying structure no longer stands out. It is worth rehearsing here, however, in order to bring out the following essential fact:

The laws of physics are fundamentally deictic.

Physical events themselves—the never-ending unfoldings of cosmic particularity—are in a fundamental sense token-

---

[21] It would be more correct to say "the initial state" rather than "the launching point." The problem, however, is that the former phrase is systematically ambiguous, in the way that so many other things in physics are: it can mean the *particular* initial state, or *the measure* of that initial state, in the sense of that (abstract) thing that this particular initial state would share with another one from which, according to the laws of physics, it was indistinguishable.

This discussion shows up why it is so important to discriminate the par-

reflexive. Moreover, it is this physical deixis that is going to ground the indexicality of reference.[22]

To see why, consider the first person pronoun 'I', a paradigmatic example of a deictic term. Semantically, we understand it in the standard two-stage way. Its *meaning*, we say, is constant: roughly, that on any occasion it is used to refer to the speaker. Because the meaning is constant, the pronoun can be learned; it is also why there is only a single entry in the dictionary. The *reference*, however, varies, according to the context of use. And the reference varies systematically—not in a chaotic or arbitrary fashion, but in a way that is governed (dictated, described, etc.) by the meaning. That is how we can know whom, on any given occasion, an utterance of 'I' refers to, without having to learn that reference as an additional fact.[23] Moreover, whereas the meaning is abstract,[24] the referents are particular (I use 'I' to refer to me; you use it to refer to you). And finally, the reference

...———————————————

ticular and the universal (first and third realms). The terms provide intuitive access to a metaphysically essential distinction that is otherwise hard to talk about.

[22]The term 'deixis' is more commonly used in linguistics than in philosophy for a phenomenon that a philosopher of language would more likely call *indexicality*. I prefer 'deixis' for the foundational phenomenon because it frees 'indexicality' to be used in an etymologically indicated way (though I will not do so here): for the more sophisticated situations, called "deferred ostension" by Quine (1971) and "deferred indexical reference" by Nunberg (1993), in which an index is used as a device with which to establish distal reference—as for example when someone says "I am parked out back," or, pointing to a book, "They don't know how to write very well."

[23]The name 'Susan' is context-dependent, too: different utterances of it, on different occasions, (often) refer to different people. But 'Susan' is ambiguous, not deictic, because there is no systematic rule of application. Each person named 'Susan' was so-named in an (approximately) independent baptism ceremony; and each use of the name 'Susan' to refer to such a person has to be based on a separately learned fact.

[24]Although "meanings" can arguably be made into individuals, most people would not call them particulars.

varies, in this systematic way, not by token, as Perry has pointed out, but by utterance or use.[25]

By the same token, consider magnets.[26] Suppose I pick up a magnet in the workshop, using it first to clean off the drill press table, then to retrieve some paper clips from the floor. In the abstract, magnetic attraction, like meaning, is systematic and constant. That is why there is only one entry for magnets in the dictionary of Maxwell's equations. Again, it is also why we know how to use a magnet in new and different situations, without having to learn any new facts. But although magnetic attraction in general is abstract, the attracted items, like referents, are particular. And once again what is attracted depends on use, not on token. I have just one (token) magnet in my workshop; but I use it on different occasions to pick up different things: yesterday, filings from the drill press; today, paper clips.

In both cases the governing law (regularity, habit) is an abstract but constant universal that maps particular occurrences — events, essentially — onto other particular occurrences or events, in a systematic way. That is by no means the end of the comparison, however. For as much might be said about any universal law. The crucial point of similarity, which is also the most difficult to say, has to do with the fact that the particularity of the "result," referent or collected item, *spreads out through space and time*, in a kind of continuous egocentric (differential) way, until it captures the first entity that relates to the source or originating particular event in the mandated fashion. If you start with a

[25] Perry's example involves two deaf mutes, so poor that they have to share a single card saying "I'm a deaf mute; will you give me some money?" (Perry 1979). His point is that the reference of 'I' is fixed by the act of handing the card to the passer-by, not by the existence of the written token. Note as usual the complex calculation involving the coordination of sameness and difference. This relates to the self-reference example in chapter 1; a community of **n** people sharing **m** cards would set up a variety of crosscutting fan-outs and fan-ins to the referent. Cf. §5.a, below.

[26] The use of magnets to illustrate this point was suggested by Adrian Cussins.

given particular, in other words, the governing laws or rules will tell you, incrementally and "egocentrically," how to move through the surrounding particular plenum, this way and that way and the other way, *but always staying fully particular*, until, finally, you arrive at the end-point—at the referent or filing, as it were, i.e., at the "object" or "target" of the given regularity.

In other words, there is more to the deixis of 'I', 'here', and 'now' than is captured in the statement that the referent depends on the context of use, even that it depends on the context of use in a systematic way. It is this "something more," this fact that it moves continuously and incrementally through the adjacent spatio-temporal plenum, that we get at with intuitions of token-reflexivity. By way of contrast, consider the aberrant word 'N', stipulated to work as follows: on its Nth utterance, in all of history, it shall refer to the Nth tallest person ever to exist.[27] Thus one could make the following true claim: "N is taller than N." This is systematic; and it depends on the context of use. But it does not depend on the context of use in the way that deictic terms do. It "takes leave" of the plenum of particularity (the first realm), and then re-enters it, at some different place, without having traveled incrementally from here to there.

What 'N' lacks, magnetism has. And what 'N' has, magnetism lacks—and not only magnetism, but the physical world in general, and not just the physical world, but the world in toto. Magnetic attraction and first-person pronouns are thus far more similar to each other than either is to the word 'N'. In both cases, one sets out from the originating particular event, the deictic "source," and travels continuously through the intervening particular plenum until one finally arrives at an equally particular

[27] This example only works if time (or at least the number of people) is finite. A more controlled version could have it that 'N' refers, on its Nth utterance, to the Nth person ever to have been born, which only requires that utterances and births be well-ordered. On this reading, "N was born before N" becomes tautological. But while this is better defined, it is more like real pronouns in being, still, though in a strained sense, token-reflexive.

"target," a target that relates to the source in a way that is continuously determined by the governing regularity. In both cases, moreover, the target is the full particular fragment of the world that exemplifies the requisite properties. When I use 'here', as I write this, I refer to a peninsula on the southern coast of Finland, replete with the uncountably many other properties it exemplifies, besides being my present location. And when I pick something up with a magnet, I pick the whole object up—scrap, birthday present, 127th object from the left corner of the table, etc.—not simply its magnetic attractiveness.

This is not an analogy. The structure is the same. Physical relations are context-dependent in the same way as elementary deictic terms. Except that that puts it backwards. Deictic terms are context-dependent, and succeed in getting at particular referents in exactly the same way that physical relations are context-dependent—namely, by parlaying their own particularity through a "spreading-out" generic regularity onto a target particularity.

2d The structure of theories

The reason the homology between deictic (indexical) reference and differential physics is not a theoretical commonplace is because the theoretic apparatus for semantics and physics has historically been formulated in such different ways (to say nothing of the fact that the enterprises have largely been carried on in different communities). Specifically, the use of the calculus in physics, and "semantic brackets" ('[[' and ']]') in logic, hides the underlying conceptual similarity.

To see how this goes one needs to track the way in which objects and properties (types) are represented in the two standard formalisms. In logic and semantics, we typically use singular terms to designate the (individual) *objects* and their types, and leave the (semantic) relations implicit. Thus consider an ordinary semantical equation, one that gives the meaning of the word 'I', assuming that contexts are modeled as structures over which such functions as 'speaker-of' are defined:

$$[\![\,I\,]\!] = \lambda context \,.\, \text{speaker-of}(context)$$

so that, in a given context c_I, the referent or interpretation can be indicated as follows:

$$[\![\,I\,]\!]\,(c_I) = \text{John}$$

What is important to note is that the relation of interpretation is represented syncategorematically, as something like:

$$[\![\,\_\,]\!]\,(\_) = \_$$

or, if one were to put it more functionally, merely as:

$$[\![\,\_\,]\!]\,(\_)$$

No explicit predicate letters are used to designate the primary semantic relation, in other words—the interpretation function, the primary subject matter of model theory, semantics' equivalent of *force* and *acceleration*. Rather, to the extent that explicit variables are used, they designate the *objects* over which this relation or function operates.[28]

In physics, in contrast, as indicated in the example given earlier, in figure 5.4 on page 162, the representational practice is almost an exact dual. The primary theoretic identifiers are used to designate the properties and relations—for example, the force of the magnetic field **B**—whereas the particulars they apply to are left wholly implicit. One would not normally ask the ques-

---

[28] The tendency to leave interpretation nameless (in equations) may be a consequence of the fact that most semantic models consider only one such function or relation (and thus do not need a syncategorematic position from which to quantify). The situation might change if models were broadened to include a third party, along with the sign and what is signified, such as an explicit interpreter or act of interpretation—or, in a computational vein, were expanded to describe the three-way relation among program, process, and subject matter, as suggested in §2 of chapter 1.

tion "Which paper clip will this magnet pick up?" in the way that one would ask "To whom does this use of 'I' refer?"

Consider the issue of coordinate system, to press the homology a bit further. In order to analyze a particular case of (first-realm) magnetic attraction, one first needs to set up a (third-realm) universal interpretation in terms of which to analyze it. This involves fixing an inertial reference frame over the situation in question, with an assumed (particular) point of origin and (universal) system of units.[29] From the magnet's point of view, however, what is attracted is a function of its own position, not of any externally imposed reference scheme. The irony is striking: a tension between, as it were, the *allocentric coordinates in which physics describes its subject matter,* and the *"egocentric" phenomena thereby described.* This subject-matter egocentricity (deixis) runs so deep in physics that it has been implicitly codified in the fact that physical laws are formulated as differential equations (what else could the "differences" implicit in the differential equations be defined over, after all, except over the system's previous particular state?). So it has never had to rise to the surface as an explicit theoretical claim.

Almost thirty years ago I asked my undergraduate physics professor what part of the content of physics was captured or carried in the differential calculus, and what part was captured or carried in the laws, the laws that were stated in that calculus. In particular, I wanted to know how much of Newton's and Maxwell's brilliance lay in selecting that formalism as the representational vehicle of choice (a lot, it seemed to me), and how much lay in formulating the laws of motion, the laws of electromagnetism, etc. This last discussion supplies the answer:

It is the deictic nature of physics (i.e., the "token-reflexive" nature of the fundamental physical force fields) that is captured in the calculus.

[29] It is essential that the origin be particular—or at least (to put the same point differently—I have made no attempt to fix the language) that there be a particular point corresponding to the universal origin.

Any physics compatible with the calculus—any physics whose laws could be expressed in differential form—would exhibit the kind of deixicity here being described.

In this way we arrive at our first moral. In virtue of the deictic nature of its constitutive regularities, the physical substrate sustains exactly the sort of token-reflexivity that Strawson and many others have seen as a necessary constituent in the particularity of object reference. Recognizing this fact, which has been obscured by differences in theoretical framing, represents a substantial step towards meeting the "world as One" mandate of naturalism. In particular, it shows one way in which physical and intentional phenomena are more similar than one might at first have thought. Perhaps it will please a Fregean physicist that the object of a magnet's reach is determined by the sense of its attraction. Or sober a proponent of situated language to realize that physics has been "situated" since the beginning.

Either way, it is clear that the major challenge, for an intentional theorist, is to figure out how even relatively context-*independent* language can possibly work. When you stand in front of me, I can refer to you in a way that is not all that different from the way in which my magnet can pick up the iron filings that are under my hand. What needs explaining is how I can miss you, when you go away.

3 Individuality

What, finally, does physics have to say about individuality?

In a word, nothing. As with logic, objectivity, truth, and various other notions essential to the (second-realm) practice of physics, but not implicated in the physical picture of the world it paints, so too issues of individuality and individuation are not a constitutive part of the subject matter of physics. Needless to say, that is not to deny that physical features may enter into the determination of an object's integrity or coherence—properties such as spatio-temporal continuity, relative discontinuity (of density or material) at the object's boundaries, and so forth. At the same time, I do not mean to imply that physically identifiable features are ever sufficient, on their own, to warrant calling something an individual. As with the relation between organic composition and life, certain kinds of physical coherence may be necessary to sustain individuality, but at the same time be incapable of explaining it. The essential point, however, is to recognize that, no matter how much or how little physical features enter into the overall equation, the essential notions—of coherence, boundary, relevant sense of continuity and discontinuity, etc.—are not themselves predicates of physical theory.

From this it might seem that an analogy between individuality and objectivity would go through intact: i.e., that physics as practiced—i.e., the second-realm phenomenon—would *presuppose*, but not *explain*, the notion of a discrete individual, just as it presupposes, but does not explain, notions of reference, representation, objectivity, and the like. That is almost right—much more right, in fact, than one might at first suspect. But at the same time the true answer is both more complex and more interesting than that suggests. Ontologically, in particular, it is not clear that physics actually does presuppose the notion of individuality. That is, it is not clear that the pure physical (first) realm is assumed by physics to be populated with any individual objects at all.

This is easiest to see on a field theory interpretation, which is one reason I have chosen to work with it. The picture of the (first-realm) world to which this conception is committed is one of infinitely extensive continuous fields of mass, charge, etc., ebbing and flowing in dynamic ways as governed by the relevant classical laws. Given the results of the previous section, we can say that the world of classical physics, at least on this interpretation, is one of infinitely extensive *continuous, particular, deictic fields*.

There is of course discreteness up one level, at the level of properties. What I am calling the third realm, in other words, consisting of the concepts and properties themselves, is wholly discrete.[30] Velocity is a discrete property, wholly distinct from mass, and equally distinct from charge. Thus it is perfectly coherent to talk of arbitrary real-valued velocities, such as 23.4589 meters per second, and arbitrary real-valued masses, such as 21.004 kilograms. It makes no sense at all, however, to talk about something that is 23.1% a velocity, but 76.9% a mass. This higher-order discreteness will be addressed in chapter 11, in an effort to understand where it comes from, determine how much it can be leaned on (in developing a general notion of discreteness and individuality), and understand what it would be like for it not to hold. For the time being, however, it is enough to focus on what would normally be called the "object" level, except that for obvious reasons that is not an available phrasing, so that (as previously mentioned) I instead call it the *particular level*.

I said just now that it makes sense to talk about "arbitrary, real-valued velocities, such as 23.4589 meters per second." It would have been easy to write the following words, instead: that it makes sense to talk of "*an object's having* an arbitrary, real-valued velocity, such as 23.4589 meters per second." But what would that object have been, that possessed such a velocity? Who brought *it* to the party? Certainly it would not have entered into any physical law. It is not just that no *particular* objects figure in the laws of mechanics or electromagnetism; there are no generic place-holders for objects, either. The equations contain no variables that range over individuals; not even, surprisingly, over space-time points, such as particular locations. Instead, as we saw in the last section, the variables range over *the measures of properties*—for example, over generic measures of the distance between locations and a fixed point of origin.

In sum, being an individual object is also not, in and of itself, an effective or even salient physical property. No physical attri-

---

[30] For a discussion of this kind of higher-order discreteness—Haugeland calls it "second-order digitality"—see Haugeland (1982).

bute holds of an individual, for example, except in virtue of its physical composition. If "to be is to be the value of a bound variable," physics will be of no help in easing the existential angst of any ordinary individuals. *For there are no physical objects.*

3a Epistemic individuals

There is something bizarre about all this, however. It is absolutely paradigmatic to conceive of the world in terms of individuals, when doing physics. Consider the trivial example discussed earlier, with a puck, table, etc. These are all discrete individuals. In fact it is daunting to imagine framing the problem in a pure, field-theoretic way. Yet the very fact that it is daunting betrays what is going on. Individuals are not an *ontological* fixture of the physical world. Instead, they are part of the *epistemic* structure of physics-the-discipline. Not only that; they are absolutely crucial, epistemically. They are necessary for us, as epistemic agents, to *calculate* anything, to *figure anything out*, to allow physics to be *useful*. In sum: they are *constructs of the second-realm* (that is why the analogy between individuality and objectivity is so close).

Consider, for example, what would be required to calculate, in the absence of any postulated individuals, what we normally conceive of as the gravitational attraction between two bodies. In such a scenario there would be no "bodies," strictly speaking; instead, there would only be an infinitely extensive real-valued density function defined over all of space—call it **M**. By the same token, since the bodies could be neither identified nor located, it is not entirely clear what the "answer" would be—i.e., exactly what is being asked. If (violating the assumptions a bit) we assume that we are interested in the gravitational force exerted on a finite region, then one can imagine that the answer should itself be a manifold, defined over the region, whose value at each point is the net gravitational force impinging on that point. The calculation thereby implied would be something like the following:

$$\iiint\limits_{region} \iiint\limits_{universe} \frac{g(\vec{s} - \vec{s}\,')M_{\vec{s}}M_{\vec{s}\,'}}{|\vec{s} - \vec{s}\,'|^3} d\vec{s}\, d\vec{s}\,'$$

Four things about this should be clear. First, except in a vanishingly small (measure zero) percentage of cases, posing the problem would require an infinite expression. Second, even if that could be done, doing the calculation would depend on an infinite amount of information. Third, even if that information were available, it would require an infinite amount of work. And fourth, the result of that work—the "answer," as it were—would, like the problem itself, be infinite, not in general expressible through finite means.

In very special cases, of course, the suffocating infinities can be elided, either by analytic means, or by the appropriate use of idealizations. Famously, for example, the gravitational force exerted by a spherically-symmetrical hollow region of uniform mass density can be proved to be zero, within the sphere, and equivalent to a point mass of equal mass located at the center, outside the sphere.[31] The very term "idealization," however, is an admission that things are not this way, which in turn betrays the fact that the idealized circumstances—alleged point masses, for example—are features of the epistemic situation, not of the ontological one. And other than in the infinitely unlikely event of a perfect arrangement of the physical world—which is to say, all the time—it is also admitted that the use not only of point masses, but every other aspect of the use of individuals, such as closed systems, discrete objects, etc., is only an approximation, that parts company with the way the world "really is." That is to say, these idealizations part company not only with the way the world is in some potentially ineffable sense, but with the way *that physical theory itself registers the world as be-*

---

[31] This is true of all $1/r^2$ forces.

ing. It is a recognition of a theory-*internal* gap or split, not a recognition of the limitation or partiality or approximateness of the theory itself. Moreover, to repeat the central point, it is a coherently structured gap, between how the theory takes the world as being, and how the theorist must register the world, in order to do any predictive or calculative or other kind of useful work.

It is of course extremely consequential, for the purposes of a theory of intentionality, to recognize that individual objects do not enter the physical world view, but instead play a role in the practice of physics for epistemic—that is to say, intentional—reasons. The original and overarching question was whether we, as students of intentionality, could gain anything from physics, regarding the notion of an individual object. The result, however, is the exact opposite. Epistemology, calculation, prediction, and the like, are *our* subject matter, not theirs:

Physicists will have to look to a theory of intentionality for an account of the notion of an individual, not the other way around.[32]

3b Discrete feature-placing

One final comment about the relation of physics to the notion of individuality. I have used the example of classical field theory because it is pedagogically simplest; in virtue of its commitment to complete continuity at the base level, it is most obviously free of any deep ontological commitments to the discreteness of individuals. There is good reason, however, to

---

[32] I have not considered a form of "indispensability" argument for individuals here: that if they are necessary, in order to do physics, then that fact alone should guarantee them a kind of reality. It is not clear to me, for one thing, that they really are indispensable, unless one takes the ability to calculate to be a necessary part of the commitment of a physicist. But anyway that is to miss the point. I am not arguing in this section that individuals are not *real*; all I am saying is that physics does not explain them. Just because I cannot buy them at physics' store does not imply that they are existentially challenged.

believe that the moral holds true of physics more generally. To see this, note that discreteness and individuality are not the same thing (although it is a nice piece of homework to spell out the relation between them). In particular, there is at least this difference. Discreteness requires only what physics has already been admitted to depend on: individuation, in the second realm, at the level of properties. Thus consider a square wave: a temporal pattern of voltage on a wire, for example, that shifts, every second, back and forth between 0 and +5 volts. Although it is easy for us to identify individual pulses—the voltage pulse between **t** and **t**+1, for example—there is nothing in the basic ontology of square waves that either requires *or justifies* that identification.

Thus the physics of square waves is what in a Strawsonian spirit I will call *discrete feature placing*. So the question to be asked is whether branches or interpretations of physics that are more superficially individuating than field theory—branches or interpretations that may look as if they work more centrally with individuated objects—do anything more than discrete feature placing. And as suggested in the accompanying sidebar (page 182), there is good reason to believe that the answer is *no*. On the other hand, I want to leave further consideration of these physical cases to another time. Here I just want to pull together such lessons as have been learned from this digression in preparation for a return to the intentional realm. It should be said, though, that the eventual metaphysical picture will undermine the sharpness of the divide between ontology and epistemology (i.e., the sharpness of the divide between the first and second realms)—a result that will soften not only the urgency, but also the facticity, of this entire question. But that does not render the current conclusions any less important, any less consequential. It simply means that we are still in the process of mapping and clearing the land, not yet of building a stable or permanent dwelling.

Reidentifiability and discrete feature-placing

Another reason to believe that the general claim that individuals are epistemic, not ontological, features of physics has to do with the notion of reidentifiability that was claimed, at the outset, to be a defining characteristic of what it is to be an individual. It was implied there that "reidentifiability" and "identifiability" are essentially synonymous: one cannot properly be said to have identified an individual, as opposed to having recognized the particular manifestation of a (potentially discrete) set of properties, unless one can distinguish the object from another that exemplifies the same set of effective properties (so that even a physically perfect replica of a Rembrandt would be of no great artistic value, for example, because of not being the one he actually painted). Given that physical laws are ahistorical, it seems almost a theorem that, with respect to their subsumption under physical regularity, equivalent exemplifications of physical properties would be indistinguishable.

None of this is to deny, when appropriate quantities of H_2O and CO_2 combine to produce a mixture of $C_{12}H_{22}O_{11}$ and O_2, that there is a fact of the matter about whether the oxygen molecules released as a gas come from the water or the carbon dioxide—or equivalent questions about electrons or quarks. Grooves in the space-time plenum are still not reidentifiable objects.

4 Conclusion

What should be taken from all this?

With respect to objectivity, universality, truth, and the like, physics had nothing *direct* to say. Relations between (second-realm) subjects and observers and the (first-realm) physical plenum were not explicit subject matters of physics. As is well known, both relativity theory and quantum theory hold intriguing consequences for such theories of the physical participant/observer. But these consequences are not explored, theory-internally, nor would their exploration seem to count as part of physics per se, but more as philosophy of science or science studies. Nor was the role of any other second-realm phenomena explored: instruments, experiments, debates, and any other quintessentially material phenomena. Nor did physics even take a stand on the metaphysical status of the second realm. Physics per se is not committed to physical naturalism, for example; physical naturalism is just one of many possible stances towards physics.

Similarly, all relations to what I called the third realm—the abstract realm of types, properties, features, numbers, mathematics, etc.—also fell outside the scope of physical theory. Metatheoretically, in sum, physics is largely mute. And in a way that is no surprise. No one ever expected physics to explain physicists.

With respect to particularity and individuality, the answer was simple: physics does provide a story about particularity, but no corresponding story for individuality. Individuals, as we saw, were epistemically necessary for physics-the-discipline, but were not part of physics' ontological claims on the world. This result can be very simply summarized:

There are no physical objects (individuals), only material ones.

That is not to say that all individuals are necessarily material; as we have seen, some individuals, perhaps even some particulars, may be abstract. What it does say is that individuality is not made out of purely physical stuff; it will have to be assembled out of some kind of more expensive ingredient.

With respect to particularity, physics did not just deal with it; it painted a very specific picture. Ontologically, this image is very important to hold in mind: of an endless ebb and flow of spatially-infinite fields of continuous, deictic, pure particularity. Except the continuity should not be taken too seriously; it was mostly useful as a pedagogical device to unseat our commitment to the discrete edges of objects. In point of fact the sorts of picture that have emerged in the physics of the last few decades—

of fractals, chaotic turbulence, and sheer ferment—are much more realistic than the smooth curves of the classicist. Fields are as likely, if not more likely, to be the locus of profuse and tumultuous chaos as of pristine smoothness. Either way, they have yet to be individuated.

If these are the substantive conclusions, what are their methodological correlates? Here the moral is cautionary, and strong. This digression into physics has only strengthened the irreductionist principle, leading to the following extremely stringent thesis:

Criterion of Ultimate Concreteness

No naturalistically[33] *palatable theory of intentionality—of mind, computation, semantics, ontology, objectivity—can presume the identity or existence of any individual object whatsoever.*

The name "Criterion of Ultimate Concreteness" is appropriate because, as will soon be evident, one of the things that individuals have, that physical phenomena lack, is concreteness's opposite: abstraction.

The most natural way in which to interpret this criterion is to see it as prohibiting the advance (pre-emptive) individuation of any discrete objects in the subject's semantic domain—in its kitchen, for example, or on its way to work, or in the office. This was one of the problems with a metaphysics of the body. "The body," as an entity, does not come for free; it is a substantial achievement, one that has to be individuated, carved out from a background, kept in shape, etc., by, among others, the subject whose body it is (and perhaps also by the cosmetics industry). The nature of this individuation, and perhaps objectification as well, is something that a metaphysical account has to explain; it is not something that can be taken for granted.

But ground-floor individuation is not the only thing that is proscribed. For the metaphysician or intentional theorist, per-

---

[33] Naturalistic in the "overall" sense embraced in §1 of this chapter: as the methodological correlate of a "world as One" construal of realism.

haps the most striking consequences of the Criterion of Ultimate Concreteness have to do with what one might think of as metatheoretic individuation, which is proscribed as well. In particular, it means that no intellectually satisfying theory can presume the identity or existence of *the subject*, let alone presume the identity or existence of any of the subject's objects—i.e., the objects that the subject will take the world as containing. For to presume the existence of the subject would be as methodologically circular, by presuming the existence of what is to be explained, as to presume the existence of their car—to say nothing of committing equally egregious errors of inscription.

Naturally enough, this boundary between subject and "the rest of the world"—a distinction between self and other (I and Thou) for the subject—will figure prominently in the subject's achievement of an objective conception of the world. It is less weighty for the theorist—a simple matter of subject-matter individuation. And yet, as the foregoing discussion has argued, and as I hope, perhaps more compellingly, in the next several chapters to show, to *presume* it vitiates any attempt to understand how reference, for example, and other forms of intentional participation, actually arise.

It is very important to be clear on the exact methodological consequences of this mandate to avoid an a priori subject-world distinction. From the point of view of the theorist, it is a requirement that the theorist take a neutral position, at the outset, on the question of realism vs. anti-realism—i.e., on the age-old issue of how responsibility is to be divided between subject and (remaining) world. But that does not mean, at least initially, that an intentional theorist need themself be metaphysically neutral. I am not, at least not yet, claiming that for a theoretician to accept the Concreteness Criterion requires that they suspend their commitment to the separation between themself and their domain of inquiry. Rather, at least initially, the requisite neutrality is neutrality about *realism for the subject*: neutrality about the way in which the territory laid out in front of the theorist is assumed (or not assumed) to be divvied up into subject and object. As usual, the aim is scrupulously to avoid inscription errors or pre-emptive registration; it is not to badger the theorist into an alien or uncomfortable theoretical standpoint.

In the long run, however, the two positions must be aligned: the position about how life is for subject-cum-world that one ends up being committed to, and one's own metaphysical standpoint, from which one has arrived at that conclusion. They must be aligned because of a different criterion, which I have elsewhere called a *Criterion of Integrity*:[34] the fact that it would be contradictory, overall, to claim that intentionality or semantics is one way, but to make that claim from a competing or alternative theoretical vantage point. It is because of that eventual alignment that the words 'at least initially' occurred twice in the previous paragraph. Nevertheless, this secondary requirement for eventual alignment should not be allowed to homogenize the primary structure of the theoretical situation.

Teasing these two metaphysical positions apart (subject's and theorist's) is important, in part because it gives the theoretician a bit of room to maneuver in dealing with a mandate for neutrality that runs extremely deep, and that otherwise might seem to be an untenable straightjacket. Vis-à-vis avoiding a distinction between subject and world, for example, the required commitment is not simply one of temporary caution or restraint, as if the answer (about the locus of the subject-world boundary) could not be assumed at the outset, but would be delivered later on. On the contrary, no guarantee is made that these particular scales will ever be weighed, so as to allocate this much to the subject, this much to world or to "other." There is no guarantee that the line will *ever* be drawn. Rather, the aim is to make room for the eventual conclusion, in the successor metaphysics, that the question of realism vs. anti-realism will itself have been shown to be ill-founded, an unanswerable awkwardness stemming from

---

[34]TMD·I and TMD·IV.

deep-seated inscription errors rooted in our methodological backgrounds.

And yet, at the same time, it would be a mistake to allow this crucial preparation to cut the investigation off at the knees—as it would do if one were to analyze the methodological position we have come to in terms of the still-reigning (i.e., predecessor) conception. The demand that an investigator take for granted the identities of *no* individual would be impossible to meet if assessed on current mythologies (specifically, on metaphysics formulated in terms of Objects, Properties, and Relations). Only when a tenable alternative at the theoretician's object or base (particular) level has been developed will it be possible to see how the meta-level can be overhauled in ways that do not lead to total collapse. And it will not collapse, at that later point, because by then it will be possible to see that the investigative methods of intellectual inquiry *have always been* as the new account claims. I.e., it will be apparent, from the vantage point of the new (successor) metaphysics, that language, discourse, intellectual inquiry, etc., have always been, including throughout the predecessor era, and will always be, as the successor theory claims.[35] This is simply an instance of the general point that it is always important to recognize that even the prior era's worst theories were the product of genuine, not mythologized, human activity.

But enough of these abstract deliberations. Let me just say in conclusion that the divide we have been talking about, between subject and object, between sign and signified, is not the only dualism to be barred by the prohibition against prior or preemptive inscription. All sorts of other standard ones are included as well: between mind and body, between nature and so-

---

[35] This is not as arrogant as it sounds. It will be apparent from the vantage point of the new position that metaphysics will always be as it claims; that is what it is to be a metaphysical vantage point (at least a vantage point that meets the integrity criterion). When, as is inevitable, the successor view is in turn replaced, then that vantage point will have to be abandoned, because it will then be seen to be, *and always to have been*, wrong.

187

ciety, between concrete and abstract (yes, even among the three realms). But the mandate is by no means wholly negative. One important benefit of "going in under" these distinctions is that it makes room for the account to recognize that objects are inexorably cultural, biological, political, psychological, social, evolutionary, historical, economic, and so on and so forth—i.e., are everything that social constructionism and critical studies have shown them to be—without, in the first (aboriginal) instance, having to pay the price of these ineliminable but nevertheless very expensive notions.

Part II · Construction

6 · Flex & Slop

Enough ground has been cleared that we are almost ready to begin construction.

The strategy in this chapter is temporarily to accept the contributions of physics as ingredients in the overall picture, and to find out what else is needed for a complete picture of intentionality, semantics, and ontology. Given the results of chapter 5, and the commitment to honor the Criterion of Ultimate Concreteness, that translates into the following more specific goal: to understand how a conception of objects can arise on a substrate of infinitely extensive fields of particularity.

Except of course that this is an untenable way to phrase it. To say "a *conception* of objects" makes it sound as if the achievement is the subject's, by assuming a split between conception and what is conceived of. It also fails by making it sound as if the achievement is cognitive. Nor is anything gained by striking a more traditionally realist stance, and asking "how objects can arise on a substrate of infinitely extensive fields." That puts the achievement too squarely on the object. Both ways of putting it violate the mandate of avoiding an a priori subject-world split.

In place of these dichotomous formulations, therefore, I will speak, unitarily, of *registering* the world.

1 Registration

By 'register' I mean something like *parse, make sense of as, find there to be, structure, take as being a certain way*—even *carve the world into*, to use a familiar if outmoded phrase. Thus, as I write this paragraph and look out the window, I register a bunch of trees, a stone barn, and a dilapidated child's bicycle thrown down on a moss-covered granite slope.

Although I will differentiate the two notions in a moment (registration is much broader), there are important ways in which registration is similar to perception. In ordinary parlance, and also as I will understand it, perception is an activity on the part of an intentional subject, and furthermore an activity that relates it to, or engages it with, something in the world. Typically this will be something in the *external* world, something outside the subject, something that may even be quite far away. Thus we talk of perceiving a sparrow, a wry look, a distant thunder-cloud—and not, except on higher-order reflection, of perceiving our perceptions or sensations. Furthermore, perception not only relates the subject to that distal object, but also implies a kind of intentional success. Perception, that is to say, is an *achievement*. To say that a sailor perceives an island on the horizon implies, unless otherwise noted, that there was an island to be perceived, and that the sailor did indeed see it. Moreover, as I will put it, it is the island itself, not an impression of the island, that figures in the *content* of the sailor's intentional state. As one would say in the philosophy of psychology, perception, at least in the unmarked case, is both veridical and "broad."[1]

Depending on how psychology goes, a perceptual claim may indirectly do other work as well: such as affirm the existence of a complex causal relation between the sailor and island, perhaps mediated by light waves and binoculars; or validate the crucial role played by sense data or sense impressions; or even just imply that a certain structure of stimuli or causal disturbances has im-pinged on the sailor's surface. But none of these things is what perception actually *is*. People do not perceive light waves, or sense data, or impressions, or causal disturbances, at least not or-dinarily. It is always possible to define some other word to mean any one of those things—e.g., to signify the relation between an agent and the structure of the impinging stimulus or sensory

[1] Fodor (1980), McGinn (1982), Dennett (1982), Pettit & McDowell (1986).

field—some word such as 'narrow perception,' or even, but unadvisedly, 'Perception.' Even if they could be proved coextensive with perception, or nomologically necessary for perception, or to be superior to perception for purposes of a scientifically respectable psychology, none of those facts would make them *be* perception, in part because they would relate the subject to the wrong thing. To say that a sailor perceives the island is to talk about two entities, several miles apart, and to say that, perhaps in virtue of some number of causally mediating processes or other psychological mechanisms, the sailor has successfully established a specific directed semantic relation towards that distal island, an island with which, as I will say, they are *intentionally engaged*.

Both of these facts—that perception reaches out into the world, and that, at least by default, it is veridical—are reflected in grammar. The direct object of the verb 'perceive' is (a term for[2]) the distal entity or situation towards which the subject ends up being intentionally or semantically directed. It is striking, however, that in the case of higher-level intentional activities—thought, conception, cognition, wondering—we have no such analogous verb. Terms like 'think,' 'conceive,' etc., usu

---

[2] There was a time, I take it, when the *subject* of the sentence 'Pat ate dinner' was a person named Pat, and the *object* of the sentence was an edible meal. Nowadays, it is almost universal to strike a syntactic stance, and to say that the subject of the sentence is the word 'Pat,' and the object, the word 'dinner.' A parallel syntactification has taken place in mathematics. When we were in high school, the velocity of the river was a constant, the angle that the boat left the dock was an independent variable, and the position where it arrived on the far shore was a dependent variable. By the time we got to college, velocities, angles, and positions were no longer variables; variables had become syntactic entities, entities that *designate* velocities, angles, and positions.

I am not fully in favor this development, which has pulled the terms 'subject' and 'object' away from their original sense, the sense in which they are being examined in this book. Hence my use of parentheses around 'a term for.'

193

ally take a thought or its content as their object (you think a *thought*, not a table). When they are used with an external situation as object, moreover, as for example in the sentence "He conceived a grand party," there is almost the opposite implication, that the conceived entity does *not* in fact exist (unless, interestingly, that object is itself a mental—intentional—construct, such as when you conceive a scheme or plan). Similarly, the more common construct with a prepositional object, such as "a conception *of* a nuclear-powered aircraft," also fails to suggest, and may even contraindicate, the existence of whatever it was that was conceived of.

My intent, in contrast, is to have 'register' be much broader than 'perceive,' and certainly to include full conception, but to retain both of these real-world characteristics of 'perceive': of similarly reaching through to the world or the referent, and carrying as well a default implication of an appropriate notion of veridicality or success or other intentional virtue or worth. Unless marked, that is, the phrase 'she registered a table' will be taken to imply not only that there was a table to be registered, but that she successfully ended up in an intentional relationship to it. Or to put it more neutrally but more adequately, the phrase will be read as implying that the overall situation of subject-cum-world was such as to sustain the truth or success or worth or virtue—i.e., the *objectivity*—of the intentional act of her taking there to be a table.

Exactly how broad registration is must await a more developed account, but my general intent is to have it include all intentional actions that can legitimately be said to have some form of *content*. How broad that is is partly an empirical question. It will at least include cognition, sensing, having intuitions about, and a number of other things—and will perhaps include willed action, action that assumes that the world is given or structured in some way. To register the world, that is, is to do or be oriented towards the world *in such a way that it presents or arranges or constitutes itself as world*.[3] Note too that although there is something right about speaking of individual subjects as the entities or agents that register, this is not to deny that in all likelihood it will be whole cultures, language communities, communities of practice,[4] or collectivities of people-and-instruments-and-organizations-and-documents-and-tools-and-other-essential-but-expensive-entities that are the full sustaining locus of this intentional achievement.

The subject matter of registration is more general than that with which the investigation started, which focused more narrowly on the notion of an object. In the special case of objects, 'register' can be taken as being related in meaning to 'individuate' or 'identify,' but a much closer synonym is 'objectify,' which shares with 'register' the useful property of not committing itself to the locus of responsibility of the resulting individuation criteria. Because objects remain in focus in the rest of the book, I will continue to consider the registration of objects as a central case, but it is important to keep in mind that registering objects is just one way of taking the world to be present or given, even if current theoretical culture takes it to be paradigmatic.[5] As a reminder once again of how narrow a case it is, however, imagine standing with a friend at the prow of a boat flying across the sea on a summer's afternoon, drinking in the air and sky and surf and islands, and reveling in the freedom and luxury of the full month's vacation opening up in front of you. It would be a trav-

---

[3] In spite of this sentence, I do not in general wish to speak of registering the *world*. The basic, simple, directed case should always govern. Forget the world; register potatoes.

[4] See Lave & Wenger (1991).

[5] Current *theoretical* culture takes Objects to be paradigmatic, not objects. On the other hand, because of the fact that so much of human practice is in part ideologically self-constituted—i.e., is in part constituted by reflective registrations on what it is to be that kind of thing—the distinction in real life between objects and Objects will not be all that sharp. Only Distinctions have sharp boundaries like that, not distinctions.

esty to reduce the ensuing registration to a process of chopping up the experience into a series of discrete individuals. So I will take registration to include quality, mass substances—even feature-placing, so long as there is reason to believe that the features are placed in a world. Remember when the Count of Monte Cristo, sewn into his friend's death sack, was unceremoniously dropped outside the Chateau d'If. In that first moment of shocked recognition, he registered, but did not individuate, the sea.[6]

The term 'register' has a number of other useful connotations stemming from its use as a term of ordinary English. Informally, for example, we say both that she did not register his anger, and also that his anger failed to register on her—implying a salutary sharing of responsibility for a subject's taking an object to be an object. Responsibility for intentional success falls on both *registrar* and *registered*, in other words, even if not symmetrically.[7] In addition, to register something implies registering it *as* something, and thus the term, like representation, carries the requisite aforementioned sense of "aspectual shape"[8] or *intensionality* (with an 's') characteristic of all intentional (with a 't') activity. Third, 'register' also carries a useful implication of alignment with the external situation, as for example in the printer's notion of registration marks (used to allow one document to be fitted exactly into place on top of another). Even without making any special commitments about lining up how the world is and how we take it to be, it is still useful to retain the residual sense of realism. Fourth, 'register' also carries a sense of involvement or engagement with the world: to register a print requires taking physical action on it. Sometimes, moreover, it

---

[6] Dumas (1894). There is of course a sense—to pedantically admit the standard stalking horse—in which he did individuate the feature *sea*.

[7] Subject and object (registrar and registered) are symmetrically *important*; that does not imply that their roles are in any way the same. Perception and registration are manifestly asymmetrical (directed) relations.

[8] See Searle (1992).

suggests not only a process of alignment, but one of active calibration, even with normative overtones.

Finally, and most importantly, the word provides a convenient way to honor the fact that the ways in which we take the world to be are in part a function of the assumptions and culture and machinery, including conceptual machinery, with which we approach it. For many reasons, some already mentioned, and some that will become more evident in succeeding chapters, I do not want to subscribe to the never-very-well-explicated notion of a conceptual scheme (primarily because I do not want to presume that all registration is *conceptual*).[9] Instead, therefore, I will adopt the nominal cognate of the verb, and simply say that different cultures, and different people within a culture, and one and the same person at different times, and indeed just about all distinct utterances, speak or talk or deal with the world *in different registers*. The idea is to suggest something like seeing the world in a different key, or of speaking in inexorably subscripted vocabularies. For example, part of the problem with specifying the content of a frog's representation of a fly, alluded to in chapter 1, is that most of us theorists, as I would put it, have trouble (to put it mildly) "speaking in a frog's register."

Some of these last connotations will surface in later discussion. For the moment, it is enough to summarize three essential properties of this notion:

1. Registration is the net activity that leads to (what we theorists register as) a conception of, or take on, or intentional attitude towards, the world as given or available—anyway, as *world*.

2. Registration is originally neutral as to the appropriate locus, if any, of two essential subject/world splits: (i) that between registrar (subject) and what is registered (object), and (ii) that between subject and supporting community (people, instruments, practices, documents, culture, etc.).

---

[9] See Davidson (1974) for an analysis of its not being well explicated.

3. Registration does not single out objects as a premier ontological category or class—or even, necessarily, require that objects count as a distinct ontological species.

From this characterization, it looks, at least on the surface, as if,
of the three properties initially identified as characteristic of objects—objectivity, particularity, and individuality—only the
first (objectivity) is a necessary condition of registration in general. But since looks can be famously deceiving, it should be considered an open question as to how much, and in what form, the
other two properties, of particularity and individuality, are essential to registration. By way of an initial hint, note the following striking duality: what in chapter 4 I called *feature-placing*
would appear, at least at first blush, to involve: particularity but
not individuality (+PARTICULARITY, −INDIVIDUALITY) in, as it
was said, the metaphysical arrangements that made the feature-
placing sentence true—e.g., in the actual rain; but individuality
and not particularity (−PARTICULARITY, +INDIVIDUALITY),
i.e., exactly the converse, in the abstract feature thereby placed.

2 Flex and slop

Here is where we stand. I started out the project, in chapter 4, by
splitting the notion of an object into two orthogonal concepts:
of individuality and particularity. I then argued that physics
supplied a picture of world-extensive cosmic particularity, but
was of no help with respect to individuality. Given that result, I
temporarily took up the (physicalist-seeming) project of seeing
how a notion of individuality could arise on a substrate of fields
of particularity. For methodological reasons I forswore a sharp
subject/object distinction along the way, but since that meshes
with a sympathy, betrayed much earlier, for the constructive intuition that objects emerge collaboratively from subject-object
interaction, that will turn out to be not as much of a felt restriction as it might otherwise have been.

Now the topic has been widened, from individuals to registration more generally. So the question on the table can be broken into two parts: (i) how does *registration* arise on a substrate of infinitely extensive fields of pure particularity; and (ii) how, and in what ways, is the registration of objects a distinct species?

And with that, finally, we are ready to start assembling a positive picture.

How to start? With this observation: that it is essential to the picture developed so far, and also an anchor of common sense, that the multi-various parts of the world do not march in lockstep together. The world is fundamentally characterized by an underlying flex or slop—a kind of slack or "play" that allows some bits to move about or adjust without much influencing, and without being much influenced by, other bits. Thus we can play jazz in Helsinki, as loud as we please, without troubling the Trappists in Montana. Moths can fly into the night with only a minimal expenditure of energy, because they have to rearrange only a tiny fraction of the world's mass. An idea can erupt in Los Angeles, turn into a project, capture the fancy of hundreds of people, and later subside, never to be heard of again, all without having any impact whatsoever on the goings-on in New York.

The world's flex and slop is so obvious that it is a little hard to talk about. As a contrast, therefore, imagine a world quite unlike ours, consisting, as suggested in figure 6·1, of nothing but an endless series of interlocked gears. Suppose, to make this precise, that every gear is constructed so as to mesh with one or more immediate neighbors, and that the entire gear universe is interconnected, but in such a way that it is still possible for them all to be turned—i.e., so that it does not lock up. Suppose, too, that the gears are perfect: no friction, no play between the teeth, and shaped so that rotating one at an even speed causes the others to rotate evenly as well, though at a potentially different speed.[10]

---

[10]In our world, so-called "constant-velocity" gears must slip against each other, and therefore have more friction than non-slip ones (requiring better oil).

One could even arrange to have an indefinitely large number of gears with relatively-prime numbers of teeth, so as to obtain a geometrically unbounded configuration space.

The gear world would lack slop. Effects would not dissipate. If one gear were to move by even a tiny amount, every other gear in the universe, no matter how far flung, would instantly and proportionally be affected.[11] Admittedly, amplified (but still non-representational) long-distance effects are possible in our world, too. That is why, famously, it is just remotely possible for a butterfly in Tokyo, with a single flap of its wings, to wreak havoc on New York's weather. Yet even if this were to happen, in our world such effects take time. And anyway, that is not how things normally work, and certainly not in this regimented and predictable way. Even if we were to discover that every macroscopically observable regularity was the product of such amplified long-distance effects of microdisturbances, it would still be true that far and away the majority of microdisturbances quickly die away. In our world, especially to the extent that we find it coherent, effects by and large dissipate. Think $1/r^2$.

FIGURE 6·1   THE GEAR WORLD

Overall, my aim in this book is to show that the world's primordial flex or play does two crucial things: (i) establishes the problem that intentionality solves; and (ii) provides the wherewithal for its solution. 'Problem' and 'solve' are prohibitively expensive words, of course; no reader should take them seriously.

---

[11] I have phrased this as if there would be time and distance in the gear world, but that is almost surely false. We claim that there is no action at a distance, but that gets it backwards. *Distance is what there is no action at.*

Nor is this the only poetic license I will take. In order to convey an intuitive picture of the relationship between slop and registration, I want to set the irreductionist principle aside, temporarily, and speak in terms of fully constituted, and thus highly expensive, objects, properties, and subjects, too—in spite of having just gone to such work to forswear them. Think of this as a temporary puppet show: as a band of marionettes being held up, not quite invisibly, with strings reaching up into the hidden recesses of the theorist's registration scheme. Though in one sense pure artifice, what is played out on stage can still unleash true imaginings about the genuine article. And anyway the show will not last long. As soon as a sense of the choreography has been conveyed, it will be important to start to untie the strings, and watch as the cast of characters learns to stand up and dance on their own.

Go back, then, to the flex or slop. Here is the problem. Because of the dissipative nature of the playing field, an enduring entity cannot, at any given moment, be affected by things that, at that same moment, are beyond what I will call *effective reach*. Effective reach is not a yes/no affair; rather, this is essentially the gradual falling off or dissipation of influence familiar from physics. Thus imagine standing on the Marin headlands looking at San Francisco, and slowly losing visual contact with the city as it is slowly engulfed in fog. The buildings only gradually fade from view, rather than vanishing instantaneously. Still, there comes a point where the effective illuminative coupling subsides below the level at which it can any longer do any work. Crucially, though, it does not follow that what is no longer within visual or tactile or other kind of effective reach is thereby rendered irrelevant. San Francisco still matters because of past connections, present interests, future possibilities. Effective connection will soon be re-established, too, when one rushes back to meet someone at Zuni's.

Moreover—and this is the essential point—when something is blocked from effective view, or removed from effective grasp, it is not thereby eliminated from one's thoughts. Intentional directedness is not held in place with physical glue. Long after the physical tie has been broken, or has stretched too thin to hold anything together, or has aged so much that it has become brittle and cracked and yellow, the semantic relation tying a subject to their subject matter will persevere, far less battered by the buffeting of circumstances, far less deteriorated by the ravages of time.

The overall pattern of separation and subsequent re-engagement, with some form of non-effective coordination maintained through the interim, is an extraordinarily important aspect of the sustenance of registration. It happens at a relatively primitive level, as well. Consider a rabbit keeping a watchful eye on a prowling coyote. While the coyote remains in view, the rabbit's tracking system can rely on causal or effective coupling to keep track of it—by implementing what amounts to a simple servo mechanism reaching all the way from the coyote itself through the atmosphere into the rabbit's retina, and from there to the muscles controlling its eyes, head, and even legs.[12] But now suppose the coyote goes behind a rock. Effective coupling is broken, but that is not the end of the story. It is still "useful" (another expensive word) for the rabbit to keep the coyote's presence and approximate position in mind—for example, by continuing to look in the coyote's general direction, so as quickly to be able to re-establish visual contact should the coyote suddenly reappear. It is a simple strategy, but a very general one, and often very useful: *to stay oriented towards what is no longer effectively discriminable*.

More fancifully, imagine that a species of "super-sunflower" develops in California to grow in the presence of large redwoods. Suppose that ordinary sunflowers move heliotropically, as the

---

[12]Note that this closed servo mechanism is easiest to recognize as a *loop* if one does not register the boundary or individuality of either the rabbit or the coyote.

myth would have it, but that they stop or even droop when the sun goes behind a tree. Once the sun re-emerges, they can once again be effectively driven by the direction of the incident rays, lifting up their faces, and reorienting to the new position. But this takes time. Super-sunflowers perform the following trick: even when the sun disappears, they continue to rotate at approximately the requisite $\frac{1}{4}°$ per minute, so that the super-sunflowers are more nearly oriented towards the light when the sun reappears. Since in all likelihood the orientation will be imperfect, super-sunflowers, like the ordinary variety, will rely on servoing to re-establish the correct causal locking, as a way of fine-tuning their positions. But because they have a leg up on the competition, in those crucial few moments when the sun is first visible again, they get just that much more benefit from the incident rays. And flourish.

What distinguishes super-sunflowers is not the fact that they track the sun. Ordinary sunflowers do that. What is special is the fact that they track something *to which they are not effectively coupled*. This behavior, which I will call "non-effective tracking," is no less than the forerunner of semantics: a very simple form of effect-transcending coordination in some way essential to the overall existence or well-being of the constituted system.

One does not need biological examples, real or fanciful, to see coordination across separation in effective coupling. It is endemic to computation in even the simplest cases. Thus consider the use of error-correction codes in computer memory systems to guard against random errors due to radiation and other forms of material decay.[13] It is a straightforward exercise to design a circuit that takes as input 32 bits of data, and outputs a 6-bit code

---

[13] 'Bit rot,' a term used to explain why programs that worked at one time no longer work, refers not to this sort of material decay, but to the inexorable effect of ongoing changes and development in the operating system and environment and other aspects of the context in which a program runs. See the discussion of boundaries and identity conditions in §s 2 & 3 of chapter 11; also Smith (1994).

indicating how many of the original 32 bits are "on."[14] Suppose this circuit is used as indicated in figure 6·2, so that whenever a 32-bit word is sent to the memory subsystem, 38 bits are actually stored. Then, when a request to retrieve the word is received by the memory system, all 38 bits are read out from the actual store, and a symmetrical checking circuit ensures that the proper number of the original 32 bits remain on. If everything matches, the word is assumed to have survived correctly; if not, an error is signaled.[15]

It will be clear to anyone that the intent of this arrangement, at least at one level of description, is for the 6-bit code to remain coordinated with the corresponding 32-bits of data during the whole period of storage. Less obvious, however, but only because it is logically prior—i.e., because it is such a basic assumption underlying the whole situation that we do not tend to

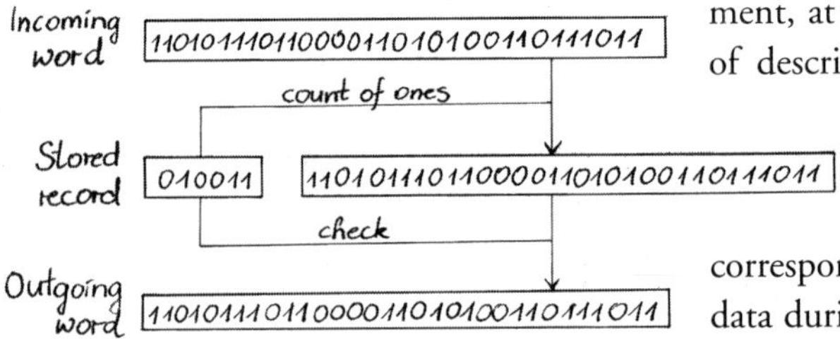

Incoming word | 11010111011000011010100110111011

count of ones

Stored record | 010011 | 11010111011000011010100110111011

check

Outgoing word | 11010111011000011010100110111011

FIGURE 6·2   SIMPLE ERROR CORRECTION CIRCUIT

---

[14] Surprisingly, six error bits are needed, not five, because there are 33 different possibilities (0–32), not 32.

[15] Real-world error correction codes are much more sophisticated than this. Not only will they detect multiple-bit errors; they can also correct them. Even more impressively, they can do so symmetrically. Thus on some computers (the DEC-20 was an early example) it is possible to remove any memory module from the machine, while it is running, and the machine will continue on without error—using the "information" encoded in the remaining modules to compensate for the loss. A similar strategy is employed in so-called "RAID" (redundant array of inexpensive disks) storage systems, in which a failure of any individual disk can be compensated for by information retained on the others. Compact disks (CDs) push correction technology in another direction: they are designed to be able to survive the loss of massive errors—hundreds of bits in a row—so that even in the presence of fingernail scratches the band can play on.

think about it explicitly—is the fact that the 6-bit code should remain *effectively separated* from the 32-bits during storage. It would not do, after all, for the 6 bits to be *invariably* correlated with the 32 bits, locked in nomologically by causal laws, like the gears in the gear world. If that were true, and a cosmic ray accidentally altered one of the data bits, the code would *automatically be updated*, rendering the entire scheme useless.

The situation is similar to that of the super-sunflower. First, code and data are effectively coupled; that is necessary to drive the original circuit. But then the two are crucially pulled apart —sufficiently separated so that effects to one (such as radiation or impurities in the magnetic material) do not affect the other. Separation means flex, in other words; the *point* of the arrangement is to allow the data, at least potentially, to flop around under some external influence without disturbing the code. Then, when the word is read, what was temporarily separated is brought back into contact in order to ensure that the coordination between the two has been maintained.

At an only slightly more complex level, consider file caches. Once again, they are governed by an interlocked pair of normative criteria. The one that normally occupies our attention is the condition that the cached version remain coordinated with the version on disk. Again, however, it is equally important, if easier to implement, for the cached version to be effectively separated from the one on disk, so that causal access to the former does not automatically engender causal access to the latter. If the second criterion were violated, the cache would be correct but useless, because it would not be able to run any faster than the disk version. As it happens, the coordination conditions are more complicated than in the memory system, because of the dynamics. Although perfect correspondence is required over the long haul, temporary misalignment can often be tolerated (e.g., in caches that do not implement what is called "write-through"), so long as care is expended to ensure that systems using the cache cannot detect the difference.

In all these situations, what starts out as effectively coupled is gradually pulled apart, but separated in a such a way as to honor a non-effective long-distance coordination condition, leading eventually to effective reconnection or reconciliation. There is a great deal more to intentionality than that, and a great deal to say about what constitutes coupling, coordination, and so on, but in various forms these notions of connection, gradual disconnection, maintenance of coordination while disconnected or separated, and ultimate reconnection or reconciliation permeate all kinds of more sophisticated example. There is nothing more basic to intentionality than this pattern of coming together and coming apart, at one moment being fully engaged, at another point being separated, but separated—this is the point —in such a way as to stay coordinated with what at that moment is distal and beyond effective reach.

Throughout, too, it is easy to see how the flex and slop are implicated. To start with, they underwrite the very notion of separation—and hence of connection, disconnection, and the limits of effective reach. If, as in the gear world, there were no flex, there would be no warrant for saying that two parts of the world had come apart. In fact there would probably be no warrant for saying that the world had parts at all, and certainly no warrant for saying that any two parts were far away from each other. Furthermore, exactly because of this slop, it is not automatic that the proximal system will stay synchronized with what is distal. This is why I said at the outset that there is a sense in which slop "establishes the problem" of intentionality.

It is an extraordinarily important consequence of this slop, moreover, that the proximal system can relatively easily adjust its own state (i.e., with modest energy expenditures, like the moth) without having to drag much of the surrounding territory with it. This is how slop provides the wherewithal for intentionality's solution (in more familiar language, it is the reason that computation is cheap). The trick, then—again, in some sense a simple strategy, but a very general one—is for the proximal system to exploit this local freedom in order to adjust itself in ways that establish or maintain a coordinating regularity with (at least part of) that from which it is separate.

The same primordial slop implies that this coordination will in general be approximate. It also implies, as I will argue later, that coordination can settle on some but not all aspects of the distal situation.[16] Even if coordination is inexorably approximate, however, it is important to note that the fact that it is possible at all puts conditions back onto the metaphysical nature of the slop itself.

If the flex were too little, as we have already seen, the world would lock up like the gear world, and everything would be correlated with everything else. Such a world would be too rigid, too straight, too stuffy; intentionality would be neither possible nor necessary. If the flex were too great, on the other hand, it would have the opposite problem: things would be too loose, everything would be random, and effect-transcending coordination would be impossible. Imagine, for example, an infinite space randomly occupied by an indefinitely large number of particles, all of which drift aimlessly around, none of which ever interact. Such a world would not have enough structure or regularity for there to be any metaphysical fact of the matter about whether these particles were of the same or different type—or even whether they were particles; it would be insufficiently regular for there to be anything coherent at all. But of course in our world we have neither problem. It is only because the world is *intermediately flexible* that there is anything like life as we know it.

---

[16]The coordinating regularity (what will ultimately become the semantic relation) and the coordinated-with regularity (what will ultimately become the type structure of the referent) will emerge together; they are not as ontologically independent as the phrasing in the text would imply.

The word 'play' is sometimes useful to describe both the world's flex and the intentional behavior that deals with it—i.e., to connote something crucially intermediate between chaos and rigidity. There must be some degree of habit or pattern or at least inchoate regularity in order for it to count as play. Yet play is neither itself, nor does it anywhere require, a straight-laced core of stringent formal rules. It lives—indeed emerges—in the middle, like a spontaneous dance, or like an improvisational session in jazz. It is as fundamental a fact as any about this metaphysics that it is based on an ineliminable notion of "playfulness"—a kind of irreducible, obstreperous, wily refusal ever to be formally captured and written down. Truly a metaphysics for Coyote. And just as a dance is not the property of one or other partner, or jazz the product of a single player, so play is not a feature of subject or object alone. As with so much in this vicinity, it is not even so much shared as it is prior to the distinction between them.[17]

That is not to say that there are not ways in which play is quite a misleading metaphor. For even if the world is unbearably light, there is nothing non-serious about these patterns of intentional coordination. Everything, it should be clear, is at stake.

Though massively too brief, this leads to the first characterization:

Intentionality is a way of exploiting local freedom or slop in order to establish coordination with what is beyond effective reach.

3 Disconnection

Because its raison d'être is to bridge gaps in effective coupling, it follows that registration, and intentionality more generally, are

---

[17] The notion of play being dealt with here stands in contrast to the much more rigid, as I would spell it, "Play" that underlies formal game theory, the notion that has historical connections with the rise of our current notions of digital computation. See Franchi (forthcoming·b). See also Haraway (1991), pp. 199 & 201, for discussion of Coyote as a symbol of irreducible metaphysical wiliness.

not effective phenomena. This will have methodological consequences. If intentionality is not a causal phenomenon, for example, it follows that it will not have a causal explanation.

This is a strong statement, but it is not the strongest statement I will make. In the wings lies another, even stronger: that objects, too, are not causal—and thus that no theory that traffics in objects will ever be entirely causal. In fact it will turn out that *no* theory is entirely causal. In a sense it should already be clear why. If what it is to be an object is in part to be constituted by regularities in which intentional subjects are participants (a thesis that was advertised or at least admitted in chapter 3, and which will presently be claimed and defended), and if intentionality requires distance and non-effective coordination, then it follows that all stories about objects, and indeed all stories in toto (since the point holds of registration, ultimately, not solely of objects) will inherently trade, more or less explicitly, in non-effective regularities.

This is all fine, from my point of view. I see no reason to suppose that anything important is thereby given up (for more details see the "causation and effectiveness" sidebar on page 210). On the other hand, independent of one's reaction to the proposal, the non-effective nature of intentionality should be perfectly familiar, especially on what is taken to be the semantical side of the story.

Thus consider what in contrast to effective reach (that near- and far-engendering bumping and shoving of the physical substrate) I will instead call the *semantic* or *intentional reach* of all registrational phenomena—the fact that, as I have been saying since the beginning, as intentional acts, they are directed, in Brentano's sense, towards something above and beyond themselves. The fact that registration reaches towards something paradigmatically other is an essential component in achieving the transcendent aspect of objectivity. The most impressive thing

Causation and effectiveness

It is claimed in the text that intentionality is not a causal phenomenon, and will not have a causal explanation, and, even more strongly, that objects are also non-causal, and will similarly not have causal explanations. Strictly speaking, this is only true to the extent that 'causal' means 'effective.' The real claims are that intentionality is not an *effective* phenomenon, and will not have an *effective* explanation, and similarly that objects are non-*effective*, and will not have effective explanations.

In TMD·III I argue that the "theories of computation" mentioned in chapter 1—i.e., a rough amalgam of the theory of effective computability, recursion theory, complexity theory, and the like—are not, in fact, theories of computation at all, because they do not deal with computation's inherently intentional character. What they *are* are mathematical theories of effectiveness, simpliciter. If effectiveness could be simply defined in terms of something else, this body of work would not be as important as it is. The way to understand it, I think, is to say that this large body of (mostly twentieth-century) work has recognized, and converged on, effectiveness as a fundamental metaphysical category.

What does that have to do with causation? Who knows, exactly? It is hard to say anything *exact* about causation, for one thing, and I claim no special insight or expertise on such a famously recalcitrant notion. I would guess, however, that the answer will be this: that what in ordinary language we mean by 'cause' (and thus 'causal') will not succumb to intellectual or scientific reconstruction, but that this recent (as it were, computational) formulation of a theory of effectiveness will eventually be regarded as its substantial scientific reformulation. There is another possibility, though: that causation is, in chapter 5's sense, a *material*, rather than a physical *or* effective, notion, and in that form will be retained.

about it is its extraordinary span: the fact that it so strikingly unconstrained by the limits of physical connection. Browning's adage that one's reach should exceed one's grasp[18] may be a difficult injunction to meet, morally or psychologically, but there is

[18] Browning's "Andrea del Sarto" (1855), l. 97.

a sense in which it is accomplished by every intentional act of registration. That semantic reach exceeds effective grasp is essentially a theorem of this metaphysical account.

By way of contrast, consider laser beams. They reach a long way, too—to the moon and back, for example, allowing us to measure precisely how far away the moon is. So do radio waves; we are just now picking up signals that were emitted by now-distant quasars only shortly after the beginning of time. But in terms of reach these phenomena do not hold a candle to reference. With a few simple syllables we can reach backwards in time, against the flow of causality, to the Pharaohs of Egypt. Or reach forward, to things that have not yet happened, such as the election of the first female U.S. president. Or to Pluto, without having to wait five or six hours for our reference to succeed. Or to Huckleberry Finn, without even needing our referent to exist. "Reference," Alonzo Church once said, "travels at the speed of logic."[19] And that is just the beginning of its mysterious powers. It also goes where reality fears to tread.

This fundamental *disconnection*, which I am taking to be essential to all registration, explains why being referred to is not physically detectable—e.g., why not even the National Security Agency, with all the money in the world, could build a meter to register when the control room in Cheyenne Mountain was the subject matter of a terrorist's intentional act. Indeed, intentionality's disconnection is so basic that it is impossible to imagine its being false. Error would be eliminated, but so would abstraction. Hypotheticals would be impossible; fantasy lives would be metaphysically banned. You could not even think about continental drift without dragging the tectonic plates along with you.

Although I have forsworn a sharp representation/ontology boundary, these examples of disconnection, in part in order that they can tap into traditional (predecessor) intuitions, have all been taken from the semantical side of the equation. Since, as I

[19]Public lecture, Stanford Center for the Study of Language and Information, May 3, 1984.

presume has been implicit throughout, I am going to take registration to be the ultimate subject matter, and therefore will not swear allegiance to a sharp representational/ontological split, it follows that anything true of semantics—i.e., of intentionality—will also and indissolubly be true of objects. Even if it is not as clear why, that is, this essential distance-transcending disconnection is in fact just as much a truth of ontology as it is of semantics.

It would be happier overall, however, to be able to tap accessible intuitions leading to the same conclusion, rather than having to argue for such a strong conclusion on what amount to relatively abstract grounds. And once the point is grasped, I believe, there is no dearth of supporting intuitions. A glimmer of one can be seen, for example, by noting how an ordinary and uncontentious property of individuals betrays their non-exclusively physical character. Part of the "gathering together as a unity" that is constitutive of an object's being an object is a *temporal* gathering—the fact that objects, by and large, endure over time. Physics, however, is intrinsically ahistorical: there is no action at temporal distance; no dependence at time **t**+1 on how the world was at time **t**-1 unless that effect is propagated through time **t**. That alone is enough to imply that being an object *cannot be a physically effective property*, since there is no way in which a temporally extended object could have a physical effect distinct from that of a non-temporally-extended instantaneous time-slice of that object. This is yet another reason to support chapter 5's contention that physics is not ontologically committed to individual objects.

In the end, this point will underwrite the entire story of registration. Abstraction, essential to the notion of an object, is like semantic reach in being physically transcendent.

What, then, do the long-distance patterns of coordination come to—and how do they arise? How do intentionality, registration, and objects take shape on the underlying playing fields?

To answer this question—even to point towards an answer —requires dismantling the puppet show. It is time to get rid of the objects, time to tell the story without the registration of any individuals. But how then is it possible to proceed? We can hardly be asked to set aside all theoretic registration, after all. That would be an impossible standard—especially for a written text (it would be easier if we could have dinner). So the first task is to figure out what options are open to us—what metaphysical and ontological resources we can avail ourselves of.

This is where the rhetorical strategy announced in the last chapter, of adopting a vaguely physicalist or with-reference-to-physics approach, begins to pay off. The overall rhetorical situation, and our position within it, are pictured in figure 7·1. Chapter 4 argued that feature-placing, both intuitively and metaphysically, was a more primitive form of language use than language committed to objects, properties, and relations—and especially that it was simpler than formal languages committed to Objects, Properties, and Relations. That was because feature-placing did not require the individuation of discrete individuals, at least not at the "particular" level. In chapter 5, it was claimed that physics, at least on a field-theoretic interpretation, could (and perhaps should) be understood as an example of such feature-placing. In presenting the physical case, I focused on continuous phenomena, because continuous feature-placing is more obviously unlike objectification (registering in terms of discrete individuals) than discrete feature-placing, and is therefore less liable to be confused with it—though I said at the time, and still maintain, that this is more a matter of convenience than of substance.

With respect to the current goal of dismantling the puppet show, this means that even if we cannot let go of all registration, a substantial option nevertheless remains open to us. As indicated at point B in the figure, we can let go of individuals, and for the next while register the world in terms of (often, but not necessarily, continuous) particular fields. Since

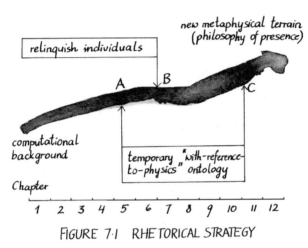

FIGURE 7·1   RHETORICAL STRATEGY

this strategy is more rhetorical than metaphysical, and is accompanied by no commitment to theory-reduction, there is no great need to worry about exactly what kinds of fields are allowed. I will therefore speak very informally about density gradients, simple space-time manifolds, and the like. Whenever it is convenient, moreover, I will let go of continuity assumptions, for example when drawing attention or analogies to turbulence and chaos.

Given this much apparatus, the aim in this and the next two chapters is to convey an intuitively accessible image of how individuation, registration, and the like might arise. Then, in chapter 11, with this feature-placing image held as firmly in mind as possible, I will let go of the physicalist props that have been used to support it, and—very quickly, before everything falls down —rearrange the assumptions underneath it, partly in order to set physics back into its proper place, but also, more importantly, in order to rest that temporarily unsupported image on a more long-term, tenable, metaphysical foundation. At that point, finally, the account will meet the requirements (about realism, pluralism, and objectivity) laid down in chapter 3.

1 Tracking

Start, then, first, with a simple case of visual tracking. Tracking, on this account, is not registration, because it is not appropriately disconnected. Or at least nothing is registration merely in virtue of tracking. Sometimes we both track and register, as for example when we consciously follow a bird's flight, or when we register a moving image on a television screen as the runner in a World Series game. By itself, though, simple tracking—by which I essentially mean no more than a causally-driven servo-loop—need not be accompanied by, and is by itself insufficient to support, this extra intentional baggage. Still, in spite of these caveats, tracking is a good example on which to gain experience in analyzing a simple situation without benefit of object registration (again, at least at the particular level)—and a far from random one. Even if tracking is not itself intentional, it is an important precursor to some of the simplest forms of behavior that are.

To be specific, therefore, and to develop some concrete intuitions, consider a frog tracking a fly.[1] Except now register the situation without any individuals or boundaries. In the spatio-temporal region of the fly, there is a differential density mass with a complex internal structure. For simplicity, suppose that a

---

[1] Strictly speaking, frogs do not track—at least not in the sense of moving their eyes (except to compensate for overall motion, as for example when sitting on an unstable lily pad). That does not really matter, here, since the point of the example is purely pedagogical, but anyway it is not *eye*-tracking that is my concern, but *attention*-tracking—or, even more minimally, the existence of some circuitry to respond to the shadow of potential prey moving across the retina, so as to orient the flicking of the tongue. And that capacity I take it frogs have.

roughly even spatially distributed flux of electromagnetic radiation (constant illumination) flows into the region. In the patch of higher mass density, various reflections and obstructions cause a local disturbance in the radiation pattern. Some of this (reflected) radiation, after making its way through an intermediating region of air, impinges on what we are tempted to register as the frog's retina. But of course there is no frog, yet, nor any retina—merely hills and valleys and spikes and skews in the various relevantly oriented feature fields, corresponding to the fly, the frog, the focusing properties of the eye, and so forth.

If, as theorists, we look in the vicinity of the frog's retina, but let go of any tendency to register objects, we can see (what amounts to a local projection of) a patch of disturbance, extended in both space and time. If we temporarily hold time still and examine a spatial region (i.e., focus on a region on the retina), we see a local distribution of activity—an increased or decreased level of nerve firings in the center, dropping back to a background level in those parts of the retina that are outside the area of disturbance. By the same token, if instead we hold space constant and watch over a period of time (i.e., study the activity at a given retinal position for a moment), we see something structurally homologous: a welling up or welling down of activity while the "fly" passes, subsiding to a level corresponding to the background, as the fly goes on by.[2]

As said earlier, this localized pattern of activity does not count as even inchoate registration, because it is a phenomenon of pure "connection." Still, it carries an important moral. A property we ultimately associate with both subject and object —that of a boundary or edge—is in the first instance *a property of their interaction*. What we register as the edge of the fly (strictly speaking, the two-dimensional projection of its three-

---

[2] The levels may be inverted, of course: less activity when coupled to the fly, more when coupled to the background. It does not matter to the argument; and anyway it is not clear that we have enough machinery to discriminate the two.

dimensional boundary tangential to the direction of illumination) corresponds directly to an "edge" of a very important column: a column of differential energy levels in the incident flood of frog-directed electromagnetic radiation, which corresponds in turn, through all the mediating mechanisms of physical coupling, to an edge of an impulse or differentiable region of energy in the retinal circuits in the frog.

The crucial point to see is that this transient welling-up of activity or difference—this local extended impulse in the manifold of sustaining physical fields—is columnar in shape, cutting at right angles to the frog-fly boundary. It is solid, too: a continuous physical disturbance, made up of a variety of kinds of material reaching all the way from retina to fly. To repeat: it is not yet bipartite. As observers we tend to chop it into two non-adjacent material parts: one out at the fly, another in the frog's eye. That is, we tend to view the mediating air as *conceptually* as well as *optically* transparent—as if it were as evacuated of theoretical significance as it is of light-obstructing material. But the transparency of air is of course not yet a "fact" for the emerging participatory scene. Indeed, the patterns of electromagnetic radiation in the air are just as thick and real as the electrical signals coming off the retina—and not yet obviously distinct from them, especially given that they are fashioned of the same (electrical) material. Indeed, as was said in the introduction, how it is that we and perhaps frogs see flies, not electromagnetic radiation, is the registration problem in a nutshell. So it is vital not to build its achievement into our conception of the initial situation. That would be a classic case of pre-emptive inscription error. Gibson was too mild: it is not just that we do not represent the tree; we are not even distinct from the tree, at least not at first.

And so the initial boundaries or edges that allow the frog to see the fly as fly—or at least allow the frog to see the fly as whatever it sees it as, i.e., in its own register—are what theory will eventually call *relational*. These boundaries matter, too; it is no

accident that edge detectors are among the first neuronal circuits to get into the registrational act. Except that to call them
edge *detectors* is both misleading and expensive. It is expensive
because it describes the situation in terms dangerously close to
the structure of the solution ('detect' being a fully intentional
word). It is misleading because all we have, so far, is a causal loop
involving subject and environment. Without further patterns of
disconnected coordination, there is no justification for invoking
the heavy language of detection—or, for that matter, for saying
that the frog *sees* anything at all. To register the circuitry in the
frog's eye as an edge detector, without paying its cost, is to over-
interpret the situation. It hides the fact that the mechanism simply involves *more accreted boundary*.

Even more specifically, consider the otherwise ordinary-
sounding claim that an edge detector in the frog's retina is *fired*
or *triggered* by the edge of the image of the fly. For a theorist to
register a frog's neuronal activity in that way is to commit to a
coincidence of three boundaries: (a) that between quiescence
and firing, being triggered or not, in the contended mechanism
in the frog (on or off); (b) the corresponding edge of the fly (*being fly*, and *not being fly*, in the mass density region several feet in
front of the frog); and (c) the edge of the intermediating pattern
of directed electromagnetic radiation. But then, once one realizes that no warrant has yet been provided for separating these
three boundaries, one sees that what is really going on is best
understood in purely field-theoretic terms: there is a single common edge to a columnar-shaped multimedia disturbance that
reaches continuously between (what we register as) frog and
(what we register as) fly.

Furthermore, if, in spite of this recommendation, one were to
insist on a discrete registration of these retinal mechanisms, it
would be more accurate and more modest, at least in the first instance, to call them edge *participators*, rather than edge *detectors*.
For they manifest just this simple property: the edges of their

own activity are aligned with, in virtue of being connected to — wired or plugged into or effectively coupled with — the edges of the target entities towards which the systems of which they are part will ultimately be said to be directed. The situation is much closer to that of a sports jacket than to that of recognition. It would be bizarre to say that your jacket "detects" your motion — even though, sure enough, it changes state in a way that is lawfully correlated with your motion. It changes state subject to the constraints of overarching physical law because it is *connected* to you — by coming along with you. So too of retinal activity and flight of fly.

Moreover, what is true of edges (difference) is equally true of stability (sameness). Think of perceptual invariants. In the first instance they too are invariants of neither the ultimate subject nor the ultimate object. They are invariances of *coupled interaction*. Again consider simple tracking. The object moves, the subject moves, a constant relation between the two is maintained. Except now relinquish the registration in terms of objects — i.e., put on your field-theoretic glasses — and look only at the wells of stability in the otherwise seething mass of activity. As before, the important stability lies *across* the boundary that will ultimately be drawn between subject and object.

2 Separation

Simple effective "tracking" — a misnomer, of course[3] — is an instructive case in which to exercise one's skills at visualizing non-individuated patternings of structure. With respect to the substantive question on the table, however, regarding the rise of registration, there are two problems: (i) ontologically, proto-subject and proto-object are insufficiently distinct; and (ii) physically, they are insufficiently separate. Neither, therefore, yet counts as an object. It will be rhetorically helpful, therefore, to refer to them as *s-region* and *o-region* respectively. Even though

---

[3]It is a misnomer because in the simple effective case there is not enough effect-spanning coordination to legitimate the term 'tracking.'

'region' is a count noun, and so may be said to have singular reference, these phrases are not strongly individualist in connotation (i.e., do not strongly signify boundaries), and so may be of some help in guarding against pre-emptive inscription.

Imagine, then, to consider a simple case of separation, the rabbit, mentioned earlier, at the instant when the coyote it is watching disappears from view. We have already seen how the tracking can, up until that point, be physically driven by the object being tracked. The causal flow—or rather, as it would be better to say, the *flow of effect*—reaches out from rabbit to coyote and back (except for the standard comment that, at the level at which the effective feedback is maintained, there is neither rabbit, coyote, nor boundary—just a feedback loop maintaining a pool of stability in the midst of the flux).

But now, suddenly, the coyote vanishes, and the causal loop is broken. In order to maintain coordination, it is *suddenly incumbent on the rabbit to take over responsibility for keeping "focused" on the coyote.* An internal mechanism has to compensate for what can no longer be relied on to be effectively provided by the environment. In a similar way, the super-sunflower, when it can no longer be driven by the incident radiation, has to employ a different, internal mechanism (some form of chemical drip, or whatever) in order to continue to "track" the sun.

This *retraction* of responsibility into the s-region, as I will call it—this shouldering of effective responsibility by the s-region, to compensate for the break in effective coupling—is no less than the origin of reasoning, representation, and syntax: the effective projection, onto the intentional agent, of the requisite arrangements for maintaining long-distance (semantic) coherence. The break for which it compensates is not a yes/no affair, of course, and so it would be better to use more gradualist language. The point, though, is that, as connection thins out, as it did with the view of San Francisco when the fog thickened, and the o-region recedes from effective reach, responsibility for

Memory and prediction

The examples used to illustrate disconnection in the text are primarily spatial, involving one mechanism (plant, animal, etc.) adjusting its state in order to stay coordinated with a contemporaneous phenomenon that is at the moment out of effective reach—i.e., is too far away to lock onto, causally. But as usual, what is true spatially is also true temporally. Because of physics' ahistoricity, any form of long-distance temporal coordination, either forward in time (prediction) or backwards in time (memory) will similarly involve a degree of disconnection.

Thus consider a simple case of prediction. In order to know now, at time t_1, what is likely to happen in the future, at time t_2, it is not possible to be effectively (causally) driven by the relevant t_2 state of affairs. To do that would either require waiting until t_2, which by hypothesis would be too late, or else depend on some form of backwards-in-time causation, contrary to physical law. Instead, one must *predict*, which involves the same sort of retraction described in the text: a shouldering of effective responsibility by the s-region in order to develop or construct local and current (i.e., *present*) structures standing in coordinated relation to phenomena that are still temporally remote.

The same holds of memory. A memory can be created in virtue of effective coupling, but it cannot be sustained—"held up"—by relying on that coupling, because the driving situation will soon go away. In order to make a memory more durable than a shadow, an s-region or subject must first allow or arrange for an appropriate impression to be formed by the event in question, but must then take responsibility for storing it in such a way as to ensure that it will continue to be effective after the event it records has dissipated. As described in chapter 8, the memory may also need to be updated appropriately, as circumstances relevant to its contextually-dependent content change, in order for it to continue, over the long haul, to signify what is no longer present.

maintaining coordination has to be retracted from the region of interaction onto the body of the s-region. Imagine, to get a feel for this, that the coordinative structure is made of silly putty stretched into some complex shape between two ends, which is then pulled apart, more and more, until it snaps. At the crucial moment, when it "lets go," a bunch of the putty that had been stretched out in the middle, between the objects, would suddenly spring back and pile up at the end. So it is with the structural responsibility for maintaining long-distance coordination. Separation between s-region and o-region is necessary for registration. (Not having it is like looking at something too closely; you have to back away, have to get enough distance, in order for an image of something as something to snap into place.) But at the same time the separation exacts a cost that the s-region must pay. What will end up being subject must make up for the fact that the now-disconnected o-region can no longer be relied on to hold up its part of the bargain, its part of the dance.

As soon as this happens, moreover, an array of properties characteristic of all registration is exhibited. Even in these elementary cases of non-effective tracking, in other words, with their relatively unsophisticated forms of coordination, features that govern much more complex cases gain an initial toehold.

First, because of the break in effective coupling, and the concomitant retraction of responsibility for maintaining coordination onto the s-region, a distinction takes hold between *what the s-region is doing* (tracking the coyote or incident sunlight) and *how it is doing it*.[4] The former gets at a non-effective regularity; the latter, at an effective mechanism whose "job" is to implement or sustain it. Among other things, this split provides a toehold for normativity to attach its tentacles.

---

[4] I have not yet justified the claim that the rabbit really is tracking the coyote, on an intentional reading of 'tracking.' The point is only that if it is tracking the coyote, which will depend on the nature and existence of various other patterns of coordination, to be described below, then the break in effective coupling unleashes this familiar explanatory split.

Second, there is suddenly the possibility for error. Because of the underlying slop, there is no reason to guarantee—and every reason to doubt—that the retracted mechanism will be able to mimic perfectly the distal regularity with which it is "striving" to maintain alignment, with which it is striving to remain registered. (Except in rare formal cases, the idea that syntax can perfectly mirror semantics is a nostalgic modernist ideal.) The problem is that the underlying flex eliminates any guarantee of alignment with what is distal. The rabbit has no way to be absolutely sure of what the coyote is doing. The super-sunflower case is a little different: the progression of celestial bodies is astonishingly regular, as it happens, which is why such accurate noneffective solar trackers can be built. But it is unlikely that any sunflower would have access to such precise mechanisms. And anyway the moral is very general: as separation increases, the chances of the s-region and o-region drifting part also increase, perhaps irretrievably. Nor is this a "new" fact, with its own metaphysical price. Being liable to drift apart is what separation is.

Third, the retraction of responsibility onto the s-region is the origin of registration's asymmetry and directedness. Note, by way of background, that an object's being an object is a collaborative affair, arising out of the registrational dance of subject and object (s-region and o-region). Logically, therefore, there is a sense in which subject and object are symmetrical in importance; neither can exist without the other. But I have never implied that the dance itself is symmetrical. On the contrary, registration is intrinsically asymmetrical and directed; it is what orients the subject towards the world (hence the use of a transitive verb). And already the origin of this asymmetry can be seen. For although the gap in effective coupling is symmetrical (if x is disconnected from y, then y is disconnected from x), *responsibility for maintaining coordination across the gap is asymmetrical*. It "falls to the s-region," one might say—except that gets it backwards. Rather: to be an s-region is to assume this re-

sponsibility. In higher cases the responsibility will assume infinitely more complex forms, but even in these aboriginal cases
registering—taking the world to be world—requires commitment.

Fourth, the example erroneously suggests that the mechanisms for coordinating with what is beyond effective reach must
be inside the s-region. This is obviously false. To maintain orientation towards an invisible sun, for example, one might establish
effective coupling with a local clock and rely on it to maintain
the long-distance synchronization. S-regions need the capacity
to track, in other words, but they need not, and generally will
not, do it alone. More generally, the "distance" over which the
s-region will be able to maintain coordination will depend on its
cleverness—not just its internal cleverness, but the total sophistication of the environmental and cultural resources on which it
can lay its hands. Maintaining coordination over vast distances,
putting in place mechanisms to "select" what is remote and to
"wash out" what is immediate, tracking the subtlest remote co-
ordinations in spite of extraordinary intermediate upheaval—
these are no less than the role of instruments, skills, theories,
inference, and civilization.

3 Stabilization   *(or: How can I miss you, if you won't go away?)*
I have tried to sketch a way in which an s-region can compensate
for separation from the o-region. But there is still a problem.
The described non-effective tracking mechanisms still suffice
only to maintain perceptual invariants: quietened, somewhat
abstract (though still particular), deictic "relations between subject and object." They *compensate* for the effective separation,
and thus succeed in maintaining relational stability. But they do
not yet *exploit* the separation—and thus do nothing to stabilize
the object as an object (or as anything else, for that matter). Im-

portant as non-effective tracking is, in other words, it is too simple, on its own, to yet count as intentional.[5]

The challenge for the s-region is to exploit the separation in order to *push the relational stability out onto the world*. In order to register an o-region as an object, that is, it is not enough for the s-region to move in synchrony with the o-region, even if that synchrony transcends physical coupling. Pointwise synchronization is just (so-called) perceptual invariance, as described above; to maintain it is just to stabilize the relation between s-region and o-region relation. To register, the s-region must do more: it must play with the relation, even at the cost of a certain amount of destabilization, so as to stabilize the far end. That is, the s-region must "sediment" or "extrude" the o-region as a discrete autonomous individual (at least partially distinct from the s-region) and thereby locate it in the wider world. *It is the o-region itself, in other words, not the relation to the object, that must be "held" in at least partial stasis.*

Doing this requires *detachment*. The s-region must "let go" of the o-region, in a very special sense of letting go: push it away, make it separate from itself. Trying to register an o-region to which you are fully coupled is like trying to see something plastered up against your eyeball. Or like holding onto a jack hammer for dear life. Or like having an insecure sycophant fall in love with you. To be welded to an object like that means being buffeted by its every vibration or variation or whim. Lacking the requisite distance to gather up and "hold" the object as a stable

[5] Though non-effective tracking can and likely will figure as an essential constituent in a larger system that is intentional.

There is something very Gibsonian about this picture: though he would say "represent" instead of "register," the point is very similar. Looming, for example—the "perceptual" phenomenon whereby an approaching object, such as a wall, casts an expanding image on the retina that is "decoded" by special-purpose circuits that play a direct role in engendering avoidance behavior, and the like—counts neither as symbolic representation for Gibson, nor as registration, for me.

unity, the s-region and o-region are instead (even if only temporarily) liable to fuse, causing both to disappear. Bringing an object into intentional "focus" is thus not only a way of coping
with gaps in effective connection; it *requires* gaps in effective
connection. The object requires these gaps, in order to settle
into being what it is, distinct from the subject, with at least a partial degree of existential independence or autonomy. And the
subject requires the gaps, too, to say nothing of a modicum of its
own autonomy or independence, *in order to register the object as
a unitary whole.* Separation—keeping things at arm's length—
allows the relation between subject and object to relax.

Separation per se is not very interesting, of course. We are effectively disconnected from virtually everything in the world,
without thereby registering any of it. Rocks are pretty disconnected, too, and they do not register at all. The issue is what
one does with one's separation—what one makes of one's
"aloneness." The trick, and it is a considerable trick, is to arrange
oneself appropriately, and dynamically, *so that the surrounding
world remains present.* By exploiting the local slop, one must arrange one's own effective structure so as to maintain coordination across the break in coupling. If done just right, one can let
go of the world without losing directedness and orientation.
More strongly: it is exactly by letting go while retaining appropriate directedness and orientation that the world "comes into
presence."

The key to this coordination, and the importance of the detachment, can be found in an remark made in chapter 4 (§1c):
that an essential act of abstraction underwrites the existence of
every individual. As was said then, taking an object as an *individual* means gathering up an extended region of the flux and
treating it as a unity. This implies that the subject must stand in
relation to what is the *same* or *in common* across the constitutive
spatial and temporal region, and by the same token must ignore
or set aside the multitudes of internal variation attendant to its

Abstraction and error

Note the intimate relation between the processes of abstraction described in the text and the aforementioned possibility of error implicit in the underlying slop. If you are not going to be able to maintain coordination with various details of the separated object, it makes sense to set those details aside. In that way an inability to track them does not eventuate in *failure*; it merely eventuates in loss of detail. It is a good thing that we have a registration of Pompeii that abstracts away from the question of exactly how many people lived there at various times, since we would otherwise be unable to register it at all.

In spite of this convenience, however, it should not be thought that the ability to abstract is a compromise, a good way of accepting limitations. A far more important fact, yet to be dealt with, is that there are regularities—stabilities—that can *only be established at these higher levels of abstraction*. This fundamental fact provides the metaphysical warrant for the so-called "special sciences," to say nothing of vitiating reductionism and validating pluralism.

parts, or across its life. When I register that passing swoosh as a hawk, I gather up its movements under a general notion of soaring, but insulate myself from the exact number of feathers, or the angle it makes with the sun. When you think of your brother's upcoming marriage, you think of him as a whole, not as a temporal cross-section, or even as a continuous evolving manifold of space-time points.

Abstraction, in other words, requires separation, in order that the s-region not be buffeted by irrelevant details. Moreover, it also imposes an important symmetric condition on the patterns of coordination. It is not enough for the s-region merely to abstract away from the excruciating particular in order to conceive of the o-region as an individual or unity or whole. In order to register the o-region as an individual, that is, it is not enough for the s-region to take the *object* to be extended (though that alone would be enough to implicate a certain amount of detachment). It is essential that the subject's own registrational state be extended as well. Subject and object must both be stabilized, in other words; both require extension. And not only that; *the two extensions must cross cut*. Each-to-each (piecewise coordination) is not enough; it must be each-to-all.

Consider an example. Today, when I think of you practicing in a loft in Vancouver, I think of a whole you, including the you that will be performing tomorrow. Tomorrow, when the concert is over, and I wonder how it went, I will again think of a whole you—including the you that sweated it out today. It would not be enough, in fact it would not count as thinking, if today I could only relate to the-you-of-today, and tomorrow could only relate to the-you-of-tomorrow. Or rather, more seriously, it would not be enough if at any particular instant, I could only relate to the-you-of-that-instant. Because there is no such thing as you-at-an-instant. You have inherent temporal extent.

Although both subject and object must be stabilized, the two stabilities cannot merely end up pointwise correlated, particular to particular, like a ruler laid down against a run of cloth. As depicted in figure 7·2, this kind of nomic (and instantaneous) pointwise correlation is how ordinary coupling in the underlying physical fields works; at any given instant, a region is impinged upon only by what surrounds it *right then*. Such is the inescapable implication of physics' ahistoricity. Only by making egregious inscription errors—i.e., by pre-emptively assuming object identities, and thereby taking out unpaid debts of temporal extendedness, as in the case of the cell in the cat's brain— could anyone imagine that intentional directedness (semantics) is anything like causal connectedness. "Sufficient unto the day is the evil thereof"[6] is curiously apt as a description of the physical world. For better or worse, but mostly for better, it cannot stand as a general characterization of registration.

[6]Matthew 6:34.

The cross-cutting nature of the extension of subject and object, in contrast, is reminiscent of Husserl's distinction between the temporality of perception and the perception of temporality, and even of Kant's distinction between the unity of consciousness and the consciousness of unity. That it is implicit in the very notion of an individual can be seen by understanding the topology of the notion of reidentification that is constitutive of being an individual (unless one can reidentify, one cannot identify —that was why reidentification was built into the initial characterization of what it was to be an individual).

Consider in particular what is involved in reidentifying at time t_2 an object x that was first identified at t_1. First, at t_1 the subject must be in such a state as to register the *whole* of x; if at t_1 it were only registering the t_1 slice of x, there would be no chance of *that* showing up again at t_2.[7] Second, at t_2 it must again register all of x, so as to be the same extended individual registered at t_1. As indicated in figure 7.3, both points in the subject extension have to span or cover the whole object extension (except that it is a mistake to think of them as "points"—see the sidebar on page 230). Third, the state of the subject at t_1 and the state at t_2 must themselves be stabilized into an enduring unit. Else there would be no warrant for the claim of *re*identification (this is the situation that was described in §4 of chapter 1). Mechanically, the stability of the subject can seem trivial, if one cheats by using unpaid-for registrations. It is the "same cell" that lights up, one says, or the "same name" that is used. Or perhaps the "same record" that was used

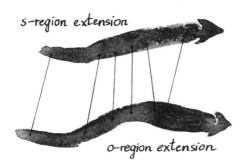

s-region extension

o-region extension

FIGURE 7.2   POINT-TO-POINT CORRELATION

---

[7] The text puts the problem *temporally*, but there is an exactly analogous spatial problem, as well: how it is that one sees a *tree*, not merely a two-dimensional presentation of leaf and bark.

229

Objects are not points

To treat an object *as* an object is (at least in part) to treat it as a unity, but that does not mean treating it as atomic—i.e., as if it lacked internal structure. Because of a common inscription error we are sometimes misled into thinking of (individual) objects as if they were "points"—so concentrated into unities as to become extensionless with respect to all relevant metrics of variation.

Thus consider figure 7·3, intended to show how states of an s-region at times t_1 and t_2 are each coordinated with the o-region as a whole. The drawing errs by suggesting that the states at t_1 and t_2 can be represented as points. As better suggested in figure 7·4, the true situation is that the cross-cutting extension mandate requires that *sub-regions* of the s-region correspond to the whole o-region—sub-regions constituting a single, whole or integral "thought" about, or act of reference to, the object. To put it in somewhat Kantian terms, the sub-regions of the s-region effect the (minimal) unity of registration; the o-region being corresponded to as a whole reflects the registration of unity. Neither will in general be atomic. Moreover, *there may be intrinsic structure in the finer-grained correspondence*, without challenge to the overarching intuition that a single thought about an object must comprehend that object in its entirety. Thus think of an apple falling from a tree. Sure enough, one can register the fall as a unity. But (at least for me), as long as one registers it as a *fall*, there is an intrinsic temporal extent to the nevertheless unitary thought—an extent that corresponds, topologically, with the temporality of the fall. Few of us, if any, can "think" or "register" a fall from bottom to top.*

Taking an object to be a point (i.e., taking 'unitary' to mean 'atomic' instead of 'integral' or 'indivisible') is a piggyback error of the sort described on p. 54 in chapter 1. Probably misled by writing, one starts by assuming that the word or representation or thought is itself atomic, lacking (relevant) internal structure. Since that word or thought must comprehend its object as a unity, it follows that the object, too, must (in all relevant ways) also be atomic, since there is (by assumption) nothing internal to the thought to correspond differentially to different parts of the taken-as-unity object. As usual, the error is in the initial inscription: that thoughts must be atomic. There is no reason why object registrations—

dynamic equivalents of terms—need be any more pointillist or homogenous than the objects they represent.†

As an example, consider Dennett's (1991) treatment of consciousness. Dennett argues against the idea that consciousness can be "found" in any particular place in the brain, or identified as any particular entity within the overall mental architecture. Superficially, it can seem as if he thereby undermines the ontological status of consciousness. If it is not *in one place*, then perhaps it does not exist—is unreal, or epiphenomenal. But no such conclusion follows (pace his own instrumental metaphysics). All his argument shows is something we should have expected, anyway: that things conscious—both the seat of consciousness, and its phenomenology—are not unitary points, but distributed and variegated. So too are rivers, lakes, watersheds. To register consciousness *as* consciousness is to treat it as a unity, and to register it as a unity is (at least usually) to abstract away from at least some of that internal (and intrinsic) variability. But registering it as a unity does not require that the thing itself be spatio-temporally or in any other way extensionless, any more than to register the Yukon River as a unity is to compress into a point a river spread out over several thousand miles. We owe as much to acts of registration themselves.

*Given a video tape of the fall, it is famously easy to "see through" the video, registering the fall, not the video itself. If one runs the tape backwards, yielding (at least arguably) a representation whose temporality cross-cuts the temporality of the fall, I can either (i) register the video, or (ii) hypothesize a non-real situation in which the apple flew up into the tree. But I am unable to "see through" this reverse video and thereby register the original fall.

†This raises a problem, of course: given that they are *not* points, what are they? And how can this be answered without committing yet another inscription error? The answer is to take the claim in the prior paragraph and read it backwards. It is not that the "two extensions must correspond," but rather, that what constitutes a "single, integral term" or a "single act of registration" is *that amount of space-time s-region that corresponds to the whole o-region*. Except how do we pay for the "whole o-region"? With *reidentification*. Only by exploiting the redundancy implicit in the multiplicity of extension-extension mappings required by reidentification is there any chance of wresting the appropriate individual boundaries out of the flux, instead of unfairly imposing them.

in the first registrational event is tied—say, with an equality sign—to the record of the second, or to the event itself. In all these descriptions, something is carried in the subject from t_1 to t_2. But once one lets go of the unwarranted inscription, one realizes that the identity of that internal individual is not God-given, not something on which the subject can unquestioningly rely. It, too, has to be achieved. Except of course it is a conceit to call it an "individual," since it is only an individual for the theorist. *Subjects have to be stable* in order to register individuals as stable, but they do not have to be *registered*, by themselves or by anyone else.

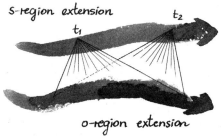

s-region extension t_2
t_1
o-region extension

FIGURE 7.3   CROSS-CUTTING EXTENSION

I have not yet said how this cross-cutting extension might be achieved. Note, though, that if it is achieved—if, that is, in virtue of such cross-cutting extensions, the subject succeeds in stabilizing an object with which, by hypothesis, it is at least partially out of effective contact—the subject thereby takes a small but decisive step towards the achievement of objectivity. It is an accomplishment, after all, as Strawson puts it, that "we think of our powers failing rather than the world fading,"[8] when the slop increases to the point that effective contact with the object is lost. Even the simpler cases of non-effective tracking begin the process of standing in coherent relation to what is distal. But it is really only when this cross-cutting extension takes hold that the subject can be said to begin to have a commitment to the continued existence of something that does not currently impinge upon it—and thus can be said to have a commitment to the *existence* of anything at all.

In this way an essential point comes into view: *the presence of an object inherently involves its absence.* The reason is simply the standard one: in order for a subject to take an object as an object,

[8] Strawson (1959), p. 74.

there must be separation between them—enough separation to make room for intrinsic acts of abstraction, of detachment, of stabilization. So it is essentially an ontological theorem of this metaphysics that no object, for any given subject, will be wholly *there*, in the sense of being fully effectively accessible. Or to put it more carefully: in order to be present, ontologically—i.e., in order to be *materially present*—an object must also be (at least partially) *absent*, metaphysically, in the sense of being partly out of effective reach.

In high-level cases, this ontological necessity of absence is almost commonsensical. Thus to recognize someone as the person they are is to register something greater than what literally confronts your eyes. "Oh, it is Randy," you say—thereby reaching out (semantically) to a wealth of relationship and extension not otherwise (effectively) available to you: relationship and extension that are irremediably different and "other." Perhaps surprisingly, the very same structure—of ontological presence requiring effective absence—holds at the level of the physical plenum. The spatial version is easier to accept, and is the one I have focused on: in order for an object to be present to a subject, it must be held a certain distance away, where distance includes physical distance. The temporal version is easier to understand in terms of extension. Because objects are in general temporally (as well as spatially) extended, there is never a moment in time in which the whole object is there, since no instantaneous time-slice can ever "capture" more than a cross-section of a temporally extended whole. It only

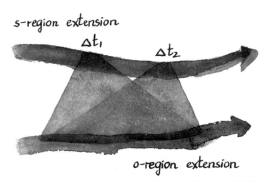

s-region extension

Δt_1

Δt_2

o-region extension

FIGURE 7·4 SUBREGION TO REGION CROSS-CUTTING

seems perverse because our apperception of time is so different from that of space. Suppose I point at an extensionless point in space, somewhere within your body, and ask "Are you all *right there*?" The question sounds a tad perverse, but the only possible answer is *no*. There is no single point in space where all of you is; you have inherent spatial extent. By the same token, to the extent that it is coherent (and I think it is largely coherent), there is no one *temporal* point where all of you is, either; you equally have inherent temporal extent.

One final comment. I have described this process as one of "stabilizing the object," but that phrasing may misconstrue the metaphysical picture, as if the object enjoyed an independent existence, and the normative weight in the situation lay on the degree to which it was "stabilized," whatever that would entail. Although that is false, the opposite is not true either; what happens is a much richer intermediate case of co-construction. As will be described in more detail in the next section, the existence of the object—including the object's continued existence while out of view—arises in part from the very achievement of registrational stability. This stability can take many forms—ranging all the way from short-term perceptual stability to long-term evolutionary stabilities of the species.

4 Intentional acrobatics

How are these patterns of cross-cutting extension achieved? Once again, I will violate one of my own methodological injunctions, this time by breaking the question into two parts: achievements of the subject, and achievements of the object. Consider the former. From the point of view of the subject, given the inherently deictic or differential structure of the substrate, what is required is a panoply of explicit compensatory mechanisms (or rather, what is required is a range of behavior or mechanism that it is theoretically convenient to register as plural). The s-region must *compensate for its own contribution to the deictic relations in which it stands to the o-region* in order to stabilize the other end. That is: it must *deconvolve the deixis*.

Think of the problem. Because they (are being assumed to) have arisen out of the underlying physical fields, the relations that have been talked about so far are differential or deictic, having to do with differences in the relative circumstances of s-region and o-region. Both sets of differences, in general, will constantly be changing. What is wanted, through this dynamic flux, is a stable way of relating to the o-region as a gathered and abstracted unity. The separation from the o-region provides the s-region with some buffer from the variation intrinsic to the o-region. What has not yet been eliminated, however, is the inevitable distraction of the s-region's own (whole) contribution to its relational stand.

Various strategies are available for isolating parts of the s-region from the inner turmoil of other parts of the s-region, or from minor perturbations that are constantly impinging on the s-region as a whole (so that violent thoughts about your advisor do not undermine your ability to think of escaping to Rio, and so that when you are cold you can still remember the friend you met last summer in Amman). For this sort of internal stability *digitality* is an excellent choice. This is why digital computation, at least at the moment, is by far the most popular species. There is a great deal to say about digitality—about its nature, its use, and its achievement, as well as about its role in registration.[9] Overall, though, Haugeland's assessment is very much on target: that digitality is "a practical means to cope with the vagaries and vicissitudes, the noise and drift, of earthly existence."[10]

But nothing about the internal structure or architecture of the s-region will enable it to insulate itself from itself as a whole, or from its overall circumstances. Thus think of the part of your registration of the house next door that has been retracted onto the s-region side of the separation, onto which responsibility for

[9] See TMD·V.
[10] Haugeland (1982), p. 217.

235

maintaining coordination has been retracted. And contrast this mental representation with a signpost, planted in the garden. Being unlikely to move, the signpost can simply say "the house next door," and thereby preserve a stable reference. Like it or not, however, what is in your head will go with you on your next trip to Paris—and so cannot have such a purely deictic structure, at least not if it is to stay referring to the original house.[11] Qua s-region, if you have reason to remember that specific house, the house next door to where you live, you have to construct something whose directedness will stay fixed on a stable referential point, in spite of, or perhaps in explicit compensation for, your own movements.

That is not to imply that external representations are any more likely than internal representations to be deictic. Deictic signs are often useful—"you are here," "next bus in 10 minutes," "campground 200 yards ahead on the right"—but so too are less indexical representations ("4421 Hingston Avenue; 5:13 A.M. Wednesday, November 29, 1950"). That way lies external (derivative) representation, documents, and writing. Skill in using and creating signs involves appropriate combination. In particular, the problem with deictic signs is that the original difficulty recurs: as soon as you drive off and become separated from the sign, it can no longer be of immediate (i.e., effective) help to you in registering the house, campground, whatever. *So in turn you may have to register the signpost.* That sounds redundant (why not just register the house directly?), but in real situations very different costs are associated with what registers what, and in what ways. As a result, complex cascades of registration, more

---

[11] A mental analogue of "the house next door" might be retained *opaquely*, as it is said—i.e., without compensation—for example in the general maxim that if, while preparing dinner, you discover that you are missing a crucial ingredient, it often pays to check with "the folks living in the house next door" (a maxim that would lose its practical force if the reference were stabilized—i.e., to use as-yet-unavailable language, if, when learned, it were interpreted extensionally).

and less deictic, are often useful, and sometimes essential. Thus you remember where the map is; the map "remembers" the directions to the lake. Or, more fully: you remember where the map is; the map "remembers" the directions to the road that runs by the lake; once there, effectively accessible (encounterable) road signs indicate the turnoff for the campground; at the campground additional (deictic) signs indicate exactly where to pitch your tent. And so on and so forth. The basic problem, however, is inescapable: (i) the circumstances of the s-region itself are vulnerable to change; and (ii) the relation between the s-region and o-region will also change. Given that the underlying fields are deictic, explicit work must be done to compensate for both so as to maintain a stable relation to the o-region.

How is this done? By analogy, as depicted in figure 7.5, imagine an acrobat leaping and jumping about on a somewhat darkened stage, putting their body through all kinds of fantastic gyrations, and yet throughout this crazed dance keeping a flashlight pointing absolutely reliably towards some fixed point—a point about four feet off the ground, say, towards the left front center of the stage. What the acrobat would need to do, through a complex series of hand and arm motions—handing the light back and forth from hand to hand, reaching it around behind themself, and so forth as appropriate—would be to do the opposite with one part of their body (arm and hand, plus flashlight) of what the rest of their body was doing (leaping and dancing), in such a way that the two, when added up together, nullified each other, leaving the focal point of illumination unchanged.

Except of course the word 'opposite' is not right. If the acrobat were to leap up four feet, it would not be necessary for them to do the exact opposite—i.e., to drop their arm down, four feet, if that were even possible—in order to hold constant the full six-coordinate position and orientation of the flashlight. In fact not a single one of the flashlight's six coordinates needs to remain fixed. It is not the *flashlight* that needs to be stabilized, after all. To freeze the position of the light outright might seem

to be overkill, and would anyway be impossible, for example if the acrobat were to rush to the other side of the stage. Ironically, moreover, there is a sense in which keeping the light itself locked in position, as if it were epoxied to a particular point in space, would be underkill, *since there would then be no way to be sure where it was pointing*. For a fixed un-

FIGURE 7·5   INTENTIONAL   ACROBAT

moving flashlight, that is, no single point along its path of illumination is uniquely singled out; all you have is a long gradually dissipating path of light.

Fortunately for the acrobat (and for registration, by analogy) there is a better way: it is only necessary to rotate the wrist in just the appropriate manner. The normative requirement is that there be a fixed point at the "end" of (i.e., at some point along[12]) the line along which the flashlight is pointing—a point that remains stably located in exocentric 3-space. So the dance does not merely compensate for the acrobat's movements; as a method for stabilizing the object, it is superior. The combined movements

---

[12] The fact that the stabilized patch is only "somewhere along" the beam of light corresponds to the fact that although we see the car, not just a two-dimensional facade, or even the pattern of incident light-waves, we do not (typically) see *through* the car and register the assembly line, or designer. But the analogy should not be taken to suggest that the phenomenon is simple: it opens up into the whole issue of the "transparency" of signs—the fact that when fluent registrars encounter external representations they typically register not the sign but what the sign represents. Semiotic transparency is almost magical; we just need to remember that part of the magic is that the transparency *stops* somewhere.

of dance and compensation together allow the s-region to triangulate in on the stable point of focus. All told, the focal point is much more stably and redundantly identifiable through the acrobat's motion than it would have been had the acrobat stayed put. And it is that one point, and only that one point, that needs to be "held" constant.[13]

Something very like this is the function of the vestibular-ocular reflex. In synchrony with rotations of our head, and with displacements in our body, we adjust the angle of the orientation of our eyes in their sockets so that a constant (distal) point of visual focus is maintained. We can even do it when we are not ourselves responsible for the body's motion. Thus imagine looking out the window of a train. It is possible to hold one's head and eyes fixed, which turns the visual field into an incomprehensible blur. The natural thing to do, however, guided by visual feedback, is to rotate our eyes and head in such a way as to compensate for the motion of the train—with, again, a net result of maintaining a stable distal point of focus. It is this sedimentation of distal stability that begins to answer the question, raised in the introduction, of why we see trees, not electro-magnetic radiation.

The mechanisms underlying visual perception are just one example of this general strategy of a subject's *computing its own inverse* (see the sidebar on page 240). When we reach out to grasp a coffee cup, we initially "think" that it is, say, 2 feet away.[14]

---

[13] The power of combined change and compensation is precursor to the common intuition that "multi-modal" perception or engagement is necessary for referential objectivity: a claim that the fact that we can touch, and smell, and use, and burn, and generally interact in all kinds of ways with a table, say, is constitutive of its being a *table* that we touch, smell, burn, use, etc.—rather than there simply being a table-surface that we touch, a table-smell that we smell, etc.

[14] Literally, we think no such thing. "Two feet away" is an extraordinarily high-level, sophisticated, and conceptual way of describing distance (see §1 of chapter 9). If distances to coffee cups are registered at all, they are surely registered non-conceptually. In the normal course of events, however, I

239

The inverse self

Although I do not want to press it here, it is possible to suggest that the "self" of a subject—i.e., its autonomy, its identity, its constitution as an individual—is in part *constituted* by the sorts of inversion process described in the text. That is, the first way in which the self is gathered together as a unity may be as a stable *locus of inversion*.

The idea is something like this: that the first emergence of the "subject" as an individual would be as a long-term integral or aggregate of *that which it must compensate for, in order to stabilize the rest of the world*. This would imply that explicit reflection upon oneself—i.e., the much later and more sophisticated taking of oneself to be an individual object (a process, it should be said, that inevitably requires establishing appropriate detachment from oneself; all the same principles apply)—would amount to the construction of a positive version of that which was initially negative.

There is clear merit to this suggestion. Arguing against any strong version of it, though, are remarks to be made later in the text, to the effect that the subject itself is by no means all that must be compensated for. On the contrary, it is really the entire embedding set of orienting circumstances that must be inverted, including the whole "registration" community of which the s-region is part, plus any instruments and documents and organizations that have been used to get at or identify the object, and so on and so forth, without apparent limit.

But as we reach forward, we similarly compensate for the motion of our hand, so that as it nears the cup, we signal it to slow down and grasp that with which it is by then in physical contact.

Nor is motion the only thing we compensate for. Think of the ideal mantra for a situated linguist, better than any T-sentence: that *tomorrow we use 'yesterday' to refer to what today we refer to with 'today.'* The shift from 'today' to 'yesterday,' in compensation for tomorrow's change in temporal

---

...

very much doubt that they are registered at all. Since physical (ocular-skeletal-muscular) coupling with coffee cups is unlikely to be broken, no disconnection needs to be transcended.

circumstances, is of the same sort as the vestibular-ocular reflex: a change in representation devised to compensate for a change of circumstance in order to allow a (distal) referent to stay constant.

5 Summary

Here then is the picture so far. The underlying spatio-temporal extended fields of particularity throw tufts of effective activity up against each other, and let them fall apart, fuse them and splinter them and push them through each other, and generally bash them around, in ways governed by the pervasive underlying (physical) laws of deictic coupling. For a subject to begin to register an object as an individual is, first, for a region of the fields (the s-region) not to be connected to another region (the o-region), but in the appropriate way to *let go* of it. Not in the sense of dropping connection forever, but in a way that maintains an overall pattern of coordination—a pattern that in all likelihood will allow it, among other things, to come back into connection with it again, at other times and places, and perhaps in other ways. The coordination requires establishing appropriately stable (extended in the s-region) and abstract (extended in the o-region) focus on the o-region, while remaining separate. The separation helps in maintaining a somewhat abstract focus on the o-region, by insulating the s-region from being buffeted by every nuance and vibration suffered by the o-region.

In order to *stabilize* the o-region as an extended unity, the s-region must employ all sorts of compensatory strategies in order to invert the contribution of every other element of the world that has been involved in obtaining access to the o-region in the first place. It must, as I said, deconvolve the deixis—precursor to the later process of shifting the registration of the object from egocentric to allocentric coordinates. This helps it to begin the long and tough process of triangulating on the object, and washing out the contribution of everything else.

The analogies with vision and pointing suggested ways in which the point of focus could be dynamically maintained in the face of the endless ebb and flow of the underlying fields. If a relatively slow observer were to watch the acrobat dance around on stage—say, by half shutting their eyes, and watching the show in just a slight mist—all they would see would be the one single point of constant illumination; the movement and acrobatic compensation would all be washed out in a blur.

So it is with the focus of registration. The speed and complexity with which we compensate for changes we undergo in orientation and access to objects is just as much of a blur— partly because they happen far too quickly for us to be conscious of (as we are reminded by the ethnomethodologists' video tapes), and partly because, not being stable, they do not end up in focus. As a result, the only thing we end up "seeing" (registering) is the single stabilized object-as-entity.

The restless dynamics of the analogy are important, too. To stabilize appropriately—*to bring the world into presence*—very much requires being alive. It is like standing on a boat in heavy seas; you must constantly dance in order to stay upright and focused on the shore. In death, on the contrary, local stability (total quiescence) obliterates the active ability required in order to stabilize the distal world. Coordination ceases, pure deixis takes over, and the only thing that any longer has impact is the press of the immediate physical surround.

There is a crucial respect in which the analogy between registration and vision breaks down, however. Light beams and visual focus are *connected* phenomena. They are all inherently constrained to operate within the pre- and proscriptions of the physical plenum. Registration is different. Not only is its directedness *able* to transcend those limits; it *must* transcend them. Go ahead, be expensive: transcending those limits is what registration is *for*.

8 · Registration – II

For almost a century logicians have focused on the normative standard of preserving truth. The examples in the last chapter illustrate what many years of wrestling with computational practice have led me to believe: that *preservation of reference* is an equal if not more important intentional achievement.[1] Given the inherently deictic nature of the substrate out of which reference arises, moreover, the preservation of reference is almost undoubtedly a prior ontological skill.

Computational practice is replete with this kind of compensatory adjustment: an (often small) expenditure of effective energy in order to maintain a stable semantic value for a deictic term. Thus consider e-mail addresses: what starts out in California as "ht@ai.edinburgh.ac.uk" is converted somewhere over (or under) the Atlantic to "ht@uk.ac.edinburgh.ai," and is then gradually stripped down as it works its way across Britain, entering a series of nested sub-domains, to "ht@ac.edinburgh.ai," "ht@edinburgh.ai," and "ht@ai"—until finally, when it reaches its target host machine, nothing is left except the atomic "ht."[2]

---

[1] As philosophers will point out, truth, at least since Frege, has been viewed as a *form* of reference, not as something opposed to or distinct from it —a perspective I myself exploit in §2, below, in arguing that context-dependent reference-preserving (term) translation can usefully be viewed as a generalization of truth-preserving (sentential) inference. But the inclusionary nature of the unifying proposal should not be allowed to obscure the differences beneath it. Hence the main point, here: that strategies for maintaining the reference of context-dependent terms designating ordinary individuals—including individuals that are subjects of predication— are not only ubiquitous and important, but have been inadequately thematized in current logical approaches.

[2] This is misleading in several ways. There are two stages to address resolution, for one thing. The "lexical" address is typically resolved first, with the help of name servers, yielding a more context-independent internet address, such as 13.0.27.446, which is sent back to the originator, which in

Context-dependent term translation

A bug in an early version of the Macintosh operating system shows what can happen when a system fails to preserve the reference of a context-dependent term.* If a user inserted an unreadable floppy into a machine with a single floppy drive and no hard disk, the following exchange took place. The system asked the user whether they wanted the unreadable disk to be formatted. If the answer was *yes*, the system tried to access the disk-formatting software. Typically it was not loaded; it needed to be swapped in from the system disk. So the first thing the system would do would be to eject the (unformatted) disk, and ask the user to insert the system disk. Once this was done, the system would load the formatting software, and then proceed to erase and reformat the system disk!

The source of the problem was roughly as follows. At the beginning of the exchange, a variable or identifier, called something like "unreadable-floppy," was bound to a value representing the unformatted disk, such as a machine analogue of "disk in drive #0." Though *bound* to this descriptor, it *referred* to the new disk, the one that satisfied the descriptor at the time, the one that the user wanted formatted (this is betrayed by the English words chosen for its name). By the time the formatting software was loaded, however, the circumstances on which that reference depended had changed. By doing nothing, the system preserved the *sense* of the descriptor, but not its *reference*. What would have honored the user's intentions would have been the dual: to go to some work to change the sense (into something like "the disk I just ejected just a moment ago"), in order to preserve the reference.

Similarly, consider processes of converting a frame offset pointer (-4) to a full address, when data is moved off the stack into main memory. Or strategies for converting a variable reference **x**, bound in the current context, into the canonical (and therefore

---

...

turn uses it to send the mail "directly." But the original moral still holds, since resolution of *that* address—the 13.0.27.446—undergoes similar processes of deictic reduction en route.

Managing the differential fan-in and fan-out implicated in such cases can get arbitrarily complex. For just a tad more detail, consider three ways of referring to such a disk: "disk in drive #0," as we just saw; "SneakerNet 3," the user's label; and "72346155236," the floppy's internally-inscribed UID number (a number that can only be written *after* the disk is formatted). The first is most useful when the system needs to read or write, but works only in a very specific context: its referent will change with every insertion and ejection. If a disk that is ejected now will be required later, one needs a way of referring to it that will span the break in access (effective coupling). The third (UID number) is relatively permanent and context-independent, but not user-friendly; "please insert disk #72346155236" is unlikely to produce good results. The second (user label) lies somewhere in between: it is more convenient than the UID number, in part because of being reusable, and also because of being part description and part name—but by that very token is potentially ambiguous. So the label will (in turn) have determinate reference in only some contexts (in this office, say), though admittedly that is a much wider set of contexts than those in which it is mounted in drive 0. No one description is best, overall; skill involves moving among them in ways appropriate to the circumstance so as to maximize operating convenience and minimize the chances of tripping up when references change.

*For a discussion of this and other similar examples—and a proposed solution—see Dixon (1991).

less context-dependent) codesignating numeral 5. Or for a more intensional example, imagine updating a counter of the number of pages that have been printed, from 35 to 36, as one more sheet of paper passes the print head. None of these changes is taken in order to perform a concrete action in the semantic realm—i.e., to inflict a permanent change on the task domain. Rather, they are all translations of terms to preserve semantic value by com-

pensating for (or sidestepping) the effects of a change of context.
(For a dramatic failure to preserve reference appropriately, see
the sidebar on page 244.)

Reference-preserving context-dependent term translation is
such an intrinsic part of computation that it has even been proposed as a core operation in terms of which to define all others.[3]
Given this potential universality—not only in the computational case, but also, as I will argue below, as a generalized model
of at least some aspects of human thinking—I want to put the
puppet show back up for a moment, traffic in fully registered
individuals, and consider half a dozen species of such translation. Although too expensively (and briefly) presented, these examples exhibit important characteristic patterns of internal
structure—structure that I will later want to extract, convert
into field-theoretic form, and use in order to tell the real (non-
marionette) story of how aboriginal subjects stabilize aboriginal
objects. The discussion may also go some way towards showing
that the procedures of "deixis convolution" introduced in chapter 7 are not just of abstruse metaphysical interest, but could be
used as pragmatic architectural principles on which to build
what has never before existed: a computer able to shoulder responsibility for its own objects.

1 Strategies of reference preservation

At least five different reference-preservation strategies can be
identified.

1a Adjusting deictic registrations

Suppose someone tells you that you have left your glasses on the
table behind you. As you turn around, without being aware of it,
you smoothly change your mental analogue of "behind me" to a
corresponding analogue of "in front of me," in order to stabilize
the place referred to, at a minor but still non-zero expenditure of
internal effective energy. This seemingly effortless mental activity, which among other things saves you from going round and

---

[3] Dixon (1991).

round in circles, is a spatial analogue of the earlier temporal example of shifting from 'today' to 'yesterday' to compensate for the passage of time. In neither case is referential stability achieved by constructing a context-*independent* representation. Just as the acrobat kept the intrinsically deictic flashlight with them, as they leapt around, constantly adjusting its orientation and angle to preserve the distal point of focus, so too in these cases the representation is kept close by, in context-dependent form. Like flashlights (and sports jackets), representations, such as memories, often come along for the ride; the trick is to adjust them to compensate for changes in circumstance, so as to stabilize and thus preserve their distal referents.[4]

1b Converting between allocentric and egocentric registrations

As well as updating deictic or egocentric registrations, we are equally adept at varying the degree of deixis, by converting back and forth between relatively more egocentric or deictic descriptions, on the one hand, and more allocentric or context-independent descriptions of the same situation, on the other— e.g., from 'the bar at the corner of Quarry Road and Route 20 at the western edge of town' to 'half a mile ahead on the right.'

Neither allocentric nor egocentric registration is better; each has its uses. Skill consists not in having expertise at one or other end of the dichotomy, but in being able to shift back and forth, appropriately, as circumstances warrant. Allocentric (context-

---

[4] In the case of changing 'behind me' to 'in front of me' (or, more plausibly, 'behind' to 'in front'—the 'me' is a distraction), the reference-preserving adjustment is in response to willed action. Most of us, but not all robots, are skillful enough to do this even if we are involuntarily turned around— though not of course if we are turned too quickly, or our eyes are closed. The passage of time from one day to another, even from one moment to another, is similarly involuntary, but such an ineliminable feature of our experience that we are skilled in the compensations it requires. What is not clear is whether these and other deixis compensation schemes are underwritten by disparate mechanisms, even if they all honor a common semantical principle, or whether there is any architectural commonality.

independent) representations are typically more stable, more portable, more comparable with other representations of a similar type, and less vulnerable to context-dependent error—all features that are especially appropriate in printed form. Deictic (egocentric) versions, on the other hand, are typically compact, and require less inferential machinery to work with, placing fewer demands on explicit representation. But by far their most important property, as many writers have noted,[5] is the fact that they are more directly "actionable," in the sense of being more easily converted into motor signals—a fact explained by chapter 5's claim that the physical world is itself intrinsically deictic. They are also more closely related to our sense of self, to our personal identity. Thus imagine reading in an almanac that a meteor will strike the earth at $37°16'57''$ N × $122°11'12''$ W at 11:54:36 A.M. GMT on November 8, 1994. The fact takes on an urgency lacking in the context-independent form, when one realizes, after convolving it into deictic form, that the meteor is predicted to strike *right here, in five minutes*. Or to take another example, suppose that upon arriving from the east you want to turn into your friend's driveway, knowing that it is on the north side of the street. It will not do to send a physiological analogue of "North!" down the nerves to your hands. Instead, you need to convert that instruction into more appropriate physiological (connected, non-representational) form. It is because the physical world is intrinsically deictic, and because physical activity therefore has only incremental (differential) effect, that what is needed is something much closer to "Right!"

Although it is easy to suggest that deictic (egocentric) and non-deictic (allocentric) representation are two distinct species, that is misleading. Allocentricity (context-independence), especially, is a matter of degree; the idea of a *completely* context-independent or "non-deictic" representation is a fiction. To shift from 'today' to 'November 21' is a step away from pure deixic-

---

[5] See e.g. Castañeda (1975), Perry (1979), Chapman & Agre (1987), and Smith (1986).

ity (physical connection), but it is only a first step along a road without end: 'November 21, 1950'; 'November 21, 1950 CE'; 'November 21, 1950 CE in the Gregorian calendar,' etc. Moreover, deixicity affects different aspects of a representation differentially. Thus "12:00 on November 8, 1994" is at once more spatially deictic, but less temporally deictic, than "noon, today, GMT."

If complete context-independence is impossible, does that undermine the utility of "context-independence" as a notion? No, for the interesting reason that context-independence itself is usually used in context-*dependent* ways, to signify the independence of a representation or registration from those aspects of the context that, from some wider "supra-context," are seen as variable. Thus from vantage point **x** a representation or registration **r** appears context-independent if it is not semantically vulnerable to shifts in context that are *visible from* **x**, even if it remains context-dependent in the same way that **x** itself is. The point is only that we are often, even usually, unaware of those aspects or dimensions of a representation that remain constant, and can therefore be deictically related to in the background. For a familiar example, note that maps are always maps *from the top*. It is not logically required that East be represented as 90° to the right of North; if one were to look *up* onto maps instead of *down*, or were to stand on one's head, East would be 90° to the left. But since it is our habit and physical constitution both to stand upright, and to look down onto roads and maps, we conventionally (and conveniently) leave the vertical dimension of maps deictic. This works pretty well on earth; it is presumably a problem in astronomy (does the earth revolve clockwise, or counter-clockwise, around the sun?).

1c Crossing the explicit/implicit boundary

A third type of reference-preserving term translation involves shifting back and forth between explicit and implicit registration. As is widely recognized, if a system (person or machine or even document) is moved out of the inevitable background context on which it implicitly depends, it is liable to break or fail, or at least be misleading. It was suggested in chapter 1 that one way to deal with such a situation is to convert the less explicit or nonrepresentational context-dependence into something explicit.

It is often convenient for this explicit representation in the first instance to be deictic; then strategies such as those discussed above can be used to convert that egocentric representation into more allocentric form. Thus 'at noon,' the unmarked case, is converted to 'at noon, today'; given that explicit representation of the day, the way is paved to create the less context-dependent 'noon on November 21.' But explicit deictic terms are not always used as intermediaries. Thus it seems possible to convert '7:03 P.M.' directly into '7:03 P.M. Pacific Daylight Time,' in a message headed for Chicago, without passing through '7:03 P.M. *here*.' Phone numbers are similarly expanded directly: from x9658, suitable within the building, to 481-9658, for local use, to 514-481-9658, for the rest of Canada and the U.S., to +1-514-481-9658, which one might want to put on one's international letterhead. Chapter 1 discussed a similar example of a data base needing an extra field to represent the university it was used in, in order to handle interinstitutional cross-registration. And to conclude with a dramatic real-world case, it has been estimated that it will cost American industry hundreds of billions of dollars to upgrade their software to deal with 21st-century dates. Unfortunately, many extant systems store dates—e.g., on employee records, in bank statements, and the like—as two decimal digits, having parochially presumed that the first two digits would always be '19'.

Adding or deleting arguments is not the only way to cross the implicit/explicit boundary. Note how some of us, in order to read maps—e.g., in order to understand which direction to turn—rotate maps so that we stand in the same orientation with respect to the map as with respect to the world, thereby allowing us, as I have elsewhere put it,[6] to *absorb* one of the map's dimensions of deixicity. Drivers, in sum, think of "right" and "left" as zero-argument functions—i.e., as egocentric constants; earthly cartographers and map readers think of them as functions of one argument; and astronomers think of them as functions of two arguments. In reality, however, as cosmologists and theoretical physicists realize, "right" and "left" are functions of (at least) three arguments: two other orientations plus a binary decision.

1d   Changing interest or belief

The first three species of translation discussed above—updating deictic registrations, converting between more and less context-independent forms, and shifting deictic dependencies into and out of explicit view—all involve the preservation or stabilization of something finer-grained than pure "reference": something more like intension or meaning. But the reference-preserving mandate has wider application.

As the fulcrum of stability or preservation moves "outwards"—away from the s-region or subject, and also away from the relation between them, and towards the o-region or referent—it is likely to preserve less of the intensional relationship (aspect or "feature") under which the referent is registered or identified, and instead to put more direct (less intensional) focus on the object itself. This pattern will especially matter later on, when we take down the puppet show: it is indicative of an objective ontological commitment to an object, rather than merely being a case of feature-placing. In the meantime, however, staying within the reference-preservation standpoint, we can see that the sorts of shifts involved take us away from what might be categorized as indexical resolution into realms more reminiscent of full traditional (sentential) inference.

Even if we do move closer into the traditional realm of inference, however, reference preservation remains a useful analytic category. Thus imagine, six months after renting a room in your advisor's house, shifting your description from "esteemed pro-

---

[6]Smith (1987) and TMD·IV.

fessor" to "chiseling landlord." Or imagine revising your opinion of what you once felt was "the best paper I have ever read" to
"one of Jones' early tries." In both cases, a description must be
updated in such a way as to be able to preserve reference *across a
change in belief.* The *context*, with respect to which the description is relative, has been widened from spatio-temporal orientation of the registrar, or even its physical location, to include its
full epistemic (judgmental) state. Similarly, "the tallest person in
the class" may have to be revised to "the second tallest person in
the class," after a new family arrives from Kenya. Here a registration has to be changed in order to preserve reference across *a
change in relevant circumstantial facts.* Now the notion of context
has been widened to include not just the full situation of the registrar, but the full described situation as well—what else is going
on in the world being registered.

   In conversation, context can also be taken to include interest-
relative facts about the communicative process itself. Thus suppose someone replies "John Etchemendy" to the question "Who
is the new dean of humanities?" and "The new dean of humanities" to the question "Who is John Etchemendy?" In both cases
they are answering a question of the form "Who is α?" with a co-
referential term β satisfying various other conversational constraints (Austinian felicity conditions,[7] a requirement to provide
new and salient information, and the like). Here it is not so
much that the change in context requires a change in registration in order to preserve reference, but rather that a change in
registration required for other reasons (interest, novelty, etc.) is
subjected to a *constraint* of preserving reference.

1e Changing register

If full inference is more complex than deixis deconvolution, but
can be unified with it, a fifth type of translation is more complicated yet—though, as so often happens, rudiments of the phenomenon can again be found in simple spatial cases. Thus
consider a situation with which we are all familiar: of saying

[7] See Searle (1983).

"Would you hand me that cup on your right?" when, facing someone, we see it in a position that, from our point of view, is to the left of them. Rather than preserving reference from within a given context-dependent system, as so many of the previous examples have done, this case involves a preservation of reference *across a shift from one context-dependent registration scheme to another.*

Spatial cases are just the tip of the iceberg. Asking a two-year old "Is the dean there?" is not likely to work as well as "Can I talk to your mom?" The point here is to shift the question to one that makes sense from the child's point of view. By the same token, if you call a restaurant, it will generally not work to ask for your brother, who just happens to be eating there, as "my brother"; instead you have to provide a description usable by someone who does not know him ("5′ 11″ with dark hair and a van Dyke beard," or whatever). Similarly, you sometimes have to shift to an entirely different language, speaking French when calling Bourg-en-Bresse, Tamil when calling Madurai. But even these cases are relatively simple, compared to what is involved in trying to convey a reference or registration across a profound difference in world view. Thus think of how hard it is to persuade someone who sees the world in psychological terms to accept an essentially political or moral conclusion. Or, within the academy, of attempting to formulate an insight in a way that will be accessible across disciplinary boundaries. Or of trying to get a hijacker or terrorist to adopt a humanitarian point of view.

All these cases involve shifting *register*. The issues involved range from the simplest facts about spatio-temporal orientation to the most fundamental problem underlying pluralism: the ineradicable fact that different people, with different experiences and different histories and different interests, see the world in different ways, or at least *can* see the world in different ways— sufficiently different that reference and registration may be arbitrarily difficult to share, at least to any degree of perfection. In both cases, in a way that the ultimate metaphysical story will have to explain (a story we have not yet come to), one struggles with a kind of "locatedness" of knowledge or viewpoint or registrational stance—a locatedness whose underlying sense of position is only partially metaphorical.[8] As in simple deictic cases, explicit attention is required in order to preserve or, as is perhaps a better word in such cases, to *convey* content across such a change in perspective.

Shifting register is not just a problem of interpersonal communication. It affects us individually as well. Some of the problems are diachronic: our earliest memories are often encoded with respect to concepts whose meaning has changed over the years (such as 'big,' perhaps because it is self-referentially deictic), challenging our ability to preserve their original content. But there are synchronic cases as well. Thus imagine the process of building a house, complete with late-night conversations about hospitality and community, early suggestive sketches, realistic perspective drawings, surveys, elevations, blueprints, even detailed working drawings—to say nothing of our initial impressions of living there, perhaps even later reminiscences. All these registrations of what is ultimately a common situation not only emphasize certain aspects over others, featuring this and eliding that, but in part constitute the house or home from differing points of view.[9] There is no reason to believe that what is essential to any given registration is capturable, even implicitly, in the others. And yet of course we try: that was the whole point of those meetings with the architect—to translate hospitality into 2×4s.

What lesson should be taken from these cases of crossing register? Primarily, not to be seduced by limit cases. Issues of multiple registration cannot be avoided: to presume that would be nostalgically to subside into Formal Ontology. Yet it is just as

[8] Haraway (1991).
[9] For a discussion of the various kinds of representation involved in architecture, see Goel (1995).

important not to be so daunted as to be brought to a halt. Sure enough, there is no general reason to suppose that perfect "translation" is possible between registers — even of the individuals involved, let alone of what is said of them. No metaphysical warrant will be issued, once we get to metaphysics, to support the idea of trans-world identicality. And sure enough, too, in pessimal cases, inter-register incommensurability can be so severe as to essentially prohibit substantive communication. But for both metaphysical and practical reasons, neither limit case matters anywhere near as much as the topology and texture, as the warp and woof, of the intermediate region. As should be clear from even as much of the metaphysical picture as has been suggested so far, *all of human communication lies in this middle region*, between identical and incommensurable registration schemes. Not only that, when we get back to the proper metaphysical story, as was promised earlier, it will emerge that, far from being undermined by it, registration is designed to cope with this middle region of partial commensurability.

In sum, it is important that shifting registers is hard. But it is not hard so much in the sense of there being metaphysical limits. What is important, rather, is that communicating across registers is *hard work*. This is what will make the metaphysical picture substantive. It is also a conclusion that underwrites a claim made in chapter 3: that developing a more adequate metaphysics is not only intellectually viable, but also politically urgent. The aim is to give metaphysical grounding to, and support for, communicative and political struggles among people whose experience of, and participation in, our world is different.

2 Coordination conditions

At the beginning of the chapter, I claimed that reference-preservation strategies are of metaphysical interest because they reveal (some of) the fine-structure of the strategies subjects use to stabilize objects. But before we can begin to extract those ontological morals, we need to consider one more generalization, this time having to do with the nature of the coupling or connection between s-region and o-region, between "subject" and "object."

Truth, it was pointed out earlier,[10] has at least since Frege been viewed as a form of reference. Traditional sentential inference, therefore, can be taken to be a *form* of reference preservation. In light of the examples given above, it is natural to consider the possibility of combining the patterns discussed above, involving deictic resolution and description adjustment, with traditional sentential inference, in order to yield something like a "general model of inference or rationality": (i) one that applies to a wide range of expression types (terms and sentences are all that have been considered so far, but the idea can be generalized to cover predicate positions as well); and (ii) one that deals explicitly with deixis and context-dependence, on some or all of the various notions of context discussed above.

2a Generalized inference

There is something very right about this generalized proposal—and also something badly wrong. It is not too difficult to imagine appropriate generalizations of soundness and completeness, for example—a major point in its favor.[11] And the amount of computation that can be collected within its grasp is truly impressive. Even if one ignores its unpaid ontological debts, however, the proposal cannot be accept as stated. There is a problem having to do with just what notion of "inference" we have by the tail.

In chapter 1, I claimed that the subject matter of anything like a satisfying intentional account of computation (and, by implication, human life) would have to be an account of the full par-

---

[10] Footnote 1, on page 243.

[11] Especially on their most general interpretations: that completeness, as John Etchemendy has put it, is *getting what you want*; soundness, *wanting what you get*. For an application to programming languages see Dixon (1991).

ticipatory engagement of an intentional system in a semantic or task domain, not merely of its projection onto reasoning or symbol-manipulation. Moreover, I argued that its participatory nature suffused computation; that it was not something that could be culled out and held off to the side, to be treated differently from the main "central" case. At a minimum, therefore, an advocate of the "generalized inference model" (at least if they wanted to do justice to computation, which I am assuming as something of a minimal standard) would want to extend that model to include what is traditionally called perception and action. Though far from trivial, this could arguably be accomplished within the spirit of "reference preservation"—by viewing perception as a process that moves from the presence of an object **x** or situation **s** to a representation **r** of that object or situation (remember: the generalized model we are temporarily working with was framed "post-ontologically," so there is no need to worry about the origin of **s** or **x** or **r**). Representation **r** would be considered "correct" or worthy or virtuous just in case it "preserved" (i.e., captured) a relevant property of **x** or **s** in some appropriate sense.

The problem is that it is not enough to include perception and action. This too was indicated in chapter 1. As an example of a familiar computational activity that fits under none of these three categories, I cited simple clocks. So the question arises of whether clocks fit within a general reference-preservation picture, and thus whether they, too, could be incorporated into the proposed general model—or rather, to turn the question around, whether the proposed model can coherently be generalized to include clocks (and whatever else they are like), along with perception, action, and inference.

The answer is *yes*, that it can be—and in an illuminating way. By comparison, think about standard inference. The underlying picture is of a stable semantic domain, with respect to which sentences or expressions in the inferential realm are evaluated.

"Stable" does not mean static or atemporal. As in the case of an inference regime designed to calculate planetary orbits, the semantic domain of a traditional inference system can be as dynamic as you please—perhaps described by a set of differential equations. Rather, "stable" means that the semantic domain does not change *from the point of view of the inference process*. It is assumed to be the same from the beginning of the inference to the end: that is, the same for the premises of a derivation as for its conclusion (the semantical interpretation function, to put the same point another way, is not itself assumed to be temporally indexed). What inference does, given this stable domain, is to yield a different "intensional stance"[12] towards it—get at it under a different description, say something new about it, represent it *as* being such and such, in an (epistemically) novel way.

Clocks—like meters, tracking systems, and other simple measuring instruments—are almost the exact dual:

Whereas traditional inference comprises a change in (intensional) stance to a stable subject matter, clocks and other measuring instruments maintain a stable (intensional) stance to a changing subject matter.

2b   Coordinated temporal realms

What is important about the clock case can be understood in terms of the relation between two temporalities. There are two time courses relevant to inference or registration: the temporality of the registration or inference process,[13] and the temporality of what is registered or inferred (the temporality of the semantic realm).

---

[12] With apologies to Dan Dennett, who of course spells his version with a 't'.
[13] In formal logic, derivability is normally treated as a relation, not as a process—and thus the "proof-theoretic" or inferential realm is not itself considered temporal at all. But from a computational perspective, inference, proof, deduction, and the like are almost always viewed as resource-limited temporal processes—e.g., in discussions of the temporal cost of Boolean satisfaction procedures.

The inability of traditional models of inference to deal with clocks (and other forms of participation) is not because they consider inference to be *atemporal*. Rather, the problem is that they take the temporality of inference to be *independent* of the temporality of the semantic domain. Doing a full calculation to determine whether a proposed satellite will escape Jupiter's gravitational field may take a long time—several hours, say, on the agency's fastest computers. And it may take a similar amount of time for the satellite to escape Jupiter's gravitational field—143 minutes, suppose. But it makes no difference whether the two times are of similar or dissimilar duration; or which comes first; or indeed any other fact about their relation. It does not matter because *the two times are not tied together*. As suggested in figure 8·1,

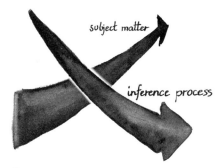

FIGURE 8·1 INDEPENDENT TEMPORALITIES

the time course of inference and the time course of the semantic domain are assumed to be orthogonal.

Needless to say, the same is not true for clocks and other similar measuring instruments. Not only are the time course of the "inference process" (i.e., of the time-keeping) and the time course of the semantic domain (i.e., of the passage of time) not independent; they are not even just coordinated. They are the *same*. That is what it is to be a "real-time" measuring system: the time of the measurement is (or at least is very close to) the time of what is measured.

As usual, most of life is in between: partly coordinated. You have thirty minutes to prepare your story until the reporter gets here; they have the same amount of time to figure out what to ask you. Then the lights go up, the microphone is turned on, and what was a partially independent pair of parallel half-hours turns into a single coordinated fifteen minute interview. Or for a different example, think about driving up to an intersection and looking both ways to figure out whether it is safe to proceed. The temporality of the "figuring out" and the temporality of what is figured out have to work together (we all know the experience of realizing that, had we rashly proceeded instead of stopping to look, it *would*, as it happens, have been safe to proceed, but now that we realize that it would have been safe, a car is coming). Similar situations arise throughout computation. In an especially complex Xerox printer, for example, built out of a network of microprocessors, a situation can arise in which one processor asks another processor to tell it, within 400 milliseconds, whether, 13 pages from *then*, it (the second processor) will have been able to render a given Postscript file into a bitmapped image, because if not, the first processor will at that point (i.e., 400 milliseconds from *now*) have to start shutting down the paper path.[14] The time course of "figuring things out" and the time course of what is being figured out are coordinated—stitch-welded together, in this case, as suggested in figure 8·2, at essential synchronization points.

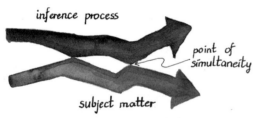

FIGURE 8·2 (PARTIALLY) SYNCHRONIZED TEMPORALITIES

This overlap of temporality—sometimes glued as closely as possible together, as in clocks; sometimes partially independent, but closely tied together at crucial points, as in traffic; sometimes more loosely coupled, as in planning between meetings—is characteristic of what is called "real-time" inference. And it of course puts temporal pressure on the "reasoning" process. It does not matter whether you could have figured out whether the car was going to hit you, if you had had more time. Nor will it do, in the last ten minutes of the exam, to use up all your time

[14] From the perspective of electronic materiality, moving sheets of paper have tremendous momentum.

figuring out what strategy would be best to employ, if only you had left some time over to apply it. So we can take that as the first lesson of clocks: the generalized model will have to deal with *co-ordinated time of registrar and registered*. And of course time is just an example. The inferential realm and the semantic realm will in general overlap in many other ways as well; this is nothing more than another consequence of symmetrical realism. So a general model will have to deal with coordination in general, as well as with effective coupling and semantic disconnection.

Given this image of tightly coupled temporalities, what about the "reference preservation" part of the original model? Is there something, in the case of clocks, that is *preserved*? Again, the answer is at least arguably *yes*, but again, doing justice to that 'yes' requires adjusting the model. For what is preserved, in the case of clocks and meters—what is the "same," from moment to moment, for a clock—is not so obviously *reference*, but something that would traditionally be taken to be more intensional: something like the *issue* that the clock addresses, something like the intension of the phrase "the o'clock property that holds of the current moment."[15] It would be presumptuous to try to work out exactly what to call it, here, not only because I do not yet have adequate tools, but also because in a moment I am going to let go of the pretense of having any supporting ontological framework at all. Rather, the image that is important to retain is that what is "preserved" (what will be "stabilized," once we take

---

[15] As implied by the fact that clocks can be right or wrong, clock faces are best read as making claims: either that a given o'clock property (being 4:14, being 4:15, etc.) holds of a given metaphysical moment, to adopt a predicative (object-property) stance; or that a feature obtains (4:14-ness, 4:15-ness, etc.), to cast it in feature-placing terms. Either way, what is "preserved" is not the intension of that predicative claim (not the "sense" of "being 4:14"), but something more abstract, more like "the current time," on an intensional (non-deictically-reduced) reading of that phrase. (In one sense, a clock always shows "the current time." In another sense, it will not show "the current time" for another 12 or 24 hours. It is the former sense we are trying to get at.) See Smith (1988).

down the puppet show) is something which, though in one sense gathered together into a stable unity, nevertheless also fans out again, as the world turns, and time goes by.

2c Intentional dynamics

Where does this leave us? At a minimum, it shows that a usable extended "preservation" model would meet the following set of conditions:

1. It would involve causal (effective) interactions with the subject matter, not just among symbolic representations; and

2. It would involve on-going temporal (and other forms of) overlap and "real-time" coordination, rather than assuming a stable (static) relation to a (potentially dynamic) semantic domain.

These two conditions—the first a consequence of the participatory nature of intentionality, the second a consequence of symmetrical realism—would be added to the two with which we started:

3. It would apply to terms and predicates and features, as well as to sentences; and

4. It would deal explicitly with all sorts of deictical and other forms of context-dependence.

The net result would incorporate not only all of what is normally considered inference, perception, reasoning, and action, but other forms of (intentional) behavior as well, of which clocks and measuring instruments were just an example.

Should the result be called inference? Was "generalized inference" an appropriate name? Who is to say? It might not matter, so long as one were clear on what was involved. But I would vote *no*. Rather than build the normative condition into the name, such as by calling it "reason" or "rationality," my own choice, when attempting to develop exactly such a model, has simply been to think of it as *intentional dynamics*.[16]

---

[16] Smith (1987) uses the somewhat unwieldy "coordination conditions on content and causal connection," abbreviated 'c⁵'. 'Intentional dynamics' is shorter, and not much less descriptive.

It even seemed like a productive direction of research, until I ran up against the ontological wall.

3 Stabilization revisited

One way to understand the problem of unwarranted ontology, inscription errors, and the like, is to understand it as an overinterpretation of the world—as a way of trying to prop up or hold together the world with more information than is really there. Reductionism is famous for acts of omission: for throwing out what is really there. What is less often remarked are its acts of commission: the fact that it is equally likely to impose what is not.

So take down the puppet show, and view these reference-preserving moves as "sleights of mind," "sleights of registration," reminiscent of the acrobat's sleights of hand. And imagine the pools of quiescence they create—sometimes close by and sometimes far away, where the compensatory actions wash out the contributions of ever-changing circumstances, leaving only a stable, distilled point of intentional focus. Imagine this, as usual, through field-theoretic glasses, letting go of any prior parse of the situation into discrete objects, discrete individuals.

As the foregoing section makes clear, the resulting pools of quiescence are constitutive not just of the "subject's" "objects," as was too simply suggested in chapter 7, but of their classificatory properties as well—to say nothing of the features and senses and intensions underlying them. For the patterns of cross-cutting triangulation we have been examining are nothing less than the processes whereby s-regions wrest ontology out of the embedding flux.

It is not that reference is *preserved*, in other words, or at least not *just* that reference is preserved—as if the objects to be referred to were independently supplied, by God or pre-emptive inscription. Rather, reference is *achieved*. These processes of preservation, maintenance of invariance, and the like, are part of the very processes of stabilization that constitute that something as a something. They are not all that is required for something to be something: in a moment I will also give credit to the object, and in the next chapter, will invoke active processes of synthesis, maintenance, and repair. This is not a story that is going to fall into pure idealism. But just because *preserving a referent* and *creating an object* are not the same, that does not mean they are independent, either.

Moreover, the benefit of having considered specific examples in this chapter is that they hint at how a more detailed story of referential achievement will go. Note, in particular, for starters, that when registered in traditional terms the locus of stability rested at various different places along what would normally be considered the referential or semantic link, from subject to object. Thus in the early deictic examples, involving changes from 'today' to 'yesterday,' '10:00 A.M.' to '10:00 A.M. GMT,' and the like, what we saw held stable was not just the traditional referent (i.e., what on a traditional analysis would be registered as the referent),[17] but also something more like the meaning or intension.[17] When the notion of "context" was broadened to include shifts in belief, interest, and situational facts, what was "stable" was less intensional, something more clearly held out at the object or o-region itself. Clocks and measuring instruments, in contrast, were different from the simple deictical cases in the opposite way: in their case the "intension" or meaning was *more* stable than the referent—at least in the sense that what is the same in content about an accurate clock, moment to moment, is more intensional than what is different.

This all has shades of more fan-in and fan-out; more cross-cutting structures of the one and the many—except note that, from where we now stand, to say "many" is not quite right, since

---

[17] I take it that theories of intensional identity (substitution *salve veritate* in modal contexts, consistent interpretation in different possible worlds, and the like) have not traditionally been applied to deictic expressions in this way.

at least in the present image the fan-in and fan-out are properties of fields, like vortices or manifolds, not yet chopped up into the discrete individuals that are prerequisite to at least a countable notion of "many."[18] (Since this field-theoretic fan-in and fan-out is going to have to be used to develop notions of individuality, there had better be a construal of it that does not require those individuals in advance.[19])

We saw other details too. Thus consider such prototypical deictic terms as 'I,' 'here,' and 'now.' It was suggested that ego-centric constants like "to the right" are implicitly defined with respect to (the direction faced by) the person who uses them. According to the cross-cutting extension story, the initial linguistic versions that use an explicit deictic pronoun, such as "to *his* right," implicitly make reference to *him*, him who has temporal extent—who is an individual, who has identity. "To his right," that is, means or implicates something like "to the right of the direction currently faced by the social, personal, historical person that he is." If we are to understand the simpler case, without a pronoun, as taking its deixis from the moment-to-moment pre-ontological (unregistered) physical substrate, then that will not make reference to a person as a whole. Thus one begins to see, as words are brought in to say what was previously left unsaid, how it is that abstractions and individuations are implicated—abstractions and individuations that reach farther out into the surround than the prelinguistic deictic ground.

Somewhat surprisingly, the picture also has a slightly essentialist feel. For if the s-region's registrational practices[20] are constitutively involved in establishing the o-region as an ob-

---

[18] As a word of English, 'many' does not require countability: there can be many clouds in the sky, without their being any metaphysical warrant for saying that there are eleven, as opposed to ten or twelve.

[19] "Field-theoretic" is not quite the right characterization. See §1 of chapter II.

[20] As I argue in the next chapter, an s-region's registrational practices are not sufficient; in general, all of its activities are implicated.

ject—if, that is, in order to be the object that it is, an object must be taken as (or quietened into) that kind of object—then it would seem, to speak in overly expensive language, as if the object will *have* to exemplify certain "properties": namely, those properties that figure in its registration as the kind of object that it is. If individuation criteria are not wholly independent of the registrational practices of the subject, that is, being *that* individual will depend (at least in part) on being so registered. To be some other individual would similarly depend (in part) on being registered in some other way—perhaps even in an incompatible registration scheme. If individuation has to do with identity, in other words, on the notion of "identity" defended in chapter 4, then identicality has to do with identity too. Identicality is not independent of aspect. *Is* is not independent of *as*.

This is not discrepant from common sense. The belt, qua belt, and the piece of leather it is made of, qua piece of leather, are not only differently registered, but have different identities—the identity of the belt having to do with its function, say; the identity of the piece of leather, with its leatherness. Is that the same belt, a year later? Yes, one might say. And the same piece of leather? No, that piece lasted only a few months. Was the belt *necessarily* a belt; could it have been a chamois for cleaning the car? The answer is not easy in the saying. Qua piece of leather, *it* could have been a chamois. But no, not qua *belt*. Not in the sense of being the entity that was still the same object a year later.

But enough of these examples. Although it is good to develop a feel for details, we cannot yet carry them through to the end; requisite preparation is still a ways off. For now it is enough to summarize this chapter's digression into reference preservation—or rather, as we are beginning to see it, into ontology-construction—by distinguishing the three kinds of entity that have played a constitutive role:

1. What is *adjusted* (e.g., the orientation of the flashlight),
2. What is *compensated for* (e.g., the movements of the acrobat), and
3. What is *thereby stabilized* (e.g., the point of illumination).

The first of these—what is *adjusted,* in order to stabilize or preserve whatever it is that is stabilized or preserved—is often an explicit representation or registration or at least part of the s-region. The second, however, what is compensated *for*, will typically involve arbitrary facts about the life and times of either the s-region or o-region or Lord only knows what else that might be relevant (e.g., who moved in from Kenya), not simply facts about the s-region's representational structures, prowess, or even movements and circumstance. Moreover, although the retraction may seem to imply that most adjustments are made locally, if not always internally, not only what is compensated for, but also, and more importantly, what is thereby *stabilized*—i.e., the crucial third type of entity—will very frequently be distal, implying that no theory that expects to get at the normative conditions on such systems can be localist or narrow. An adequate theory of reference preservation, therefore—or rather, an adequate theory of intentionality and metaphysics—in order to do justice to all three in relation, will have to consider the full, embodied, participatory life of the subject, not simply its intentional projection.

4 The achievement of the object

So far, in this chapter, I have emphasized the compensatory strategies of the subject in order to highlight the contribution of the s-region to the resulting stabilization or ontological achievement. This strategy is dangerous. By compensating for common sense (or rather by compensating for received Ontology), it puts too much weight on one side of what is ultimately a collaborative endeavor. It is time, therefore, to apply a rhetorical corrective, and give due credit to the object.

For no matter how clever the compensatory practices of subjects—no matter how inventive their use of instruments, for example, to obtain effective but ingenious access to the o-region, orchestrated in such a way that the peculiar contributions of those instruments can themselves be washed out by yet further compensatory practices—there is no reason to believe that the world is such that arbitrary patches of it can be appropriately stilled. This is one reason why the account is not purely idealist. Stability is equally an achievement of the o-region.

It is here that traditional intuitions about the constitutive conditions on being an object would find their place—intuitions, for example, about objects being a common cause of multiple external events, and of being the loci of appropriate forms of internal coherence—all forms of "sameness across difference" (more fan-in and fan-out). One way to get a sense of this, without paying too high an ontological price (for "external events," "coherence," "cause," etc.) is by analogy with the now-famous vortices and basins of attraction of non-linear dynamics. As an example, think of an eddy in a fast-flowing stream: even though it exists happily without clear boundaries, it pulls a certain amount of structure or coherence into itself, thereby developing something like an internal center of gravity, in terms of which it both insulates itself from the buffeting of external events, and in virtue of which it exerts its influence on that surrounding region. It is along such lines that intuitions about self-organization and other structural configurations investigated in research into artificial life would come into play.

Three caveats need to be posted, however, against a possible misinterpretation of these and other earlier intuitions.

First, as already indicated, and as will be examined further in chapter 9, the assumption that stability is conveniently separable into actions of the s-region and actions of the o-region is a fiction. Part of what it is for a subject to stabilize the o-region is to intervene, bodily, as it were, so as to ensure that the o-region remains stable enough to be registered. Except that even to say "intervene" takes too strong a position as to the locus of agency. The achievement is collaborative, through and through, not wholly attributable to either party.

Second, as suggested in chapter 4, since what it is to be an object cannot in general be separated from what it is to be registered as an object, "being an object" is not a *local* property of the o-region, not something that inheres within it.[21] A teacup's exemplification of the property of being a teacup does not inhere in its meager six ounces; it reaches back into British society. Nor is a computer's being a computer something that can be got at by getting out a microscope and taking it apart. Being a computer is a question of *fit*, not of architecture. As is everything else.

Objects cannot be objects on their own, to answer a question asked at the beginning of chapter 3. The achievement is not one of *self*-organization, as imagined in so much of the current fashion with artificial life. There are also no intrinsic properties. All of these facts are entailed by the comment made above that presence and absence are indissoluble. Objects, in order to *be* objects, not just in order to be *taken* as objects, require being separated from. This is why they are not *effective*, and will never be understood through wholly effective (physical) glasses.

Third, as all these points make clear, the fundamental picture being painted is one in which the world, primordially whole or entire, is gradually but only partially broken down or separated or *articulated* into objects, through complex and partially disconnected practices of registration. This is the opposite of a bottom-up story—the opposite of a view in which the world is

---

[21] At first blush, one might claim that the property of being an object is *relational*. At second blush, that might seem untenable—circular or contradictory—if relations are viewed as holding between and among objects. But at third blush, the claim has some sense to it, after all—if what it is to be an object and what it is to "be in relation" emerge together, as ontological coconspirators.

assembled, piece by piece, from a foundation of objects (or Objects). Imagine, instead, a scenario in which one starts with the world as a whole, and slowly takes it apart into objects—pulls them apart, separates them, makes distance between them, as it were, but only gradually, the way a potter would gradually pull pots out of a prior mass of clay. *The pieces are (partially) sedimented or extruded from the whole; the whole is not put together from the pieces*—a fact of great significance, implying for example that there are infinitely many unregistered (and hence unseparated) connections and ties and kinds of connective tissue tying everything together, more than can possibly be imagined, or than could possibly be the result of any given articulation.

But then imagine the same thing, except this time remove the external observer—the potter. The fields must be sufficiently dynamic and restless to do all this separating out on their own.

5 The registration of particularity

In chapters 3 and 4, objects were analyzed in terms of three notions—particularity and individuality, primarily, at least imaginatively on the part of the object, against a backdrop of objectivity, on the part of the subject-object relation. As a final exercise for this chapter,[22] it is instructive to consider a single more complicated case: what it is to register objects in the sense described in those chapters—i.e., to register them *as* individual and particular.

With respect to particularity, note first that the particularity of neither registrar nor what is registered, of neither s-region nor o-region, is in question. Particularity is inescapable; it derives directly from the flux. Do anything, point to anything, be anything—and it will be particular. In a sense, that is, particularity is the one free lunch: the one characteristic that does not need to be paid for. On at least one interpretation, therefore, "the registration of particularity" is not in itself much of an achievement,

[22] For those with the requisite technical appetite. Some readers may prefer to skip directly to chapter 9.

beyond the achievement of having successfully registered any-thing at all.

Registering something *as* particular, however, is considerably more complex. In part it is ontologically more complex, because it demands more sophisticated forms of cross-cutting extension than we have yet seen. But it is also methodologically more com-plex, in the sense of being more difficult to analyze. And it is more difficult to analyze, in turn, because of lurking inscrip-tion errors.

To see why, return to the case of the super-sunflower, the vari-ety that was able to non-effectively track the sun. More specifi-cally, imagine that we, qua theorists or observers, watch a particular such flower for a few moments—late one afternoon, say on May 7, 1995—as it slowly turns, while, obscured by a mountain or building or tree, the sun, too, moves across the sky, in at least rough synchrony.

In and of themselves, these two processes, flower and sun, are wholly particular. That much is virtually tautologous; there is no sense to the idea of their being anything else. But now sup-pose we inquire about the "content" of the super-sunflower's states.[23] Suppose, moreover, in order to sharpen intuitions, that a critic raises the following challenge: claiming that, in spite of the particularity of both flower and sun, the *content* of the flow-er's angular position, at any given moment, should be counted as *generic*, rather than particular. The suggestion might be de-fended by arguing that the flower cannot distinguish between the actual sun and any other exemplar of something pointing at it from that direction. "The flower would be in the same state," the critic claims, "in the face of any equivalent incident sun-

---

[23] That the super-sunflower's states or movements have at least some rudi-mentary form of content is assured by my describing the situation as one of "non-effective tracking"—although of course there is no reason to suppose that I can register that content, in English, in anything like the way in which it presents to the flower itself. I cannot speak in the register of sun-flowers.

light." The content of the flower's orientation, they go on to argue, is not the particular situation of the sun's now being at exactly that incident angle (N-74°W, say), but rather the abstract property of *there being incident radiation at* N-74°W.

Though superficially seductive, this argument fails, because of what in chapter 1 I called piggyback errors. It fails, that is, for the same reason that the argument failed about cats' abilities to reidentify their masters. And it is straightforward to see why. By way of preparation, note that the facts on the ground (i.e., in the garden) involve *100 percent point-wise correlation of particularity*, of exactly the sort that was indicated in figure 7·2. That is how we set up the problem. At a particular instant in time, a particular instance of a particular super-sunflower's pointing in a particular direction is distally coordinated, across a gap in effective coupling, with the particular incident light of a particular sun. There is no gap in particularity across this chain of correspondence.

But if there is no gap in particularity, what intuition underlies the critic's suggestion—a suggestion which does after all have some intuitive appeal? The answer is very simple. The critic's intuition has grip *because it registers the flower generically*. It assigns content not to a *particular* state of the flower, but to a *type* of flower state; namely, to what it registers as a generic *orientation*. This is betrayed by the critic's use of the phrase 'the *same* state' in their claim that the flower "would be in the same state." The phrase 'the same state' in that statement means the same state *type*; it does not mean the very same metaphysical (particular) space-time instant. The critic was not making a claim about what would be true if the universe's time arrow magically turned around, mid-course, and—contrary to metaphysical possibility—were to return the flower to the exact same particular state it was in (if that even makes logical sense). Rather, they were referring to the fact that, in a situation in which the flower was in the same generic state (in the same state *type*), then the content—that with which it was non-effectively coordinated—would similarly be in the same generic state. And that indeed is true. I admitted at the beginning that the case involved *100 percent point-wise correlation between particular and particular*. By an equivalent argument, it is easy to show that, at least with respect to a natural registration of types, there is *also 100 percent point-wise correlation between type and type*.

Does that make the content generic? It depends on what you mean. If, as is the common practice in semantics, you define as "content" something that *holds* of different particular uses—i.e., if you register the flower generically—then reason dictates, as just argued, that you will likely identify something equally generic on the other side, as the semantic value. But if the question, as I have been assuming, is about the interpretation in a particular situation, then it would be correspondingly reasonable to identify something equally particular on the other end. In a way, the situation is structurally identical to one in which a magnet picks up iron filings. And likewise it is the same as in cases of feature placing. In each case, qua theorist, you can register a generic-to-generic relation, or you can register a particular-to-particular relation. Each has its use. Each time I say "It is foggy" I make a different particular claim—now when I say it, I mean that it is foggy now; when I say it, here, just a little bit later, I mean that it is foggy here; and so on and so forth. On the other hand, there is something more generic—something I earlier called the "meaning"—that one can associate with the sentence type "It is foggy."

Given this general picture of pointwise correlation, return then to the original question, about registering something *as* particular. Since the beginning, I have admitted that particularity is essential to the notion of a concrete individual, and thus that registering something *as* particular must be part of registering a concrete individual as the concrete individual that it is. Moreover, as I have said several times, the task in the case of reg-

Degrees of particularity

Consider the question (posed in chapter 1) of whether or not to count computational self-reference as indexical. As the registrational prowess of a system increases, it exploits its local effective freedom in order to establish cross-cutting patterns of intentional directedness. That is the essence of registration. Typically, moreover, such activity, with respect to particularity, involves *both an aspect of fan-out and an aspect of fan-in*, as first suggested in several examples presented in chapter 1, and then again here in chapter 8. To the extent the subject achieves any cross-cutting directedness at all, then the following theoretical situation presents itself.

If one registers the state of the subject with common fan-in as the semantically evaluable entity, that will count as an appropriate reduction in particularity, and "particular registration" will be warranted. If instead one registers the subject more abstractly, then the fan-in across that wider extent will fail to converge, and so the appropriate semantic "value" will cease to be considered particular. The analysis in chapter 1 illustrated just this structure, except that it was complicated by the introduction of two semantic entities, rather than one: meaning vs. interpretation. The result, however, was structurally the same: the more abstract registration (trans-machine types) passed beyond the point where the fan-in converged on a

istering something as an individual is to refer, consistently, *to a particular object over time*—i.e., over a period of time, to reidentify it, to take it as the *same* particular individual. As this way of putting it makes clear, the situation requires something above and beyond what is required in simple cases of tracking (effective and non-effective). It needs exactly the sorts of cross-cutting regularity discussed in previous sections. But now we can state that requirement more carefully. What the analysis shows is that to register something *as* particular requires that a generic *type* of registrational act have a *particular* object as its content.

The registration of something *as* particular, in other words, requires a *reduction (fan-in) in particularity across the registration*

single taken-as-unitary region, thereby justifying the label of indexicality (generic *meaning*, as opposed to generic *content*).

In the case of the super-sunflower as described in chapter 6 (point-wise correlation of particularity), there is essentially no fan-in, and so no motivation to register the state of the flower any more abstractly than as a particular instantaneous state, without thereby registering the semantic value abstractly as well. The symmetry of the situation is what impresses itself onto analysis. This is what was conveyed by saying that the coordination structure of the super-sunflower was of particular to particular, and of type to type. In other cases, however, as fan-in grows, wider and wider ranges of behavior will be seen to orient to the same particular referent. There is no reason to suppose that this is a binary process, or that there is any sense to be made of a notion of the "most" abstract registration (a mistake endemic to various traditional philosophical distinctions, such as that between "narrow" and "broad" content). The crucial point is to see this as an instance of a general moral (§s 2–3 of chapter 11) about gradualism: *particularity of content is not an all-or-nothing accomplishment.* It has to do with the extent of the cross-cutting directedness—which will always be a matter of degree.

link, from registrar to registered. This reduction is necessary in order for *different* uses or instantiations of a registrational type to have the *same* particular referent or content. This is why taking an individual to be an individual requires something above and beyond the simple point-wise correlation of feature-placing. It is also why identification of something as an individual is logically the same as being able to reidentify it as an individual.

Once started, moreover, the process multiplies productively. Indeed, these are the origins of the "calculus of sameness and difference" alluded to in §1c of chapter 4, towards the development of which this work is now in part aimed. Space does not permit the pursuit of more complex examples here (though see the "degrees of particularity" sidebar on page 274). But reason would suggest, as I have anyway tried to indicate informally, that the most appropriate or useful mathematical calculus for these phenomena will primarily want to traffic in generalized fan-out and fan-in, and (reminiscent of the way in which relativity theory takes synchrony to be perspectival) allow individuality to be perspectival. And in a way this same conclusion is required by an argument given in the final chapter: that the very *distinction* between particularity and universality is ultimately a matter of negotiation and degree.[24]

---

[24] None of this is to imply the possibility of, or even to admit a longing for, an entirely "formal," non-perspectival mathematics. See §3c of chapter 12.

So far—except during puppet shows—the discussion has been conducted at a relatively low level. Talk about "subjects" and "objects" has remained within shudder quotes; not enough structure has emerged to warrant unmarked use of those terms. Because of working at this low level, and because of still operating under the temporary expedience of an underlying physical feature field, I have also been informal in choosing theoretic categories for registering what the subject registers—i.e., for registering the "object" or o-region towards which the s-region is directed. In these aboriginal cases, there is no point pretending that we elaborated theorists and our minimalist "proto-subjects" can even begin to share or even overlap registers. Admittedly, this lapse into pre-emptive registration limits analysis. But as long as we remember that all analytic and descriptive categories are ours, not theirs, and strive to minimize unwarranted theoretical projection, we can stay out of too much trouble. Certainly none of the described situations has been complicated enough for there to be any danger of outright conceptual clash (of the sort discussed at the end of the introduction).

But one cannot live in the basement forever. At some point, the discussion needs to move "upwards," towards more sophisticated forms of registration. We saw glimmers of these upper reaches in chapter 8: of proto-feature-placing in the workings of clocks, for example, where what was stabilized was more of an intensional invariance or object-less-property than an independent individual with an autonomous claim on being a referent. And with respect to object registration, we saw some of what was involved in using a process of deconvolving deictic relations to stabilize a distal point of directedness beyond effective reach. Still, there would be a ways to go before one could make good on the promise of building a registering machine.

1 Conceptual registration

One of the most important ingredients in a more complex story will be an explanation of the construction of the logical structure of property exemplification—i.e., an analysis of what is involved in the ability of a subject to interact with the world in such a way as to allow it to register that world in terms of (or to take it to consist in) properties and relations holding of objects. This introduces a second kind of cross-cutting topology into the story, a topology taken to live wholly in the "semantic domain"—i.e., in the vicinity or realm of the o-region (though that is not to say that the full *achievement* is there; for many reasons, including some discussed in this chapter, part of the achievement may be the subject's).

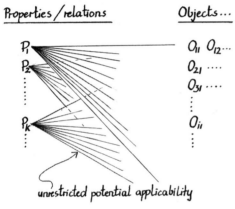

FIGURE 9·1   CONCEPTUAL REGISTRATION

The initial cross-cutting topology introduced in the last chapter was simpler and logically prior: it had to do with tying parts of extended s-regions to whole extended o-regions (rather than the even simpler point-to-point relations directly sustained in the underlying fields), necessary en route to the registration of a proto-individual. Taking the world to consist in properties holding of individual objects, and relations holding between and among objects, requires something more complex: not just relating to the world via a cross-cutting topology, but seeing the world as itself at least partially *consisting in* a (different) cross-cutting topology.

More precisely, the ability to register a specific property's holding of a particular object (or a specific relation's holding among two or more particular objects)—what I will call *concep-*

tual registration—is widely assumed to rest on a general ability to register (within reason) *any* property as holding of *any* object. Thus, at least for subjects in possession of the requisite concepts of *blue, lake, big*, and *cup*, to register a cup as blue, or a lake as big, is taken to depend on a background ability, in contrast, to register the lake as blue, or the cup as big. Using expensive language, one could say that objects and properties and relations must form something like the basis set of an algebraic structure of possible propositions.[1] Or more formally and more epistemically, that conceptual registration involves satisfying the following criterion, diagrammed in figure 9·1, and called a "generality condition" by Evans:[2] in order for a subject S to register an object **x** as being P, then (i) for any other objects **x′**, **x″**, etc., that S is capable of registering, it must also be able to register **x′**, **x″**, etc., as being P, and (ii) for any other properties P′, P″, etc., in terms of which S is also capable of registering, S must also be able to register **x** as being P′, P″, etc. (Instead of "register **x** as P" Evans would say "entertain a thought about **x** to the effect that it

---

[1] Conceptual registration is cross-cutting not only in this algebraic sense of requiring that an arbitrary predicate potentially apply to an arbitrary object, but also in another more metaphysically demanding sense that the notion of "locality" for properties or types is in some intuitive sense metaphorically based upon, but at the same time conceptually orthogonal to, the original case of spatio-temporal proximity or continuity. Thus to register or "carve the world" in such a way that violet is closer to blue than to yellow, that rutabagas are closer to parsnips than to blueberries, that melancholy is closer to ennui than to spunk, and so on and so forth, is to separate the world's underlying richness into manageable pieces according to measures or metrics substantially different from those of ordinary space-time.

[2] See Evans (1982). Strawson (1959) takes something like this to be the logical structure of objects and properties. Essentially the same requirement is called by Fodor the systematicity or productivity of thought; see Fodor & Pylyshyn (1988) and Fodor & McLaughlin (1990). It is also one of the things that is connoted by the term 'compositionality,' though the language/world ambiguities of that notion, talked about in the next few paragraphs in the text, make it perhaps the least useful of the three.

279

is **P**," and Cussins "represent **x** as being **P**," but the point survives translation.)

Accounting for conceptual registration would be just part of a higher-level account. Such a story would also want to tease apart different *kinds* of object—or different ways in which singular terms refer—so as to distinguish processes from events, mass terms from properties, composite objects from sets, and so forth. It should also explicate such familiar issues as: the nature of, and interaction between, negation and denial; how homophony, indexicality, ambiguity, and vagueness are alike, and how different; what fictional reference is, and how it works; how language and thought relate, and whether either has logical or ontological priority—and so on and so forth, up through and including the whole panoply of topics normally studied under the banners of semantics, epistemology, and the philosophy of language.

Important as these questions are, however, it would be premature to pursue them here. We do not yet know nearly enough about the lower levels. This metaphysical ignorance is especially hazardous in the face of such theoretically familiar questions. The conjunction—of subject-matter ignorance and methodological familiarity—makes it almost impossible to proceed without being derailed by the classic Realist Ontology of Objects, Properties, and Relations.

1a Character, coverage, and closure

Three problems stand out, that would need resolution en route to a tenable (irreductionist) account of conceptual registration. The first has to do with the *character* of conceptual registration's ingredients: the nature of the logical or ontological "primitives" in terms of which the generality condition is typically formulated. In a spirit of reclamation, I remain committed to lower-case versions of these upper-story notions—to objects, properties, and the like, as lived, in-the-world, workaday categories. But of course I cannot take them as primitive, or even as atomic.

All I have said in a positive vein about these lower-case categories, however, is that ontological boundaries, at least in general, will not be nearly as "clear and distinct" as Ontological Boundaries. By itself, this is not enough to resist the seduction of classical formalized borders. Thus consider the discussion, above, of how predicating **P** of **x** depends on a background ability to predicate **P′**, **P″** of **x**, and **P** of **x′**, **x″**. Crucially, this statement does not *require* a formal conception of **P** and **x**, yet it is almost guaranteed to *receive* a formal interpretation, given its almost algebraic formulation—especially in these modernist theoretical times, unless buttressed by a sturdy non-formalist alternative. But a non-formalist alternative has yet to be supplied.

Conceptual registration's second problem has to do with *coverage*: with how much of the world can or should be corralled under such categories, even in lower-case form. So far I have explicitly named only one exception: feature-placing, introduced in chapter 4. But chapter 6's image of riotous fomenting fields, to say nothing of the overall tenor of the discussion, suggest that feature-placing is not unique. Moreover, much recent cognitive science argues to the same conclusion. Thus think of what Cussins calls "non-conceptual content," applicable not only to informal drawings and sketches but also to thoughts, such as when we imagine two objects *a certain distance apart*, comprehending the distance *as such*, not mediated via its conceptualized equivalent of a number and standardized distance to which it is related by a signified mathematical ratio—such as "3½ feet." Or what Smolensky calls *sub-symbolic* interpretations of connectionist networks. Or the Churchlands' focus on non-propositional content. Or even Dreyfus' avowal of implicit knowledge and skill, in place of explicit conceptualized structure.[3] Remember, too, more directly, that blown spray on a summer afternoon. Earlier I decried the prospect of force-fitting such phenomena

---

[3] Strawson (1959), Evans (1982), pp. 159, 227, etc., Cussins (1990, 1992, & forthcoming), Smolensky (1988), Churchland (1986 & 1992), Churchland (1989), Dreyfus (1992), Goel (1995).

into Conceptual Ontology, but it would still be a travesty, even if a lesser travesty, to subjugate them to what it is natural to call *conceptual ontology*: the ontology of objects, properties, and relations, even in lower-case dress.

Third, there is a question about *closure*. At issue is whether conceptual registration, and the thought and inference and behavior processes it involves, are coherent on their own terms—and thus, even if they are not complete, nevertheless form a well-behaved and partially autonomous sub-region of a larger overall registrational space—or whether, as seems more likely, especially given the spirit of what has been suggested, that that sort of internal closedness is only characteristic of Ontology. Traditional models of rational inference, to come at this from another side, including most formal logics, are what we might call *Conceptually Closed*. They assume that all applicable normative properties—Truth for Propositions, Warrant for Judgment, Validity for Inference, etc.—can be semantically evaluated with respect to the presence or absence of relevant Properties and Relations holding of relevant Objects (perhaps aided with Sets, Types, Functions, and other ordnance of Mathematics). Such Closure is metaphysically indicated, from Logic's point of view, since Conceptual Ontology (Objects, Properties, Relations, etc.) is all that is assumed to exist.

There is no reason why someone who embraces non-conceptual registration need accept even a more modest lower-case version of the thesis, however: that rationality or inference be *conceptually closed*. Think of the truism that someone possessed only of "book knowledge" of a given subject matter, especially one far from common sense and experience, is liable to reach spectacularly dumb conclusions. Or that a constant diet of perception and action is needed in order to keep inference from gradually drifting astray. These homilies suggest, and I will soon argue, that the coherence of conceptual inference is not wholly sustainable "internally"—within conceptual ontology alone (even in lower-case dress). On the contrary, "in the wild" high-level conceptual inference will turn out, essentially and inextricably, to rest on a constant underlying connective tissue of non-conceptual content, between and among and through all the explicit conceptualized steps.

1b   Representation and ontology

All three questions—about character, coverage, and closure—should be answered, not presumed, by an analysis of conceptual registration. But doing so without inscription error is hard. A moment ago, for example, I said that the rise of conceptual registration involves the development (existence, emergence, achievement) of a certain almost algebraic compositional structure. As will have been noticed, I described that structure in two ways. First, I described it *ontologically* as a space of (possible) facts or worlds: consisting, for any given object, of a spate of properties holding of it; and for any given property, of its holding of a spate of objects. Second, I described the same thing *representationally* or *epistemically* as a space of possible syntactic or grammatical or linguistic representational states: different terms governable with the same predicate; different predicates governing the same term.

In Logic and Semantics, both structures are posited, as if independent, and then related. This is the famous "syntax mirroring semantics." First, the world is alleged to have a certain (Logical) structure, consisting of Objects, Functions, Properties, Relations, etc., fitting together in a certain combinatoric way—helped along by metaphysical Conjunction, Disjunction, and the like. Second, the representing subject is held to employ a certain syntactic (grammatical, linguistic) representational system, consisting of Terms and Predicate Structures and Operators, which again fit together in a certain combinatoric way—this time helped along by such things as open terms, concatenation, and dominance. Then, taking both structures as given, traditional Semantics frames the normative question as one about the extent to which these structures *correspond* (at least on a correspondence theory)—with Truth obtaining when they do.

A prior question, however, has to do with their respective ontological or metaphysical status. *How independent are these two combinatoric structures—one of word, one of world?* Did God make them separately: starting on Tuesday with the compositional structure of objects and properties and relations, and then turning, independently, on Friday, to a second form of composition, of predicates and terms? Or (to skip a few hundred pages), did predicates and terms—i.e., λόγος—come first? Is one structure subsidiary to, or a reflection of, the other? Or, more in line with what is being suggested here, are they neither dependent nor independent, but instead *partially* independent metaphysical cohorts? And what does "partially independent" even mean?

It is difficult to imagine a more metaphysically basic issue. By embracing registration as a logical alternative to representation and ontology, I have distanced myself from *having* to take (the compositional structure of) word and world as independent. By committing myself to the constructive intuition that subjects play a partially constitutive role in creating the ontology of the worlds they inhabit, I have suggested that they are *not* independent. And simply to *presume* that they are independent, as I have implied throughout, is at best pre-emptive, and at worse an inscription error. In particular, by projecting an essentially linguistic or representational categorical framework onto the world,[4] it is liable to "overdimension" it, by assuming that it contains more information or distinction than in fact exists.

---

[4] Many so-called property theories, such as Barwise and Perry's situation theory (1983), are in my view guilty of this form of linguistic projection—for example in distinguishing the type *tiger* from the type *being an* **x**, *such that* **x** *is a tiger*. "There is less in heaven and earth than is dreamt of in their philosophy," if I can borrow a Goodmanesque critique (1983, p. 34). Especially in virtue of not being admitted, such linguistic projection (inscription) is different from the view being argued here: that anything warranting the name 'ontology' must reflect the registrational practices of subjects.

And yet it would be madness to suggest the opposite: that the combinatoric structure of language and the combinatoric structure of the world are the same. First, they are token distinct. There is still a robust sense, compatible with the best in constructivism, in which it is possible to discover that object **x** exemplifies property **P**—e.g., to notice that the sun has just set— in a way that is neither reducible nor homologous to a syntactic property of a representational vehicle. And of course it is also possible to be wrong. Second, neither are they categorically isomorphic. Not many, I suspect, especially this late in the century, would be willing to subscribe to such a strong "picture" theory of semantics as to require bestowing ontological reality onto non-existent individuals, or even (pace Lewis) giving metaphysical reality to other possible worlds, let alone populating the world with referents for unadorned quantifiers and naked modal operators.

What is odd about this discussion is that it has considered only two possibilities: (i) completely independent structures— at least metaphysically independent, even if subsequently tied by semantical regularity; and (ii) totally dependent structures— i.e., identical structures, i.e., really only one structure, or at least only one kind of structure or form of combination. Fortunately, however, these two options do not exhaust the space of possibilities (even if they are the only things that present themselves to a formalist imagination[5]). A vast territory opens up between them: a territory of *partial interdependence* or *partial co-constitution*—a territory, especially on reflection, that is likely to include all of reality. Indeed, as will become increasingly clear, the opportunities provided by this intermediate space of are a source of great optimism. This should come as no surprise; it is hardly a secret, after all, that mature adult relations require exactly this kind of mix of partial interdependence and partial autonomy. The problem is that pragmatic familiarity, especially in the

---

[5] See §2 & 3 of chapter 12.

realm of human interaction, is different from theoretical rigor. It is still unclear what a conceptual territory of partial interdependence might be like, especially in its middle regions.

1c   Partial separation

It is time to pause, to take our bearings. In considering the sorts of issues that would be involved in moving the story upwards, into the realm of conceptual registration, we ran into the general epistemological issue of *how the order of explanation relates to the order of phenomena*. In the conceptual case, the question had specifically to do with the nature of the relation between two rather abstract combinatoric (lower-case) structures: an ontological one of objects and properties and relations, and a representational one of terms and predicates. By adopting a notion of registration, I avoid committing myself to a sharp (formal) dichotomy between the two. But I still need *some* distinction in order to keep word and world from collapsing. Something intermediate is needed: something like a notion of partial distinction.

But that is very suggestive. For I have already pointed to something else that is partial: *the separation between subject and object*. That raises the following obvious question: of how the two relate. Specifically, how does the partial separation (coordinated partial disconnection) between subject and object, constitutive of registration, affect the epistemological issue of (perhaps partially interdependent) word-world order? What is the metaphysical (not just semantic) relation between property exemplification and term predication? Though admittedly abstract, the question is of extreme metaphysical importance. And it is because I am not yet ready to answer it that it would be premature, at least at this point, to drive the story upwards.

So we need to stay in the basement for a little while longer. And in a way, that is just as well. For something else calls out for attention. Even though the scope of the discussion was broadened at the beginning of chapter 6 from objects to registration in general, it is still too restricted. Not so much restricted to a particular species of registration (such as feature placing or conceptual registration) as restricted to registration itself—to the exclusion of the rest of life. This was especially a problem in the previous two chapters: the microscope was focused too closely on the disconnected (semantic) tie that binds subject to object. It is time to widen the view.

2 Participation

The picture of registration conveyed in the last several chapters was too narrow. It was too cognitive, as if registration were a function of (proto-)brains. It was too individualistic, as if registration were an achievement of individual "subjects." And it was too specific, as if registering the world were the only thing these subjects ever did. All three assumptions are false. We also eat, take shelter, make things, run away, laze about, get old, and argue about politics. We write, make signs, operate instruments, read newspapers. And we do these things in community—not only with other *people*, but "in communion" with the whole rest of the world: with newspapers, meals, instruments, and organizations, as well as with family and friends.

Coming at it from above, one can say, as I have said many times, that an account of full-scale intentionality, as opposed merely to registration, must be an account of *participation* or *engagement*—not just of cognition, and not even just of experience. Planting a garden, driving across the tundra, and spilling dioxin in the water supply are aggressive and violent acts, not capturable by being described as a way of experiencing the world. And as suggested in chapter 1, a participatory moral is also a clear result of studying computation in the wild. In spite of the fact that the theoretical frameworks passed down to us from intellectual history, especially those inherited from the formal tradition, by and large treat computation as detached symbol manipulation, in actual fact computers are inextricably *involved* in their subject matters, whether that is a world of documents, electronic mail, network servers, microwave ovens, keyboards, or computerized brakes. No model of them as purely representational, or even as purely experiential, can begin to do them justice.

Adopting a participatory stance cuts deep, deeper even than has yet been admitted. The point is not simply that machines (and people) are doing things, as well as representing and reasoning about and sampling the world—as if those forms of activity could be conceptually teased apart. The idea, rather, is that a full spectrum of behavior is ontologically implicated in a system's ability to individuate and register. We need to acknowledge the extraordinarily complex networks of actors and activities and "actants"[6] that make up the compensatory behavior necessary in order to triangulate onto an object. This is the realm of history, documents, instruments, social practices, organizations, beliefs, settings, interests, money, lawyers, and the like, whose ontological importance sociology and social studies of science have been at such pains to point out.[7] Scientific examples may be the easiest to see, partly in virtue of the fact that the resultant stabilized entities are relatively far from common sense, and partly because the machinery necessary in order to stabilize them, to hold them quiescent in our view, is often both visible and expensive. But the moral is as true of the mundane as it is of the abstruse. Fairy stories and grudging invitations to dinner are at least as sophisticated ontological achievements as the discovery of penicillin or the use of gamma rays.

Objects are not stabilized only through acts of disconnected focusing, in other words. Nor are they stabilized merely in virtue of their own integrity or achievement, or even of the two phenomena together. They are also stabilized by *force*, through the travails of those who register them. And not solely through the

[6] A semiotic term for people, machines, and any other social agents or agencies.
[7] See the references listed in footnote 1 of chapter 3 (p. 86).

efforts of individuals, or even institutions, but with the full complicity of the surrounding community of practice.[8]

So that is the territory to be reached for: not just higher-level (conceptual) ontology or traditional epistemology, but the full social and material and political and historical web of life. And yet, crucial as these observations are, there is a problem with proceeding in this explanatory vein. The problem is the usual one: the image is being painted with overly expensive paint. Whence these organizations? these scientific practices? these social and political forces? Until we know their cost—the violence they wreak, the biases they betray, the blinders they impose—we cannot take responsibility for them. And until we can take responsibility for them, we cannot invoke them in metaphysical reconstruction. As much is implied by the irreductionist mandate.

But what, then? Does this bring analysis to a halt? Is this a more profound, ethical version of the ontological wall?

No. It would be, if intellectual work were solitary. But just as any adequate successor account must acknowledge the sociality of registration, so too intellectual work should be conducted in full appreciation of the sociality of *inquiry*. And I am not claiming that no one can take responsibility for such institutions; only that the general metaphysician, or at least this metaphysician, cannot, since I, in particular, am not a social theorist. So I will take my task as one of reaching towards those who can shoulder such responsibility, in a spirit of collaboration, and of offering them the best account I can of what it is to be metaphysically grounded—rather than attempting to account for how we are grounded in this or that institution, or even, more abstractly, for how we are grounded in institutions at all.

Given that I am still working under a semi-physicalist framework, that translates into a requirement to see, currently from a field-theoretic viewpoint, but soon without that restriction, how such organizations and scientific practices and political

---

[8] See Lave & Wenger (1991).

forces could arise, and what role they could play in underwriting registrational practice.[9] And this is task enough. For until one gets underneath ontology, it turns out to be impossible to understand the nature or purpose of this whole surrounding web of histories and forces and practices and organizations that play such a role in stabilizing objects. Only by getting in under ontology (and in part under registration) can one understand what in general I will call the *participatory surround*.[10]

3 Connection and disconnection

Go back, then, to the original image: of parts or regions of the deictic fields continuously pulling apart from other parts, and then subsiding back into them, sometimes being overwhelmed or absorbed, sometimes staying separate, sometimes aligning and becoming stronger, sometimes being fractured or scattered irretrievably. Throughout, the picture was of a fomenting sea of riotous activity—so riotous and dynamic, in fact, as to defy unique or even finite registration.

Above, when using expensive language to get at this picture, I claimed that people and computers are engaged or involved in the world. This engagement was fundamental—even constitutive—to the picture of intentional life as participatory. But it was not explained. So we need to figure out what engagement

[9] In a sense, one can imagine the space-and-time-filling fields (in this chapter; full flux, in chapter II), as *extensive* in a way that must underwrite the extension of the social and political and historical. Some readers will feel that the present account is insufficiently social; that it has concentrated too much on individuals. That is an impression I have tried to avoid, without simply repeating words such as 'social,' etc., though to some extent there is an inevitable problem with language, especially language under a modernist interpretation. But note that I have not yet assembled sufficient equipment with which to individuate or restrict the fields to individuals. So the presumption that the text has focused on individuals cannot be quite right.

[10] The Integrity Criterion (TMD·I) requires that an account of grounding *itself be grounded*. This form of grounding is something I neither pretend nor want to avoid. That was one of the motivations for chapter I.

looks like, through our field-theoretic glasses. What dimension does it add, what contribution does it make, to the pictures of gap-transcending coordination sketched in chapter 7?

The answer is plain. From the relatively minimalist perspective of fomenting deictic fields, an admission that engagement is constitutive can be understood as a recognition of the fact that the emergent patterns of activity we theorists register as subjects, objects, registration, dinner, etc., involve as much *connection* as *disconnection*. In the initial descriptions of registration I emphasized disconnection, or rather the effect-transcending coordination across gaps in connection, because such disconnection is a precondition to anything's taking anything to be something (and also because, of the two, especially recently, disconnection has been less adequately theorized[11]). But to focus on disconnection alone, even coordinated disconnection, is to skew the picture. First, disconnection is inevitably partial. Second, even that partial disconnection is only part of the story.

This is a philosophy of separation, in other words, *but it is equally a philosophy of encounter.* You can hardly cook for dinner something that is fictional, or that will only exist in the future, or that lives a long way away. Or lean on it, or bump into it on the street, or keep it in a drawer as a memento. Or wrestle it to the ground. What you *can* do with a fictional or future or faraway thing is to refer to it, wonder about it, or entertain it in a hypothetical. You can do those things because referring and wondering and hypothesizing are forms of intentional directedness, and intentional directedness, as we have already seen, is disconnected. Cooking and leaning on and wrestling with, on the other hand, are ways of *connecting*. And—this is the point—cooking and leaning on and wrestling with are also constitutive parts of the processes that stabilize objects as objects. They are part of *life*. And it is our lives, ultimately, that determine our ontologies.

In spite of anything that was implied in the previous chapters, that is, the participatory substrate—the grounds of intentionality—is not wholly constituted by patterns of disconnection. It is equally constituted by patterns of connection. In fact it is not quite right even to separate them in that way. It is the indissoluble patterning of connection and disconnection together that makes the whole thing work. That is why the metaphor of a dance was so appropriate. You touch, and then you let go; but you also touch.

So the story must be broadened, and made more symmetrical: to include patterns of connection and encounter, as well as coordinated patterns of disconnection and separation.

Except to say just that much is too easy. Or rather it makes things look too easy. For this sentence hides one of the trickiest facts about any metaphysical picture of this general sort (e.g., any picture compatible with symmetrical realism), having to do with what is symmetrical and what is asymmetrical within the overarching picture of an otherwise balanced, endless dance of partial connection and partial disconnection.

Connection or encounter is important, first, because this is where things happen; this is even what it is to happen—the locus of all struggles and trials and engagements and meetings, the pure and unvarnished bumping and shoving of the world. This is the realm of the effective, of which so much of computer science (or so at least I claim) is a nascent theory. This is what has to be *implemented* if you want to build something that plugs into the wall and gets something done. It is what was lacking in the properties Searle attributed to the wall in his office. And it is the locus of what is right about physicalism (though physicalism gets its own intuition wrong by trying to formulate it *ontologically*). The connected is the realm of force, struggle, energy, encounter. Connection or encounter is how the whole thing *works*.

On the other hand, *connection is also ineffable*. It is ineffable because, qua pure encounter, connection is inherently unregistered. It is unregistered in virtue of not being sufficiently separated for there to be any room for registration's inherent abstraction and stabilization to get purchase. The only way to get at it intentionally—e.g., through thinking or speaking—is by indirect triangulation. We can register it, in other words, but we register it inaccurately, at a loss, *at a distance*. Thus consider Latour's "trials of strength and of weakness"[12]—a phrasing he not so much qualifies as bursts open with a string of parallel ontological categories: of political battles, biological fermentation, physical effect, causality, late-night meetings, wars, face-to-face encounters, the taking of action, being effective. Connection, I take it, is what Latour is talking about; the point of the spray of terms is to evoke its utter familiarity while at the same time reminding us of the intrinsic paucity of any attempt to capture it in a single word.[13]

What does this have to do with registration? Just this: by far the most important fact about the essential coordination that gives rise to subjects, objects, culture, ice cream cones, and the like, is that it rests on a balance of partial connection as much as partial disconnection. As we have seen, systems continuously pull apart from other parts of the world and mesh back into them in complex temporal patterns. If they are to survive, these parts or regions cannot fuse wholly together; that would be too connected, too buffeting. Nor can they pull wholly apart; that would be too disconnected, too uncorrelated, too formal. Success, rather, is always an indissoluble mix of more or less separation, more or less engagement, so that the registered world, including all of ontology, is coordinated or *held in a kind of middle distance*.

As before, analogies from vision are helpful. Earlier I noted

[12] See Part Two of Latour (1988), e.g., pp. 158, 183, etc.
[13] Some may think that physics is, or provides, exactly what I am saying does not exist, or cannot be provided: a theory of pure encounter. See §1 of chapter 11.

that it is impossible to see something plastered on your eyeball; it has to be held away from you. But it is equally true, even banal, that you cannot see something that is out of view, or even just too distant. In order to be held in visual focus, objects have to be held in a literal middle distance—not too close, but not too far away. Registration is the same. If its object is too close it is buffeting; the requisite distance for stabilization and abstraction is missing. If it is too far away it cannot be coordinated with. There is too much flex, too much slop, and it is lost. It is in the middle where registered and registrar both live—constituted by an indissoluble mix of more or less separation, more or less engagement.

4 Separation and engagement

Throughout, I have used metaphors from physics to hint at features of much more sophisticated metaphysical situations. Some readers, it was admitted, will have worried that this will breed reductionism, though I have promised to let go of the physicalist crutch in chapter 11. In this section, however, just to keep things in (or perhaps out of) balance, I want to turn this practice around, and use sophisticated human examples to illustrate characteristics that I will then argue are shared by even the simplest objects.

The point is simple: we are wholly familiar, in conducting human affairs, not only with intrinsically partial notions of connection and separation, but also with managing a balance of the two—to say nothing of the maturity that such balancing acts require if we are to achieve our ends or virtue. Thus think for example about how, in managing a project (in business, research, family, whatever), one needs to balance enthusiastic involvement (connection) with a degree of perspective and detachment (disconnection) in order to avoid the pitfalls of either extreme: being either too reactive or close, or too oblivious and far away, from local events and contingencies. And think as well about how each member of a group has to both connect and disconnect from the group as a whole—i.e., must balance collaborative spirit with independent initiative. By the same token, notice how strongly we react against people who embody either extreme: people who want too much connection in their human relationships, people who fuse themselves to our affections, from whom we all shy away; and also people who in contrast are too separate, who take autonomy to pathological limits, who fail to be members of community at all. Like so much in this story, ordinary human interaction involves appropriately negotiating a seething middle ground.

Early on I said that objects are things on which one can have a perspective. This is again entirely familiar in human affairs: establishing and maintaining appropriate perspective on a situation involves a balance of connection and disconnection. Like visual perspective, it also requires being somewhere; it is a relational property, not an unlocated one. Thus part of what is involved in developing an appropriate perspective on a social or political situation is to recognize that one is somewhere, to take responsibility for one's proper place in the world. But it also requires detachment. Consider any sort of challenging or trying human relationship. If we are too involved, or get too upset, we may need to go on a trip, or leave the room, or count to ten, in order to gain some perspective on the situation. By the same token, human relationships sometimes suffer for lack of attention or contact; in such a case we may need to sit down and talk, get out on the floor, come along for the ride, put our shoulder to what needs doing. Moreover, it is again obvious, in these human cases, that the extremes are no ideal. Everyone knows that appropriate detachment does not mean cutting oneself off entirely or severing involvement; such states would better be called autism, estrangement, or death. Nor does appropriate involvement mean relinquishing dispassion or moving in too close or surrendering utterly; doing that is a sign of immaturity and insufficient autonomy.

To come at the same issue through a different kind of example, think about the homespun injunction to "think globally, but act locally." This homily is almost a *theorem* of the metaphysical view being advanced in these pages. In virtue of its inherent disconnection and abstraction, thought is inherently large-scale; it establishes long-distance relations, at an intrinsic cost of immediate detail, by a special form of separation. Action, on the other hand, in its most immediate and potent form, at the instant of taking effect, is concomitantly intrinsically local—so local in the limit as to defy adequate description. To achieve the right balance remains a trick; but the fact that a situation of "thought and action" is a situation *requiring* balance is by the present lights metaphysically guaranteed.

In citing these examples I am not trying to say anything new or surprising about the pattern of human relationship. The aim is just to point out the profound continuity between these "high-level" practices and the perhaps-only-apparently simpler practices involved in registering ordinary material objects. Patterns of partial engagement and partial separation, stabilization and coordination, are characteristic of an astonishing array of intentional behavior. Imagine a mountain lion streaking after a hare: the lion would employ a blend of connected servoing (when the rabbit is visible) and disconnected tracking (when the rabbit is out of sight), and even "predictive leaping," in order to land at a point where the rabbit is "expected" to be. Even chapter 1's computational examples exhibited this middle-ground participatory structure. Memory and file caches need to be connected to their underlying backing systems, in order not to get out of step; they also need to be detached, in order to run faster. Internet gateways must similarly stay apprised of the load on their neighbors in order to make intelligent routing decisions (whether a packet originating in Detroit should be sent to Tokyo via Honolulu or Anchorage). But they cannot stay in too close contact. Not only would this run the danger of having the checking process clog the system; it would also be senseless to spend more time searching for an optimal route than would be thereby saved. Or consider processor failure in distributed systems, to take a final example: in many situations it is reasonable for a client to wait for "output" (connection) from a server; but it is also important to design in enough "detachment," so that the client does not "hang" if the server is down.

Three comments will help place these last examples in context. First, none of this is to deny that human and social examples are more complex than simple graspings of coffee cups; or to deny that other considerations, such as of moral responsibility, play a more significant role in employee disputes than in reaching for a pen, let alone in updating a router table. But we should never forget what the ethnomethodologists' video tapes so reliably remind us: that even what we think of as the most trivial actions, on inspection, are almost stupifyingly complex. So we should at least be on guard against a pro-human ideological prejudice that our interactions with each other are so much more special than our involvement in the material world, or in its own internal interactions. Granting the human its due does not require subscribing to a formalist hierarchy of nature.

Second, it should be clear in all these cases, from simple to complex, familiar to remote, that connection and disconnection are not enough to constitute intentional participation alone, even if they are partial (as much holds of any sticky substance). The trick is not only to remain coordinated while apart, which we have seen in prior chapters, but also, as the social examples in this chapter have made clear, to make effective use of one's connection when together. The latter condition is particularly consequential, since it puts normative constraints onto action, even if that action is unregisterable. More generally—and this begins to show what would be involved in a more complete theory of participation, as opposed to a partial one of registration—the point is to connect in such a way as to support appropriate (coordinated) disconnection, and to disconnect in such a way as to support appropriate prior or subsequent connection. How this works is naturally complex. Think of how one recognizes someone from the perspective of a (nonconceptual) registration, but also of how, during the encounter, one lets go of the registration's intrinsic abstraction, in order to let the person's ineffable details fill in the lack. It is in order to make room for such achievements that I have used, but not yet attempted to analyze, the terms 'separation' and 'engagement.' My intent is to use *engagement* to signify something like "intentionally appropriate disconnection-oriented connection," and *separation* to signify "intentionally appropriate connection-oriented disconnection," in such a way that we can inquire into the nature of the separation and engagement that are characteristic, even constitutive, of intentional life.

Third, and finally, it is no accident that human relations are such a rich source of intuitions about this middle ground of participatory involvement. As much, after all, was one of chapter 3's desiderata for an adequate metaphysical picture: that human and social and ethical affairs—the right-hand side of figure 3·1, on page 90—be as solidly underwritten by any picture to be developed as electrons or numbers. Far from being on a different plane or in a different realm from the worlds of tables, fishing, and the achievement of objectivity, or being merely a metaphor, these familiar habits of dynamically balancing our affairs are both similar to and continuous with—in fact, at an important level of abstraction, are *the same as*—what is involved in taking a simple coffee cup to be a simple coffee cup.

5 Life in the middle lane

How can these expensive but intuitive pictures of middle-distance practice—these mixtures of partial separation and partial engagement—be brought back into the main stream of the story? In the long run, that will require the support of the full metaphysical account; for now, while we are still reaching towards that point, it will help to record a handful of the consequences that spill out from this picture of "life in the middle."

5a Construction

I said at the outset that I wanted to do justice to what was right about constructivism. I also said that constructivism could not be passed off as the claim that how the world *appeared* was (at least in part) dependent on facts about us perceivers, but had to be recognized as the stronger claim that we collaborate in determining how the world *is*. That this must in a very general sense be so was shown to be required by the "one world" symmetrical reading of realism. But that did not say how it would go; and anyway those claims were all desiderata, rather than substantive proposals.

Some of this has already been accomplished. That the subject is intrinsically involved in the act of registration was already made clear in the last chapter. But a stronger and perhaps deeper kind of construction—construction in the original sense of that word, involving authentic intervention and building in the world—is implicated by the present participatory story. Because the ineliminable relations that connect the web of practice to what is registered are in part *connected*—implying that a kind of ineliminable and unregistered "effective connective tissue" holds up every registerable thing, every act of registration—it follows that registration is not simply a process of selecting or filtering the world. On the contrary, it may, and usually will, also involve shaping the object in such a way that it can be seen as world. Participatory processes are as much violent as they are descriptive: we adjust the objects so that our theories are true of them, as well as adjusting our theories so that they are true of the objects. Stabilization is not just a process of standing back in order to let the object quieten; it also involves reaching out and bashing the object into shape, so that it will be stable enough to register. Programming is a vivid example. Though called computer "science," it is not a very good model of the empirical method. As in sculpture and painting, when word and world disagree, the practitioner is at least as likely to debug the world as to revise the word. By the same token, think about how hard electronics companies work in order to ensure that the resistors they produce are correctly described by Ohm's law. Or notice, to pick up on the example in the preface, how you have to get down on your knees and root around in the soil to till and maintain a garden, in order for the garden to continue to be "garden." *You have to work in order for it to continue to be the kind of thing that it is.* Processes of intervention, maintenance, tilling, and stabilization of this sort are in general necessary in order to sediment any object as an object. In their inexorable in-the-primordial-world-ness, the stuff of objects is by nature unruly. It is a collaborative achievement for them to hold, or be held, still enough to be brought into focus.[14]

A real-world example will illustrate. In the late 1980s, the Xerox Corporation began to wrestle with the consequences of the upcoming technological shift from optical (light-lens) to digital (electronic) copying. It was evident that the company's core business was in for radical change. As soon as an image of an original can be scanned electronically and stored on disk, many of the assumptions in the traditional model of copying no longer hold. There is no need to scan the original more than

---

[14] There is a famous children's sermon according to which a clergyman says to his neighbor, "That is an impressive garden you and God have there." "Thanks," says the neighbor; "you should have seen it when God had it alone." When I was young the theology perplexed me; now it seems like a wonderful ontological tale.

once, when making multiple copies. Copying speeds can be increased by running multiple print heads in parallel, rather than having to develop expensive, single high-speed paper paths. There is no need for the printer to be local; it can be upstairs, or across town, or thousands of miles away. In fact there is no need to print at all, right now; it may be more convenient to store the image and print it out later, on demand. And while you are at it, why leave the image intact? Why not crop it, or enhance it, or translate it into Telugu? All these shifts, Xerox noticed, were going to wreak havoc with the traditional business model—ranging from how charges are calculated, to such idiosyncrasies as recognizing that if the user is in Tokyo, but has requested printing in Delhi, it will not do much good to display the "printer is out of paper" message in Tokyo.

Informally, it was easy to see that what had been a unitary operation of "copying" was being broken down into a series of parts: scan, store, and print; or perhaps scan, store, modify, and print; or even scan, store, modify, retrieve, and print. But what about the objects these operations were defined over (or, perhaps more accurately, the objects these operations defined)? "Documents," one could (they did) call them—but that is just a name. What are documents? and what are their identity conditions? To make retrieval work, you need an answer that the user can understand. But as to what that answer should be, that is far from clear. If you modify an image, for example—clean up ink splotches on it, or crop it, or translate it into German, is it still the same document? Or is it a *copy* of the original? If the latter, has copying returned in a different, albeit abstract, guise?

For several years, a group of Xerox researchers tried to sort these things out, finally producing a four-volume specification of a new "document processing architecture." The result was so unwieldy as to be impossible to use. The team went back to the drawing board, where they continue to work. Meanwhile (as this is being written), the first "multipurpose" document machines are reaching market. People will learn how to use them; but no one will claim they are conceptually clean.

What is the moral? Xerox was trying to *construct compositionality*. They were trying to identify or construct or invent a modest set of operations or properties, **P, P′, P″**, etc., and an equally modest set of object types **x, x′, x″**, etc., that would sustain exactly the sorts of cross-cutting algebraic structure discussed at the beginning of the chapter. Doing that is *hard*. It takes argument, consensus, sweat, design—and sometimes blunt imposition on the market. It is also a struggle that makes a mockery of the idea that compositionality is "out there," for free. Compositionality is an extraordinary achievement—as much of construction as of discovery.

It is not so easy to find phrasings that convey the collaborative nature of this ontological achievement, yet preserve the (normatively) directed asymmetry of the registration relation. Words are not always helpful: it sometimes seems as if they take hold of distinctions and push them towards one or other extreme, as if binarism or dichotomy were built into writing. Perhaps that is a reflection of the times. Even the words I have used for what we do to objects ('sediment' and 'extrude,' when activity was in focus; 'still' or 'quieten' or 'stabilize', when the passivity of the result was relevant; as well of course as 'register') place responsibility too heavily on the subject. Traditional intentional terms like 'see', 'refer to,' 'recognize,' 'perceive,' 'discover,' etc., place it too heavily on the object. As suggested by the garden example, above and in the preface, agriculture is a useful source of metaphors: words such as 'grow,' 'till,' 'shepherd,' and the like, convey a salutary sense of collaboration between farmer and farmed—and thus of the resultant phenomenon's being located in an appropriately textured middle region.[15] 'Steward' might

[15] A long time ago, "naming" or "calling" was viewed as a sacred act, on the belief (or fear) that to utter something's name was to call it into existence. *Referring*, that is, was very close to *summoning*. Those images were perhaps not as wrong as they seem to a modernist imagination.

also be pressed into service. And then of course there are images of dance. Throughout, the aim is to convey the sense that ordinary objects are like life (participation, registration, having dinner, etc.) in being complex and risky patterns choreographed and executed in the middle of the dance floor.

5b Participatory surround

Because a surrounding web of practice or activity or sustenance or use is necessary to support any and all acts of registration, it follows directly that those practices are not themselves registered. That is, they do not work in virtue of being registered; they are what they are in order to allow something to register, in order to allow something (else) to be registered. Like everything else, the supporting activity *can* be registered, but only in a reflective or observing kind of way, from within another practice, complete with its own surround of unregistered history and instruments and documents and practices—at a price, too, and partially. And also with separation, and with violence: stemming both from the abstraction intrinsic to any registrational act, which implies that it will and must do an injustice to its particular subject matter, and also from the necessity for connected — i.e., effective—intervention.

In this way a tacit but materially consequential background of sustaining practice for all registration—for both representation and ontology—is built into the basic metaphysical picture. Note, too, that because no purpose-specific hypotheses are required in order to frame it, it comes at no extra cost.

5c Normative virtue

Perhaps the most challenging aspect of this entire picture of life in the middle, even more than the shifting patterns of connection and disconnection and of sameness and difference that sustain a configuration of subjects and objects, has to do with the normative standards that govern the whole process. Or rather, if 'normative' is at once too expensive and too limited a word, with what notions of truth or beauty or goodness or virtue or fidelity are appropriate to this mediate, vaguely Confucian (or perhaps even Greek) way of life.

There is no reason to suppose that there will be any "unsub-scripted" answer to this normative question. Different spheres of human activity—politics or science or religion or psychology, professional life or personal life, prose or poetry—get at virtue or fidelity in their own partially overlapping but partially incommensurable registers. And each of us, in our own ways, knows that it is a mistake to misappropriate one subscripted version of virtue into another sphere of life—to aestheticize religion, for example; or to hold scripture accountable to notions of truth imported from prose or poetry; or to analyze political injustice in psychological terms. Still, some very general things can be said, at least by way of pointing in some directions in which our standard notions will have to be adjusted.

I will start by considering a very small example, so simple as to run the danger of caricature, but one that nevertheless opens up into a much larger and more suggestive sphere. It is also familiar from earlier discussion. The example has to do with the conditions governing the use of simple indexical terms. Because action is connected (ineffably connected, at the very front lines), and because the physical world is deictic, the signals in terms of which a person physically operates their body—e.g., the signals that you send down your nerves to the muscles in your arm—need to be in completely reduced deictic form. This was implied, in an earlier discussion of what a driver has to tell their hands, in order to cause the car to turn right. On the other hand, in order to carry on anything like a disconnected or even objective discourse, more stabilized (less deictic) terminology is required.

Skill, therefore, at least in this minuscule domain, is not exhausted or even captured by conditions governing only a particular given degree of connectivity. Rather, *skill involves the ability to move back and forth, plastically and seamlessly, between and among different degrees of connectivity*—being able to convert back and forth between allocentric abstraction and egocentric action, and being able, for distal reasons, to register present particularity in relatively abstract ways that coordinate with other events, other times, other places.

What makes indexical terms like 'here' and 'now' interesting, in this light, is that they are manifestly "boundary" objects,[16] playing a mediating role not only between and among different registrations—e.g., in mediating egocentric-allocentric coordinate shifts—but between registration and unregistered activity. They are very close in their reference (and connection) to the underlying physical deixis, and yet they have been shaped, like words, to fit into more abstract representational contexts. This is why they are involved in the first step in articulating, in language, the disturbance that your stomach sends to your brain. (If your stomach were to speak, it would say "hungry," not "I'm hungry"; but of course it does not speak, since it is not sufficiently disconnected.)

This example of indexicals points the way towards a much more general condition. Go back to the characterization of objectivity given in chapter 3: as involving recognizing, as I said then, or registering, as I would now say, a transcendent but immanent (inclusive) world, as mandated by symmetrical realism. As already suggested, one of the most important facts about the inherently participatory picture of registration being painted here is that the form of objectivity available to it cannot be achieved by mistakenly trying more and more to completely disconnect from the world, in a vain attempt to achieve the infamous view from nowhere.[17] On the contrary, the ability to register—*the ability to make the world present, and to be present in the world,* which is after all what this is a theory of—requires that one inhabit one's particular place in the deictic flux, and partici-

<hr>

[16] Star (1989).
[17] Nagel (1986).

pate appropriately in the enmeshing web of practices, so as to sustain the kinds of coordination that make the world come into focus with at least a degree of stability and clarity.

It is important to understand that the ideal limit cases—of pure connected action or unvarnished encounter, and of pure disconnected "objective" language—do not at all fit into the picture. It is not just that they are in practice unobtainable; that is true of almost all idealizations. Rather, the point is that neither the operative regularities nor the best explanations are framed in their terms. Trying to understand the structure of registration and participation in terms of 100 percent connection and 100 percent disconnection would be a little like trying to understand the structure of photography in terms of two ideals—pure blackness and pure whiteness—instead of recognizing that the constitutive regularities that actually matter, of shadows, specular reflection, texture and grain, and so forth, are all middle level categories. By the same token, remember the useless physics formula in chapter 5 (on p. 179), involving the double triple integral, from which all base-level individuals had been eliminated. One begins to glimpse, in its utter futility (in the fact that it required infinite information, would be impossible to work with, would yield up an answer of no conceivable use, etc.), what happens when one pulls word and world too far apart. It is no accident that physics is the only theory we have that even begins to approximate "totally disconnected" form.

Once one recognizes that the aim is not to "escape reality," moreover, as if that could even be thought, but is instead to be present and make things present, and to operate in and from a location, the way is paved for a much deeper kind of "located responsibility" than could be made sense of in the predecessor view—a kind of responsibility that involves being where one is, acting from there, reaching out (as all registration does, more or less) to encompass a more global view, but never taking leave of one's roots, one's grounding, one's proper location.[18] In a sense,

---

[18] Suchman (1994), Haraway (1991).

the ability to register is like the ability to fly: it involves knowing how to take off and land, how to return to the earth for food and fuel, how to survey the surrounding landscape, how to fly at different altitudes for different purposes, how to accommodate to and even exploit local weather and air currents, how to carry things that are not too heavy and will not be damaged en route. Not only is the aim not to fly at infinite speed and infinite altitude in a perfectly straight line disconnected from any earthly landing; that "Logical" idealization would also be of no great use (achieving it would be both impossible and useless). For flight, and by analogy for registration, the normative issue has much more to do with how these skills are integrated into the conduct of a tenable life.

5d   Reconciliation

I have claimed throughout that *disconnection* is involved in registering anything as anything. In order to register, a subject (or s-region) must pull away or withdraw. Disconnection is humanly familiar, too. We pull away or withdraw from other people, and know what it is to have someone else pull away from us—far enough, sometimes, *to treat us as an object*. In every case disconnection extracts its toll—has its price, a price that can only be repaid, and then only partially, by a committed kind of return from this withdrawal, a coming back from the "being away" or being out in the cold that underlay the registrational act.

This picture of registration enmeshed in committed action, balanced by thick restorative connection, reveals in its symmetry another inadequacy in the ways in which traditional analytic frameworks treat intentionality. Everyone, in fields from logic to computer science to philosophy to art, speaks of *abstraction*—the process (as I would put it) of letting go of a patch of pure particularity in order to register it, to find it coherent, to set it up in relationship with other patches in other places. In this framework, perception is viewed as a paradigm site of this kind of abstracting process. It is manifest, however, that abstraction—going from being enmeshed in the world to a partially detached registration of that world—is only half the story. Its opposite is equally important: the process, which I will in general call *reconciliation*, of coming back into effective contact with what has been registered, and filling in the details.

"Action," one might think this is called, and set in opposition to perception, as if perception—registration of what is encountered—were not itself an action. But that is not the point. It is not the perceptual act itself for which I am commending an opposite, at least not on the view that perception is a process that goes from an object's *being* φ to a registration of it *as* φ. By that account, action is indeed a natural opposite, at least in a general sense that includes construction and doing: a process of going from registration of something as being φ (being in my office, say, or dinner's being on the table) to its actually being so. Rather, I want to uncover and highlight a counterpart to the act of abstraction that is so commonly recognized as part of perception.

Abstraction is a process of going from the ineffably rich microdetails of a particular circumstance to an abstract or categorical characterization of it, a characterization that washes out 95 percent of those details and places it alongside other circumstances in a general conceptual typology. But what about the reverse? What happens when one acts, in a particular circumstance—a circumstance that, like all circumstances, is awash in its own unique and conceptually overwhelming detail? What happens to all the details that were washed away on "input"? Because the distinction between detached representation and committed action is gradual, there is room in this metaphysics for *reconciliation*, for action to *reattend to the details that were lost in the disconnection of registration*—room to fit in and accommodate and respond and adjust and negotiate and gradually become inextricably enmeshed and no longer distinguishably separate.

As an analogy, imagine picking up a cloth that lies draped over a complex surface or terrain. As one pulls the cloth away, all the local details that previously deformed it, this way and that, would be lost—details, let us assume, that it would be hopeless to try to describe in language, at least with finite resources. In just this way any registration (any attempt at effability) loses touch with the fine and thick texture of any particular situation it describes. We know that; such loss is intrinsic to abstraction.

But now imagine laying the cloth back down onto the terrain again—either in the same place, perhaps at a later time, or perhaps in a new place altogether. On the traditional mythology of action (i.e., Action), in which action is performed in accordance with a rational registration of the target situation, it would be as if the cloth, after being picked up, had not only been smoothed and ironed and laid out exactly flat, but had then been converted into steel plate. According to that traditional model, to "do" the action, to act in accord with the registration, would be like pressing that flat piece of steel back onto the terrain—either squashing the details, or perhaps landing skewed and partially bent, but basically not fitting very well, and likely doing damage. This is what it would be to (falsely) imagine that action could be exhaustively described as being in accordance with a registration of the target situation—e.g., as *acting in strict accordance with plans*. Whereas on the alternative being described here, the idea is much more that the cloth, even if cleaned and dried, is laid back down in such a way as to once again pick up, as appropriate, ineffable details of the new situation.

That is not to say that action is necessarily *soft*; here the analogy is misleading. Better to consider how we grip things with our hands: there is strength, but there is also adaptation, to the angle and orientation and texture and a million other contingencies of the grasped object. Plasticity is in no way at odds with strength; on the contrary, it is in virtue of flexible adaptation that we hang on strongly. By analogy, I certainly mean to include the possibility of re-engagement and reconciliation that does violence; these are trials of strength and weakness, after all, not wimpy handshakes. Nonetheless, just this point, if I understand her correctly, is Suchman's:[19] conceptual registrations, such as articulated plans, can be resources, even very powerful resources. But *as one increasingly engages with the particularities of the situation in which one is acting*, one invariably adopts inventive strategies, adapts to, and adjusts in accordance with, and generally enmeshes oneself in, the constantly renegotiated, phenomenally complex, impossible to describe, and even more impossible to predict, particularities and contingencies and sheer peculiarities of how things are bent and rearranged and otherwise part company with anything quite imagined in the abstracted version.

This is all entirely familiar. Once again, human involvement is a good source of examples. Imagine you have a simple idea about how to deal with power struggles in your start-up company, or propose a simple egalitarian principle at your faculty meeting to govern the allocation of departmental offices. In the event, when you go to implement your ideas in the excruciating particularity of the given, concrete situation, some of the connectedness that was lost in the process of abstracting and letting go must be regained, as you fit yourself back into the unregistered details of a purely particular case. It is accessible to common sense, too, that as one works one's solution into the actual fabric of the situation, there is a sense in which one's commitment to disconnected registration (to the "letter of the law") slips away. And yet, if one loses one's sense of where one is headed, the local and situated action can lose focus, and founder. As always, the virtue is in the balance.

Although introduced with respect to action, reconciliation is

[19] Suchman (1987).

not bonded to that notion alone (except in the sense that every-thing is an action). The aim, rather, in using the word 'recon-ciliation,' is to emphasize the pattern of abandoning one's registrational abstraction and re-engaging with the ineffable de-tails of the world. This process—of "letting go of letting go," as it were—holds of our entire participatory connectedness; it is as much characteristic of listening and meandering as it is of more directedly doing or accomplishing. Thus think of how one allows oneself to submit to or to submerge into the wealth of surrounding detail, as one wanders along the sidewalk, muses on something one sees, attends to what is happening across the street, eases one's way through a crowd. With respect to norma-tivity, moreover, the crucial point is this: there is at least as much virtue in proper reconciliation—in fitting back into the world—as there is in obtaining the right abstraction in the first place.

The traditional notion of representational or linguistic Truth, in sum, apart from any other limitations as a capitalized idealization, such as being defined with respect to an indepen-dent, not merely transcendent, reality, fails because it is so one-sided.

If abstraction is virtuous withdrawal,
we equally need virtuous re-engagement.

This is the entrée into a more symmetrical form of virtue, al-luded to in chapter 3, in which the normative condition on a registered statement as much involves what it is to *live by that statement* as *whether that statement is true*—i.e., the path from registration back to the world, as much as the path from the world to the registration. Only with the two in dynamic balance will one approach that to which I alluded earlier: a stable and present form of "living in truth." And yet—it is very important to get this right—the recommended symmetry or balance of life cannot be allowed to undermine the asymmetry of the underlying directedness of virtue. Directedness in the intentional sphere is formulated as the directedness or "pointing" of semantics; in the moral sphere, as granting priority and significance to the world—to the world as a whole, rather than to the self or to the world as other. As always, these and other subscripted variants of normativity must be hammered out, as appropriate, in different spheres of human endeavor. But a common spirit of deference or directedness underlies them all.

Finally, to echo the standard refrain, the fact that things work out in this way—with respect to the nature of action and reconciliation, with respect to the power and limitation of plans, and with respect to the symmetrical virtue of participation—all these things are once again a consequence of the single underlying metaphysical picture. It falls out, as I have said, and can therefore be had without additional cost.

6 Conclusion

With luck, these few comments—about construction, ineffable connection, participation, symmetrical virtue, reconciliation, and the like—will have conveyed a sense of how a successor account can be built on a new foundation. Except for one thing: we do not yet have the new foundation. Since chapter 7, I have been assuming an underlying space of physical feature fields—fields that were never paid for, and which anyway are about to be discarded. Before discarding them, though, it is worth noticing how useful they have been, even if they were provisional, in giving us a picture of what it is like to work without a preordained cast of individuals. For think about how little would have been visible if we had stayed under the strictures of Standard Ontology: cross-cutting correspondence, continuous fan-in and fan-out, partial separation, gradual coming together and coming apart, overwhelming particular detail washed out in registrational abstraction. Had we stayed with the Ontology of model theory, none of these regularities could have been seen.

The fields will go. But the patterns will remain: restless patterns of stabilization and coordination, of invention and description and activity and design, of struggle and submission and conquest and peace, sometimes collaborative, sometimes singular. All these participatory activities arise out of ineffable connection and subside back into it, at a different place or different time or under different circumstances, often benefiting from the perspective of abstraction and registration, but never escaping from the located, the directed, and the exquisitely particular.

10 · Transition

Adam Lowe
CR 29 (Studio with phone), 1993
Collection of Adrian & Charis Cussins
Oil and resin on board, 123 cm × 123 cm

One task remains. It is time to make good on the underlying metaphysics.

1 Higher-order registration

Go back to chapter 5, to the discussion of what could be inherited from physics. Physics, it was claimed, at least on a field-theoretic interpretation, contains no ontological commitments to first-realm (particular) individuals. This is what was meant by the statement that there are *no physical objects*—no individuals at the particular or base level. Yet at the same time it was pointed out that the situation is very different at higher levels, in the "third realm" of pure abstraction. Even when interpreted field-theoretically, physics makes crucial use of fully individuated properties—or, as I preferred to call them, because of their independence from objects, fully individuated *features*: force, mass, acceleration, spin, charge, etc. Furthermore, the individuation of this feature space was both precise and strict, as well as being, in some important sense, abstract. Indeed, these third-realm physical categories are as clear and distinct as any this side of mathematics.

At the time, however, that chapter said nothing about where those abstract entities came from, or how they were paid for. That was because no appropriate machinery was available. By now, though, the answer—or at least the overall shape of the answer—should be clear. Indeed, it is essentially preordained from what has already been said:

We individuate properties and relations in the same way as we individuate ordinary (particular) individuals—through analogous processes of separation, stabilization, long-distance coordination across breaks in effective coupling, and the like.

317

We extrude the *types*, in other words, along with the individuals that exemplify them—through similar processes of alignment and observation and restriction to appropriate circumstance, with the same support of the participatory surround, and sometimes, too, by boxing the world on the ears in order to ensure that it behaves.

None of this should be news. It is the simplest possibility, for one thing, and thereby the least expensive. It fits with common sense, making direct contact with personal and professional attempts to find concepts and categories that fit our lived experience. And it is intrinsic to the picture that has already been painted. For pulling the world apart in this way—between and among types, as well as into objects vs. types—was itself recognized to be a part, and a sophisticated part at that, of high-level or "conceptual" registration. Indeed, it is exactly this cross-cutting structure of objects and properties, and concomitant generality condition, that was mentioned at the beginning of chapter 9 to be a second- or third-floor achievement. Separating out exemplified features may in some ways be a bit simpler, but it is essentially similar in kind.

Physics, in other words, as was clear all along, is just one more registration of the world. This is not to deny that in some ways it is special—special in ways that will never be explained by analyses that traffic solely in power, money, or politics (see the sidebar on page 320). None of this special character, however, takes anything away from the fact that physics, like all registrations, is one way, among many, in which located, embodied, participatory subjects register the world. As a result, all remarks that are true of registration in general hold of it more specifically as well. It is true, for example—necessarily true, according to the picture being painted—that the registrations of physics, like all registrations, must be held up by a complex surround of participatory forces. This is exactly what social studies of science have been telling us: physical claims are enabled by, grounded in, and warranted via the mediation of a spectacularly complex pattern of policies, practices, institutions, and instruments.

So I lied. Physics does not come for free. Everyone knows that. Still, the discussion was useful for having provided a picture of continuous, world-extensive, deictic, particular fields. That image, which I hope has by now become familiar, was only a stepping stone en route to the real metaphysical picture, towards which this account has been aiming. So the entire discussion in terms of "fields of particularity" was only a temporary expedience. Just as we let go of individuals at the beginning of chapter 7, we can now, as promised, let go of physical registration as well. Thus we reach point C of figure 7·1, reproduced here as figure 11·1.

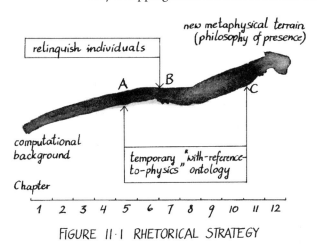

FIGURE 11·1 RHETORICAL STRATEGY

What then is the real picture? Get at it by induction. As I have said so often, the field-theoretic interpretation of physics yields a picture of the world in which individual objects are eliminated at the particular or base level, replaced by continuous fields of pure particularity. This was not a registration one could compute with, but it was still a registration one could imagine. When one *did* imagine it, moreover, the experience was a little like that of having fallen overboard: of looking out on an endless enveloping sea, textured with waves and swells and cross-cutting undulations, potentially of great complexity, and perhaps even foaming in turbulence or sucked in at places with eddies and

Physical registration

No account of physics can claim to be satisfying unless it can explain why more people, or at least more post-Enlightenment academics, have believed that physics, more than any other master narrative, is the single story of all there is. Many things might be considered: the precision of its measurements, its seeming insulation of influence from phenomena registered under other schemes, the power of the notion of supervenience (that no two things can differ on any other registration scheme unless they differ on the physical one).*

But a more intriguing suggestion lurks in the present story. Physics aims to be what chapter 9 proscribed: *a complete theory of local encounter.* Except that, in that aim, it faces an insurmountable problem arising from a conflict among three things: a goal of explanatory perfection, a subject matter interest in pure connection, and the intrinsic disconnection and loss endemic to all registration.

So what does physics do? Two things, to make headway. First, as noted in chapter 5, it rids itself of ontological commitment to particular-level individuals. This is an extraordinary achievement, though it exacts a cost already seen: a discrepancy between what the theory officially claims to exist (infinite spatio-temporally extensive perhaps probabilistic fields of pure particularity) and anything *epistemically viable,* such as closed systems, point mass idealizations, and individuals. Second, physics is forced downwards, towards ever smaller and more basic features, in the hope of shedding as much abstraction as possible. But it can never shed *all* abstraction, again for two reasons: (i) it remains hobbled by epistemic limitations—to be useful, it must traffic in approximate calculations, idealizations, individuals, etc.; and (ii) it does not let go of individuals at the property level (i.e., in the third realm)—or at least it has not done so yet, and cannot easily be imagined as doing so. And so, if my claim is right, physics will never be able to capture *everything,* because properties and relations are also the result of participatory registrational practices, and hence also involve disconnection and loss. In a way this is already evident: most of the world's "information content," even according to physics, is crowded into the infinite, inaccessible, and ultimately (for similar epistemic reasons) ineffable boundary conditions.

How does physics' ultimately unreachable attempt to capture the world differ from the present metaphysical project? In some ways my project is more ambitious, because it attempts to get underneath *everything*: not just objects and properties, but features, fields, the works. But in other ways my ambitions are less. I admit to inexpressible loss, for one thing; no attempt is being made to say (nor equipment being provided with which to say) how things are, *in particular, completely, somewhere, right now.* Even if it is a picture of a world sans (or prior to) abstraction, it employs abstraction in picturing that world, so has claim neither to unique truth nor to complete information. At best the story I am telling is *a* metaphysical tale; it is not *the* metaphysical tale.

More importantly, though, the projects differ in respect to grounding. The present metaphysics is grounded in what I call *immanent induction* (§6 of chapter 12), stemming from the fact that we are in and of the world. Physics aims for purely ratiocinative grounding, and for the ultimately unavailable position of an entirely third-person stance; immanent induction is in contrast a way of being grounded that is ultimately unregistered, inexorably participatory (partially *connected*), and to a degree ineliminably first-person.

*Suppose you receive two physically indistinguishable gifts (two copies of the same book, say), one from a friend, one from a foe. It may matter to you which copy came from whom. This would seem to be a situation in which two physically identical objects exhibit different properties. Does this challenge physical supervenience? No, for two reasons. First, the two books are not, strictly speaking, *identical*; else they would be one. So 'physically indistinguishable' must mean something like "nonidentical but instantiating the same physical! types," where physical! types are a subset of physical types, excluding those that have to do with location, relation to other objects, etc. (the assumption being that physical laws make reference to only this restricted set). If such a type restriction could be identified, and supervenience characterized in its terms, the example would challenge a *local* reading of supervenience. But supervenience is usually interpreted *globally*: as a claim that the world-as-awhole could not be different from *any* point of view, without being different from a physical point of view. This wider (weaker) reading does not require restriction to physical! types; location can be included. But according to it the two books are not identical, after all; so the example poses no actual metaphysical threat.

attractors, but nevertheless stretching on and on, without limit, in all directions, to the (deictically defined) horizon.

At all higher reaches, however, the image was almost diametrically opposite. Even on a field-theoretic interpretation, only the particular (concrete) first realm was continuous; the abstract third realm consisted of a small number of discrete, individual, punctuated entities—features, types, properties, and relations. These were the entities that I described at the beginning of the chapter as being as clean as any in mathematics. And these abstract individuals were necessary—not only in terms of which to state physical laws, but even in order to sustain the idea that the first level was in fact continuous, world-extensive, and the like (even to sustain the idea that it was particular). Unlike the first-realm image of a turbulent sea, the image of the higher-order third-realm was of a vast, mostly deserted space, populated by a few widely-separated, immovable, homogenous, and eerily silent monoliths—a scene reminiscent of the movie *2001*.

Not only were the third-realm individuals perfectly discrete, moreover, immovable, and silent; so too were all the (higher-order) distinctions among them—between the particular (base) level and the level of features above it, and so on, successively, above that. Even the idea of "realms" or "levels" is discrete. Whatever their origin, these ramified levels, at least as imagined so far, were indisputably the work of a master digital craftsman. This is not the province of ambiguity or indefiniteness. According to the images I have used, there has been no uncertainty about what is at the particular level, what is at the level of features (force and mass), what is at the level above that (derivatives and Hamiltonians), and so on and so forth, without limit or loss.

So what then is the right metaphysical picture? Get at it, as I said, by induction. The metaphysical picture is just like the physical picture, except that what in the physical case is true only at the particular (base) level, is in the metaphysical case taken to complete generality. The metaphysical picture is of a *wholly particular world—not individuated at all*. Rather than consisting, at the bottom, of continuous and extensive but otherwise neatly-classified fields, surmounted by a perfectly discrete, abstract, classificatory hierarchy, the metaphysical picture is instead of a world filled with particular, deictic flux, riotous and differentiable at every rank—in fact riotously *ranked*, not committed to any a priori registration whatsoever. Not neat, not close, not anywhere.

How can one understand this image? What seems inaccessible at first soon grows easy and familiar. Perhaps one could start with images of Anaximander's *apeiron*: unbounded, limitless, undifferentiated, wherein one cannot predicate. But that is not quite right, because what I have in mind is the opposite of a blank or neutral slate. Not so much undifferentiated, as on "the other side" of differentiation: such a feisty and fertile and fomenting ground that a virtual infinity of registrational practices can (and do) erupt from within it.

So the whole book should be rewritten, or at least re-understood, with 'fields' replaced by 'flux,' with the suggestion of neat orthogonal categories dimensioning those fields washed away, and with the underlying image of the disruptive and unregistered flux pulled even further away from the ossifying grip of a rigid and formal conceptualism.

2 Indefiniteness

Among many other things, the metaphysical picture is shot through with a fundamental and ultimately unregisterable lack of abstract sharpness, lack of clear discreteness (or at least with a lack of its necessity or inevitability). This lack of sharpness is as important as it is difficult to describe. Temporarily, therefore, for this one section, I will say that all boundaries and distinctions are, in the end, intrinsically *indefinite* or *gradual*—rather in the way in which a bump on a curve, such as a Gaussian distribution, has no definite starting point. This is the complete opposite of what, in another context, I have identified as the essence of formalism: the idea that things can be chopped up, neatly, without any middle regions. Formality, that is to say, is a completely general (and thus higher-order) version of the law of the excluded middle—a version applicable to any conceivable distinction whatsoever (including logical properties). Crucially, formality is not itself a formal property; it is a prior stance or attitude:

Formality is discreteness run amok.

On the picture being painted here, in contrast, the world is not presumptively discrete—indeed, it is as completely opposite of formal as it is possible to imagine. It is instead permeated by:

1. Indefiniteness *at the edges of given objects*, such as the boundaries of the region on the wall where I ask you to write your name (there being no metaphysical need for determinate edges);

2. Indefiniteness *between and among objects of the same type*, such as whether you are standing on this sand dune or the neighboring one; or whether the massif above our campsite consists of three mountains or four;

3. Indefiniteness *among different types*, such as among chutzpah, bravado, ego, self-confidence, and brashness;

4. Indefiniteness *among the notions 'concept,' 'type,' and 'property'*—as for example in debates between philosophers and psychologists on the nature of concepts: about whether they are mental or abstract, and about what it is that people can and cannot share (do we share a concept of red? do we each have private concepts that represent the same abstract property? or do we all have different concepts?);

5. Indefiniteness *between objects and the types they exemplify*, implying that the "instance-of" relation is itself approximate, contested, and potentially unstable—as for example in

whether the headache you have this morning is the same one you had last night, or a different one of the same type; and similarly for patches of color, fog, and "the rain"; and

6. Indefiniteness *between and among different realms of human endeavor*, such as the political, the social, the technical, the religious, the esthetic, the psychological, etc.

The ubiquity of this gradualism shows once again why it was so important to avoid making sharp theoretic distinctions in advance. This was especially true in the case of the classical dualisms: between subject and world, mind and body, abstract and concrete, nature and society. I initially motivated avoiding these binarisms for two reasons: in order to avoid making inscription errors, and in order to keep theoretician's and subject's ontology (registration) distinct. Third, I avoided them because of their expense. But as was also suggested early on, there is a fourth reason not to be committed to them in advance: namely, to make room for the possibility of not being committed to them later on, either. This applies not only when a predecessor distinction is elided in the successor account (as electromagnetic theory elides the distinction between magnetism and light), but also when the *nature* of a successor distinction is inaccessible in advance. It was in part in order to make room for this current disruption/eruption in the very nature of distinction that it was so important not to inscribe any sharp or categorical distinctions in advance.

3 Zest and spunk

Except that 'gradual' and 'indefinite' are entirely the wrong words. There is nothing necessarily smooth about this picture of disruption and distinction. Variation may sometimes be relatively gradual or even, but it is just as likely to be as rough as sandpaper, sharp as a thorn bush, tangled as a mangrove swamp.

Go back to chapter 6, this time, to where I said that a certain flex or slop—an ultimate refusal to be tied down into formal neatness—was fundamental to the metaphysical picture. This ineliminable flex, this irremediable and often eruptive *playfulness*, was shown to be at the root of all registration (constituting the problem and enabling the solution). The same flex is implicated here, in the idea of distinctions being gradual or indefinite, or anyway not formal or sharp. It is because of this prior pluck or playfulness, this irrepressible spunk or spirit, that the words 'gradual' and 'indefinite' are untenable. In fact it is easy enough to see how neither concept could possibly be right.

Gradual, first, implies a shading of one thing to another. To say that the boundary between **x** and **y** is gradual is to license talk of being "partly **x**," or of being "more **x** than **y**." But the coherence of that idea, in turn, requires the existence of a metrical higher-order property: a property, one level up, in terms of which the notion of an amount or degree of exemplification of **x** or **y** makes sense. But this fundamentally violates the spirit of what is being said. The whole point—indeed, one of the most important ways in which this metaphysics differs from physics and (at least our myths[1]) of predecessor science—is that there *are no* properties upstairs, at least *no properties available in advance, without achievement, at no cost.* As I keep saying, the metaphysical picture is not suspended from above via an infinitely expensive sky-hook. Historically, the dream of a single, pure, governing abstraction has captured people's imagination, from Babel to the ramified theory of types. But to the extent that we participants succeed in constructing higher reaches of abstract conceptualization, they are always plural, subsequent, approximate, and contingent. Like Joseph K,[2] we wait in vain. All we can be sure of is the underlying, primordial, (bottom-level) cosmic particular flux.

Indefinite is even more wrong. Think about the cloth, discussed in chapter 9, draped in complex ways over the variegated irregularities of a lumpy surface underneath it. Just because the

[1] See Dupré (1993).
[2] Kafka (1925/1992).

local intricacies were not easily classifiable with a coarse-grained equivalence metric (i.e., in terms of conceptual properties), it did not follow that there was anything metaphysically indeterminate about the shape of the cloth itself. Suppose, by analogy, that one were restricted to categories chosen from the following set: "is 3 inches above the table," "is 4 inches above the table," "is 5 inches above the table," etc. And suppose further, to be concrete, that the cloth was draped in a disheveled manner over a complicated bunch of stuff—over a project table in a child's bedroom, say, strewn with dolls and small furniture and screwdrivers and glue and string and the odd assortment of clothing. How should we classify the cloth: as 3 inches, 4 inches, or 5 inches from the surface? Since no available answer is clearly good, someone might argue that the question is indeterminate or indefinite—or perhaps that it has no determinate or definite answer. What I want to block, however, is any inference from that fact to the (false) conclusion that the cloth's *position or shape* is in any way indeterminate. It is perfectly determinate; it is just that in this example, by hypothesis, we lack any way to *describe* it.[3]

It is not hard to see how indefinitely rich local (effective)

---

[3] Some will object that, if it cannot be described, then it cannot be usefully said to exist, either. But to believe that argument is to make two mistakes: (i) it gives inappropriate advance priority to language; and (ii) it assumes that the divide between language and non-language is sharp (formal). The only reason to suppose that existence implies effability is either to *assume* that language can explain any difference, which is what is being contested, or to suppose that the "life of language" (e.g., reason and theory) is wholly separate from the metaphysical world it describes, and therefore that if any difference cannot enter the realm of reason *as* language then it cannot enter at all. But neither position is one I accept.

For evidence of an opposing view, note the argument two paragraphs forward, in the text, about what your friend can say in a café: differences can make *particular* differences, and perhaps even be *particularly* referred to, without implying that any person can (or has yet been in a position to) register such a difference's *type*.

structure can be consequential. Arbitrary subtleties can catalyze large-scale change or features, as is seen so often in examples from non-linear dynamics. Extraordinarily fine subtleties can affect human registration, as for example when apparently uncategorizable features of a cartoon betray Abraham Lincoln, or when we recognize that an out-of-focus photograph is in fact a picture of someone in our family.[4] Moreover, attesting to its universality, this propensity for the details of particular situations to outstrip the conceptual classificatory powers of language holds of language itself. For ironically—or so at least it seems to a "modern" imagination—this phenomenon of signifying something more precise than can be captured in conceptual properties is *true of ordinary discourse.*

Imagine you are sitting in a café, across the table from a very particular friend, hours after the musicians have packed their instruments and gone, talking about a person you have discovered you both knew well, though in very different circumstances. At a certain point, your friend may utter a single word ('rumpled,' say, or 'schlemiel,' or 'poofy') that will in your estimation get them *just ever so exactly right.* The experience of the power of an excruciatingly precise observation is familiar to us all.

But now suppose that, pedantically, one were to ask what property your friend thereby refers to. The crucial point is this: sustained by the wealth of riches established by and available in that particular context, the friend's utterance may have signified something *more specific than any generic answer can relate.* Just as

---

[4] The point is not the following: given one cartoon **x** that people register as Abe Lincoln, and one **y** that they do not, that no categories exist in which to classify the differences between **x** and **y**. A complete characterization of the figures as two-dimensional black-and-white images could probably do that, at least to any requisite degree of accuracy (e.g., in terms of bitmaps or splines or generalized lines). Rather, what is (at least potentially) not conceptually classifiable are the regularities underlying such differences — what geometrical properties ϕ *in general* must hold of a cartoon, such that all cartoons that are ϕ will be registered as Abe Lincoln, and all cartoons that are not ϕ will be not be so registered.

the cloth had a determinate but unclassifiable shape, so too the governing metaphysical picture in this linguistic situation, as in any situation, is one of determinate particularity that swamps the ultimately rather coarse-grained classificatory powers of bare lexical items. It is a conceit to assume that the meaning of discourse is built up out of the atomic or stable meanings of words, as we are classically taught. There is every reason to believe that the meaning of the words is just as much affected—adjusted, focused, stretched, made more precise—by the meaning of the embedding discourse. Why not, after all? Absent a bias towards formal construction, it is the most natural possibility: that generic and particular constrain each other, rather than requiring that all work be done, asymmetrically, from one end.[5]

If this is the underlying picture, what are we to say about borders? about boundaries? about the limits of categories?

One way to point towards the answer is once again via an analogy with physics—this time with quantum mechanics. Empty space, it is said, is not really empty if you look *very very hard*. Instead it everywhere and always (to say nothing of already) boils and bubbles, toils and troubles, with countless millions of subatomic particles and their antimatter opposites seething in a somewhat random but thoroughly intermixed pattern of activity. At even quite a low level of statistical averaging, all this activity cancels itself out, adding up to nothingness— adding up, that is, to what we idealize with our formal notions of "Empty Space" and "Vacuum." But au fond space is more unruly than that. Even in this rather extraordinary limit case of what is classically thought to be pure nothingness—and *nothingness* is surely a case on which one might reasonably have

---

[5] It has often been asked whether music and art are representational. By far the best answer, it seems to me, is this: that yes, music and art are at least sometimes meaningful, or at least significant in a non-subscriptable way, but that each instance—a given string quartet, say, or a single performance—signifies something *so exquisitely particular* that there is no way even to imagine saying it in clunky abstract words.

thought formal categorization would get at least a toehold of adequacy—the world proves too wily, too obstreperous, and too locally riotous to let itself be so neatly tied down.

It is because of this overwhelming specificity, and the concomitant metaphysical unruliness, that I have often used the word 'play.' Several things recommend the term. On the one hand, play connotes a lack of exactness—as when one talks about play in a mechanism or gear, implying that the tolerances are loose, and that there is room for things to slop around. This lack of exactness is part of what was implied by 'gradual' and 'indefinite' (to say nothing of being a metaphysical precondition to the possibility of registration). Real play, too—ironical play, play-in-the-wild—connotes the canny, the inventive, the active, the "playful," as in unpredictability and delight. But the word has its detractions, too, especially its inevitable connotation of frivolity. This connotation is sometimes avoided, for example when one says that something (an operating procedure, say) is "in play," but as a general characterization of the nature of boundaries the word ultimately fails for failing to convey that everything is at stake—for failing to make evident that these eruptive non-tie-downable aspects of things also involve fight and contention and struggle. Coyote was wily, all right; but Coyote was consequential, too.

There are dangers in using any single term; it can turn into an ideology. Sometimes, in unapologetic back-formation, I will use *feist*, though that has a tone of nastiness that it would be unfortunate to spread too widely. Sometimes I will focus on eruption; sometimes (as discussed below) on criticality. But most often I will call it *zest* or *spunk*, this often-eruptive nature of the intrinsic bounds of distinction. Boundaries that are not wholly chaotic, but neither wholly regularizable. Boundaries that disintegrate upon close encounter, that break open into a thousand parts, like a wave smashing on a rock and falling apart into a turbulence of drops and rivulets and spray. This is what the edges of our concepts are like, and for that matter what their middle is like, too; their appropriateness and application rarely fades away evenly, uncontested and gradual, like evening light. Much more often, they disintegrate into such a profusion of specificity that not enough discipline or coordination remains to sustain the governing abstraction.

4 Criticality

At several points, throughout the book, I have set up comparisons with physics. Positively, I exploited physics' registration of the world in terms of continuous particular fields, using it as an inspiration for, and stepping stone en route towards, a more encompassing deictic flux. At the same time, I contrasted physics' ontological commitments with those of common sense, focusing especially on its lack of support for material individuals. By now we have mostly dropped the temporary underlying reliance on physical fields, but I want to lean on physics one more time, again with both a positive and a negative spin. Specifically, a comparison with non-linear dynamics and chaos will help to convey the nature of the underlying metaphysical zest.

In recent work in artificial life and theoretical biology, it has been hypothesized that much of life, if viewed as a dynamical system, occupies a "critical region" between stability and chaos. "Stable" does not mean static or passive; rather, the contrast is between behavioral regions that are linear or at least smoothly regular, in ways we have studied for centuries in classical dynamics, and only much more recently theorized regions of genuine chaos or turbulence. It is the boundary between the two that is called *critical*, poised unstably between these two extremes.

In some ways, the character of criticality is reminiscent of the metaphysical picture I have been pressing here. Descriptions of critical systems tend to evoke images of the same sorts of eruptively complex boundary as I have been describing: in some ways impossible to tie down, and exquisitely vulnerable to underlying structure, yet at the same time sufficiently regularizable to sustain abstraction, coherence, etc., rather than collapse into too much flex, unpredictability, or heat. No matter how hard or close one probes, the amount of structure and differentiation seems to outstrip one's attempt to control or contain it. And yet, as in life, neither is the situation so tormented as to defy coherence completely. This underlying coherence is why dynamics is a science; a great many regular and abstract things can be said about such apparently complex structures.

And yet, although there is something similar, perhaps even shared, between criticality and spunk, the comparison is also misleading, as shown by contrasting Lowe's painting in chapter 10 with the by-now-popular pictures of chaos, fractals, self-embedding structures, and the like. In most cases, it is immediately evident (at least to this viewer) that published images of non-linearity are undergirded by a cold, mathematical precision that the painting lacks. Or to put the same point another way, it is plain that Lowe's painting is not just locally non-linear, but that its abstract regularities—the higher-order patterning of textures and regions and marks, even the distinctions or boundaries between what is one region and what is another—are eruptive or turbulent as well. It is also clear, I take it, that the painting is more like what one encounters when one wakes up and stumbles down to breakfast, much more like the political situation one struggles to resolve at the office—much closer, in general, to the stuff and substance of life.

Moreover, the reason for the difference is not hard to find. The regularities we have come to associate with scientific dynamics—of fractal sets, infinitely self-embedding structure, criticality, etc.—are regular and precise because they are *higher-order formal*, in a way that Lowe's painting is not, and in a way that is the opposite of the sense of the metaphysical base that I am trying to convey. For think about how most scientific images of non-linearity are generated. They are the computer-generated output of simple non-linear equations—and so at best illustrate turbulence, or the movement from regularity through criticality into chaos, only *at the particular (first) level*. At higher levels they are liable to be clean, precise, and mathematical—perfectly discrete. If one were to lay out their conceptual topology, that is, only the first level would manifest a tumultuous, variegated structure. At the level of the properties themselves, at the level of the sets they are (thought to be) defined in terms of, at the level of the distinctions between the types and instances, and all the rest, they would continue to carry the signature of that master digital craftsman.

The kind of fundamental metaphysical play or spunk that I claim lies in between and among and through and around our concepts and categories—the kind of spunk that characterizes, au fond, the world we conceptualize and categorize and live in and till—is in general nothing like so controlled. It is much more often hot, ironic, rambunctious. In fact one could think of the entire metaphysical project being argued in this book in the following way: as an answer to the question of what it would be like for *everything to lie in a critical region, poised between regularity and chaos*—not just base-level mathematical particulars, but the whole shooting match: distinctions among different categories, distinctions between objects and the categories they instantiate, distinctions among objects—and so on and so forth, without restriction and without limit. What would it be for *logical* distinctions to be critical? What would it be for mathematics itself to emerge? What would it be for *the very notion of distinction* to be won, at a price, from a partially regular, partially turbulent, noisy and critical background—rather than for a formally first-order critical region to be defined on top of, or hung from, a perfectly structured infinite silence?

What would our theories of dynamics look like if, top to bottom, assumption were interchanged with achievement?

5 Politics

Some will object. The categories of our daily lives are neither so imprecise nor so ragged, they will say. Planes fly unproblematically from Boston to San Francisco. Today is Tuesday; it is raining outside; the hall light is turned on. There is nothing vague or unruly about these facts, nothing ambiguous about whether this keyboard that I am typing on really is a keyboard, nothing uncertain about whether or not eleven friends sat around the table, last night, for Thanksgiving dinner. Sometimes, the critic will claim—often, even—we make a decision and stick with it. Everything is not always up for grabs.

That is true, and importantly so. But there are three thing to be said.

5a Digitality as achievement

First, it is not my intent, in presenting this somewhat irreverent metaphysical picture, to deny that some categories are amazingly regular, some distinctions extraordinarily robust, some issues of individuation and identity astonishingly clear-cut. Rather, the claim, first and foremost, is that the world is not *in general* like that. Plus, to repeat a point made many times, in those cases where regularity and precision do reign—as for example in the numbers on the front of a MasterCard—the digitality should be viewed as an achievement. In a sense, to believe that the metaphysical foundation is formal is to rob the formal (scientific, digital) tradition of its highest accomplishment: of having wrested a robust, non-error-prone distinction out of the underlying flux. To pretend that the world comes already formal is like a bourgeois theory of history that defines the notion of a citizen to be middle class, thereby "disappearing" the class struggles and battles that were (and remain) necessary in order to sustain it. Or like a theory that simply defines biology to be the study of kingdoms, phyla, classes, orders, etc., without any recognition of what it took for these categories to develop, or even what sustains them.[6]

---

[6] Dupré (1993).

Moreover, the formalist is almost bound to fail to see that such digital achievements are propped up by practices that are necessarily unruly, but not for that reason any less creditable — practices whose very purpose is to manage the underlying flex and slop, ebb and flow. MasterCards and social security numbers are good examples, but for a more vivid case think about flight controllers at a major international airport.[7] Though ultimately discrete, the decision about whether or when a plane is ready for take-off or landing is far from neat; it is collectively produced by a highly skilled cadre of people out of a bewildering mess of supportive facts.[8] As is evident in these cases, too, the discrepancy between the flux and the digital achievement is filled by *commitment*, commitment that is intrinsically *non*-formal, and thus invisible to the formal foundationalist.

5b Idealization vs. ideology

So yes, some formal categories are won—some "immutable mobiles"[9] hammered out, first, and then sustained, with constant attention and nourishment, like formal English gardens. At the same time, however—and this is the second thing to say to the critic—the tendency towards inscription error, so often raised here, must never be underestimated, especially for those of us born and bred in the formal tradition. Far, far less in the world is regular, precise, and (higher-order) discrete, I am convinced, than the over-schooled among us were given any reason to expect.[10] Nothing, of course, is ever *completely* discrete, per-

[7] Suchman (in press).

[8] It is misleading to call them "facts," if facts are taken to be individuated along conceptual lines. Better, perhaps, to call them reality.

[9] Latour (1987), p. 227.

[10] I have been a critic of formality for approximately twenty years. Every year, up to and including the present (and I have no reason to believe the end is in sight) I have been amazed to realize that my conviction that certain distinctions were clear and precise was the result of ideological bias. The most recent example, or at least the one that currently most occupies my imagination, is that between types and their instances. Originally I believed that this distinction was clear; then I thought that it was usually

fectly precise, totally robust. It is not just a question of an idealization failing at the edges. Sure enough, everything is not always up for grabs; but everything, as was evident in the original discussion of pluralism, is *potentially* up for grabs. In the end, one cannot hold any distinction, boundary, or categorical limit as forever out of bounds without becoming an ideologue or zealot.

5c Politics as dynamic negotiation

Finally, there is a third answer for the critic—a moral having to do with politics, and if anything more important than the first two. As a consequence of this metaphysical picture, decisions, categories, ontological commitments, etc., must be agreed or wrestled or fought out, through ongoing struggle, in the political sphere. This non-optional conclusion is entailed for two reasons. First, categorical zest is as much *temporal* as anything else. The potentially eruptive boundaries are *dynamically* unstable, not just vague or indefinite or unruly on some non-temporal dimension. To believe otherwise would be reductionist with respect to time. Second, as registrars, *we too are implicated in the zest*—we are not outside it looking on, the way one might look at a sunset far away and comment on a cloud's ragged edges. The point is nothing more than the usual participatory one: that the governing characteristic (spunk, in this case) holds of the whole act or process or practice of registration; it is not a fact about the object of that registration, not a fact about one allegedly isolated end.

···

clear, being vague or indefinite only in rare exceptions, such as in the case of headaches, an example I use at various points in the text. Recently (i.e., in the last year or two), I have come to believe that, first impressions notwithstanding, it is almost always unclear. If prior experience is any guide, it will probably settle down, a few years from now, to be somewhat more clear than it is now, but nowhere near as clear as I originally thought—and also to be not very much like what I was originally committed to, in basic metaphysical nature.

My experience of this gradual process of "letting go" of in-bred bias has remained as astonishing as ever—and sobering, to boot.

It would be a mistake, in other words, upon recognizing the spunk intrinsic to a concept's boundary or metaphysical warrant, to succumb to nostalgia for the (modernist) view from nowhere, and assume that one could somehow take a neutral or protected position with respect to that uncertainty, and thereby hold it safely at bay. For example, suppose that sex and gender are imperfectly correlated concepts, and also that neither has entirely clear determination conditions (I take it both claims are true). Suppose, furthermore, that upon discovering this, someone were to think, "Goodness! These notions are not very well defined!"—and were then to falter, withdraw commitment to decisions based on them, or conclude that they should (forthwith) be cleaned up. The problem with this familiar reaction is not just its treatment of uncertainty and spunk as *bad*; the more serious difficulty stems from viewing them as *external*. It is almost as if the unruliness were smelly or radioactive or something—as if, by pushing it as far away as possible, one could distance oneself from an unsavory aspect. In the long run, such a view leads to an arrogant resistance to the participatory nature of the metaphysics, a moral drawn as early as in chapter 1's discussion of computation. As an interim position, it can simply reflect partiality of understanding. For it is the same mistake as thinking that in place of saying, "This is a cup," one should instead say, "This is a region of the metaphysical flux that in virtue of my history and experience I register in terms of the culturally and politically assimilated concept of 'cup'." That is not right. As Zen masters know, one should simply say, "This is a cup"— but then recognize, if perhaps with a smile, that, yes, sure enough, to do so is to register a region of the metaphysical flux in terms of a social and historical concept.

What is the difference? Modesty is only part of it. The problem is that if one does not realize that one simply says, "This is a cup," rather than the longer gussied-up version, one does not know what it is to utter the longer version, either. There is no way to extract oneself from the world, no way to avoid participating—by adding extra verbiage, piling on hedges, or for that matter by doing much of anything else. *No direction leads away from the world.* There is no way to be safe; no way to be sure. Rather than attempt the impossible, one should instead bow to the inevitable, accept one's location, participation, and take a stand. This blend of humility and responsible action is one of the most important consequences of the participatory view. It is why saying of a cup that it is a cup, or indeed saying anything at all, is a *commitment*—a commitment to be defended, appropriately; a commitment one may always, and sometimes even should, lose.

Ontology involves commitment; commitment involves risk. C'est la vie. Commitment is necessary because one must live *within* the ambiguity, within the spunk; there is no sense to the idea of getting "outside." This is one more reason why this is a philosophy of presence: it is as much a question of *being present* as it is of making the world present (in fact the two can never be wholly separated). In a way, too, it is all a consequence of symmetric realism—which has always been a much stronger thesis than it looks. Symmetric realism is strong for a simple reason: it is the metaphysics of nowhere to hide.

The satirist was right.

> *You play, you win;*
> *You play, you lose;*
> *You play.*[11]

6 Paying the price

In chapter 2, as part of the irreductionist mandate, I claimed that one must be prepared to "pay" for any decisions that one makes. Since then, I have primarily used the notion negatively, criticizing various flavors of reductionist program for making

---

[11] Anonymous.

ideological decisions, or committing pre-emptive acts of inscription, without paying for them. I have been notably silent, however, on paying prices myself, or even admitting much debt. Clearly, this will hardly do, especially in the long run. Some of the problem will be repaired in the next chapter, when I take stock of the notions of connection, disconnection, deixicity, etc., that have been used to characterize the allegedly uncharacterizable deictic flux. Mostly, though, I have not paid because it has not been clear what "paying" comes to. Finally, however—given the overarching fact of inexpressible particularity, the general perspective of a participatory stance, a recognition that committed action is a constitutive part of registration, and an understanding of the notion of reconciliation—it begins to become clear what it is to pay for a decision.

Registration involves abstraction. Abstraction involves loss. So registration does violence. This much is ineliminable. Violence is intrinsic—to our words, to our thoughts, even to our wonder. Yet in spite of this irredeemable loss, we are not thereby rendered finite. The significance of located, particular action continues to outstrip any possibility of abstract registration. This gap, invisible to a formalist, is crucial: between the restraining limits of registration, on the one hand, and the inexpressible located significance of action, on the other. In that gap lies the possibility for reconciliation. Not the ability to avoid doing violence, which is at best impossible, and at worst a nostalgic ideal. But the raw materials for owning up to and taking responsibility for the violence that one has, in fact, thought or said or done.

In a way, the nature of the responsibility is obvious, given the overarching metaphysical picture. Responsibility is a constitutive part of an irreductionist attitude to registration; it is not an addition to it (as if one could glue conscience onto value-free reason). The most important thing, in understanding it, is to

recognize the importance of locatedness.[12] For part of assuming
responsibility for a commitment to a given registration is to take
responsibility for the ways and extent to which the abstraction
on which it is based does an injustice to the (potentially inexpressible) particularities of the circumstances out of which it is
extracted, and into which it is subsequently injected.

6a   A political example

Suppose, to consider an example, that over coffee someone asks
us to help them with a political problem. A community they be-
long to restricts voting rights to permanent members. There is
one person, however, who has been a full-fledged participant
for many years, but who has explicitly never been made permanent, in order not to trigger some recherché clause in their
immigration status. Should this person be granted suffrage? Denying it seems unfair, since everyone recognizes that, except for
the legal technicality, they would have been made permanent.
But allowing them to vote also seems problematic, since violating (at least the letter of) the rules is liable to open up the situation to endless bickering and contention among others in the
group — perhaps especially among a group of medium-term visitors. As chair of the voting rights committee, our friend wants
to know what to do.

Who knows, exactly? Without being part of the situation,
we can hardly be expected to answer in detail. But some commonsensical suggestions would occur to any of us. At a minimum, for example, most of us would recommend sitting down
with the medium-term visitors, to see whether an appropriate
sense of the difference between their own and the long-term
individual's state could be developed and collectively held. This
we should presumably do with an open mind, listening to see
whether they have legitimate reasons for treating the two cases

---

[12]The need for a located responsibility is made explicit by such writers as
Suchman and Haraway; as always, the aim here is to show how that locatedness arises directly from the foundations, rather than having to be added,
or even posited, as an independent phenomenon.

similarly. Perhaps, after due consideration, a decision would need to be made, pro or con. If that were done, we might be tempted to suggest that it be made as straightforwardly and un-apologetically as possible, communicating the reasons to every-one involved, and embedding it in a larger overall situation (i.e., by aligning it with other decisions of a similar type) in such a way as to maximize justice and fairness over the long haul. But deciding "up or down" on the case as originally framed is not the only possibility. Instead it might be more appropriate to ques-tion the original rule—of only allowing permanent members to vote—in order to see whether it is outmoded, elitist, or for any other reason should be eliminated. Perhaps the organization should be reconceptualized, resulting in a different (less hierar-chical) allocation of responsibility or authority. In particular, it would seem important to understand, and admit, whether the problem really is one about the nature of "permanent member-ship," or even about voting, or whether the rule is not being used as a guise for an elite subset of the group to hang on to power and control.

Or a raft of other things. My concern is not with what to do, which is anyway, as I said, commonsensical. Overall, it might be summarized as follows: that one should reconcile the expressed principle with the exigencies of the prevailing circumstances so as to do maximum justice to the widest variety of concerns, commensurate with the community's overall goals—something on that order. What matters here—the reason I have gone to such trouble to set up the example—is that I mean 'reconcile,' in that sentence, in literally the same sense as was introduced at the end of chapter 9. This kind of political, moral, and social "reconciliation" is *constitutive of the metaphysical / ontological sit-uation*. The political recommendations are continuous with, even constitutive of, what it is to pay for the ontological com-mitment to voting, permanence, suffrage, etc.

For note the overall structure. First, I said that we cannot be expected to provide a detailed answer, because we are not part of the situation. This is consonant with the metaphysics: it is a consequence of an irreductionist view that an adequate answer can be undertaken only by an at least partial participant. Or rather, to put it more carefully, a recommendation or answer will be appropriate only to the extent that the person or people who make it can take (ultimately ineffable) responsibility for its consequences, at the level at which it was made. *Only those who participate can pay.* So the metaphysics generates what common sense already knows: that to make a more specific recommendation from the outside than one can accept responsibility for will retain an ineliminable aspect of imposition or ideology.

Second, no one is entirely outside. The boundaries of "being part of" or "belonging" are as eruptive and dynamic as those of any other category. So the participatory moral cannot be used as a way of ducking involvement. This is especially urgent as the global community grows more interconnected, and the ties among us thicken. It was the questioner's and our common membership in a wider community that led, in the example, to recommendations of process rather than outcome. For these recommendations (once again this is clear to common sense) can only be made by someone who has experienced, or participated in, situations of a similar sort. To the extent that our own communities and the questioner's community differ—if they were from another culture, say, or from a religious community whose ways were foreign to us—our ability to offer helpful suggestions would to that extent be reduced (and, if we nevertheless insisted, would shade into ideology and inscription).

Third, the question, at least as originally framed, was in part an ontological one: about the boundaries of the concept *permanent*. Because of the situation's intrinsic dynamics, the participatory nature of the metaphysics, and the constraints of symmetrical realism, we should expect what is in fact the case: that the boundaries of this category require constant negotiation, adjustment, and maintenance. Some may object, saying, "No, the friend came to us with a *political* issue, not an ontological one." But that is a mistake. Ontological issues *are* political issues. To deny that, and pretend that they can be divorced, is to violate (the second branch of) irreduction.

Fourth, and finally, as the discussion proceeded, it began to emerge, or at least the possibility emerged, that *permanence* was not the issue. At a minimum what was at stake was suffrage, or the ability to vote—or even, beyond that, elitism, power and control. This shading of one notion into another, or even the hiding of one notion behind another, is again metaphysically expected. It is also one reason why "knowledge" is not enough — why one would ultimately need to live in and be part of the community, and participate in the deliberations and surrounding actions, in order to be accountable. This connected participation is necessary in order to allow the limits of abstraction implicit in the ontological category, and endemic to the rule, to be reconciled with the particulars of the situation. Again, this is mandated by irreduction: one "pays the price" of the concept by reconciling its limited and limiting abstraction with the particular situation's ineffable exigencies.

12 · Conclusion

To say that this book has opened more doors than it has closed is not to say much, since anyway it is an argument against closed doors. Still, an attempt has been made to tell a coherent story, a story it will pay to review. For one thing, it is important to see how many of the desiderata laid down in the first few chapters have been met. Since I have barely scratched the surface of a positive proposal, it is also important to understand what work remains to be done. And a number of other loose ends need to be attended to, to bring even this much of an introduction to a close.

1 Project

Overall, the project was to develop what I called a *successor metaphysics*, one that would honor the following pretheoretic requirements:

1. Do justice to what is right about:
   a. *Constructivism*: a form of humility, or so at least I characterized it, requiring that we acknowledge our presence in, and influence on, the world around us; and
   b. *Realism*: the view that adds to constructivism's claim that "we are here" an equally profound recognition that we are not all that is here, and that as a result not all of our stories are equally good.
2. Make sense of *pluralism*: the fact that knowledge is partial, perspectival, and never wholly extricable from its (infinite) embedding historical, cultural, social, material, economic and every other kind of context. The account of pluralism must:
   a. Avoid devolving into *nihilism* or other forms of vacuous relativism, and in particular not be purchased at the price

of (successor notions of) excellence, standards, virtue, truth, or significance; and

    b. Not license radical *incommensurability*, provide an excuse to build walls, or in any other way stand in the way of interchange, learning, communion, and struggle for common ends.

Two additional criteria were applied to how these intuitions are met:

3. Be *irreductionist*—ideologically, scientifically, and in every other way. No category, from sociality to electron, from political power to brain, from origin myth to rationality to mathematics, including the category "human," may be given a priori pride of place, and thereby be allowed to elude contingency, struggle, and price.

4. Be nevertheless *foundational*, in such a way as to satisfy our undiminished yearning for metaphysical grounding. That is, or so at least I put it, the account must show how and what it is to be grounded *simpliciter*—without being grounded in α, for any category α.

Along the way, the account should:

5. *Reclaim* tenable, lived, work-a-day successor versions of many mainstay notions of the modernist tradition: *object, objective, true, formal, mathematical, logical, physical*, etc.

Needless to say, these five criteria interact. The modernist "hierarchy of nature" tradition, for example, which views everything as built up out of the formal ingredients of particle physics, held together with the abstract epoxy of set theory, logic, and mathematics, stakes a claim to realism and foundationalism, but (at least at first blush) does so at the expense of pluralism and irreduction. Some room for pluralism is provided by theories of supervenience and other ways of accommodating "special sciences" on top of a physicalist or causal base. But they run the danger of incommensurability, are asymmetrically pluralist, and fail on irreduction. Certain forms of post-modern criticism avoid foundationalism, but sacrifice realism in the process, and curiously enough remain reductionist, particularly with respect to categories of text, discourse, sign, and the like.

2 A philosophy of presence

The solution proposed to meet this suite of requirements—my specific proposed instance of the general type—I call a *philosophy of presence*.[1] Its overarching metaphysical viewpoint is one of *symmetrical realism*: a commitment to One world, a world with no other, a world in which both subjects and objects—we and the things we interact with and think about and eat and build and till and are made of and give away as presents—are accorded appropriate place. At its most basic level, that world is depicted as one of cosmic and ultimately ineffable particularity: a critically rich and all-enveloping deictic flux. Neither formally rigid nor nihilistically sloppy, the flux sustains complex processes of *registration*: a form of interaction, subsuming both representation and ontology, in which "s-regions" or subjects stabilize patches of the flux, in part through processes of intervention, adjusting and building them and beating them into shape, and also through patterns of disconnection and long-distance coordination, necessary in order to take the patch to be an object, or more generally, to be something *in and of the world*. The constitutive patterns of partial connection and partial disconnection,

---

[1] One merit of dividing the project into type and instance, in this way, is to provide some structure for on-going discussion. Some readers may disagree with the type itself, arguing for example that our human yearning for grounding (criterion #4) is intrinsically sentimental and must be overcome, or rejecting the irreductionist mandate (criterion #3), perhaps along lines that any metaphysical account that grounds human life must take the category *human* to be sacrosanct (which I do not believe). Someone else might accept the type, choosing instead to argue that my proposal fails to meet its criteria (for example, by claiming that my philosophy of presence is ultimately reductionist about locatedness and connection), or proposing a different instance entirely—such as one that rejects the ultimate deixicity of the flux.

of interwoven separation and engagement, while in detail so infinitely various as to defy description, nevertheless reveal regularities across a wide range of cases—from high-level political struggles for autonomy to simple error correction regimens in low-level computer circuitry.

Among the most important characteristics of the constitutive cross-cutting structures of registration are what I call metaphysical *zest*: the fact that all distinctions and stabilities—empirical, conceptual, categorical, metaphysical, logical—are taken *not*, at least not necessarily, and not in the first instance, to be "clear and distinct," sharp, or in any other way *formal*, but instead to be, or at least potentially to be, wily, critical, obstreperous, contentious, and in general richly eruptive with fine-structure. As well as having profound implications for (or rather against) all binarisms and dualisms—between and among different subjects, between the linguistic and the ineffable, between the abstract and the concrete, and so on and so forth—this fine-structure is sustained by an enveloping flux of cosmic particularity, one that meshes with the everyday sense that, in detail and in particular, located actions and particular circumstances always outstrip their classifiability under abstract categories.

3 Consequences

All sorts of consequences spill over from this picture of cosmic particularity, metaphysical spunk, lack of ultimate ontological or categorical decisiveness, and consequent political action. In this section I want to mention just four, to give a feel for the territory where we have arrived.

3a Representation and ontology

The first consequence is already familiar. It has been waiting in the wings since the beginning—and has even, from time to time, made forays onto center stage. It has to do with the characterization of the project arrived at in chapter 1, born of computation's needs: that a comprehensive theory that does justice to computation in the wild will have to be a full theory of semantics and intentionality, on the one hand, and of ontology and metaphysics, on the other. As has been implicit since the beginning, however, and especially since the introduction of registration, the fundamental metaphysical gradualism defuses any sharp split between representation and ontology. Indeed, the "middle distance" aspect of registration shows up those prior analytic categories for what they are:

Ontology is the projection of registration onto the world. Representation is the projection of registration onto the subject or vehicle.

Neither projection is ultimately tenable. Given that registration is logically indissoluble, even if it (necessarily) involves a degree of partial separation, it is no surprise that we have never had an intellectually satisfying theory of either half. Nor will we. Registration is the only rooted subject in the vicinity.

That is not to say that it is a mistake to call something a representation. Representation is an important category for a successor theory to reclaim—as important as any of the other mainstays of modernism: 'object,' 'truth,' 'objective,' 'mathematics,' even 'formal.' It is hard to imagine a plausible theory of scientific practice, for example, that does not make reference to the complex representational practices that are characteristic, perhaps even constitutive, of that discipline. Such theories will benefit from the development of a notion of representation that gives it substantial, work-a-day significance, one that is intellectually and morally and politically tenable.

What can be said about such a successor notion? Three things, for starters: (i) even a reclaimed notion of representation will not be able to stand as an ultimate explanatory category on its own; (ii) representation is not a phenomenon that can be explored without investigating its concomitant ontological commitments; and (iii) the distinction between representation and ontology is indefinite, vague, unstable, etc. As much has been clear throughout: one cannot press on the *whats*, the *whethers*, the *whys*, and the *wherefores* of representation without facing up to the ontological and metaphysical commitments of the people who use them to register. And one cannot do these things because representational practices and metaphysical commitments are not independent phenomena. That is why registration is such an important category.

There is a more specific moral, as well. In current writing, especially in the philosophy of mind, representation is often pressed into service as if it were a general label for intentionality. Thus commitment to the so-called "representational theory of mind" is often taken to be essentially synonymous with a commitment to intentionality full bore.[2] Once registration's central place in the theory of intentionality is recognized, an appropriately reclaimed notion of representation can emerge as a more specific and subsidiary notion—and more useful, for that.

On the proposed view, the original intentional act is taken to be one of *registration*: a process whereby the world *presents*, directly—or at least as directly as is metaphysically possible. As mandated by symmetrical realism, such presentation depends on the located "presence" of both subject and object—presence of the subject in the sense of its being located, responsible, and aware; presence of the object in the sense of its presenting as object, as in and of the world. It is for this ultimately indissoluble presence that the proposed philosophy is named.

---

[2] The presumptively wider representational view is typically contrasted with the presumptively narrower computational theory of mind—the latter being viewed as more specific in virtue of its commitment to what is known as the *formality condition*: the idea that the agent (mind, computer, etc.) works in virtue of the constitutive representations' syntactic properties (Fodor 1975, 1980). The condition counts as a *species* of formality, by my lights, because of its assumption that the category of syntax is second-order discrete, and also because it is defined in opposition to semantics (though I deny that computers-in-the-wild are formal in this sense).

This overall picture allows representation to return to its etymological roots—to be *re*-presentation, to involve "presenting again." This usage is far more natural. For think of what representation is informally taken to signify: something that stands for or symbolizes the world, something that is a realistic image or likeness or depiction of something else, where that "something else" is assumed to be already or otherwise metaphysically secure. Informal use, that is, separates metaphysical responsibility for the entity itself in its "primary" presence or presentation in the world, and this intrinsically secondary representation of it as being a certain way. Thus one imagines making a *presentation* of a new building project, for example, when the audience has not encountered it before, and using a "representation"—say, a picture of how it will look once the ivy has grown and the scars in the earth have faded away—in order to influence the way in which people go back and register it. Similarly: "she *presented* her new assistant, *representing* him as a financial wizard." This relative indirectness of representation, compared to registration, is even reflected in the grammar: we say "represent **x** *as* **y**," but "register **x**," directly.

Distinguishing representation and presentation (registration) opens up a considerable amount of room in our ability to describe intentional systems, especially when combined with two other moves already made: (i) a shift in emphasis away from purely conceptual (propositional) representation to include a much wider variety of non-conceptual forms; and (ii) a general commitment to view registration as an emerging capability, occurring in more and less sophisticated form, rather than as restricted to very-high-level human species. Consider, for example, one of the most contested claims in cognitive science research, from Gibson to post-modern AI, that direct interaction does not require representation.[3] Because the term 'representation' has been so overloaded, and because of a lack of alternatives, such remarks are often interpreted as fully anti-

[3] Gibson (1979), Neisser (1989), Chapman & Agre (1990), Brooks (1991).

intentional, triggering intense debate. They have even led some of their proponents to embrace various forms of eliminativism. Under pressure, though, it often turns out that what is being rejected is only conceptual registration, or only secondary representation, or some other species.

Discussing a case of looming, for example, a neo-Gibsonian might argue that an agent registers its approach to a wall or solid object, even if it does not do so in a conceptual register, and even if it does not construct an internal representation. Someone else, however (such as I), might argue or attempt to demonstrate that it does not do even that, because there is insufficient separation between agent and wall—and thus no fact of the matter as to what the agent registers it *as*, to say nothing of no theoretical need to invoke more than patterns of causal coupling. I might not even admit to enough distinction in the case to warrant *separating* agent and wall. Whereas in a more sophisticated case, perhaps one involving prediction, I might admit non-conceptual registration but argue against anything like a (conceptual) generality condition. Whatever; the point is only to see how a richer theoretic vocabulary allows one to make sense of a much more compelling range of alternatives than are accessible on a traditional (Ontological) view.

3b Constructivism

There are many other arenas, or so at least I would claim, in which the proposed metaphysics makes eminent sense, retroactively, of what, from the predecessor viewpoint, seemed to be a binary opposition, outright disagreement, or outrageous claim. Nowhere is this more obvious than in the sometimes fractious debates between realists and constructivists, both of whose underlying intuitions I am sworn to honor. Traditionalist realists, in particular, reliably founder on the counter-intuitive vocabulary of antirealists. Thus one reads such claims as that electromagnetic fields did not exist before Maxwell, or that penicillin did not exist before 1941, or that physicists created the neutrino.

Such claims shock, often usefully. It is tough, though, once one has admitted the ineliminable role that we play in registering the world, to square these phrasings with any sort of residual grip on a "larger than us" world—i.e., to square them with the characterization of symmetric realism given in chapter 3. It may be, of course, that their proponents do not want to square them with any form of realism, including this one. But it is much more likely, I would contend, that it is Realism that is being rejected—i.e., the modernist construal, that I, too, have tried to set aside. The problem, though, is that the act of rejection is more successful than the presentation of a positive alternative.

Constructivism has recoiled from Realism, that is, only to succumb to its equally untenable opposite. This post-modern dilemma is an inevitable consequence of speaking in fully registered language. It is a dilemma stemming from a failure of imagination: an inability to talk about the world except in terms subsequent to the registrational achievement. And that in turn has led to three insurmountable problems. First, it has meant that the constructivist's only option in describing the world prior to the act of registration is to deny that what was only then registered ever existed (this is the source of the shock). Second, even more seriously, it supplied no apparatus with which to describe the true nature of the registrational achievement, thereby somewhat ironically denying the constructivist any way to describe the metaphysically constitutive act of construction. Third—this was perhaps the most obvious of all, to the outsider—it failed normatively, giving one no handle on what was important or significant.

As admitted at the outset of chapter 3, it was in part exactly to address these difficulties that the present account of registration was developed. And as a measure of its success, note how easy it is, in the new language, to make the original claims. Thus we can say, without undue strain, that electromagnetic fields were not registered before Maxwell, or that it was only in this century that physicists registered the neutrino. To the extent that it is common sense to assume that the achievement belongs to the object, these descriptions of registration can then seem like discovery, and are thus more likely to please the traditional realist than the traditional anti-realist (though it is not my brief to please *any* traditionalist, especially). But to argue that time was not formally registered until the invention of the clock, or that intelligence became a registered phenomenon only in the twentieth century, begins to convey more of the appropriate constructive sense, especially when it is understood that registration is violent, creative, and inevitably supported by an ineffable participatory surround.

3c   Mathematics

Compared to the partial merger of representation and ontology, and the attempt to steer a tenable course between constructivism and realism, the third consequence of the metaphysical lack of categorical decisiveness may seem less important. But it is still dramatic enough. Mathematics will need to be overhauled.

To see why, note first how present-day (i.e., modernist) mathematics orders its explanations:

1. Discreteness is assumed to be primitive and absolute, exemplified for example by sets, natural numbers, and many other such properties (being even, being irrational, etc.);

2. Continuity is then defined in terms of discreteness, with the usual apparatus of Dedekind cuts, convergent Cauchy sequences, and the like; and

3. Finally, if at all, vagueness, or at least a little bit of vagueness, is modeled (as for example in the current fashion for fuzzy logic[4]).

---

[4] Fuzzy logic defines or models first-order fuzziness or indeterminacy in terms of exquisitely precise second-order real numbers. As a consequence, at least from a metaphysical point of view, it remains extremely close to standard mathematics. It is almost wholly formal. With respect to ultimate metaphysical warrant, it is still assumed to hang from a pristine, clean-and-precise, abstract sky-hook. As an attempt at ultimate metaphysical

This is the world view captured in Kronecker's famous dictum: that "God made the integers; all else is the work of man."[5] If my metaphysical picture is right, Kronecker's order of explanation is *close to backwards*. Metaphysical indefiniteness is the base case, continuity needs to be extruded from the flux, and then discreteness won, at a very high price, from that.

That is to put it metaphysically. It may be more revealing to approach it epistemically, however—or at least we should look at it from that angle as well, given that two are never wholly separable. At a minimum, the proposal will require exhuming mathematical practice, as recommended for example by intuitionists, and explicating this *achievement* of mathematical results by giving mathematicians partial ontological as well as partial epistemic responsibility for their acts—some ontological responsibility, rather than none; some epistemic responsibility, rather than all. This is not to give unrestricted license to idealism or formalism, because of realism's second constraint: mathematicians themselves, the very ones to which this metaphysical respect is to be granted, must be recognized as part of the same reality as the numbers they extrude.

This recognition that mathematicians are as much part of the world as the numbers they study puts the lie to the sharpness, and perhaps even to the coherence, of the distinctions among three allegedly alternative ways in which mathematics is traditionally understood:

··· vagueness, it does not hold a candle to the sort of rearrangements being suggested here. And anyway, as discussed in §3 of chapter 11, fuzziness and vagueness are not the right notions.

[5] Leopold Kronecker, quoted by Michael Beeson (1985, p. 429) as *Die ganzen Zahlen hat der liebe Gott gemacht, alles andere ist Menschenwerk*. Beeson in turn refers to p. 160 of Struik (1962), where it is said that Kronecker made this statement at a meeting in Berlin in 1886.

One might regret the sexism in (the translation of) Kronecker's remark, but it adds spice to the claim that he got it backwards.

1. *Empirical:* true of the physical or material world, even if at a relatively abstract level or high order;
2. *Platonist:* true of an independent mathematical realm; and
3. *Intuitionist:* characteristic of our native mental or cognitive capacities.

At a minimum, on the present metaphysics, the first and third positions, empirical and intuitionist, begin to merge. For suppose that the empirical view is right: that (what we come to register as) mathematical properties are high-level abstractions of ordinary material situations. Suppose, that is, that "threeness" is first and foremost a property of those worldly states of affairs that we register as consisting of three individuals. This essentially empirical view is compatible with the intuitionist's claim, to put it into current language, that our ability to register situations as exemplifying threeness depends, inexorably, on architectural facts about our native registrational capacities.

This compatibility is a straightforward consequence of an overarching participatory view. It is almost trivially a consequence of the present metaphysics. For if properties are the result of a certain (conceptual) kind of registration, and registration is an inexorable collaboration between (what we register as) subjects and (what we register as) objects, taking properties to be "abstractions of ordinary material situations" already implicates subjects, since ordinary material situations are not (as they are registered to be) independent of us. But the same conclusion can be reached along much more general participatory lines, without needing to advert to an even vaguely constructionist attitude towards properties. For suppose, as was suggested in chapter 1,[6] that our ability to register situations as comprising a plural, countable number of individuals depends on our being able to

---

[6] The suggestion made in chapter 1 was for computers, not for subjects in general. But it is not much of a stretch to suppose that the same may be true of us—especially if one takes seriously the moral of cross-cutting boundaries (thus consider the sidebar on page 70 in conjunction with figure 8·2, on page 260).

exemplify that same plurality in our thoughts—i.e., that our ability to *register* threeness depends, among other things, on our being able to *manifest* threeness (reminiscent of the way in which a Goodmanesque swatch represents gabardine in virtue of being gabardine).[7] If this were true, then once again both empiricist and intuitionist would be right: sure enough, arithmetic properties would be (higher-order) properties of the material world; and sure enough, too, our ability to engage in mathematical registration would depend, intrinsically, on the structure of our minds. Nor is this a remote suggestion. It has much to recommend it, especially from a symmetric realism perspective— so much so that it can make other alternatives seem forced, or outright bizarre, by comparison. Consider Hardy's remark, for example, that "mathematical truth is part of objective reality. [Mathematical propositions] are not creations of our minds."[8] Once one has come to live for a while from the perspective of symmetric realism, it seems bizarre to deny that creations of minds are part of reality.

These deliberations touch on the place and the warrant of a successor mathematics, but they say nothing about its content. This is an enormous topic, one that will have to be left to future investigation, though two general points can be made. First, no advance (reductionist) credit can be given to Frege's injunction that the content of the Pythagorean theorem should not depend on the sodium content of our brains. The consequences of the metaphysics are strong: it will not be enough to give an ethnomethodological or critical theory of mathematical practice, but leave the content intact.[9] If the notion of registration is worth its salt, it should put theorems at risk.

---

[7] Goodman (1976), pp. 52 ff. Naturally, it would be bizarre to argue that the one could not represent, for example, the number 143,293,033,854 without first exemplifying it. But we are talking about the grounding of arithmetic intuition here, not about its full exercise.

[8] Hardy (1929), cited on p. 329 of Monk (1990).

[9] As for example seems to be implied by Livingston (1986) and Leith (1990).

Second, if the world itself is not fundamentally precise or discrete, but instead irreverent or spunky or critical, why should mathematical concepts be required to be so neat and clean? Or should they not? But if not—i.e., if mathematics is not restricted to the clear and precise (higher-order formal)—what does restrict it? What makes mathematics *mathematics*? Something must give it identity. Perhaps mathematics is a theory of the complete abstract—unless of course nothing is completely abstract.

Even if a final answer cannot be predicted, an analogy from computation may hint at what it would be like to travel down this path. A few centuries ago, before the advent of modern technology, you could reliably assume that anything that uttered recognizable words of English would be something you could befriend, invite to supper, and share a minimal cultural inheritance with—i.e., would be a *person*, in the full biological and ethical and political sense of that word. Starting with the arrival of recording technology, the ability to vibrate air in ways that can be registered as English has no longer been a reliable indicator of human presence. But as long as we dealt only with recordings, the *origin* of linguistic sound remained human; technology only displaced its temporal and spatial presentation. But that is no longer the case. Toyotas ask you to buckle your seatbelt; telephone systems utter phone numbers no person has ever spoken; automated financial advisors regale you with the day's activity on the Street, using speech synthesizers and a line from Dow Jones. It is still the case that the underlying selection of words is still largely due to human choice, but needless to say that will not last. Natural language research systems are already starting, even if crudely, to assemble and pronounce minimal English sentences "of their own design."

The consequence of these developments, to put it in computational jargon, has been that we have to *unbundle* our conception of what it is to be human. What has for centuries been an aggregated mass of properties, features, etc., needs to be teased apart, the closer we get to building or simulating intelligence. As best as I see it, the ultimate consequences of a participatory metaphysics for mathematical practice will be a little like the consequences for logic and philosophy of the advent of computers: they will disrupt its boundaries, splitting what has seemed an integral study into a web of cross-cutting currents that not only interpenetrate with others inside the mathematical realm, but that weave and course through the rest of society's intellectual practice as well.

3d Computation

One of the practices with which mathematics will be (and is being) interwoven is that with which the whole exercise started: computation in the wild. As a final consequence of the overall metaphysical picture, it is worth taking a second look at this original subject matter.

In chapter 1 I said that years of study have convinced me that computation is not a distinct or autonomous *subject matter*, but is instead a complex *practice*, involving the design, construction, maintenance, and use of intentional systems. At the time that seemed like a negative result—since it seemed to put theoretical computer science in jeopardy. Overall, though, I struck an optimistic tone, claiming that in many ways it made the advent of computation on the intellectual scene more interesting, rather than less.

By now, I hope the grounds for this optimism are clear. I also hope that computation's integrity has begun to emerge. For the constructive aspect of computational practice—the fact that it involves design, architecture, construction, engineering, and the like, along with observation and description—is fully consonant with the balanced intellectual picture described above, of adopting a partially (dis)connected stance towards a partially (dis)connected subject matter.

Furthermore, modern practice is bursting with possibility, as designers, playwrights, artists, journalists, musicians, educators, and the like are drawn into the act, along with the original scientists and engineers, and now also anthropologists, linguists, and sociologists. In fact few fields, if any, are being left behind. And to repeat something said earlier, it would be a mistake to think that these people are just *users* of computation. On the contrary, they are participating in its invention—creating user interfaces, proposing architectures, rewriting the rules on what it is to publish, disrupting our understanding of identity. Moreover, the line between specifically computational expertise and general computational literacy is fading, as the medium grows ever more accessible, especially to children.

This is all just as the story predicts. For if we are expanding our registrational capacities—building instruments and other devices that mediate[10] our full participation in the world—we should expect traditional theoretical categories to be disrupted. We should especially expect this to happen if, as I have suggested, the intellectual role of computation is to serve as a disruptive catalyst, causing the collapse and requiring the replacement of the predecessor era's methodological and metaphysical assumptions. For the boundaries between computation and mathematics are by no means the only ones that are crumbling. Not only are notions of mathematical proof being revised; literary forms and conceptions of publishing are being overhauled; music, composition, journalism, and the like are in transition; notions of money, market, and value are increasingly vulnerable. Some distinctions are being opened up, such as between determinism and predictability, in part because of intrinsic computational limits. Other distinctions are collapsing, such as those between and among theories, models, simulations, implementations, and the like. As I admitted in an early chapter, I once thought this intentional disarray was evidence that the

---

[10] Perhaps one should coin a verb and say 'immediate' (ĭ–mē´–dē–āt´), in the sense of "making things immediate or present that were, or would otherwise be, remote."

field was confused. I should have given it more credit. It is palpable evidence of the ineliminable wiliness underlying even our most sacred logical distinctions.

In suggesting that this profusion of practice has a certain plucky integrity, I am not pretending that we are in good theoretical shape. I am still hungry for more adequate intellectual understanding. But it is telling that it was part of the original metaphysical desideratum to ease the boundary between academic theorizing, on the one hand, and the playful, the inventive, the literary, and the erotic, on the other. Practice leads the way. It is sobering, too, to realize in retrospect that the computational theory of mind, which at one point seemed (at least to me) to be about as major a theoretical challenge to our sense of self as one could imagine, and thus to be computation's biggest potential impact, seems from this new perspective rather narrow and conservative. It is conservative in its supposition that *mind* is all that is at stake, as opposed to full participatory, social, and material life. It is also conservative for being phrased as a *theoretical* hypothesis. If computers are allowed to run their course, they promise to disrupt, rather than lay claim to, our concept of mind; and to disrupt, rather than lay claim to, our notion of theory.

As for what the consequences of *that* will be on intellectual life, it is hard to imagine. Newton, it has been said, was not the first of the new scientists, so much as the last of the great magicians.[11] In light of its theoretical infancy, it can be tempting to say that computer science is in a "pre-Newtonian" phase: that we do not yet know the fundamental regularities governing the subject, or even very clearly what sort of tiger we have by the tail.

---

[11] John Maynard Keynes describes Newton as "the last of the magicians, the last of the Babylonians and Sumerians, the last great mind which looked out on the visible and intellectual world with the same eyes as those who began to build our intellectual inheritance rather less than 10,000 years ago . . . the last wonder-child to whom the Magi could do sincere and appropriate homage." Keynes (1947), p. 27, as quoted in Fauvel et al. (1988), pp. 6–7.

That was my position for many years. But the problem with current computer science may be just the opposite: that we are *post-Newtonian*, in the sense of being inappropriately wedded to a particular reductionist form of scientism, inapplicable to so rich an intentional phenomenon. Another generation of scientists may be the last thing we need. Maybe, instead, we need a new generation of magicians.

4 The middle ground

One could talk about consequences forever. But I want to return to a more focused review. How, more specifically, were the processes of registration envisaged to work?

Given the intrinsically deictic nature of the underlying flux, the challenge for a subject or s-region, in registering something *as* something—i.e., in taking something as *other*, yet at the same time part of the One world—was to stabilize it by exploiting its own freedom (its metaphysical allotment of slop) so as to compensate for the deictic irregularities standing between it and the o-region, and thereby "bring the object into focused existence" as an objective part of the encompassing reality. We saw a variety of patterns of cross-cutting extension implicated in these stabilization processes, from the very simplest feature-placing and stabilization of a single extended patch of the flux, up towards the more sophisticated, almost algebraic structures associated with a full conceptual deployment of objects, properties, and relations. Even in these more complex cases, ineliminable dependencies on the participatory surround, on non-conceptual registration, and on a residue of ineffable circumstantial particularity kept the resulting ontology from achieving the sterility of the predecessor metaphysics' formal (capitalized) ontology of Objects, Properties, and Relations.

When registration was first introduced, we were operating under the temporary expedience of assuming a substrate of deictic physical fields, instead of deictic metaphysical flux. From that point of view it emerged that objects, because of the requisite patterns of registrational disconnection, were never entirely physical. Once the proper metaphysical picture is introduced, the same insight gives rise to two conclusions: not only are no objects entirely physical; none are entirely *local*, either. Nothing is what it is solely in virtue of what inheres in it, since to be an object is in part to be registerable as that object, and registration requires separation and distance.

It followed that material objects—and the material world more generally—occupy what we might call a *middle ground*,[12] halfway between (the predecessor era's notion of) the physical world, and (the predecessor era's notion of) the intentional world. The resulting *median nature of materiality* has numerous theoretical consequences, only a few of which have even been touched on here. For example, it undergirds the fact that objects themselves, not just their representations, are culturally, historically, and socially plural—and yet not just products of the imagination or intentional whim of a person, society, or community, either, but made of the stuff of the world, as resistant and wily and obstreperous as the rest of us. As described in the sidebar on page 364, the middle-ground nature of ontology also leads to the following rather curious result: registration and materiality, on this metaphysics, play a role that *syntax* was asked to play in the prior metaphysics—a role that, from this new vantage point, it is clear syntax could never possibly have played.

Since registration subsumes both representation and ontology, and because registration is inextricable from the full participatory life of the registrar's community, it also follows that, to the extent that this is a theory of meaning, it is a theory of meaningfulness, rather than of a static or objectified notion of meaning on its own. Moreover, because ontology is inseparable from intentionality, *all objects* are enmeshed in these normative considerations. Because of the inexorable pluralism, I have not focused on any single normative notion: truth, beauty, goodness,

[12] Cf. Wild & Damiris (in preparation).

Impossible demands on Syntax

The traditional theoretical approach to intentional phenomena has been to "naturalize" them, on something like the following conception: (i) the underlying "natural" world is taken to be physical, to include ordinary material objects, and to be theoretically unproblematic; (ii) a higher-level intentional realm, of language and content and psychology and representation and mind and the like, is, in contrast, viewed as metaphysically problematic; and (iii) naturaliza-tion is taken to be a methodolog-ical stance or practice of reduc-ing or explaining the latter in terms of the former. In particu-lar, naturalizing intentionality is understood to be an issue of *bridging* from a presumptively higher level of thoughts, sen-tences, dreams, contents, etc., to a presumptively lower level of physical, material, causally re-spectable, metaphysically safe, "natural" objects.

How are these two realms to be bridged? As depicted in the above fig-ure, this was assumed to be the role of Syntax. On the one hand it was pulled from below: assumed to be concrete, causal, "non-semantic" (on the reigning view of formality), and thus naturalistically palatable. On the other hand Syntax was also pulled from above: assumed to correspond to Properties, refer to Individuals, and the like (so that the operations could mirror semantics). Provided both requirements were met, the machine could be understood as working "naturally," and at the same time as meet-ing the normative constraint of having content. All in all, it is a neat struc-ture: inherit causal efficacy, and thus naturalistic palatability, from below; inherit appropriate individuation (ontological palatability) from above.

But it could never work. In the wild, the tensions are simply too great. Negatively, this conclusion is part of my argument that computers are not formal symbol manipulators.* But it is the positive alternative that matters here. The notion of syntax cannot survive. But the proposal is not to get rid of syntax, and to leave the two realms unconnected. On the contrary, I am arguing that *all of ontology* lives in the intermediate realm. You can see this in the moves I have made. On the one hand, I have "lifted" material objects up from the bottom, claiming that they depend inherently on intentional (registrational) practices of subjects. At the same time I have driven semantics and content down, claiming that thought is intrinsically material, giving priority to non-conceptual content, arguing that connected practices are a constitutive part of intentionality, and the like. It is the thick participatory mix to which I have given the label "middle ground."

Once the integration is complete, there is no longer much need for a special syntactic category. That is not to belittle the difference between effective connection and disconnected coordination; the retraction of coordination onto the s-region, discussed in chapter 8, remains an essential ingredient in the overall intentional story. But retraction does not generate an *ontologically* isolated realm—as suggested by the discussion of clockworks as effective mechanisms for tracking disconnected o'clock properties.† Moreover, 'effective' is a much better term than 'syntactic' for this kind of causal efficacy. Overall, syntax turns out to have been something of a metaphysical band-aid—a solution to a misconceived problem. Once the two extremes are recognized to be theoretical fictions, the full participatory intentional subject matter is allowed to return to the middle ground, where it belongs, and the divisions between the realms are allowed to heal, then the need for a special ontological category rather evaporates. As usual we can take a lead from computational practice, which has not by and large found it necessary or useful to predicate the higher-order property 'syntactic' of a machine's internally effective states.

*See TMD·II.

† One could, of course, call clockworks syntactic—but as soon as you do that, you end up having to apply 'syntactic' to every mechanically effective property there is.

function, meaning, value, political ramification, and the like. Each of these, and a wealth of others, is a subscripted version, always and everywhere at least potentially subject to negotiation and refinement. Overall, it may do the least damage to use the word *significance* to signify the full range of normative, semantic, aesthetic, religious, and other long-distance coordinative characteristics of registration—so that we can ask about the *significance* of an utterance, of an event, of an object. Everything there is, from bicycles to meetings to multiply-targeted warheads, not least in virtue of being so registered, is as much the locus of significance as a statement or a question. It is not a metaphor, that is, how one treats something. Being an object matters. Moreover, it follows from the general picture of cosmic particularity that significance in a particular situation will always transcend what can be said. Like everything else, significance, in any given situation, is *exquisitely particular.*

5 Theory

The fact that objects must be held by subjects in a middle distance, not too close and not too far away, and also the fact that the material world is of an intermediate degree of intentionality, neither wholly physical nor wholly non-physical, are just two instances of a much more general pattern of restoring balance to a world view that the modernist era has allowed to grow askew. A third balancing act has to do with the status of theory itself.

At the end of chapter 5 I embraced what I called the *Criterion of Ultimate Concreteness*—claiming that an intellectually satisfying account of registration must presume the existence of no individuals whatsoever. At the time, that seemed like an impossible mandate to honor. In some limit sense it *is* impossible to honor, though not in a way that detracts from its truth. But it is nevertheless much *less* impossible than might first seem. I hope that the mandate's utility will already have been informally illustrated, at least to some degree, merely in the effect it has had on this discussion. But it also depends for its impact on a more serious methodological point, stemming directly from the form of the emerging theory. It has to do with the consequences, for intellectual inquiry itself, of the participatory nature of registration.

There are two sides to the story. Consider a theory of any intentional phenomenon, such as registration, language, or computation. In terms of the subject matter or content of that theory, I have already said that the story being told here implies that the constitutive regularities will not be entirely local, or effective, or causal. It follows that to be a computer, to take just one salient example, is not an issue of having this or that internal architecture, not an issue of manifesting this or that effective internal arrangement. As I said in chapter 8, it is a matter of *fit*, not of architecture—a matter of coordinating appropriately with embedding circumstances. There is no more reason to suppose one could determine whether a particular lump of silicon was a computer by examining its inner arrangements than to imagine that one could determine whether someone was in Kansas by giving them a catscan, whether they were within 200 miles of Boston by opening them up and looking inside. The same is true of all ontology. *No registered thing is as it is registered to be solely in virtue of its local or purely connected structure.* In a way this is the dual of what was said above: that the limit case of pure encounter is utterly ineffable.

That in turn implied, as has again already been admitted, that no theory of computation, language, registration, etc., will be entirely expressible in causal language. Taking something to be something—registering the angle of a ski slope, noticing whether the coffee is ready, seeing a friend coming to the door— is not a matter of standing in a causal relation to it. This has been a theme throughout the discussion: registration as much involves patterns of disconnection as of connection. This has implications for such endeavors as the recent upsurge in interest in neuroscience, mentioned in the introduction, and for the co-alescence of interest among connectionists, dynamicists, and proponents of artificial life. To the extent that they focus purely on patterns of arrangement and effective behavior, they will at best be enabling theories of the implementation of registration, not theories of registration itself.

In terms of *content*, in other words, one enduring theme or effect of the present story of registration is to *push towards disconnection*: to highlight the importance of separation, of the non-effective, of what is at one level of remove. I have highlighted the argument for separation in part because of the times: this particular text, at this moment in history, is being written against the background of a causal, physical, reductionist intellectual environment. Ironically, however—and this irony is important to see—*at the meta-level I am pushing in exactly the opposite direction*. At the meta-level, that is, with respect to the nature of theories themselves, my emphasis is almost exactly the reverse: towards a much more *connected* view than usual of how theory and subject matter relate.

My seeming to push in opposite directions—towards separation, in the subject matter; towards engagement, at the level of the theory—is not intended to drive the two apart. On the contrary, it is intended to bring the whole intellectual situation back into balance. The irony is not mine, in other words; it exists in the predecessor situation. It exists because of the following somewhat bizarre fact: the predecessor era's reductionist or naturalistic "theories" are imagined to be entirely *disconnected* accounts of entirely *connected* phenomena. Logical axiomatizations of physics are a perfect example. The semantic relation tying the axioms themselves to the physical situations they are thought to describe—i.e., the relation between the (disconnected) third and (connected) first realms—is *exactly not* the kind of relation that physics is thought to account for. As much was admitted in chapter 5.

The picture being painted here, in contrast, is much more integrated. Registration is taken to involve complex patterns of *partial* connection and *partial* disconnection—not limit cases of either. And what is true for registration in general is true for theoretical inquiry, which is after all a form of registration. If registration is participatory, so too must theory construction be.

This makes all sorts of sense. It makes sense, for example, of the widely accepted but never very well explicated platitude that one must be at least partially involved in a subject matter in order to understand it. It also gives reign to a pragmatic conception of the virtue or worth of a scientific theory, since, like all normative value, it will be discharged at least in part into the patterns of activity or way of life to which it gives rise. But it also, somewhat more technically, gives credit to what in chapter 1 I suggested may be computer science's most important contribution to intellectual life: its development of a *synthetic* methodological stance towards registrational and intentional systems. As any practitioner would admit, it is not at all immaterial that we build, use, and maintain these systems. Nor was it fatuous to say that much of our current understanding of them resides partially in the bones of practitioners—the product of endless late-night debugging sessions, and decades of sheer practical experience. This is nothing else than the requisite participatory surround that enables our registration of these systems to work—which explains why all standard theoretical intentional terms ('semantics,' 'representation,' 'reference,' 'language,' etc.) inevitably take on novel meanings as this explosive practice develops. It also makes sense of the intuition, felt by many, that one of the best ways to understand systems that understand the world in radically non-standard registers is to understand how they are built—provided, at least, that the twist is added that an intellectual understanding of how to build something is no substitute for having actually participated in the construction process.

6 Grounding

All these deliberations lead back to the most important overall
question: how the account measures up to the mandate first formulated in chapter 2, of supplying irreductionist foundations
— of being grounded, simpliciter, without being grounded in α,
for any α.

The most important fact has to do with the participatory nature of registration, theorizing, and indeed all other forms of activity. Registration, it has been claimed since the beginning,
involves distance, disconnection, separation—and thus the introduction of a boundary between subject and object. Crucially,
however, the separation is *partial*. For as has been clear since the
beginning, but was especially highlighted in chapter 9, although
the *focus* of registration crosses a (created) gap, it is surrounded
by a web of connection. And since connection is unregistered
and unregisterable, the boundary of an object, and the boundary of a subject, is itself only partial. When the subject is gathered together as a unity and registered as a subject (whether in a
form of alterity, or in self-conception), boundaries are invariably
imposed—though throughout they remain lower-case, non-
formal boundaries: feisty boundaries, eruptive boundaries,
boundaries that are challenged and negotiated and forever re-
drawn. In virtue of its connection, however, the subject itself
shades inexorably into unregistered contact with what is *around*
it, with what it is *made of*, with the overwhelming particularity
of its ineffable local surround.

To *be*, therefore—to be a subject, an object, to be anything
or any way at all—is a little bit like being a drop of ink on a blot-
ter. Even if there is a center, a core—a resolute and defensible
facticity about there *being* an ink blot, here and now—it nevertheless always turns out, on sufficiently close inspection, that the
boundaries of the ink drop are not black and white (discrete, formal). Instead, the ink spreads out, gradually and ineluctably
into the surrounding paper, until it so thoroughly fades into

fuses with the fibers that for all intents and purposes there is no longer any distinction to be drawn. *So too of existence.* Boundaries are only features of registration, and registration requires separation. In our local connectedness, au fond, we are inseparable from the world—rather in the way that a Gaussian distribution is inseparable from the whole line, or an ink blot is inseparable from the paper.

Except in one way the analogy is radically misleading. In the case of Gaussians and ink blots there is a *dimension* to the spreading out. The way in which we are continuous with the world, the way in which we arise up out of and subside back into and are never wholly separate from it, is much more fundamental. In chapter 6 I said that intentionality's directedness outstripped physical pointing—that whereas it was (at least arguably) difficult to point outside your light cone, intentionality was capable of "pointing" discontinuously across time, space, and even possibility. But even intentionality's directedness is limited; there is no way, even semantically, to point "out of the world." In a way, it was this impossibility that defeated the attempt to achieve a view from nowhere—there being no axis along which "nowhere" is far away. By the same token, there is no axis, no registerable dimension, along which the distinction between us as bounded registered individuals, and our non-individuated participation in the world, is gradual (except perhaps the unregisterable dimension of registerable-or-not).

In a way the point is obvious. Even adherents of an irreconcilable distinction between noumenal and phenomenal worlds would admit that subjects, in virtue of existing, are noumenal, too, or at least have a noumenal "aspect." The most serious problem with this most elite of metaphysical distinctions is that it, too, is taken to be formal: absolute, inviolable—whereas in fact, or at least so it is being claimed here, nothing is that totally divided, nothing is that formal, and so we are not so totally divided from its (our) noumenal essence. In a way the theoretical admission made above, about locatedness and the grounds for connection and disconnection, points towards the same conclusion.

Someone might think that this inextricability of existence is impossible to understand—impossible to imagine, impossible to describe, impossible *even by its own admission*. But that worry is transitory; it only seems to be a problem from an intermediate, and ultimately untenable, phase. For it would be impossible only if logical and metaphysical distinctions were formal—only if existence were sundered from the world. According to the present account, however, being shades continuously into exactly the sort of ineffable contact that grounds reference, meaning, practice, being. This, in turn, is why the Concreteness Criterion—the mandate to eschew all advance registration—is, if not wholly possible, not wholly crazy, either.

Forget transcendental deduction, in other words. Let go of the pretense, once and for all, that we can hang a metaphysical story from a rope that somehow reaches up into a magical abstract heaven—an image that is disturbingly like, and about as plausible as, that enduring image of a fantastical sky-hook. Forget it if for no other reason than to satisfy the mandate of naturalism. For naturalism, after all, at least in the form in which I embraced it, was a mandate to avoid the metaphysically spooky. And surely nothing is as spooky as the unfortunately familiar idea that properties, numbers, types, sets, propositions, variables, and the like somehow rain down on us from a God-given heaven, a heaven beyond the reach of any empirical science.[13]

The picture painted here, in contrast, is grounded from the opposite direction. Very simply, it is rooted in the One world. Moreover this way of starting has since the beginning had very pragmatic consequences. Since our registrational practices derive from, and are never fully separated from, our unregistered

---

[13] In chapter 3 I pretended that my construal of naturalism was weak; but for the second time I lied. Naturalism had better be strong enough to rout this most entrenched of all dualisms.

connected participation—our encounter of and our being in the world—the way is paved for something I will (only somewhat ironically) call *immanent induction*: a continuous process by which we can partially let go of prior registrations and pick up new ones, without disappearing or collapsing in the process. This is why there is any substance at all to the suggestion made in §1 of this chapter, that we do field-theoretic physics one better, and let go of individuals at the property level as well. Only because we are not wholly registrational—and not wholly individuated from everything there is—is there any chance of our surviving that injunction, and thereby triangulating on what registration is.

7 Pluralism

That, in turns, brings us full circle, to the relation between the limits of effability and the overarching desideratum of doing justice to pluralism. As stated, it is an essential part of the picture that registration in general, and conceptual registration more specifically, is itself an only partially extruded activity—still inextricably tied, though in an ultimately ineffable way, to a prior form of grounding in the world. By the same token, subjects, too, are only partially extruded from the world. The putty attaching us to the One world is never stretched so far as to break.

Moreover, this boundary between our registration of the world and our unregistered participation is not only gradual, or indefinite, or playful; it is also crucial to our ability to register. Our registrational practices are continuous with, and au fond are grounded in, our pre-registered embodied existence. Except that it is a conceit to call that existence *our* existence, for at that level we are not even distinct or separated from the world as a whole. *This is immanence with a vengeance.* It is not just that no one ever cut the umbilical cord. Every breath we breathe, every word we speak, every step we take, is fashioned from, but not entirely broken away from, everything there is.

Naturally, this places limits on effability—though it also means that those limits are not nearly as serious as one might suppose. It is not so easy to say exactly what the limits come to, not only because they, too, have no exact boundaries, but because the picture affects the notion of what it is to say something—i.e., affects to the very core a successor notion of "effability." It is difficult, if not impossible, for example, to retain any very precise notion of explicit content. In its place, genuine communication can be seen to involve a more radical form of cohabitation than is required on traditional models, which in turn, in a kind of second pass, reinfuses the notion of "effability" with a richness that it lacks on those same traditional models— including the respectful ability to grant that friend in the café their untranslatable exquisite articulation. The very notion of "what it is to say something" changes—in a way that, among other things, is necessary in order to explain how the phrase 'unregistered flux' can coherently be uttered. Of course the words 'unregistered flux' can be uttered; of course the underlying unregistered flux can be referred to—*everyone knows that, even those who claim it cannot be*. If it did not have accessible content, people would have no intuition suggesting that it cannot be said. No, the *content* is not the problem; it has been known for a very long time what it is to see through a glass, darkly, and to understand, in our bones, that it is a glass, and dark. What evades understanding is not the saying itself, but an understanding of how we can say things like this; what keeps us from collapsing in paradox; why we smile.

But these are all deliberations for another time. For the moment, the crucial point is only that every real thing—registrar and registered, indissoluble—is constituted of the one, same, infinite, underlying, ineffable deictic flux, a flux we can knowingly refer to, even as we truly say that there is no adequate way to *describe* it.

Registration is inexorably plural, in other words, though not discrete; the flux from which it arises is inexorably singular. This playfully gradualist dialectic is key to the entire story. It is those two facts, in conjunction with the recognition that our way of inhabiting the world is inherently participatory, that answer the condition set in chapter 3: of making room for what is deep and right about commitments to pluralism, theories of social construction, and the like, while at the same time retaining what is right, and indeed moral, about the foundations of realism. For the account has supplied

FIGURE 12·1 PLURALISM

what would otherwise have been impossible: *ontological pluralism sustained by metaphysical monism.*

There is only one world—that is what was important about realism. But its unity transcends all ability to speak.

Indexes

Sections

379

Figures

Page numbers to the right indicate where each figure appears; those in brackets following the title indicate references to the figure in the text (59 s refers to the sidebar on page 59).

Sidebars

Page numbers at the right indicate where each sidebar appears; those in brackets following the title, references to the sidebar in the main text.

Topics

References have the following form: **197** indicates a page on which a technical term is introduced or defined: *238* (fig. 7.5), figure 7.5 on page 238; 240 s, the sidebar on page 240; and 265 n, the footnote on page 265, with footnote numbers explicitly indicated (e.g., 336 n. 10) only if necessary for disambiguation.

Names

References are to page numbers where authors or their works are cited (for references to specific works see the reference index, beginning on page 411). Footnotes are indicated (e.g., 258 n. 12) only if the name does not appear in the main text. 245 s refers to the sidebar on page 245.

References

Page numbers in brackets at the end of each reference indicate places in the text where the given work is cited. Footnotes are explicitly indicated (e.g., 284 n) only in cases where the author is not cited by name in the main text. 245 s refers to the sidebar on page 245.

Agre, Philip E. (1996): *Computation and Human Experience*, Cambridge: Cambridge University Press · [140 n]

Akins, Kathleen (1993): "What It Is Like to Be Boring and Myopic," in Bo Dahlbom, ed., *Dennett and His Critics*, Oxford: Blackwell, pp. 124–160 · [68 n]

Aydede, Murat (1993): *Syntax, Functionalism, Connectionism, and the Language of Thought*, doctoral dissertation, College Park: Univ. of Maryland · [35 n. 13]

Barrow, John (1991): *Theories of Everything*, Oxford: Clarendon · [144 n. 6]

Barwise, Jon and John Perry (1983): *Situations and Attitudes*, Cambridge, Mass.: MIT Press / A Bradford Book · [31 n. 8, 284 n]

Bawden, Alan (1993): *Linear Graph Reduction: Confronting the Cost of Naming*, doctoral dissertation in computer science, Cambridge, Mass.: Massachusetts Institute of Technology · [41 n]

Bechtel, William and Adele A. Abrahamsen (1991): *Connectionism and the Mind: An Introduction to Parallel Processing in Networks*, Oxford: Basil Blackwell · [64 n. 37]

Beeson, Michael (1985): *Foundations of Constructive Mathematics*, Berlin: Springer-Verlag · [355 n. 5]

Bellah, Robert (1985): *Habits of the Heart*, Berkeley: University of California Press · [91 n]

———— (1991): *The Good Society*, New York: Knopf (distributed by Random House) · [91 n]

Berger, Peter L. and Thomas Luckmann (1966/1980): *The Social Construction of Reality: a Treatise in the Sociology of Knowledge*, Garden City, New York: Doubleday (1966); New York: Irvington Publishers (1980) · [86 n. 1]

Bloor, David (1976/1991): *Knowledge and Social Imagery*, Chicago: University of Chicago Press · [86 n. 1]

—— Boyd, Richard (1979): "Metaphor and Theory Change: What Is 'Meta-phor' a Metaphor For?" in Anthony Ortoni, ed., *Metaphor and Thought*, Cambridge: Cambridge University Press, pp. 356–419 · [33 n. 9]

Brentano, Franz Clemens (1874/1973): *Psychology from an Empirical Standpoint*, New York: Humanities Press · [111, 209]

Brooks, Rodney A. (1986): "A Robust Layered Control System for a Mobile Robot," IEEE *Journal of Robotics and Automation*, Vol. **2**, pp. 14–23 · [50]

—— (1991): "Intelligence Without Representation," *Artificial Intelligence*, Vol. **47**, Issues 1–3, pp. 139–159 · [20 n. 20, 351 n.]

Butler, Sir William Francis (1982), as quoted in the *Wild Rivers Survey* series of pamphlets, Parks Canada, Ottawa, Canada · [vii]

Callon, Michel (1986): "Some Elements of a Sociology of Translation: Domestication of the Scallops and Fishermen of St. Brieuc Bay," in J. Law, ed., *Power, Action, and Belief: A New Sociology of Knowledge?* London: Routledge and Kegan Paul · [86 n. 1]

Castañeda, Hector-Neri (1975): *Thinking and Doing: The Philosophical Foundations of Institutions*, Dordrecht, Holland: Reidel · [248 n]

Chapman, David and Philip Agre (1987): "Abstract Reasoning as Emergent from Concrete Activity," in Michael P. Georgeff and Amy L. Lansky, eds., *Reasoning about Action and Plans: Proceedings of the 1986 Workshop*, Los Altos, California: Morgan Kaufmann, pp. 411–424 · [248 n]

—— (1990): "What Are Plans For?" in Pattie Maes, ed., *Designing Autonomous Agents: Theory and Practice from Biology to Engineering and Back*, Cambridge, Mass.: MIT / Elsevier, pp. 17–34 · [351 n]

Chisholm, Roderick M. (1957): *Perceiving: A Philosophical Study*. Ithaca, New York: Cornell University Press · [111 n]

Churchland, Patricia Smith (1986): *Neurophilosophy*, Cambridge, Mass.: MIT Press / A Bradford Book · [11 n, 281]

—— (1992): *The Computational Brain*, Cambridge, Mass.: MIT Press / A Bradford Book · [11 n, 281]

Churchland, Paul M. (1989): *A Neurocomputational Perspective*, Cambridge, Mass.: MIT Press / A Bradford Book · [11 n, 281]

—— (1995): *The Engine of Reason, the Seat of the Soul: A Philosophical Journey into the Brain*. Cambridge, Mass.: MIT Press / A Bradford Book · [46 n. 21]

Constable, Robert L., et al. (1986): *Implementing Mathematics with the Nuprl Development System*. New Jersey: Prentice-Hall · [30 n. 5]

Crick, Francis and Christof Koch (1992): "Towards a Neurobiological Theory of Consciousness," *Seminars in Neuroscience*, Vol. **2** · [145 n]

Cussins, Adrian (1990): "The Connectionist Construction of Concepts," in Margaret Boden, ed., *The Philosophy of Artificial Intelligence*, Oxford: Oxford University Press, pp. 368–440 · [20 n. 20, 46 n. 21, 65 n. 39, 281]

———— (1992): "Content, Embodiment, and Objectivity: The Theory of Cognitive Trails," *Mind*, Vol. **101**, No. 404, Oct. 1992, pp. 651–688 · [281]

———— (forthcoming): *Constructions of Thought* · [42 n, 50 n. 25, 140 n. 4, 281]

Davidson, Donald (1974): "On the Very Idea of a Conceptual Scheme," *Proceedings and Addresses of the American Philosophical Association, Vol.* **47**, reprinted in Donald Davidson, *Inquiries into Truth and Interpretation*, Oxford: Clarendon Press (1984), pp. 183–198 · [197 n]

Dennett, Daniel C. (1982): "Beyond Belief," in Andrew Woodfield, ed., *Thought and Object: Essays on Intentionality,* Oxford: Clarendon Press · [192 n]

———— (1987): *The Intentional Stance*, Cambridge, Mass.: MIT Press / A Bradford Book · [10 s, 73, 258 n]

———— (1991): *Consciousness Explained*, Boston: Little, Brown and Co. · [231 s]

Derrida, Jacques (1967): *Writing and Difference* (*L'écriture et la différence*), Paris: Editions du Seuil.

Dixon, Michael (1991): *Embedded Computation and the Semantics of Programs*, Xerox Palo Alto Research Center Report SSL–91–1, 182 pp. · [35 n. 11, 77 n. 1, 245 s, 246 n, 256 n. 11]

Dretske, Fred I. (1981): *Knowledge and the Flow of Information*, Cambridge, Mass.: MIT Press / A Bradford Book · [13 n. 13, 31 n. 8]

———— (1985): "Machines and the Mental," Presidential Address to the 83rd Annual Meeting of the Western Division of the American Philosophical Association, Chicago: *APA Proceedings* **59**, pp. 23–33 · [10 s]

———— (1994): "If You Can't Make One, You Don't Know How It Works," in Peter French, Theodore Uehling, et al., eds., *Midwest Studies in Philosophy*, Notre Dame, Indiana: University of Notre Dame Press, pp. 468–482 · [21 n, 147]

Dreyfus, Hubert L. (1992): *What Computers Still Can't Do: A Critique of Artificial Reason*, Cambridge, Mass.: MIT Press · [7–8, 281]

Dreyfus, Hubert L. and Stuart E. Dreyfus (1988): "Making a Mind Versus Modeling the Brain: Artificial Intelligence Back at a Branchpoint," *Dædelus* special issue on artificial intelligence, Winter 1988; issued as Vol. **117** No. 1 of the *Proceedings of the American Academy of Arts and Sciences*, pp. 15–43 · [7–8]

Dumas, Alexandre (1894): *The Count of Monte Cristo*, Boston: Little, Brown & Co. · [196 n. 6]

Dupré, John (1993): *The Disorder of Things*, Cambridge, Mass.: Harvard University Press · [326 n. 1, 334 n]

Dupuy, Jean-Pierre (1994): *Aux origines des sciences cognitives*, Paris: La Découverte · [III n]

Evans, Gareth (1982): *The Varieties of Reference*, Oxford: Oxford University Press · [65, 125 n, 279, 281 n]

——— (1985): *Collected Papers*, Oxford: Oxford University Press.

Fausto-Sterling, Anne (1993): "The Five Sexes: Why Male and Female Are Not Enough," *The Sciences*, Vol. **33** No. 2 (March-April), pp. 20–25 · [79]

Fauvel, John, Raymond Flood, Michael Shortland, and Robin Wilson, eds. (1988): *Let Newton Be!* Oxford: Oxford University Press · [361 n]

Fodor, Jerry A. (1975): *The Language of Thought*, Cambridge, Mass.: Harvard University Press · [7–8, 350 n]

——— (1980): "Methodological Solipsism Considered as a Research Strategy in Cognitive Psychology," *Behavioral and Brain Sciences*, Vol. **3** No. 1; March 1980, pp. 63–73. Reprinted in Fodor, Jerry: *Representations*, Cambridge, Mass.: MIT Press, 1981 · [7–8, 192 n, 350 n]

——— (1984): "Semantics, Wisconsin Style," *Synthese*, Vol. **59**, pp. 231–250 · [13 n. 13]

——— (1987): *Psychosemantics*, Cambridge, Mass.: MIT Press · [13 n. 13, 31 n. 6]

Fodor, Jerry A. and Brian McLaughlin (1990): "Connectionism and the Problem of Systematicity: Why Smolensky's Solution Doesn't Work," *Cognition*, Vol. **35**, pp. 183–196 · [35 n. 13, 279 n. 2]

Fodor, Jerry A. and Zenon Pylyshyn (1988): "Connectionism and Cognitive Architecture: A Critical Analysis," in Steve Pinker and Jacques Mehler, eds., *Connections and Symbols*, Cambridge, Mass.: MIT Press (a *Cognition* special issue), pp. 3–71 · [35 n. 13, 279 n. 2]

Franchi, Stefano (forthcoming · a): "Intentionally True," unpublished ms. · [III n]

——— (forthcoming · b): *Endgames: Game and Play at the End of Philosophy* (working title), doctoral dissertation in philosophy, Stanford: Stanford University · [208 n]

Frege, Gottlob (1892/1993): "On Sense and Reference," reprinted in A. W. Moore, ed., *Meaning and Reference*, Oxford: Oxford University Press, pp. 23–42 · [43 n, 243 n. 1, 256]

——— (1893/1980): *The Foundations of Arithmetic : A Logico-Mathematical Enquiry into the Concept of Number*, second revised edition, Evanston, Illinois: Northwestern University Press · [131 n]

Gell-Mann, Murray (1994): *The Quark and the Jaguar*, New York: W. H. Freeman and Co. · [19 n. 17]

Gibson, James J. (1979): *The Ecological Approach to Visual Perception*, Boston: Houghton Mifflin · [217, 225 n, 351]

Gleick, James (1987): *Chaos*, New York: Viking · [19 n. 17]

Goel, Vinod (1995): *Sketches of Thought*, Cambridge, Mass: MIT Press / A Bradford Book · [46 n. 22, 254 n. 9, 281 n]

Goodman, Nelson (1976): *Languages of Art: An Approach to a Theory of Symbols*, second edition (first published 1968), Indianapolis: Hackett Publishing Co. · [357]

——— (1983): *Fact, Fiction, and Forecast*, fourth edition (first published 1954), Cambridge, Mass.: Harvard University Press · [31 n. 6, 284 n]

Grice, H. Paul (1989): *Studies in the Way of Words*, Cambridge, Mass.: Harvard University Press.

Halpern, Joe (1987): "Using Reasoning about Knowledge to Analyze Distributed Systems," *Annual Review of Computer Science*, Vol. **2**, pp. 37–68 · [31 n. 8]

Haraway, Donna (1991): *Simians, Cyborgs, and Women: The Reinvention of Nature*, New York: Routledge—especially the article "Situated Knowledges: The Science Question in Feminism and the Privilege of Partial Perspective" · [4 n, 86 n. 1, 208 n, 254 n. 8, 306 n, 340 n]

Harding, Sandra (1986): *The Science Question in Feminism*, Ithaca, New York: Cornell University Press · [86 n. 1, 93 n. 11]

——— (1991): *Whose Science? Whose Knowledge: Thinking from Women's Lives*, London: Open University Press · [86 n. 1]

Hardy, Godfrey H. (1929): "Mathematical Proof," *Mind*, January 1929, pp. 1–25 · [357]

Haugeland, John (1978): "The Nature and Plausibility of Cognitivism," *Behavioral and Brain Sciences*, Vol. **2**, pp. 215–260 · [5 n. 4]

——— (1981): "Semantic Engines," in John Haugeland, ed., *Mind Design: Philosophy, Psychology, Artificial Intelligence*, Cambridge, Mass.: MIT Press / A Bradford Book (1981), pp. 1–34 · [10 s]

——— (1982): "Analog and Analog," *Philosophical Topics* (Spring 1981); reprinted in J. I. Biro & Robert W. Shahan, eds., *Mind, Brain, and Function: Essays in the Philosophy of Mind*, Norman, Oklahoma: University of Oklahoma Press (1982), pp. 213–225 · [177 n, 235]

——— (1985): *Artificial Intelligence: The Very Idea*, Cambridge, Mass.: MIT Press / A Bradford Book · [10 s]

——— (1991): "Representational Genera," in William Ramsey, Stephen P. Stich, and David E. Rumelhart, eds., *Philosophy and Connectionist Theory*, Hillsdale, New Jersey: Lawrence Erlbaum Associates, pp. 61–90 · [46 n. 21]

Hutchins, Edwin (1995): *Cognition in the Wild*, Cambridge, Mass.: MIT Press · [6 n. 5]

Jackendoff, Ray S. (1987): *Consciousness and the Computational Mind*, Cambridge, Mass.: MIT Press · [7 n]

Kafka, Franz (1925/1992): *The Trial*, New York: Knopf · [326 n. 2]

Kauffman, Stuart A. (1993): *The Origins of Order*, New York: Oxford University Press · [19 n. 17]

Keller, Evelyn Fox (1985): *Reflections on Gender and Science*, New Haven: Yale University Press · [86 n. 1]

Keynes, John Maynard (1947): "Newton, the Man," *Newton Tercentenary Celebrations*, Cambridge: Cambridge University Press · [361 n]

Kirsh, David (1987): "Putting a Price on Cognition," in *Southern Journal of Philosophy*, Vol. **XXVI**, supplement.

——— (1991): "Today the Earwig, Tomorrow Man?" in *Artificial Intelligence*, Vol. **47** No. 1–3, pp. 161–184. Entire issue reprinted as David Kirsh, ed., *Foundations of Artificial Intelligence*, Cambridge, Mass.: MIT Press / A Bradford Book · [46 n. 21, 65]

Kitcher, Philip (1992): "The Naturalist's Return," *Philosophical Review*, Vol. **101**, pp. 53–114 · [138 n. 1, 140 n. 4]

Knorr-Cetina, Karen (1981): *The Manufacture of Knowledge: An Essay on the Constructivist and Contextual Nature of Science*, Oxford and New York: Pergamon Press · [86 n. 1]

Kripke, Saul (1976): "Is There a Problem about Substitutional Quantification?" in Gareth Evans and John McDowell, eds., *Truth and Meaning: Essays in Semantics*, Oxford: Clarendon Press, pp. 325–419 · [45 n]

Kuhn, Thomas (1962/1970): *The Structure of Scientific Revolutions*, Chicago: The University of Chicago Press (1st edition 1967, 2nd edition 1970) · [86 n. 1]

Kundera, Milan (1984): *The Unbearable Lightness of Being*, New York: Harper & Row · [208]

Latour, Bruno (1987): *Science in Action: How to Follow Scientists and Engineers Through Society*, Cambridge, Mass.: Harvard University Press · [79 n. 4, 86 n. 1, 335 n. 9]

——— (1988): *The Pasteurization of France*, Cambridge, Mass.: Harvard University Press · [77, 86 n. 1, 293]

——— (1993): *We Have Never Been Modern*, Wheatsheaf, New York: Harvester Press · [87 n. 3]

Latour, Bruno and Steven Woolgar (1979/1986): *Laboratory Life: The Social Construction of Scientific Fact*, London: Sage (1979). Reprinted (without the word 'social' in the title) Princeton: Princeton University Press (1986) · [86 n. 1]

Lave, Jean and Etienne Wenger (1991): *Situated Learning: Legitimate Peripheral Participation*, Cambridge and New York: Cambridge University Press · [195 n. 4, 289 n]

Leith, Philip (1990): *Formalism in AI and Computer Science*, New York: Ellis Horwood · [357 n. 9]

Lettvin, Jerome Y., Humberto R. Maturana, Warren S. McCulloch, and Walter H. Pitts (1959): "What the Frog's Eye Tells the Frog's Brain," *Proceedings of the IRE*, Vol. **47** No. 11 (November), pp. 1940–1959. Reprinted in Warren S. McCulloch, *Embodiments of Mind*, Cambridge, Mass.: MIT Press (1965/1988), pp. 230–255 · [149 n]

Levy, David M., Daniel C. Brotsky and Kenneth R. Olson (1988): "Formalizing the Figural: Aspects of a Foundation for Document Manipulation," *Proceedings of the ACM Conference on Document Processing Systems*, New York: Association for Computing Machinery · [48 n]

Livingston, Eric (1986): *The Ethnomethodological Foundations of Mathematics,* London: Routledge & Kegan Paul · [357 n. 9]

Locke, John (1959): *An Essay Concerning Human Understanding*, Dover Publications, unabridged, 2 volumes.

Longino, Helen (1990): *Science as Social Knowledge,* Princeton: Princeton University Press · [86 n. 1]

McAlister, Linda L. (1974): "Chisholm and Brentano on Intentionality." *Review of Metaphysics*, Vol. **XXVIII** No. 2, pp. 328–338 · [111 n]

McGinn, Colin (1982): "The Structure of Content," in Andrew Woodfield, ed., *Thought and Object: Essays on Intentionality*, Oxford: Clarendon Press · [192 n]

Marcus, Mitchell P. (1980): *A Theory of Syntactic Recognition for Natural Language*, Cambridge, Mass.: MIT Press · [61 n]

Marcus, Mitchell, Don Hindle, and Margaret Fleck (1983): "D-Theory: Talking about Talking about Trees," *Proceedings of the 21st Annual Meeting of the Association for Computational Linguistics* · [61 n]

Marcus, Mitchell and Don Hindle (1990): "Description Theory and Intonation Boundaries," in G. Altmann, ed., *Computational and Cognitive Models of Speech*, Cambridge, Mass.: MIT Press · [61 n]

Millikan, Ruth (1984): *Language, Thought, and Other Biological Categories*, Cambridge, Mass.: MIT Press · [13 n. 13]

——— (1989): "Biosemantics," *Journal of Philosophy*, Vol. **LXXXVI** No. 6, June 1989, pp. 281–297 · [13 n. 13]

——— (1990): "Compare and Contrast Dretske, Fodor, and Millikan on Teleosemantics," *Philosophical Topics*, Vol. **18** No. 2, Fall 1990, pp. 151–161 · [13 n. 13]

Monk, Ray (1990): *Ludwig Wittgenstein: The Duty of Genius*, New York: Penguin Books · [357 n. 8]

Montague, Richard (1963): "Syntactical Treatments of Modality, with Corollaries on Reflexion Principles and Finite Axiomatizability," *Acta Philosophica Fennica*, Vol. **16**, pp. 153–167 · [45 n]

Nagel, Thomas (1974): "What Is It Like to Be a Bat?" *Philosophical Review*, Vol. LXXXIII No. 4 (October), pp. 435–50 · [67 n. 40]

—————— (1986): *The View From Nowhere*, Oxford: Oxford University Press · [305 n. 17]

Neisser, Ulric (1989): "Direct Perception and Recognition as Distinct Perceptual Systems," in Meeting of the Cognitive Science Society, Ann Arbor, Michigan: August 1989 · [351 n]

—————— (1994): "Multiple Systems: A New Approach to Cognitive Theory," *European Journal of Cognitive Psychology*, Vol. **6**, pp. 225–241.

Newell, Allen (1980): "Physical Symbol Systems," *Cognitive Science,* Vol. **4**, pp. 135–183 · [7–8, 74]

Newell, Allen and Herbert A. Simon (1976): "Computer Science as Empirical Inquiry: Symbols and Search," *Communications of the Association for Computing Machinery*, Vol. **19** (March 1976), No. 3, pp. 113–126. Reprinted in John Haugeland, ed., *Mind Design*, Cambridge, Mass.: MIT Press / A Bradford Book (1981), pp. 35–66 · [7–8, 74]

Nunberg, Geoffrey (1993): "Indexicality and Deixis," *Linguistics and Philosophy*, Vol. **156**, pp. 1–43 · [169 n. 22]

Perry, John (1979): "The Problem of the Essential Indexical," *Nous*, Vol. **13** · [170, 248 n]

Pettit, Philip and John McDowell, eds. (1986): *Subject, Thought and Context*, Oxford: Oxford University Press · [192 n]

Popper, Karl R. and Eccles, John C. (1977): *The Self and Its Brain*, Berlin: Springer-Verlag · [158–59 s]

Putnam, Hilary (1981): *Reason, Truth, and History*, Cambridge: Cambridge University Press · [86]

—————— (1987): *The Many Faces of Realism*, La Salle, Illinois: Open Court · [86, 112–13 s]

——————, edited by James Conant (1990): *Realism with a Human Face*, Cambridge, Mass.: Harvard University Press · [86, 96, 112–13 s, 142]

Quine, Willard von Orman (1953): "Three Grades of Modal Involvement," *Proceedings of the XIth International Congress of Philosophy*, Vol. **14**, pp. 65–81 · [45 n]

—————— (1964): *Word and Object*, Cambridge, Mass.: MIT Press · [138 n. 1]

—————— (1971): "The Inscrutability of Reference," in D. D. Steinberg and L. A. Jacobovits, eds., *Semantics,* Cambridge: Cambridge University Press · [169 n. 22]

Reichenbach, Hans (1947): *Elements of Symbolic Logic*, New York: Free Press · [157, 167]

Rosenschein, Stanley (1985): "Formal Theories of Knowledge in AI and Robotics," *New Generation Computing*, Vol. **3** · [31 n. 8]

Rudwick, Martin J. S. (1985): *The Great Devonian Controversy: The Shap-

ing of Scientific Knowledge among Gentlemanly Specialists, Chicago: University of Chicago Press · [86 n. 1]

Searle, John (1980): "Minds, Brains, and Programs," *Behavioral and Brain Sciences*, Vol. **3**, No. 3, Sept. 1980, pp. 417–458 · [7 n, 10 s, 28, 30 n. 4]

———— (1982): "The Myth of the Computer: An Exchange," *New York Review of Books* · [10 s]

———— (1983): *Intentionality: An Essay in the Philosophy of Mind*, Cambridge: Cambridge University Press · [252 n]

———— (1984): *Minds, Brains, and Science*, Cambridge, Mass.: Harvard University Press · [7 n, 10 s, 28, 145 n]

———— (1992): *The Rediscovery of the Mind*, Cambridge, Mass.: MIT Press / A Bradford Book · [29 n. 2, 31 n. 6, 43, 145 n, 196 n. 8, 292]

Shapin, Steven and Steven Schaffer (1985): *Leviathan and the Air Pump: Hobbs, Boyle, and the Experimental Life*, Princeton: Princeton University Press · [86 n. 1]

Smith, Brian Cantwell (1984): "Reflection and Semantics in Lisp," Salt Lake City: *Proceedings of the 11th Annual Principles of Programming Languages Conference (POPL)*, pp. 23–35 · [37 n. 16, 77 n. 1, 102 n]

———— (1986): "Varieties of Self-Reference," in Joseph Y. Halpern, ed., *Theoretical Aspects of Reasoning about Knowledge: Proceedings of the 1986 Conference*, Monterey, California, March 19–22, 1986, Los Altos, California: Morgan Kaufmann, pp. 19–43. Also available as Center for the Study of Language and Information Technical Report No. CSLI–87–76, Stanford: Stanford University · [77 n. 1, 248 n]

———— (1987): "The Correspondence Continuum," Center for the Study of Language and Information Technical Report No. CSLI–87–71, Stanford: Stanford University, 59 pp. · [34 n, 58 n. 31, 77 n. 1, 251 n, 262 n]

———— (1988): "The Semantics of Clocks," in James H. Fetzer, ed., *Aspects of Artificial Intelligence*, The Netherlands: Kluwer Academic Publishers, 1988, pp. 3–31. Also available as Center for the Study of Language and Information Technical Report No. CSLI–87–75, Stanford: Stanford University, March 1987 · [74 n, 261 n]

———— (1994): "Discreteness Run Amok," in Joan Fujimura and Lucy Suchman, eds., *Vital Signs: Cultural Perspectives on Coding Life and Vitalizing Code*, Department of Anthropology, Program in History and Philosophy of Science, Stanford University, June 2–4, 1994 · [203 n]

———— (forthcoming): *The Middle Distance: An Essay on the Foundations of Computation and Intentionality*, a series of books in the philosophy of computation · [8 n. 8, 23 n] Tentative titles:

　Volume I: Introduction · [72 n, 186 n, 290 n. 10]

　Volume II: Formal Symbol Manipulation · [9 n, 14 n. 14, 15 s, 365 s]

　Volume III: Effective Computability · [12 n. 12, 210 s]

Volume IV: The Correspondence Continuum · [34 n, 42 n, 58, 77 n. 1, 186 n, 251 n]

Volume V: Digital State Machines · [235 n. 9]

Smolensky, Paul (1988): "On the Proper Treatment of Connectionism," *Behavioral and Brain Sciences*, Vol. **11**, pp. 1–23 · [20 n. 20, 46 n. 21, 64 n. 37, 65 n. 39, 281]

────── (1991): "Connectionism, Constituency, and the Language of Thought," in Barry Loewer and Georges Rey, eds., *Meaning in Mind: Fodor and His Critics*, Oxford: Basil Blackwell, pp. 210–237 · [35 n. 13]

Snow, Charles Percy (1964): *The Two Cultures and the Scientific Revolution* and *A Second Look: An Expanded Version of 'The two cultures and the scientific revolution,'* Cambridge: Cambridge University Press · [3, 94]

Star, Leigh (1989): *Regions of the Mind*, Stanford: Stanford University Press · [305 n. 16]

Strawson, Peter (1959): *Individuals*, London: Methuen · [65 n. 39, 124, 175, 232, 279 n. 2, 281 n]

────── (1992): *Analysis and Metaphysics*, Oxford: Oxford University Press.

Struik, Dirk (1962): *A Concise History of Mathematics*, London: G. Bell · [355 n. 5]

Suchman, Lucy (1987): *Plans and Situated Actions*, Cambridge: Cambridge University Press · [310]

────── (1994): "Working Relations of Technology Production and Use," *Computer Supported Cooperative Work*, Vol. **2**, pp. 21–39 · [306 n, 340 n]

────── (in press): "Centers of Coordination: A Case and Some Themes," in L. Resnik, R. Saljo, and C. Pontecorvo, eds., *Discourse, Tools, and Reasoning*, Berlin: Springer-Verlag · [335 n. 7]

Taylor, Charles (1989): *Sources of the Self: The Making of the Modern Identity*, Cambridge, Mass.: Harvard University Press.

Vico, Giambattista (1744/1984): *The New Science of Giambattista Vico*, Ithaca, New York: Cornell University Press · [21 n]

Weinberg, Steven (1993): *Dreams of a Final Theory*, New York: Pantheon Books · [144 n. 6]

Wenger, Etienne (forthcoming): *Communities of Practice: Learning, Meanings, and Identity* · [36 n. 14]

Wild, Helga and Niklas Damiris (in prep.): *The Writing Condition: Bodies, Language, and the Emergence of Social Praxis*, Stanford: Stanford University Press · [363 n]

Designed by Shelley Evenson and Brian Cantwell Smith.
Typeset in Adobe Garamond text with Frutiger Ultra Black display
by Melissa L. Ehn at Wilsted & Taylor Publishing Services.